SHIV'IM:

Essays and Studies in Honor of Ira Eisenstein

SHIV'IM:

Essays and Studies in Honor of Ira Eisenstein

Edited by
Ronald A. Brauner

Volume 1

Publications of the Reconstructionist Rabbinical College

RECONSTRUCTIONIST RABBINICAL COLLEGE
PHILADELPHIA, PENNSYLVANIA

KTAV PUBLISHING HOUSE, INC.
NEW YORK
1977

Library of Congress Cataloging in Publication Data

Main entry under title:

Shiv'im.

(Reconstructionist Rabbinical College Press publications; 1)
Includes bibliographical references.
CONTENTS: Biblical civilization: Caine, I. Teaching Biblical civilization. Kaplan, M. M. Interdependence of religion and science. Miller, A. W. Claude Lévi-Strauss and Genesis 37-Exodus 20. — Rabbinic civilization: Brauner, R. A. Rabbinics and rabbinic education. [etc.]
1. Judaism—History—Addresses, essays, lectures. 2. Jews—History—Addresses, essays, lectures. 3. Eisenstein, Ira, 1906-   I. Brauner, Ronald A. II. Eisenstein, Ira, 1906-
BM42.S497   296   77-5583
ISBN 0-87068-442-6

MANUFACTURED IN THE UNITED STATES OF AMERICA

פתח דבר
PREFACE

This collection of essays and studies is occasioned by the seventieth birthday of Rabbi Ira Eisenstein, editor of *Reconstructionist* and president of the Jewish Reconstructionist Foundation and the Reconstructionist Rabbinical College. It is a fitting and appropriate expression of the admiration and affection of the students and colleagues of one who has labored for more than fifty years on behalf of the Jewish people. Well-recognized it is that the fabric and substance of American Jewry have been profoundly affected by the thinking and activities of this man who, together with Rabbi Mordecai Kaplan, is a prime mover and leading exponent of Reconstructionism.

To you, Ira Eisenstein, we offer these contributions to Torah in the prayerful hope that you may see many more years of health, that you may be granted the strength and inspiration to continue your endeavors for *K'lal Yisrael* and that all the works of your hands may be blessed.

כל מקום שנאמר אחד גדול הוא, **בישראל** כתיב (במדבר רבה, י.)

R.A.B.

4 Kislev, 5737

November 26, 1976

ACKNOWLEDGMENTS

Grateful acknowledgment is made of the generous financial support of the following for the publication of this volume. These people have demonstrated their love of Torah in a most substantial way and in so doing, have brought honor both to their friend Ira Eisenstein and to the Jewish people:

Mitchell and Maxine Aigen
Lavy and Augusta Becker
Samuel and Adele Blumenthal
Louis and Ann Bunis
Peter and Carol Kessner
Leonard and Clarice Leveton

"Torah is a source of life to those who offer it support; those who sustain it find good fortune."

Proverbs 3:18

CONTENTS

Biblical Civilization

E Saias gesendet war/
      Das er GOTTES Wort offenbar/
Dem ein Engel den Mund auff thut
    Mit einer Zang/ vnd durch ein Glut
Anzündt/ das er ist düchtig worden
    Zu predigen. In solchen Orden
Die bruffen find/ hat auch der Geyst
Gestärckt mit seinem Fewr allermeist.

מקים דבר עבדו ועצת מלאכיו ישלים האומר לירושלים תושב
ולערי יהודה תבנינה וחרבותיה אקומם
(ישעיהו מד: כו)

TEACHING BIBLICAL CIVILIZATION

By

IVAN CAINE

DEDICATION

This essay on teaching Biblical Civilization is gratefully dedicated to Rabbi Ira Eisenstein, a gentleman exemplary in his devotion to the Jewish people and in his commitment to the preservation and progress of its cultural contributions to the growth and enlightenment of humanity. It is a personal pleasure to offer this statement in his honor. He has been a faithful friend and gentle guide. Thanks to his acceptance of the onerous responsibility to found and maintain the Reconstructionist Rabbinical College, the opportunity has been mine to shape and implement a total program in the field of Bible, in an environment which seems to me virtually ideal for the study of Torah in our day.

BACKGROUND

The three non-Orthodox American rabbinical schools share a screening process which assures that candidates are granted admission only if they indicate general competence, with a fine undergraduate degree, as well as a commitment to serve the Jewish community as a vocation. The other two seminaries have larger staffs, and the students are matriculated full-time. By contrast, the Reconstructionist Rabbinical College has very modest facilities, with a small teaching faculty, and the students have a double program, working for a graduate degree in a local university.

These data define, in terms of realistic goals, the task of training students to be rabbis. The question we must answer is what to do with the temporal and spiritual resources at our disposal during the five years of training. The answer, beginning with the method of the Reconstructionist movement, is the linear study of the history of the civilization of the Jewish people, starting with the period of the Bible. Each core director has a mandate to offer a program of integrated study in a specific period.

What follows reflects my experience in teaching the Bible year in this civilization plan. As a Reconstructionist institution only eight years old, RRC has a high rate of evolution. The program today is not what it was when the first adventuresome dozen entered the school in September 1968, although the goal has not changed.

The task is insuperable. There is no way, in the span of an academic year, to train a prospective rabbi in the civilization of the Israelites becoming Judeans on their way to becoming "Jews." It is necessary, in the spirit of Judaism, at least in its pessimism, to despair. Then, out of desperation, with the exhilaration that comes from the awareness that "yours is not the task to finish, but that does not exempt you from the effort," the enterprise becomes exciting, even captivating. After all, no institution today can offer a complete training, combining the competence in text that a yeshiva student would have had in Europe with the finest observations of modern scholarship. The goal must be to concentrate on the issues and dynamics of the biblical heritage, combined with the material culture as unveiled by the sciences of the past. Beyond this, one must hope for the motivation to study further, as a life-task, to broaden and deepen comprehension, and to offer a creative contribution to the understanding of a period in the life of the Jewish people.

CORE CONCEPTION

The concept of a core curriculum is not original to the Reconstructionist movement. Nor is the search for the dynamics of the historical development of the Jewish people. Nonetheless, the combination of features in the curriculum of the Reconstructionist Rabbinical College is fully original, and it deserves description. What follows applies to the first of these sequential core curriculum conceptions, as it has evolved from the inception of the school, during which period I have had the privilege of serving as director of the Biblical Civilization program.

Strangely enough, in the limited time available, it seems to me important to stress language competence rather than pass over to the second level of scholarship, and leave the future rabbi dependent on the treatment of the text as well as its interpretation at the hands of other people, competent and creative though they may be. In the language program, the text is studied with the full range of tools offered by the history of commentation and criticism. In the Bible year, insights are welcome from any source, without prejudice. In the case of traditional commentary, beginning with the sages of the rabbinic period, our interest ends at the border of midrash. We are vitally interested in the insights of rabbinic literature insofar as they touch the plain sense of the Bible text (*pshat*); the creative exposition (*drash*), much of which reflects attempts to meet contemporary needs, is the proper study of the Rabbinic Civilization Core. Similarly, the particular application of the Bible to the needs of the Middle Ages is the proper study of that core program, and the exposition that reflects modern problems and needs is germane to that core program.

CORE COMPONENTS

The core courses are: Biblical Grammar, Bible Text, and Biblical Civilization Seminar. My conviction is that a thorough grounding in the grammar of Bible Hebrew is indispensable. Our text has been *Introduction to Hebrew* by M. Greenberg (2d ed., 1965), chosen for its approach, academic level, and brevity.

BIBLE TEXT

The aim of this course is to equip the student to study any Bible text. The goal is quality of comprehension, not quantity. A translation is used: the new materials of the Jewish Publication Society are required as available. A lexicon is used: students choose between the exemplary but obsolete Brown-Driver-Briggs and the contemporary work by L. Koehler. Two modern commentaries are used: the classical work of the *International Critical Commentary* (parallel to the first lexicon mentioned), and a contemporary series, as available, *Anchor Bible* or *Old Testament Library*. Highly recommended is the current series *Da-at Miqra,* published in Jerusalem by a circle of traditional scholars. Finally, for technical training and convenient summary, the recitation in class uses the apparatus of the *Biblia Hebraica* (ed. Kittel), reprinted with Dead Sea materials. Students are required to mechanically read Greek words.

The outline of assignments follows, where possible, that of the seminar (see below). When the subject of the week is a major figure in the prophetic corpus, such as Isaiah, or the anonymous prophet(s) known conveniently as Deutero-Isaiah, the text for that week will be a chapter or two from that book, or a series of short selections (as in the case of Jeremiah). In cases where the subject reflects the narrative material in the Bible, especially in the early part of the syllabus, the poetical chapters of those books are assigned (Gen. 49, Deut. 32 and 33, Judg. 5), or material from Psalms. In addition to materials in biblical Hebrew, special weeks are devoted to the following: the history of the alphabet, reading in class the Moabite Stone in paleo-Hebrew characters; a practical introduction to biblical Aramaic, with an assignment in Daniel; a session devoted to the Dead Sea Scrolls, with reading from a photograph of *Pesher Habakkuk*.

In the last session, we have a *siyyum* with the study of the Ten Statements, read synoptically in Exodus 20 and Deuteronomy 5. Assigned are: on Exodus, S. R. Driver (Cambridge), the *OTL* volumes by Noth and Childs, and Cassuto; on Deuteronomy, S. R. Driver (*ICC*), von Rad (*OTL*), and D. Hoffman (Hebrew trans., 1959). The entire text of the Septuagint translation is to be read; the aim is the satisfaction to be gained from finding that mere mechanical reading, with the Hebrew original for comparison, is enough to understand most of the Greek translation. For *pshat*, RaShBaM (ed. D. Rosin) and S. D. Luzzato are assigned; and for a combination of *pshat* and *drash*, Rashi (ed. Berliner) and, in the modern key, S. Goldman (ed. M. Samuels, 1956).

SUPPLEMENT

Text study in the Biblical Civilization program does not include narrative texts. Some students enter with competency in this material; others acquire the tools for such mastery in the course in Biblical Grammar. Each student, before graduation, has the option of preparing the narrative portions of the Torah for an oral examination on the grammar, vocabulary, text problems, and basic commentary; or a course in Torah with Rashi. In the former option, the assignment is: Genesis 1–48, 50; Exodus 1–20, 32–34; Numbers 11–25, 27, 31–32, 36; Deuteromony 1–11, 27–31, 34. In the latter case, the course in Torah with Rashi has a cycle of five years, to accommodate the length of the program at the RRC, according to the "fifths" of the Torah. In this course, we examine the dynamics of the Rashi material, both *pshat* (original commentary) and *drash* (anthology of rabbinic exposition), for the problems in the text. An attempt is made to indicate the common motivations to seek solutions in these traditional sources and in modern scholarship, contrasting the solutions in the "prescientific criticism" of the Jewish tradition and the "scientific criticism" of the moderns.

These requirements should result in the understanding of the language, its application to the study of Bible text, and the range of commentary as it attempts to elucidate lower critical problems and summarize aspects of higher criticism. What is lacking from the complex of courses taught by the core director is the systematic study of a book of the Bible, applying all of these techniques. That course is taught by a faculty colleague, Dr. Ronald Brauner, who serves as director of the Rabbinic Civilization Program. Again, there is a cycle in five years: Isaiah, Jeremiah, Ezekiel, The Twelve, and Psalms. This course, required for students of the Biblical Civilization year, is also open (as is the course on Torah with Rashi) to students of other years, as an elective course.

SEMINAR

The core of the "core program" is the seminar. Meeting in weekly sessions for three hours, the students discuss major issues in Bible scholarship, with a background in material culture, utilizing the research in cognate cultures. The task of organizing the materials is formidable, both for the core director, who structures the seminar and moderates the discussions, and for the students, who are presented with much more material for study than can be mastered, and must judiciously mix assigned readings with optional selections. The backbone is a chronological line, and the text is J. Bright, *A History of Israel* (2d ed., 1972). Into this chronological grid, the other materials are fitted. As is clear from an outline of the syllabus, divided into twenty-eight sessions, some weeks are thoroughly organic, while others include a combination of diverse materials.

In addition to the historical outline, there are two main sources of seminar materials: Yehezkel Kaufmann, expecially *Toldot Ha-Emunah Ha-Yisraelit* (1937–56, 8 books in 4 vols.); and the *Encyclopaedia Judaica* (16 vols., 1972, + 2 yearbooks). While the students are urged to use the original Hebrew of Kaufmann's magnum opus as well as his commentaries on Joshua (1959) and Judges (1962), the material available in English is required: *Great Ages and Ideas of the Jewish People* (1956, ed. L. Schwarz), pp. 3–75; *The . . . Conquest of Palestine* (trans.

M. Dagut, 1953); the series of volumes translated from book 8 of *Toldot* by C. W. Efroymson (first volume published in 1968); and the adaptation of books 1–7 of *Toldot* by M. Greenberg, published in 1960 as *The Religion of Israel*. The last is a text in the seminar, with part 1 (pp. 1–149) assigned as background reading, and the remainder fitted into the course outline.

As is often the case with composite books, the *Encyclopaedia Judaica* is an uneven work, and it is not intended for students specializing in Bible. Nevertheless, the work is a valuable reference tool for rabbinical students, and the arrangement is appealing. As a result, every substantial entry in the set that bears on the study of Biblical Civilization is noted on the syllabus, in a suitable place.

The insistence on Kaufmann is a reflection of the course orientation. The syllabus includes sources, mainly in English but occasionally in Hebrew or European languages, from the various approaches: classical critical, neo-German, American, contemporary Israeli, and Kaufmann. It is important that rabbis-in-training be exposed to currents in modern scholarship, with the equipment to understand and criticize these materials. Some students have background in the field from their university training, while others do not. For both groups it is necessary to study secondary sources that are balanced against each other. The critical work of the classical German school of Kuenen-Graf-Wellhausen and the neo-German school of Alt, Noth, and von Rad is indispensable, but not more important than the conservative reaction of Kaufmann, the moderate outlook of the Albright school, or the congeries of materials in archaeology and cognate cultures that do not directly serve any of the systematic formulations.

SUPPORTING TEXTS

In addition to a Hebrew Bible, a modern translation, Bright, Kaufmann, and selected articles from the *Encyclopaedia Judaica*, RRC students must use various reference works and read a variety of material from books and journals.

Since it is often difficult to include aspects of material culture, such as dress and living conditions, students must regularly use *Views of the Biblical World* (ed. B. Mazar, Jerusalem, 4 or 5 vols.), with reference to J. B. Pritchard, *Ancient Near Eastern Pictures Relating to the Old Testament*. A book on archaeology, such as *Biblical Archaeology* by G. E. Wright (rev. ed., 1962), and an atlas, preferably *The Macmillan*

Bible Atlas by Aharoni and Avi-Yonah, are beneficial, although material from these sources is built into Bright's history text.

Other reference works include the collection of texts in translation, brought up to date on a continuing basis, by Pritchard, *Ancient Near Eastern Texts Relating to the Old Testament*; the translation, with additional bibliography, by P. Ackroyd, of *The Old Testament: An Introduction,* by O. Eissfeldt; R. de Vaux, *Ancient Israel* (trans. J. McHugh); *Interpreter's Dictionary of the Bible* (4 vols., 1962). The Israeli series, *World History of the Jewish People,* not for reference but for regular study, is especially adapted to the needs of our program.

SYLLABUS

The organization of the course is reflected in the reading list, which includes the weekly assignments in Bible text. For each week there is a subject, or a combination of subjects, with readings from the reference works and course texts referred to above. This is followed by a list of materials, drawn from the available literature in books and journals, followed by the germane articles from the *Encyclopaedia Judaica.* All items on the list are on reserve in the library of the college, and Mrs. Jennifer Gabriel supervises their use so that all students are assured access to the material of a given week.

The list of readings is stratified with symbols: two stars mark an assigned reading, one star a recommended reading, and the unmarked items are optional. Participants in the seminar have the task of surveying the materials and preparing those which seem most appealing, outside of the assigned work. Students are also encouraged to reach beyond the syllabus, and bring in relevant materials from other sources.

The syllabus cannot be reproduced here, but the list of weekly topics follows:

1. Orientation: prehistory of Israel; Bible scholarship; Ancient Near East; material aspects of biblical civilization; introduction to Semitic languages.
2. Patriarchs. Genesis.
3. Eisodos; Egyptian history and culture; the people Israel; exodus; Book of Exodus.
4. Law in the Ancient Near East; law in the Bible; treaty and covenant; revelation; YHWH; slavery.
5. Wilderness trek; conquest of Canaan; Book of Joshua.

6. Settlement in Canaan; amphictyony; Judges; Ruth; intermarriage; aliens.
7. Samuel and Saul; kingship; Books of Samuel; Canaanite and Israelite religion; Philistines; nazirite.
8. David and his period; Chronicles, an introduction.
9. Solomon and early divided monarchy; Proverbs; Kings.
10. Elijah and Elisha; alleged Hosea A (chaps. 1–3); ritual purity.
11. 850–750 B.C.E.; prophecy; Jonah.
12. 750–630; Amos; Hosea.
13. Isaiah 1–39; Micah; Jerusalem.
14. 630–550; five minor prophets; Song of Songs.
15. Deuteronomy and "the Deuteronomist"; "the priestly work"; priesthood; Levites.
16. Jeremiah; Lamentations; women; family.
17. Ezekiel; demonology and apotropaics; circumcision.
18. 550–520; Isaiah 40–66; concept of the anointed; servant of the Lord and "the servant songs."
19. 520–450; Haggai; Zechariah; Malachi; tabernacle, temple, and cult; the synagogue.
20. 450–400; Ezra; Nehemiah; Chronicles and "the Chronicler."
21. 400–200; Kohelet; Esther and Purim; Elephantine and other documents.
22. 200–60 B.C.E.; the Hasmoneans and Hanukka; Daniel; wisdom.
23. Psalms; music.
24. Calendar and holidays; Job.
25. Noncanonical literature; Ben Sira; Samaritans.
26. Dead Sea Scrolls.
27. Bible text; canon; burial.
28. Summary; transition to Rabbinic Civilization.

ORIENTATION

In my introductory remarks to entering students, I indicate that my responsibility in the seminar is limited to providing a reading list and guiding the class discussions. While this may be an overstatement, it expresses my orientation. Education is a combination of ingestion and evaluation, and the principal medium is reading. In studying Biblical Civilization, skills are the responsibility of the instructor—fundamentals and refinements in grammar, and total use of textual tools—but the seminar is the responsibility of the participants. The study of Bible materials at the RRC has had many exciting moments, with original ideas presented by students and faculty alike. Hopefully, this excitement of discovery will continue, and novellae will be offered in print in future publications of the college.

OUTLOOK

As H. M. Orlinsky has been at pains to point out, bias is widespread in academic interchange, and the problem is particularly acute in the study of sacred scripture. In my view, bias is inevitable, and pure knowledge is a chimera. Our charge is to make clear the position from which we work, and to equip our students to intelligently disagree, by exposing them to the most convincing formulations of views that are in opposition to our own, and by entertaining in class the free expression of any view that is grounded in primary sources.

We live in a remarkable time, when the intelligent and intellectual study of the sacred text is not only rewarding but respectable. The amanuensis view of revelation, that Moses wrote the Torah at the dictation of the Almighty, dominated Jewish and Christian belief for over a millennium and a half in the common era. A century ago, the antithesis held sway under the aegis of Welhausen: that the preponderance of the Torah is post-exilic, the material of the Bible is largely counterfeit, and the Israelite religion developed from a carefree earthiness, through an elite ethical monotheism, to a hieratic organization which presided over a post-exile population obsessed with guilt and dominated by sacrificial expiation.

The time of the synthesis has arrived. It is tolerably clear that the "thesis" is a point to which we cannot return, while the "antithesis" is generally viewed as extreme. We now have the enviable task of incorporating the swelling mass of new materials in a mediating manner, in appreciation of the Bible as a source of information and inspiration, through an understanding of its place in the evolution of Israelite civilization, within the greater context of world history and culture. It is a time when many traditional texts, the Bible and Homer among them, command renewed respect, and it is timely to be skeptical, within reasonable limits, of skeptical criticism.

CONSERVATISM

In the study of the text, my position is conservative. While I do not imagine that our present printed books represent *ipsissima verba,* and the principles of transmission errors must be mastered, I do not think that scholarly emendation (especially without support in manuscript, recension, or early translation) is likely to reflect an original. The practice of emendation is a valuable heuristic exercise, but the notion that such restoration takes us back to a written or oral original is hybris, despite the instances in which modern discoveries, notably the scrolls from the Judean Desert, have provided readings that coincide with emendations suggested by scholars who were dead when the materials were found. The more complicated a restoration, the more unlikely, in geometric progression. We must scrutinize the text with all the critical means at our disposal, but our aim should be to elicit the least unlikely meaning of a masoretic reading or give up a text as incomprehensible; sometimes, both of these.

If there is an analogue in the realm of civilization, it too applies. The Bible material should be tirelessly researched (the Hebrew term is *d-r-sh*), and all reasonable reconstructions entertained. But the onus for such reconstructions falls on those who offer them, and the further removed a formulation is from the Bible as we have it, the more unlikely that reconstruction is, in geometric progression. Y. Yadin finds the skepticism of M. Noth arbitrary, and so do I. Y. Kaufmann thought the German criticism, of the classical and modern schools, needlessly artificial, and so do I. There are those, including me, who think the severely critical treatment of the German scholars reflects a religious bias, oscillating between naked anti-Semitism and subtle efforts to undermine the value of the Hebrew Bible in favor of Christian sources.

Any scholarly position may be true; future discoveries will support some of those offered and shake the foundations of others. The preliminary reports of the dramatic discoveries in Syria suggest that the thesaurus of documents from Tel Mardikh will bolster the conservative approach. In any case, it seems to be necessary to entertain the most audacious theories, but to weigh them carefully and suspend acceptance until the information of the data is coercive.

CONCLUSION

In 1934, Mordecai Kaplan, in *Judaism as a Civilization,* undertook the awesome task of reconstructing Jewish life and returning to Judaism those who had become disaffected. Kaplan was prepared to work with the most unfavorable results of biblical criticism, and formulate a conception of Judaism that would not be undermined by such a negative evaluation of the Bible. Soon after, Yehezkel Kaufmann, using the methodology of the Graf-Wellhausen school, undertook to reverse its main conclusions regarding the authenticity of the biblical corpus.

The contribution of these two creative minds should define our mandate. Judaism does not lose its meaning if the theses of German critical scholarship prevail, but neither are we constrained, in the current climate of scholarship, to rest content with those conclusions. The modern enlightened conservatism of a line of scholars, including Cassuto, Kaufmann, Speiser, and Albright in the last generation, and in our own, Sarna, Greenberg, the Israeli "school," and students of Albright, offers a respectable base from which students of *mikra* can comfortably operate, and rabbinical schools should be particularly grateful for that opportunity.

INTERDEPENDENCE OF RELIGION
AND SCIENCE

By

MORDECAI M. KAPLAN

In 1934 I wrote (in *Judaism As a Civilization*): "To steer clear both of rigid traditionalism and irreligion, the Jew will have to realize that religion is rooted in human nature, and the belief in the existence of God, and the attributes ascribed to Him, must be derived from, and be made to refer to the experience of the average man and woman. The ability to negotiate the transition from the theurgic to the rational conception of religion is but a phase of the larger problem of spiritual adjustment which has prevailed since the days of Copernicus, and which has been accentuated with the acceptance of the Darwinian theory.

"Whatever Jews' conception of the physical universe may be, assuming that man must come to terms with life and justify his spiritual striving, it should be possible to work out an affirmative spiritual adjustment in Jewish life in terms of the evolutionary conception of religion.

"The reorientation which is essential to the survival of Jewish religion cannot be effected merely by trying to harmonize the traditional teachings of religion with the results achieved by modern science. It calls for nothing less than an approach to the religious interpretation of life with the same unbiased empirical attitude as that which constitutes the spirit of science, that spirit which regards truth not as something absolute and final, but as an active process of the mind whereby error is gradually eliminated. A conflict betweeen science and religion is possible only when we falsely assume that our knowledge of God originates not from our understanding of the universe and human life, but from some supernatural

15

revelation which is entirely extraneous to the natural powers of the human mind. However, once we take for granted that our knowledge of God is necessarily based upon experience, and develops with it, all conflict between science and religion is precluded; for then all that is necessary to keep religion vital is to permit it to grow concurrently with experience.

"The inclusion of religion within the scope of scientific thinking pre-supposes a much broader conception of science than that of a method of measuring phenomena or tracing their sequences. The scientific spirit is synonymous with the application of intelligence to everything within the range of human experience, including ends as well as means, social and spiritual life as well as physical existence. So understood, it is in the interest of religion to submit itself to the scientific approach. To state the matter more concretely, it is to our advantage spiritually to submit all our religious ideas, habits, and emotions to the scrutiny of intelligence." [1]

In brief, it is my purpose in this essay to apply the scientific approach to religion. At once two important questions arise which must be answered: (1) What is the scientific approach? and (2) What are the implications of applying the scientific approach to the question of Revelation?

The *Funk and Wagnalls Dictionary* defines science as follows: "Science is knowledge gained and verified by exact observation and correct thinking. It is exact knowledge of facts (historical and empirical) plus exact knowledge of laws obtained by correlating facts and exact knowledge of proximate causes."

The first prerequisite to an understanding of the scientific approach, therefore, is to recognize that it demands knowledge. Emile Durkheim, in his classic *Elementary Forms of the Religious Life,* stated the attitude of science toward religion with matchless clarity: "That which science refuses to grant to religion is not its right to exist, but its right to dog-matize upon the nature of things and the special competence which it claims for itself for knowing man and the world. As a matter of fact, it does not know itself. It does not even know what it is made of, nor to what need it answers. It is itself a subject for science, so far is it from being able to make the law for science. . . . However, it seems destined to transform itself rather than to disappear." [2]

More recently, Albert Einstein put the matter succinctly: "Science without religion is lame. Religion without science is blind." [3] In order fully to understand the implications of Einstein's epigram, one must recall the second of the two questions posed at the beginning: What are the implications of applying the scientific approach to traditional, "revealed" religion?

The answer to that question is contained in the recognition of the uniqueness of the ancient Hebraic conception of how salvation (the central theme and function of religion) is to be achieved. The Hebrew Bible clearly sets forth the view that salvation is acquired by wisdom, by knowledge and intelligence. The God of Israel, in the Bible, is referred to 273 times as the "God of salvation." According to Durkheim, "the first article in every creed is the belief in salvation by faith." [4] The only religion which is an exception to Durkheim's generalization is that of the Hebrew Bible, where *not* faith but wisdom is the key to salvation.

Thus, Psalm 19:8 reads: "The decree of YHWH is trustworthy, making wise the simple." Jeremiah, chapter 22, addresses the King Shallum in the following words: "Your father ate and drank like you but he practiced honesty and integrity, so all went well with him. He used to examine the cases of the poor and needy, then all went well. Is not that what it means to know me? It is YHWH who speaks."

A rereading of the early chapters of Genesis, from a scientific point of view, yields new illumination on the real meaning of the myths which characterize those chapters. We should interpret Elohim or El in the story as the reification of the idea of the Creative Laws that make the universe a cosmos rather than a chaos. Nature is thus made possible. The opening chapter, therefore, conveys the idea that Nature's God, the personification of the process of Creative Law, produced a creature which would, in its turn, function like the Creator Himself, creatively, transforming the chaos of violence into order.

The identification of the law, or the orderly process of life, with the name Yah, in chapter 2, denotes the phenomenon by which Law reveals God—unlike the traditional notion that God revealed the Law.

Yah's purposes are frustrated by the fratricide of Cain. Thenceforth violence gains momentum. This is attributed in the mythological narrative to the seduction of Eve by the serpent—the embodiment of Satan. The basic sin was the acceptance of the belief that the human species could manage its own affairs in accordance with *its* laws, without relying upon the Laws revealed in Nature, the Laws by which the world was created, the Laws that reduced chaos to order.

In order to understand the difference between man's laws and the Laws that reveal God, it is necessary to point out that, for the most part, man's laws stem from the desire for power, while God's Laws are designed to lend power to the right. Since man's laws generally deal in terms of the right of power, philosophers like Aristotle have been misled into thinking that man is by nature a "political" animal—that is, one who ever seeks power over his fellowmen. The fact is that man is an animal that cares about maximum life. He is a salvation-seeking animal. This distinction, as Professor Harry A. Overstreet has pointed out, goes to the "roots." In saying this he approved the distinction which I made in an early paper; he added: "It should invest science with the dignity of being co-explorer with [philosophy and religion] in man's quest for salvation."

The sad truth is that the history of the Jews is a history of God's "frustration." Again and again, God is described as trying to impart His wisdom, and constantly failing. Even the Prophets, who were the most eloquent spokesmen for God's Laws, failed to impress their contemporaries.

One may say that the rejection of Wisdom on the part of those who adopted the Hebrew Bible as their own eventually produced the Holocaust of the twentieth century. And as we move on into the twenty-first, the price to be paid for the lack of wisdom becomes ever more prohibitive; indeed, with atomic power at man's command, the destruction of the world is now possible.

How could God have failed to impress man with the absolute necessity of achieving wisdom and practicing it? Interestingly enough, even from the traditional point of view, God was not omnipotent. Having given man the right to choose between good and evil, His powers were curtailed.

The issue before us, then, is: Where can wisdom be found? The answer to this question is available today as it never was before. Men sought wisdom in mythology, in revelation, even in philosophy, but never in human experience. That is where we must now look for wisdom.

This means that we must examine man in a critical and scientific manner, analyze his nature and his needs, and then work out the means whereby his needs can be fulfilled. Salvation today must mean the fulfillment of the needs of all men.

What are those needs?

The first of the needs is a combination of five needs subsumed under one category:

1. The vital needs—for sustenance, for security, for health, for diversion, for sexuality.
2. The need to experience certain feelings, like that of belonging; a sense of power, of love, of cooperation, the feeling of being needed.
3. The need to experience the existence of *oughts:* basically justice, the control of greeds for power, pleasure, and license.
4. The need to apply wisdom to satisfy these needs, leading to
5. The need for ethical religion.

These needs, it is asserted here, are without doubt present in all people.

In order to satisfy the above needs one must know the facts about them and hence about ourselves:

—One must understand one's thoughts, one's psychology.

—One must be able to distinguish between imagination and reality.

—One must apply reason, and check reason with all the available methods of science.

Finally, man needs the will to achieve salvation.

—He must be moved to action, moved by the need to experiment, using his intelligence in all techniques, and in the arts.

There is nothing in Jewish tradition approaching Einstein's conception of religion as blind without science. On the other hand, the Hebrew Bible insists upon vision, knowledge, and intelligence as indispensable to the achievement of salvation.

Both Isaiah's and Micah's visions of the end of days imply that the human species will ultimately succeed in having man the political animal cooperate with man the animal in quest of salvation.

For a fuller formulation of the "science of religion" the discipline called Soterics is essential. When fully developed it will (in the words of Harold Schulweis) be a "this worldly normative science of human life in all its aspects, from the standpoint of verifiable experience."

NOTES

1. *Judaism As a Civilization,* p. 307.
2. *Elementary Forms of the Religious Life* (London: Allen & Unwin), p. 430.
3. Einstein, *The Universal God,* ed. Carl Hermann Voss, p. 41.
4. *Elementary Forms of the Religious Life,* p. 416.

CLAUDE LÉVI-STRAUSS AND GENESIS 37–EXODUS 20

By

ALAN W. MILLER

"There have been three major developments in the modern study of myths," writes Geoffrey S. Kirk:

> The first was the realization, associated especially with Tylor, Frazer, and Durkheim, that the myths of primitive societies are highly relevant to the subject as a whole. The second was Freud's discovery of the unconscious and its relation to myths and dreams. The third is the structural theory of myth propounded by the great French anthropologist Claude Lévi-Strauss.[1]

This structural theory of myth is developed by Lévi-Strauss in a number of works, ranging from an article on the Bororo Indians, published in 1936,[2] through his tetralogy *Mythologiques,* the last volume of which appeared in 1971.[3]

His general thesis has two aspects. Myths are not random. Under analysis they all manifest rigorous structure. That is the most generally acceptable part of his thesis, although even here the critics have their serious reservations with regard to the issue of universality. The other aspect relates to the notion of a mental algebra subsumed under the concept of *esprit*, variously translated as "mind" or "reason."[4] When reduced to their basic elements, the relationships in myths manifest an invariant and transformational type of thinking about the world.

This latter concept, unfortunately, is highly ambiguous. Most of the critics have great difficulty with it, especially with its claimed universality and exclusivity. "Although I feel reasonably safe with Lévi-Strauss's concept of structure," observes Edmund Leach, perhaps the master's most brilliant exegete,

> I am quite out of my depth when it comes to the related but subtler notion of *esprit*. . . . *esprit* seems to be a kind of limiting characteristic of the human brain mechanism and appears as part of an extremely involved interchange relationship in which it (*esprit*) is the causal force producing myths of which its own structure is a precipitate. . . . I have to confess that, when it comes to the crunch, I have no clear idea of what it is that Lévi-Strauss is really talking about.[5]

The titles of the first two volumes of *Mythologiques* may best serve as a preliminary exemplification of the general thesis. Raw and cooked, honey and ashes express fundamental polarities which exist in the social life of the South American Indians whose myths provide the central subject matter for these volumes. Drawing on Roman Jakobson's model of binary linguistics, which in turn was influenced by the work of Ferdinand de Saussure, Lévi-Strauss sees myth as reconciling opposites, especially opposites deriving respectively from nature and culture. In the titles, *raw* and *honey* represent the natural, and *cooked* and *ashes* (tobacco) represent the cultural. But his concern is less with the referents of the mythical elements, at least theoretically speaking, than with their structural relationships. At times he denies all interest in the external referents, but then at times he contradicts himself. His main burden appears to be that myth-making is governed by rigorous laws, almost on the analogy of falling bodies being governed by gravity.

In a footnote to *The Raw and the Cooked* Lévi-Strauss quotes Tylor: "If law is anywhere, it is everywhere." He goes on, approvingly: "Such was the conclusion reached by Tylor in the passage that I used seventeen years ago as an epigraph for *Les Structures élémentaires de la parenté*." [6] Just in case we have missed the point he stresses on the next page: "I therefore claim to show, not how men think in myths, but how myths operate in men's minds without their being aware of the fact." [7]

And in the Author's Preface to the French edition of *Anthropologie Structurale* he quotes, obviously with satisfaction, Jean Pouillon: "Lévi-Strauss is certainly not the first nor the only one to have emphasized the structural character of social phenomena, but his originality consists in taking that character seriously and in serenely deriving all the consequences from it." [8] To which Lévi-Strauss adds: "My hopes would be fulfilled if this book could induce other readers to share this judgement." [9] He welcomes Paul Ricoeur's criticism that his structuralism is "Kantism without a transcendental subject." [10] He adds:

> But far from considering this reservation as indicating some deficiency, I see it as the inevitable consequence, on the philosophical level, of the ethnographic approach I have chosen; since, my ambition being to discover the conditions in which systems of truth become mutually convertible and therefore simultaneously acceptable to several different subjects, the pattern of those conditions takes on the character of an autonomous object, independent of any subject.[11]

Elsewhere he speaks of *"l'architecture de l'esprit."*
Michael Lane, discussing structuralism in general, clarifies further what Lévi-Strauss is about.

> . . . there seems to be general, if implicit, agreement among certain structuralists, notably Lévi-Strauss in anthropology, Roman Jakobson in linguistics, Jean Piaget in psychology and Francois Jacob in biology, that there is in man an innate, genetically transmitted and determined mechanism that acts as a structuring force. Moreover, this inherent quality or capacity is so designed as to limit the possible range of ways of structuring. It has been pointed out, for example, that the structures of natural languages (that is, those that actually exist) represent only a very restricted spectrum of the possible structures of language. If this is the case (and it is still being vigorously debated by scholars in the various disciplines), then we can imagine a hierarchy in which the innate structure generates a specialized structure for a particular type of activity—language, myth or kinship systems, say—which in turn produces the observable pattern of speech, story or marriage.[12]

> The structuralist method, then, is a means whereby social reality may be expressed as binary oppositions, each element, whether it be an event in a myth, an item of behavior or the naming and classification of natural phenomena, being given its value in society by its relative position in a matrix of oppositions, their mediations and resolutions.[13]

If Lévi-Strauss's thesis is correct, there will be homologous relationships within a given culture between, for example, modes of eating (raw or cooked), modes of dressing (clothed or naked), patterns of etiquette (table manners), modes of exchanging women (licit or illicit), modes of barter, and other modes of communication, such as language and myth. There will also be homologous relationships and, most importantly, transformational relationships between these modes from one society to another.

It is as if, of the spectrum of possible civilizational choices, each culture contingently, on account of natural environment and internal collective "genetic" constitution, must choose one particular segment out of which it constructs meaning. Within that segment communication is possible only because the law of identity obtains. It is only because each culture develops rigorous binary oppositions within its limited spectral range in all its modes of communication, and then keeps those oppositions equally rigorously apart by mediators, that any meaning and communication is possible (structure). The principles governing the construction of such civilizational complexes, Lévi-Strauss argues, are universal and invariant (*esprit*). It is, of course, crucial to understand that for Lévi-Strauss culinary, sartorial, mensal, sexual, economic, and linguistic patterns all serve equally as modes of human communication.[14]

Edmund Leach develops the spectrum metaphor. "I postulate," he writes,

> that the physical and social environment of a young child is perceived as a continuum. It does not contain any intrinsically separate "things". The child, in due course, is taught to impose upon this environment a kind of discriminating grid which serves to distinguish the world as being composed of a large number of separate things, each labelled with a name. This world is a representation of our language categories, not vice versa. Because my mother tongue is English, it seems self-evident that *bushes* and *trees* are different kinds of things. I would not think this unless I had been taught that it was the case.
>
> Now if each individual has to learn to construct his own environment in this way, it is crucially important that the basic discriminations should be clear-cut and unambiguous. There must be absolutely no doubt about the difference between *me* and *it,* or between *we* and *they.* But how can such certainty of discrimination be achieved if our normal perception displays only a continuum? . . . by means of a simultaneous use of language and taboo. Language gives us the names to distinguish the things; taboo inhibits the recognition of those parts of the continuum which separate the things . . . [15]

What taboo is, on this argument, for language, Lévi-Strauss's mediating categories are for myths.

The critics have recognized that important though structure is to Lévi-Strauss, *esprit* is even more important. They have faulted him for not living up to his promise of providing an invariant algebra of myth. Mythology, they argue, cannot be compared to language with the structuralist algebra serving as the functional equivalent of syntax. Language is based on combinations of phonemes and morphemes, myth on combinations of relations which in their "pre-mythical" state already have meaning. The meaning of a linguistic proposition is not its syntax, yet Lévi-Strauss would have us believe that the meaning of a myth is its structure.[16] Roland Barthes, acknowledging the contradiction, has endeavored to deal with the problem of the relationship of language to myth in a more satisfactory fashion.[17]

More importantly for our purposes, Paul Ricoeur has drawn attention to the fact

> that Lévi-Strauss's examples of mythical thought "have been taken from the geographical areas of totemism and never from Semitic, pre-Hellenic, or Indo-European areas." Ricoeur felt that Sumero-Akkadian, Hebrew, Egyptian, Mycenean, Iranian and Indian myths might behave quite differently: that, as E. R. Leach expresses it, Lévi-Strauss's myths are those "in which there is a notable confusion between human beings and animals but which are characterised by the absence of any setting within an historical chronology, real or imaginary. Ricoeur suggests that there may be a fundamental contrast between 'totemic' myths of this kind and the mythologies of civilized peoples." [18]

Moreover, although he denies it, Lévi-Strauss is clearly interested in the applied aspect of myth as well as in the purely algebraic or architectural aspect.

In spite of these criticisms, it is generally agreed that Lévi-Strauss is on the right track. Mary Douglas, notwithstanding her many critical reservations, generously but rightfully endorses the validity of the basic approach.[19] Edmund Leach, somewhat less generously, observes: "In my view the end product is in large measure fallacious, but even the study of fallacies can prove rewarding." [20]

Ricoeur's criticism was leveled in 1963. But in 1955 Lévi-Strauss had already anticipated that criticism in part by applying his structural technique to the Oedipus myth. The effort is not entirely successful. At the last minute he leaves us up in the air, with his usually tortuous style reaching new heights (or should we say depths) of relentless obscurity.

However, there is no doubt at all about the general outlines of what he has to say.

In order to understand the structural analysis of the Oedipus myth, we must first understand two crucial concepts, one of which Lévi-Strauss draws from the *Course in General Linguistics* of Ferdinand de Saussure, and the second from the realm of music. Both are closely related. The first concept is the dichotomy of *langue* and *parole*. Lévi-Strauss proceeds to apply this dichotomy to the realm of myth (illegitimately, according to his critics, for, as we have noted, the basic elements of myth, and especially of the Oedipus myth, are meaningful propositions and not phonemes or morphemes). The second concept comes from the world of symphonic composition and conducting.

According to Ferdinand de Saussure, *langue,* or "language", is a system of signs and is "the norm of all other manifestations of speech." [21] *Parole,* or "speech", is the "executive side" which is performed by the individual, whereas "language is not complete in any speaker; it exists perfectly only within a collectivity." [22]

> "The English language" denotes a total system of words, conventions, and usages; from the point of view of any particular individual speaker it is a "given"; it is not something he creates for himself; the parts of the language are available for use, but they do not have to be used. But when I, as an individual, make an utterance I use "speech"; I select from the total system of "the language" certain words and grammatical conventions and tones and accents, and by placing these in a particular *order* I am able to transmit information by my utterance.[23]

Language is synchronic, speech diachronic.

> Diachronic facts are then particular; a shift in a system is brought about by events which not only are outside the system . . . but are isolated and form no system among themselves . . . synchronic facts, no matter what they are, evidence a certain regularity but are in no way imperative; diachronic facts, on the contrary, force themselves upon language but are in no way general.[24]

In a discussion of Bachofen's use of symbolism, Raymond Firth observes:

> Moreover, with Bachofen the Romantic tide came to a flood. In his study of symbolism he went beyond the classical conventions of his day in mak-

ing much more articulate abstract statements about the nature of his subject. . . . He argues that human speech is too poor to convey all the thoughts aroused by such basic problems as the alternation of life and death and the sublimity of hope. Only the symbol and the related myth can meet this higher need. The symbol awakes intimations; speech can only explain. *The symbol plucks all the strings of the human spirit at once,* speech is compelled to take up a single thought at a time. Into the most secret depths of the soul the symbol strikes its roots; language skims over the surface of the understanding like a soft breeze. The symbol aims inward; language aims outward. *Only the symbol can combine the most disparate elements into a unitary expression* . . . . [italics added][25]

Whether or not under the influence of Bachofen but certainly under the influence of de Saussure, Lévi-Strauss takes up the metaphor of music to account for the structure of myth as well as for its meaning.[26] He avers his intention

to treat the sequences of myth, and the myths themselves in respect of their reciprocal interrelations, like the instrumental parts of a musical work and to study them as one studies a symphony. The legitimacy of this procedure depends on the demonstration of the existence of an isomorphism between the mythic system, which is of a linguistic order, and the system of music which, as we know, constitutes a language, since we understand it, but whose absolute originality and distinguishing feature with regard to articulate speech is its untranslatability.[27]

Mythology occupies an intermediary position between two diametrically opposed types of sign systems—musical language on the one hand and articulate speech on the other; to be understood it has to be studied from both angles.[28]

Just as music makes the individual conscious of his physiological rootedness, mythology makes him aware of his roots in society. The former hits us in the guts; the latter, we might say, appeals to our group instinct (TRANSLATOR'S NOTE: The original reads: *L'une nous prend aux tripes, l'autre, si l'on ose dire, "au groupe."* [29]

Armed with the dichotomy synchronic/diachronic and the musical metaphor, Lévi-Strauss now proceeds to break up the Oedipus myth into units of simple relations. These units are unfolded diachronically, that is, irreversibly and unilinearly, in the narrating of the myth. However, the meaning of the myth cannot be found on the level of these simple units.

It is not the separate elements of relations but the "bundles of such relations" which carry the *real* meaning of the myth. The bundles of relations are to be "read" synchronically. That is to say, the myth cannot be understood by reflecting only on the sequential and isolated relations of Kadmos seeking his sister, Oedipus marrying his mother, Antigone burying her brother, the Spartoi killing each other, Oedipus killing his father, Eteocles killing his brother, and so on. The meaning of the myth resides in the realization that the first three relations together constitute a "bundle" which must be read synchronically. Likewise, the latter three relations must be read as a "bundle." The first "bundle," according to Lévi-Strauss, speaks of "the *overrating of blood relations.*" The second "bundle" speaks of the *"underrelating of blood relations."* It is a pleasure to be able to quote Lévi-Strauss in one of his more lucid moods.

> Let us first suppose that archaeologists of the future coming from another planet would one day, when all human life had disappeared from the earth, excavate one of our libraries. Even if they were at first ignorant of our writing, they might succeeed in deciphering it—an undertaking which would require, at some early stage, the discovery that the alphabet, as we are in the habit of printing it, should be read from left to right and from top to bottom. However, they would soon find out that a whole category of books did not fit the usual pattern: these would be the orchestra scores on the shelves of the music division. But after trying, without success, to decipher staffs one after the other, from the upper down to the lower, they would probably notice that the same patterns of notes recurred at intervals, either in full or in part, or that some patterns were strongly reminiscent of earlier ones. Hence the hypothesis: what if patterns showing affinity, instead of being considered in succession, were to be treated as one complex pattern and read globally? By getting at what we call *harmony,* they would then find out that an orchestra score, in order to become meaningful, has to be read diachronically along one axis —that is, page after page, and from left to right—and also synchronically along the other axis, all the notes which are written vertically making up one gross consituent unit, i.e. one bundle of relations.[30]

Lévi-Strauss argues that the Oedipus myth may be reduced in this fashion to four columns of "bundles of relations." As we have seen above, the first column speaks of overrating blood relations. In different ways Kadmos, Oedipus, and Antigone are overinvolved with their blood relations. By the same token, the Spartoi, Oedipus, and Eteocles underrate blood relations by killing, respectively, each other, Laios, and Polynices.

The third column of relations, or "bundle" (Kadmos kills the dragon, Oedipus kills the Sphinx), affirms *"the denial of the autochthonous origin of man,"* and the fourth column, in which reference is made to the lameness of Labdacos, Laios, and Oedipus, affirms *"the persistence of the autochthonous origin of man."*

The argument is not entirely clear, but the general gist of what Lévi-Strauss is saying is evident. The myth tells a story which can be broken down into simple units of relations which, when the myth is read as a story, emerge diachronically, irreversibly, sequentially. But something else is also happening. At specific intervals "harmonies" appear, emerging relations which correlate with relations already established. From the standpoint of synchronicity, the myth is making four distinct statements which fall into two parts. Overrating of blood relations stands in relation to underrating of blood relations as denying the autochthonous origin of man stands in relation to insisting that man is, indeed, autochthonous.

The notion that man is vegetal, that he is not born from the union of a man and a woman and then issues forth from the womb of the woman, but that he emerges from the ground, is well attested in the classical sources in particular as well as in world mythology in general. Some cultures maintain that "originally, men lived as embryos or larvae in the body of the Mother, that is, deep in the bowels of the earth . . . that, one fine day, man found an opening in the Earth's crust and crawled out onto the surface, and began to enjoy living in the open air." [31] Mythological details such as Jason's sowing of the dragon's teeth reflect this preoccupation. But if men come from the ground, then immediately after they emerge they must be like other "beings" originating from the ground—plants—which are weak and tend to wilt until they have been warmed by the sun and enabled to stand up straight and become fully rooted. Lévi-Strauss perceives in the etymology of the names Labdacos (lame), Laios (left-sided), and Oedipus (swollen-foot), which constitutes his fourth column, overtones of the notion that when men, conceived of as having an autochthonous origin, first emerge from the earth they are unable to walk properly and hence stumble, giving the appearance of being lame.

The dragon, according to Lévi-Strauss, is "a chthonian being." (Could it be that the ancients who first saw volcanoes erupting or who heard tell of volcanoes erupting assumed that these "fire-breathing" mountains were some species of fire-breathing animal? The mistake would be natural in a pre-scientific age.) Lévi-Strauss sees in this "bundle" of relations an insistence that man is *not* of autochthonous origin. Man kills dragons which are chthonian creatures. (Evidence of extinct volcanoes?) This is a denial of man's autochthonous origin.

What, then, does the myth mean? According to Lévi-Strauss, the culture in which this myth arose was a culture which accepted the autochthonous origin of man as part of its cosmology. Daily reality contradicted cosmology. Men could see all around them that children, in fact, were born from the womb and not from the earth. For whatever reason, the culture needed to believe in its cosmology rather than accept reality. (It was not unique in this regard.) It "created" a myth in which, by juxtaposing two oppositions, the genuine tension between what the culture wanted to believe and what was, in fact, the case, was alleviated by being placed next to another tension. The second tension, less intense than the first, drew off some of the original tension. We may compare the process to what happens when a pain in one part of the body is alleviated, but not entirely removed, by creating another kind of pain in another area, which gives "the impression" of having diminished the intensity of the original pain. Pressing onto a gum in the vicinity of an aching tooth is a case in point.

> The myth has to do with the inability, for a culture which holds the belief that mankind is autochthonous (see, for instance, Pausanias, VIII, xxix, 4; vegetals provide a *model* for humans), to find a satisfactory transition between this theory and the knowledge that human beings are actually born from the union of man and woman. Although the problem obviously cannot be solved, the Oedipus myth provides a kind of logical tool which, to phrase it coarsely, replaces the original problem: born from one or born from two? born from different or born from same? By a correlation of this type, the overrelating of blood relations is to the underrating of blood relations as the attempt to escape autochthony is to the impossibility to succeed in it. Although experience contradicts theory, social life verifies the cosmology by its similarity of structure. Hence cosmology is true.[32]

The critics were not entirely happy with Lévi-Strauss's interpretation of the Oedipus myth, and for obvious reasons. "All the majestic themes which we had previously thought the Oedipus myth was about—destiny, duty, and self-knowledge, have been strained off, and we are left with a worry about how the species began," complained Mary Douglas.[33] Nor were the critics mollified when Edmund Leach ingeniously applied structural analysis to the first three chapters of Genesis.

When Edmund Leach applies the same technique to the Book of Genesis, the rich metaphysical themes of salvation and cosmic oneness are replaced by practical rules for the regulation of sex. When Lévi-Strauss has finished with the Tsimshian myth it is reduced to anxieties about the problems of matrilateral cross-cousin marriage. . . . It seems that whenever anthropologists apply structural analysis to myth they extract not only a different but a lesser meaning . . . [34]

Reductionism is, perhaps, too harsh a judgment. The meaning of myths is clearly "overdetermined" in the Freudian sense of the term. There is more than one single causal explanation for any myth and probably also for any part of a myth. What cannot be gainsaid is that the structure which Lévi-Strauss and Leach see in this material is there. It is not a figment of their imagination. The myth may have other meanings in whole and in part, but the structural element cannot be ignored. Mary Douglas is well aware of this. "Some may have doubted that myths can have an elaborate symmetrical structure," she observes in her critique of Lévi-Strauss's *The Story of Asdiwal.* "If so, they should be convinced of their error." [35] The approach is invalid only if it is used exclusivistically.

Edmund Leach, perhaps also piqued by Ricoeur's criticism, applied Lévi-Strauss's technique to another section of the Bible. "My purpose," he writes,

is to demonstrate that the Biblical story of the succession of Solomon to the throne of Israel is a myth which "mediates" a major contradiction. The Old Testament as a whole asserts that the Jewish political title to the land of Palestine is a direct gift from God to the descendants of Israel (Jacob). This provides the fundamental basis for Jewish endogamy—the Jews should be a people of pure blood and pure religion, living in isolation in their Promised Land. But interwoven with this theological dogma there is a less idealized form of tradition which represents the population of ancient Palestine as a mixture of many peoples over whom the Jews have asserted political dominance by right of conquest. The Jews and their "foreign" neighbours intermarry freely. The synthesis achieved by the story of Solomon is such that by a kind of dramatic trick the reader is persuaded that the second of these descriptions, which is morally bad, exemplifies the first description, which is morally good. [36]

Without denying that theologians find other meanings in these texts, Leach insists that his analysis "reveals only a patterning of arguments about endogamy and exogamy, legitimacy and illegitimacy as operative in the thought-processes of Palestinian Jews of the third century B.C." [37]

To the very best of my knowledge, neither Lévi-Strauss nor any of his colleagues or disciples has recognized that another important segment of the Bible is susceptible to the structural method of analysis, namely Genesis 37-Exodus 20. I cannot claim to have unraveled all the details or to have clarified every aspect of the structural arrangement. But the evidence overwhelmingly points to the fact that we are here in the presence of another "mediation" of a culturally determined binary opposition.

I propose to show that this entire biblical sequence may best be conceived as a segment of a larger myth, namely, the Pentateuch as a whole, which, when broken down into its simple units of relation and then into "bundles" of relations, may be read synchronically as mediating a major and fundamental biblical opposition or contradiction.

The myth of the Pentateuch is basically the myth of the Bible as a whole. Those parts of the Bible which were produced after the redaction of the Pentateuch are an extension of the original myth. That core myth, which may be found in the Pentateuch, is the story told by the Jewish people in the fifth pre-Christian century to account for its reality situation. Perhaps it would be better to say that the myth expresses how the Jewish people *experienced* its reality situation in the fifth pre-Christian century. While not going as far as Lévi-Strauss in his notion that myths think through men rather than that men think through myths, I wish to dissociate myself from any view which sees intellectual deliberation or cognition involved in the creation of myth. The Pentateuch as myth is a collectively unconscious response on the part of the Jewish people to the twin traumas of the loss of the northern kingdom of Israel in 721 and the loss of the kingdom of Judah in 586. "Literary and historical criticism," observes Vriezen,

> will have to take into account the fall of Jerusalem in 586 B.C., much more than it has done hitherto. The destruction of the holy city in A.D. 70 had an enormous influence on the development of the Jews, on the defining of the canon of Old Testament writings, on the genesis of a *textus receptus* and on theology as a whole (characterized by opposition to further development and by radical and traditionalist tendencies). The same applies to the first destruction of the temple in 586 (with the previous downfall of Samaria in 722, and the subsequent restoration of the religious life of the people after 539). It would be of great importance if the study of background were to pay more regard to these data and thus show clearly the *"Sitz im Leben"* of the writings separately and of the canon as a whole. Even a superficial inspection of the dates of these

writings suffices to show how the classical writings of the Old Testament centre round these events.[38]

And even more succinctly:

> . . . the Old Testament is not merely a collection of ancient Israelite religious texts, but is the book of the religion of Israel as it was reformed in the period of the exile under the influence of the prophets whose critical insight was formed under the guidance of the Spirit of God in times of great distress.[39]

According to Salo Baron, the syndrome of trauma to which the Pentateuch is a mythological response antedates the fall of the Northern kingdom. "For a century before Tiglath-pileser reached Palestine," Baron writes,

> Assyria cast its shadow over the shores of the Mediterranean. In fact, the first definitely datable event in Israelitic history was Ahab's participation in the battle of Karkara (853–852). According to a contemporary Assyrian inscription, Ahab served as an ally of the king of Damascus, commanding the relatively large contingent of 2,000 chariots and 10,000 infantrymen. This battle seems to have ended in a deadlock or perhaps even in Assyria's defeat, but it underscored Israel's subordinate position. *From that time on Israel and Judah, irresistibly drawn into the whirl of western Asiatic affairs, were impotent to direct their own destinies.* [italics added][40]

The "trauma," then, to which, it is my contention, the Pentateuch is a mythological "reaction," is bounded by the historical parameters of the battle of Karkara in 853–852 and the destruction of Jerusalem in 586.[41] Throughout this entire period, but cumulatively so and coming to a head in the aftermath of the destruction of the Temple, it became ineluctably evident to the spiritual leaders of the people, specifically the prophets, that Israel's sovereign and autonomous future was doomed. It was only a matter of time before this small political entity, which had established itself at a time when there was a power vacuum in the Middle East—the interest of Egypt in Palestine having waned and the interest of Assyria as yet not having emerged, a period extending approximately from the twelfth through the ninth pre-Christian century— would lose its independence. To couch the problem in cognitive terms which would have been unavailable to the prophets, the situation was

clear. Either Israel would differentiate and become a totally different
kind of political entity or Israel would go the way of all those other small
principalities which had taken advantage of the political interregnum
to establish a footing in, or in the vicinity of, Palestine. The prophetic
response was to see Israel as the Chosen People of the Creator of heaven
and earth. This is the story that the Pentateuch in particular and the
Bible in general tell—-that the God of All chose Israel, that Israel proved
faithless, that God therefore punished Israel by exiling her, but that in
the fullness of time God would redeem His people and restore them to
their land.

Precisely at that moment in time when the myth of Israel's Election
was being articulated in its most systematic fashion, the fortunes of
Israel had fallen to their lowest ebb. There is almost an inverse relationship between Israelitic messianic aspirations and the reality situation. The
thirty-seventh chapter of the Book of Ezekiel, with its vision of the valley
of dry bones, epitomizes what must have been the dominant mood of
the Babylonian exiles. If Israel is the Elect, why does it suffer so? The
Bible tells the story of God's choice of Israel and of His promise that He
will never forsake His people. But the reality of the Jewish people in the
middle of the sixth pre-Christian century belies this promise. The reality
situation of the captives in Babylon is in stark contrast to an Elect people
living in the Promised Land. The opposition between fact and fantasy,
between reality and illusion, between "social system" and "cultural system," [42] is mediated by the idea that God's plan from the beginning of the
world, culminating in the coming of the Messiah, is to work through
impotence. Therefore, *actual* impotence (the condition of the exiles in
Babylon) need not negate fantasied potence (the biblical myth). This
idea operates through the notion that biblical succession is invariably
through the younger and weaker rather than through the elder and the
stronger. What appears weak is strong, and what appears strong is weak
(Abel, Abraham, Perez, Isaac, Ephraim, Moses, David).

The centrality of this myth is attested in the time-honored tradition in
Jewish families, which dates back to talmudic times, of blessing the
children on the Eve of the Sabbath. The blessing for boys runs: "God
make thee as Ephraim and as Manasseh" and is taken from Genesis
48:20: "And he blessed them that day saying: 'By thee shall Israel
bless, saying: God make thee as Ephraim and as Manasseh.' And he set
Ephraim before Manasseh." Genesis 48 is inexplicable unless we see
in it an embodiment of a central mythical mediation of the Bible. By
right, Manasseh, who is the firstborn, should have received priority in

the blessing. This is clearly the wish of his father, Joseph. Jacob deliberately places his right hand on the head of Ephraim, which entails self-consciously crossing his hands, since Joseph had placed the two boys in front of him so that his right hand would have naturally fallen on the head of Manasseh.

It is to be seriously doubted whether, in the pre-modern period, Jews were ever aware of the full implications of this myth.[43] It served as a constant unconscious[44] mythical mediation of the disparity between the Jewish notion of Israel being God's chosen people and the reality situation of the Jew being the most despised of men.

It is interesting to observe that the dichotomy diachronic/synchronic, so valuable for the elucidation of problems in semiology in general and linguistics in particular, is clearly adumbrated in the biblical myth. On one level the *res gestae* of Israel are worked out diachronically in irreversible, sequential, historical time. But on another level an entirely different time factor is operating, a synchronicity based on the preexistent plan in God's Mind which is worked through in the Bible. Man experiences history as irreversible and unilinear. God as the Cosmic Conductor reads the score "diachronically along one axis . . . and also synchronically along the other axis" in terms of His Grand Cosmic Plan. This is especially evident in P but is also present in the overall text of the Bible. The dichotomy may well have Mesopotamian antecedents. It is typically exemplified in such texts as: "And in the fourth generation they shall come back hither; for the iniquity of the Amorite is not yet full." [45] The Bible, thus conceived, is a preexistent ideal symphonic messianic score of Divine composition, waiting to be "played" by the Composer, rather than an evolutionary and emergent Darwinian process of unilinear mutational "jumps." On this view Jewish history is the result of preformation rather than of epigenesis.

There is a further analogy with psychoanalysis. On one level the neurotic lives his life diachronically, irreversibly. From the standpoint of the analyst, however, what is experienced by the neurotic as diachronic is seen, in fact, to be a synchronic "playing" of "harmonies" and "rhythms" "composed" in early childhood (neurotic patterns deriving from trauma). Psychoanalysis mediates the Pauline opposition between "the good that I would I do not: but the evil which I would not, that I do" by making the patient aware of his personal "responsibility" for his present "behavior." Resolution takes place when the synchronic can be seen in the diachronic and ultimately anticipated and hence "defused." Since, as Freud realized, there is no total cure for the human con-

dition, the opposition healthy/sick is mediated but never entirely resolved. Psychoanalytic theory as an implicit therapeutic model relieves
the tension of the insoluble problem. The biblical dichotomy of syn-
chronic/diachronic almost certainly derives from an intuitive awareness of this psychological paradox.

Before demonstrating that Genesis 37–Exodus 20 is susceptible to
a structural analysis, some remarks are called for on the nature of the
myth under discussion in particular and on the legitimacy of speaking
of myth in connection with the Bible in general. Lévi-Strauss has argued
that no matter how many times the myth is told, the structural approach
still holds. "Thus, our method," he writes,

> eliminates a problem which has, so far, been one of the main obstacles to
> the progress of mythological studies, namely, the quest for the *true* ver-
> sion, or the *earlier* one. On the contrary, we define the myth as con-
> sisting of all its versions; or to put it otherwise, a myth remains the same
> as long as it is felt as such. A striking example is offered by the fact that
> our interpretation may take into account the Freudian use of the Oedipus
> myth and is certainly applicable to it. Although the Freudian problem
> has ceased to be that of autochthony *versus* bisexual reproduction it
> is still the problem of understanding how *one* can be born from *two:*
> How is it that we do not have only one procreator, but a mother plus a
> father? Therefore, not only Sophocles, but Freud himself, should be in-
> cluded among the recorded versions of the Oedipus myth on a par with
> earlier or seemingly more "authentic" versions.[46]

How does this argument apply to the biblical material? Does it matter
how many recensions the material we are discussing underwent? Oddly
enough, in responding to Paul Ricoeur's criticism that he, Lévi-Strauss,
had ignored Oriental, Egyptian, and Hebraic material and concentrated
on totemistic religious myths instead, Lévi-Strauss appears to write off
the biblical material.

> He advances the rather curious proposition that Old Testament mythology
> has been "deformed" by the intellectual operations of Biblical editors and
> he seems to imply that, on this account, a structural analysis of such mate-
> rials must prove to be largely a waste of time.[47]

> . . . he sidestepped Ricoeur's objection about Old Testament myths by
> claiming that they have suffered from redactors and intellectual inter-

preters, and therefore their *"residu mythologique et archaique"* has been overlaid.[48]

It seems strange that whereas Lévi-Strauss maintains that even Freud's version of the Oedipus myth is susceptible to a structural analysis, the biblical myths do not qualify. If he were consistent, then surely he would allow Thomas Mann's trilogy to be included with Genesis 37–Exodus 20 in a structural analysis of the Joseph story and its subsequent developments. It stands to reason that our text has been "deformed." The Joseph story has acknowledged Egyptian antecedents. Yet within the framework of the Bible it surely deserves to be treated on its own merits. Edmund Leach has demonstrated that at least *some* biblical material is susceptible to structural analysis. Or does Lévi-Strauss, the Jew, have problems with "Jewish" material?

As far as the legitimacy of using the term *myth* in connection with the Bible is concerned, it would seem that there is no longer any possible objection. Time was when biblical scholars avoided using the term *myth* in connection with the Bible. Myth was falsehood by definition. This has changed. "For the past fifty years at least," writes Mircea Eliade,

> Western scholars have approached the study of myth from a viewpoint markedly different from, let us say, that of the nineteenth century. Unlike their predecessors, who treated myth in the usual meaning of the word, that is, as "fable," "invention," "fiction," they have accepted it as it was understood in the archaic societies, where, on the contrary, "myth" means "a true story" and, beyond that, a story that is a most precious possession because it is sacred, exemplary, significant. This new semantic value given the term "myth" makes its use in contemporary parlance somewhat equivocal. Today, that is, the word is employed both in the sense of "fiction" or "illusion" and in that familiar especially to ethnologists, sociologists, and historians of religions, the sense of "sacred tradition, primordial revelation, exemplary model." [49]

One remembers Gunkel's embarrassment ("myths—let no one shrink from the word") in his *Commentary on Genesis*. Myths for Gunkel are stories of the gods.[50] He compromises in referring to "mythical" parts of the Bible by speaking of "faded myths." [51] Likewise Sarna betrays the same embarrassment: ". . . God . . . has no myth; that is, there are no stories about any events in His life. Magic plays no part in the worship of Him." [52]

These views are no longer tenable. Even on Gunkel's narrow defi-

nition of myth, the Bible is full of myth. Henri Frankfort has perceptively observed that the central biblical myth is that of the Will of
God. "Hebrew thought did not entirely overcome mythopoeic thought.
It created, in fact, a new myth—the myth of the Will of God." [53] As for
the claim that there are no stories about any events in God's life in the
Bible, it is simply not true. Even Gunkel admits as much.[54] John F. Priest
has boldly and insightfully suggested that "the history of Israel is the
biography of Yahweh."

> Yahweh did not, to any considerable extent at least, interact with the
> other gods. He had no consort or, in this early period, any defined heavenly
> entourage. But he did have a life, a life most distinctly discernible in the
> accounts of his dealings with his people Israel. Thus Yahweh's biography
> and the resultant Yahweh myth was indistinguishable from the history of
> Israel itself. *One can say that the history of Israel is the biography of
> Yahweh* and this insight provides the justification for the contention that
> history was in fact the mode of the Israelite expression of myth.[55]

But there are any number of other ways in which one can now speak
of myth in connection with the Bible. Nor are we thinking of vestigial
traces of Mesopotamian myths, such as references to Rahab the dragon
and the like, which scholars of the ilk of Alexander Heidel delight in
justifying and in apologetically explaining away.[56] The Bible is myth
in terms of its aetiological explanations. It is crucially myth conceived
as a whole in terms of Malinowski's charter theory of myth. "I maintain," writes Malinowski,

> that there exists a special class of stories, regarded as sacred, embodied in
> ritual, morals, and social organization, and which form an integral and
> active part of primitive culture. These stories live not by idle interest, not
> as fictitious or even as true narratives; but are to the natives a statement
> of a primeval, greater, and more relevant reality, by which the present
> life, fates, and activities of mankind are determined, the knowledge of
> which supplies man with the motive for ritual and moral actions, as well
> as with indications as to how to perform them.[57]

> The function of myth, briefly, is to strengthen tradition and endow it with
> a greater value and prestige by tracing it back to a higher, better, more
> supernatural reality of initial events.[58]

From the standpoint of Durkheim, one important function of the Bible
is to affirm the collective identity of the Jewish people. From the stand-

point of the "ritual" school, the annual recitation of the Pentateuch in synagogue may be seen as a functional equivalent of the annual recitation of the *Enuma Elish,* the Babylonian "Genesis," at the Babylonian New Year festival of Akitu. (As for the insistence that magic plays no part in the Jewish worship of God, that may be true of the Bible, but Gershom Scholem has shown conclusively that from the time of the appearance of the Book *Bahir* [ca. 1180], "a stratum of myth" in its narrowest sense, including magic, reappeared in Judaism itself.)[59] I take it, therefore, as axiomatic that we may legitimately regard our material as myth and approach it from the standpoint of Lévi-Strauss's definition of myth as a structure that affords meaning by mediating opposites: ". . . the purpose of myth is to provide a logical model capable of overcoming a contradiction . . ."[60]

We now turn to the biblical material, which we will first break down into units of relations prior to constructing columns of "bundles of relations."

1. Jacob chooses Joseph.[61]
2. Joseph has two dreams.[62]
3. The brothers reject Joseph.[63]
4. Joseph is thrown into a pit.[64]
5. Joseph is declared dead by Jacob on account of the blood-stained coat of many colors which the brothers bring to him.[65]
6. Judah chooses Joseph.[66]
7. The brothers reject Judah.[67]
8. Judah marries exogamously.[68]
9. Tamar plays the harlot but only in order to have issue.[69]
10. Tamar is almost thrown into the fire but is rescued at the last minute.[70]
11. Tamar reveals her true identity by producing the signet, cords, and staff given her by Judah.[71]
12. Potiphar chooses Joseph.[72]
13. Potiphar's wife chooses Joseph.[73]
14. Joseph insists that he is a respectable and responsible steward and not a lecher.[74]
15. Potiphar's wife tears off Joseph's cloak.[75]
16. Potiphar is convinced of Joseph's guilt on the evidence of his cloak, which Potiphar's wife claims she tore from him while defending her virtue.[76]

17. Potiphar's wife rejects Joseph.[77]
18. Potiphar's wife claims that Joseph attempted to see her nakedness.[78] The verb translated into English as "to mock" means "to act sexually promiscuously." [79]
19. Joseph is thrown into prison.[80]
20. The keeper of the prison chooses Joseph.[81]
21. The butler and the baker have dreams. The former's dream will lead to his metaphorical elevation. He will be restored to his post. The latter's dream will lead to his literal elevation—by hanging.[82]
22. The butler rejects Joseph.[83]
23. Pharaoh has two dreams.[84]
24. Pharaoh chooses Joseph.[85]
25. Joseph is "thrown" into the royal chariot.[86]
26. Joseph marries exogamously.[87]
27. The brothers are "thrown" into Egypt on account of the famine.[88]
28. Jacob chooses Benjamin.[89]
29. Joseph rejects his brothers.[90]
30. Joseph dissimulates.[91]
31. Joseph accuses his brothers of coming "to see the nakedness of the land." [92]
32. Joseph chooses Benjamin.[93]
33. Joseph's brothers are thrown into prison.[94]
34. The brothers acknowledge their guilt.[95]
35. Simeon is thrown into prison.[96]
36. Joseph reveals himself to his brothers.[97]
37. Jacob chooses Ephraim over Manasseh.[98]
38. Pharaoh rejects Israel.[99]
39. Pharaoh orders all male Hebrew children thrown into the Nile.[100]
40. Moses' mother "throws" him into the Nile.[101]
41. Moses "throws" the Egyptian into the sand.[102]
42. The shepherds drive Jethro's daughters away from the well.[103]
43. Yahweh reveals Himself to Moses in a burning bush.[104]
44. Yahweh chooses Israel.[105]
45. Yahweh rejects Pharaoh and the Egyptians.[106]
46. Yahweh chooses Israel.[107]
47. Moses throws the rod onto the ground.[108]
48. Zipporah throws the foreskin of her son at Moses' feet.[109]
49. Yahweh reveals Himself to Moses as Yahweh, formerly known as El Shaddai.[110]
50. Aaron throws down his rod.[111]

51. The Egyptian magicians throw down their rods.[112]
52. Yahweh rejects the Egyptians (the plagues).[113]
53. The Egyptians are thrown into the sea.[114]
54. Yahweh reveals Himself to the people on a burning mountain.[115]
55. Yahweh gives the Law to the people.[116]

This does not claim to be an exhaustive list of every single relation in the material treated. Where there were only a few synchronic relations, it did not seem feasible to suggest that a major statement was being made. The repetition of the fact that God made everything that Joseph did prosper [117] is a case in point. Moreover, some of the relations have been defined loosely. From one point of view, there is a considerable difference between throwing a man into prison, throwing a baby into the Nile, and burying a man in the sand. But when the evidence is cumulative that a major statement is being made, it seemed important to try to itemize every possible variation on this theme. The same liberties have been taken with the idea of election or choosing. In all instances there was present the notion of separating one person from among all others as an act of favoritism, but the intensity and the nature of the choosing differed from case to case. Yahweh's choosing of Israel is clearly not on the same level or of the same order as Judah's endeavoring to be partial to Joseph as against the brothers' legitimate complaints against him. Nevertheless, the evidence is overwhelming that the theme of election is central to this material, and it was therefore deemed wise to endeavor to extract every possible relation which might conceivably be subsumed under this theme.

As we have already indicated, there is no way of knowing whether or not this material has been altered in the course of transmission. On the basis of the evidence, we have selected six conspicuous "bundles of relations," which, on further analysis, can be reduced to three major "chords," or "harmonies," when the material is read synchronically as opposed to diachronically.

The first column seems to consist of relations which involve election or choosing of one form or another. Some individual or group is chosen above others or some kind of favoritism or selectivity is involved.

Jacob chooses Joseph.
Judah chooses Joseph.
Potiphar chooses Joseph.

Potiphar's wife chooses Joseph.
The keeper of the prison chooses Joseph.
Pharaoh chooses Joseph.
Jacob chooses Benjamin.
Joseph chooses Benjamin.
Jacob chooses Ephraim over Manasseh.
Yahweh chooses Israel.
Yahweh chooses Israel.

The second column consists of relations which involve rejection of one sort or another.

The brothers reject Joseph.
The brothers reject Judah.
Potiphar's wife rejects Joseph.
The butler rejects Joseph.
Joseph rejects his brothers.
The new Pharaoh rejects Israel.
Yahweh rejects Pharaoh and the Egyptians.

The third column involves someone or something being thrown into something else. From these relations we shall select those which seem to underline the notion of rejection.

Joseph is thrown into the pit.
Tamar is almost thrown into the fire.
Joseph is thrown into prison.
Joseph's brothers are thrown into jail.
Simeon is thrown into jail.
Pharaoh has all male Hebrew children thrown into the Nile.
The Egyptians are thrown into the sea.

The next two columns are ambiguous, that is, they involve opposites. In the fourth column we have election and rejection expressed in dreams.

Joseph has two dreams, in both of which someone is elected and some-one rejected.
The butler and the baker have two dreams, the former of election, the latter of rejection.
Pharaoh has two dreams involving rejection (famine) and election (plenty).

ALAN W. MILLER   43

In the fifth column we also have ambiguity. The general theme of this group of relations is that something which appears to be the case is, in fact, not the case. We propose to describe this syndrome as dissimulation.

Tamar to Judah: You don't recognize me, but I am Tamar your daughter-in-law and not a harlot.

Joseph to the butler and the baker: You don't know who I am, but I am Joseph, son of Jacob, and not a rapist.

Joseph to his brothers: You don't recognize me, but I am Joseph your brother and not Zaphenath-paneah.

Joseph to Potiphar's wife: You don't know it, but I am Joseph, son of Jacob, and not one of your run-of-the-mill lecherous slaves.

The Israelites to the new Pharaoh: You don't know who we are because you are new, but we are the descendants of the man Joseph who saved this country by his foresight. We are not a bunch of ingrate foreigners.

Yahweh to Moses: You think that this is a burning bush but it isn't. It's Me!

Yahweh to Moses: You and the children of Israel think that I am El Shaddai, but I am much more than that. I am Yahweh. You have only known me as El Shaddai, but all along I have been Yahweh also. Now I disclose to you my true and complete identity.

We have taken some liberties with the relations by expressing them in a common formula, but the argument still stands on the weight of the cumulative evidence.

The sixth column seems to deal with recognizing identity through the presence of symbols. This may best be presented as follows:

Joseph is dead, and to prove it, here is his coat of many colors ripped to pieces and stained with blood.

I am Tamar the woman you had sex with, and to prove it, here are your signet, cords, and staff.

I am Zerah the firstborn, and to prove it, here is the scarlet thread tied round my hand by the midwife as evidence that part of my body, my hand, came out of the womb first.

I, Potiphar's wife, am the wronged party, and to prove it, here is Joseph's coat, which I succeeded in tearing off him as he attempted to rape me.

I am Joseph your brother, and to prove it, I show you my circumcision (I have taken the liberty here of including a rabbinic eisegesis,[118] which, for Lévi-Strauss, would qualify as part of the myth).

I am Yahweh, and to prove it, the bush is not consumed.

I am Yahweh, and to prove it, I will perform miracles.

There remain elements of relations in this material which I am unable to account for but which afford clear evidence of minor "harmonies."

There would appear to be some connection between Judah marrying exogamously and Joseph marrying exogamously.

There would appear to be some relationship between Joseph's coat, which is torn off by his brothers, and Joseph's tunic, which is torn off by Potiphar's wife.

There would appear to be some connection between Judah's "seeing the nakedness" of Tamar, Potiphar's wife wanting Joseph to "see her nakedness," and Joseph's accusation leveled against the brothers that the real reason they came to Egypt was not because they were hungry and needed corn but because they wanted "to see the nakedness of the land." The phrase "seeing the nakedness of" is a common biblical metaphor for sexual immorality.[119]

There appears to be a relationship between Joseph's insisting on his innocence, Tamar's insisting on her innocence, Potiphar's wife insisting on her innocence, and Judah's admitting his guilt with respect to Tamar and the brothers' admitting their guilt with respect to Joseph.

Surveying the six columns as a whole, we cannot avoid the challenge of Lévi-Strauss's claim that "repetition has as its function to make the structure of the myth apparent."[120]

Ignoring the peripheral "harmonies" and dividing the six columns logically, it is my contention that we are in the presence of three major "chords" or "bundles of relations" in the Lévi-Straussean sense of those terms. The opposition is between election and rejection. The mediation is through dissimulation. That which appears to be the case is not, in fact, the case. From the standpoint of our presentation, we would suggest that the myth gives evidence of the kind of structure which Lévi-Strauss claimed to find in Amerindian myths as well as in the myth of Oedipus. In addition to its *architecture de l'esprit,* indeed, arising out of it, the myth serves the purpose of reassuring the Babylonian exiles in the following fashion: We are the Chosen People of God (Election). But we find ourselves at the lowest point of our national history (rejection). What appears to be the case is not the case. Our downcast state is due to our sins. We are still the Elect of God, only in a temporary condition of rejection. Although it doesn't look like it, God still loves us, and to prove it, here is the Torah in which His Divine Promise may be seen by all who care to look, our signet, cords, and staff, our coat of many colors, our veritable *lettres patentes.*

If we may assume that the Pentateuch was edited during the Babylonian exile, we may also assume that the ethos behind that editing derived from Israelitic collective experience which long antedated the
destruction of Jerusalem. The dominant fear in the hearts of the
exiles was that they had been utterly rejected by God.[121] It was the
task of the editors of the nascent Bible to strengthen the morale of the
people. Whether they created the myth or the myth created itself through
them is immaterial. There is overwhelming evidence that the Lévi-
Straussean structuralist approach draws our attention to hitherto unnoticed tensions in a central segment of the Pentateuchal narrative or
myth. Although the myth appears to be of the past, its function is of
the present: It looks as if you are finished, O House of Israel. Be not
afraid. God will redeem you. He will save you. Appearances are not
everything. The rejected will be the chosen. "The stone which the
builders rejected is become the chief corner-stone." [122] It is not without
significance that the second-born offspring of the union between Tamar
and Judah, Perez, is the ancestor of the Messiah.[123]

The above-cited evidence must be placed next to Lévi-Strauss's insistence that "Old Testament mythology has been 'deformed' by the
intellectual operations of Biblical editors . . ." [124] It is difficult to believe
that the "bundles of relations" we have observed in Genesis 37–Exodus
20 are not illuminated by Lévi-Strauss's own structural method of reading myth synchronically to elicit its true meaning, at least one of its
possible true meanings.

Was there a reason for the greatest anthropologist of the twentieth
century ignoring his own Jewish tradition and cultivating instead the
aboriginal vineyards of North and South America? Freud's ambivalence
toward his Judaism has been the subject of frequent comment.[125] A rare
passage in *Tristes Tropiques* may throw some light on our subject. In
that book Lévi-Strauss asks:

> . . . how can the anthropologist get free of the contradiction implicit in
> the circumstances of his choice? Under his very nose, and at his disposi-
> tion, he has a society: his own. Why does he decide to disdain it, reserving
> for societies distant and different from his own the patience and devotion
> which he has deliberately witheld from his fellow-citizens? It is not by
> chance that the anthropologist is rarely on terms of neutrality with his
> own social group . . . He has, in fact, become an anthropologist for one of
> two reasons: either he finds it a practical method of reconciling his mem-
> bership of a group with his severely qualified acceptance of it—or, more
> simply, he wishes to turn to advantage an initial attitude of detachment

which has already brought him, as we say, "half-way to meet" societies unlike his own

But if he tries to think straight, he will have to ask himself whether he is really justified in setting such great store by exotic societies (and the more exotic they are, the more he will prize them). Is this not rather a function of the disdain, not to say the hostility, which he feels for the customs of his own milieu?[126]

No doubt Lévi-Strauss was thinking of French society when he penned these words, the French society which, when the Nazis came, would not protect him because of his Jewish origin. That he did not even consider applying his genius to his Jewish background is evident from the following:

> . . . my only contact with religion goes back to a stage in my childhood at which I was already an unbeliever. During the First World War I lived with my grandfather, who was the rabbi of Versailles. His house stood next to the synagogue and was linked to it by a long corridor. Even to set foot in that corridor was an awesome experience; it formed an impassable frontier between the profane world and that other world from which was lacking precisely that human warmth which was the indispensable condition to my recognizing it as sacred. Except at the hours of service the synagogue was empty; desolation seemed natural to it, and its brief spells of occupation were neither sustained enough nor fervent enough to overcome this. They seemed merely an incongruous disturbance. Our private religious observances suffered from the same offhand quality. Only my grandfather's silent prayer before each meal reminded us children that our lives were governed by a higher order of things. (That, and a printed message which hung on a long strip of paper in the dining-room: "Chew Your Food Properly: Your Digestion Depends On It.")[127]

It took field work among the Bororo Indians to afford Lévi-Strauss his first experience of the sacred. One wonders what might have been the outcome had Lévi-Strauss received an authentic Jewish experience as a child. Instead he becomes one more distinguished representative of the lost intellectual tribes of the House of Israel of the modern era.

A distinguished Aggadist of the late third and early fourth century draws our attention to the fact that Perez was the ancestor of the Messiah and that this fact is integrally related to all the other events transpiring in the segment of the Pentateuch which we have been discussing.

Rabbi Samuel the son of Nahman commented as follows: *For I know the thoughts that I think toward you, saith the Lord* (Jer. 29.11). The tribes (that is, Joseph's brothers) were busy selling Joseph; Joseph was busy wearing his sackcloth and fasting (presumably in prison); Reuben was busy wearing his sackcloth and fasting (presumably because he had gone to the pit to find Joseph and Joseph had already been removed by the Midianites); Jacob was busy with his sackcloth and his fasting (in the belief that Joseph was dead); Judah was busy finding himself a woman—whilst the Holy One, Blessed Be He, was busy creating the light of the Messiah.[128]

Although Samuel ben Nahman's idiom would not have permitted him to express his homily thus, what he was really saying from our point of view was: If you read history diachronically you can almost give up hope. It is only when history is read synchronically that hope becomes possible. Functionally, the Jewish belief in the Messiah represents the unquenchable refusal on the part of the Jewish people to permit current frustrations to dampen future hope or quench past significance. It was left to the grandson of another rabbi, the rabbi of Versailles, to afford us the structural method whereby that ancient hope, expressed within the pages of the Bible, might be seen in a new light—the structuralist implications of the messianic hope.

NOTES

1. G. S. Kirk, *Myth: Its Meaning and Functions in Ancient and other Cultures* (University of California Press, 1975), p. 42.
2. For a biographical note, see Edmund Leach, *Claude Lévi-Strauss* (New York: Viking Press, 1970), p. ix.
3. The four volumes of *Mythologiques* are *Le Cru et le cuit* (Paris: Plon, 1964), English trans. *Introduction to a Science of Mythology, Volume I, The Raw and the Cooked,* trans. by John Weightman (New York: Harper & Row, 1970); *Du Miel au Cendres* (Paris: Plon, 1967), English trans. *Introduction to a Science of Mythology, Volume II, From Honey to Ashes,* trans. by John and Doreen Weightman (New York: Harper & Row, 1973); *L'Origine des Manières des Tables* (Paris: Plon, 1968), English trans., *Introduction to a Science of Mythology, Volume III, The Origin of Table Manners* (forthcoming); and *L'Homme Nu* (Paris: Plon, 1971), English trans., *Introduction to a Science of Mythology, Volume IV, Man Naked* (forthcoming).
4. Michael Lane, ed., *Introduction to Structuralism* (New York: Basic Books, 1970), p. 436.
5. Ibid., p. 248.
6. Claude Lévi-Strauss, *The Raw and the Cooked,* p. 10.
7. Ibid., p. 12. "Nous ne prétendons donc pas montrer comment les hommes pensent dans les mythes, mais comment les mythes se pensent dans les hommes, et a leur insu." Quoted in Kirk, *Myth,* p. 44.
8. Claude Lévi-Strauss, *Structural Anthropology* (New York: Basic Books, 1963), p. vii.
9. Ibid.
10. Lévi-Strauss, *The Raw and the Cooked,* p. 11.
11. Ibid.
12. Lane, *Introduction to Structuralism,* pp. 15–16. For the concept of spectrum see also Ruth Benedict, *Patterns of Culture* (Boston: Houghton Mifflin, undated), pp. 23–24.
13. Ibid., p. 32.
14. Kirk, *Myth,* p. 42.
15. Edmund Leach, "Anthropological Aspects of Language: Animal Categories and Verbal Abuse" in *Mythology,* ed. Pierre Maranda (Harmondsworth: Penguin Books), p. 47. Leach's concept of continuum is clearly related to the Freudian model. Compare Margaret S. Mahler, Fred Pine, and Anni Bergman, *The Psychological Birth of the Human Infant* (New York: Basic Books, 1975), chap. 3. Compare also John S. Dunne, *Time and Myth: A Meditation on Storytelling as an Exploration of Life and Death* (New York: Doubleday, 1973), p. 54.

16. Mary Douglas, "The Meaning of Myth With Special Reference to *La Geste d'Asdiwal*," in *The Structural Study of Myth and Totemism*, ed. Edmund Leach (London: Tavistock Publications, 1969), p. 50, and Kirk, *Myth*, p. 43.
17. Roland Barthes, *Mythologies* (New York: Hill & Wang, 1975), pp. 109 ff.
18. Kirk, *Myth*, p. 49.
19. Douglas, "Meaning of Myth," p. 56.
20. Leach, *Claude Lévi-Strauss*, p. 120.
21. Ferdinand de Saussure, "Course in General Linguistics," in *The Structuralists From Marx to Lévi-Strauss*, ed. Richard and Fernande DeGeorge (New York: Anchor Books, 1972), p. 61.
22. Ibid. p. 65.
23. Leach, *Claude Lévi-Strauss*, p. 44.
24. De Saussure, "Course in General Linguistics," pp. 78–79.
25. Raymond Firth, *Symbols Public and Private* (Ithaca, N.Y.: Cornell University Press, 1973), p. 105. For more on the "musical" metaphor in connection with myth, see also Giorgio de Santillana and Hertha von Dechend, *Hamlet's Mill: An Essay on Myth and the Frame of Time* (Boston: Gambit, 1969), pp. xiii and 346. Compare also the observation of M. Auguste Bailly quoted in Stuart Gilbert, *James Joyce's Ulysses* (New York: Vintage, 1958), p. 15: "The life of the mind is a symphony. It is a mistake or, at best, an arbitrary method, to dissect the chords and set out their components on a single line, on one plane only. Such a method gives an entirely false idea of the complexity of our mental make-up, for it is the way the light falls upon each element, with a greater or a less clarity, that indicates the relative importance for ourselves, our lives and acts, of each of the several thought streams."
26. Lévi-Strauss, *The Raw and the Cooked*, p. 26.
27. Ibid., p. 26.
28. Ibid., p. 27.
29. Ibid., p. 28.
30. Claude Lévi-Strauss, "The Structural Study of Myth," in *The Structuralists from Marx to Lévi-Strauss*, ed. Richard and Fernande DeGeorge (New York: Anchor Books, 1972), p. 176.
31. Amaury de Riencourt, *Sex and Power in History* (New York: David McKay, 1974), p. 19.
32. Lévi-Strauss, "Structural Study of Myth," p. 180.
33. Douglas "Meaning of Myth," p. 63.
34. Ibid.
35. Ibid., p. 56.
36. Edmund Leach, "The Legitimacy of Solomon: Some Structural Aspects of Old Testament History," in Lane, *Introduction to Structuralism*, p. 252.
37. Ibid., pp. 248–49.
38. Th. C. Vriezen, *An Outline of Old Testament Theology* (Oxford: Basil Blackwell, 1958), pp. 40–41.
39. Ibid., pp. 14–15.
40. Salo Wittmayer Baron, *A Social and Religious History of the Jews, Volume I, Ancient Times, Part I* (New York: Columbia University Press, 1952), p. 67.
41. For a further example of a "sociological trauma" refracted through myth, see Riencourt, *Sex and Power*, p. 94.
42. Compare John Murray Cuddihy, *The Ordeal of Civility: Freud, Marx, Lévi-Strauss and the Jewish Struggle with Modernity* (New York: Basic Books, 1974), p. 176: "An intellectual or priestly class, we learn from history, emerges with the differentiation of the culture system and its beliefs and values from

the social system. Their job is to legitimate the social facts by means of the cultural myths and values. If there is a gap they bridge it."

43. For the distinction between *"la parole de face"* and depth knowledge with regard to the transmission of myth, see Marcel Griaule, *Conversations with Ogotemmeli: An Introduction to Dogon Religious Ideas* (Oxford University Press, 1972), p. xv.

44. Compare Pierre Maranda, *Mythology*, p. 16: " . . . we could say, inspired by Rousseau, that human communication is a social contract which rests on a body of subliminal laws, and that a culture's myths contain its semantic jurisprudence."

45. Gen. 15: 16.

46. Lévi-Strauss, "Structural Study of Myth," p. 181.

47. Leach, "Legitimacy of Solomon," p. 251.

48. Kirk, *Myth,* p. 50.

49. Mircea Eliade, *Myth and Reality* (New York: Harper & Row, 1968), p. 1.

50. Hermann Gunkel, *The Legends of Genesis: The Biblical Saga and History* (New York: Schocken Books, 1970), p. 14.

51. Ibid.

52. Nahum M. Sarna, *Understanding Genesis: The Heritage of Biblical Israel* (New York: McGraw-Hill, 1966), p. 3.

53. Henri Frankfort et al., *Before Philosophy: The Intellectual Adventure of Ancient Man* (Baltimore: Penguin Books, 1973), p. 244.

54. Ibid., p. 13.

55. John F. Priest, "Myth and Dream in Hebrew Scripture," in *Myths, Dreams, and Religion,* ed. Joseph Campbell, (New York: E. P. Dutton, 1970), p. 56. Compare also Randolph Crump Miller, "Empiricism and Process Theology: God Is What God Does," *Christian Century,* March 24, 1976, pp. 285–86: " . . . the Bible is not centered on humanity. Although it is a record of the human search for God, the emphasis is on God. It provides historical data open to human interpretation, but the theme is the acts of God."

56. See Alexander Heidel, *The Babylonian Genesis* (Chicago: University of Chicago Press, 1972), pp. 82 ff.

57. Bronislaw Malinowski, *Magic, Science and Religion* (New York: Anchor Books, 1954), p. 108.

58. Ibid., p. 146.

59. Gershom G. Scholem, *On the Kabbalah and Its Symbolism* (New York: Schocken Books, 1972), p. 93.

60. Lévi-Strauss, "Structural Study of Myth," p. 193.

61. Gen. 37:3. Biblical references throughout are to the Jewish Publication Society of America's translation.

62. Gen. 37:5–10.

63. Gen. 37:11–36.

64. Gen. 37:24.

65. Gen. 37:31–33.

66. Gen. 37:26.

67. Gen. 38:1.

68. Gen. 38:2.

69. Gen. 38:14.

70. Gen. 38:24–26.

71. Gen. 38:25.

72. Gen. 39:1–6.

73. Gen. 39:7–12.

74. Gen. 39:8–10.
75. Gen. 39:11–16.
76. Gen. 39:17–19.
77. Gen. 39:13–18.
78. Gen. 39:17.
79. Compare Exod. 32:6.
80. Gen. 39:20.
81. Gen. 39:21–23.
82. Gen. 40:1–23.
83. Gen. 40:23.
84. Gen. 41:1–7.
85. Gen. 41:38–45.
86. Gen. 41:43.
87. Gen. 41:45.
88. Gen. 42:1–2.
89. Gen. 42:4.
90. Gen. 42:7.
91. Gen. 42:7.
92. Gen. 42:9.
93. Gen. 42:15.
94. Gen. 42:17.
95. Gen. 42:21.
96. Gen. 42:44.
97. Gen. 45:3.
98. Gen. 48:13–20.
99. Exod. 1:8–14.
100. Exod. 1:22.
101. Exod. 2:3.
102. Exod. 2:12.
103. Exod. 2:17.
104. Exod. 3:2.
105. Exod. 3:7–10.
106. Exod. 6:6.
107. Exod. 6:2–8.
108. Exod. 4:3.
109. Exod. 4:25.
110. Exod. 6:2–3.
111. Exod. 7:10.
112. Exod. 7:12.
113. The ten plagues, Exod. 7:14 ff.
114. Exod. 14:27.
115. Exod. 19:18.
116. Exod. 20.
117. Exod. 39:3 and 39:23.
118. Genesis Rabbah 93:10.
119. See Lev. 18 passim.
120. Lévi-Strauss, "Structural Study of Myth," p. 193.
121. Ezek. 37.
122. Ps. 118:22.
123. Ruth 4:18–22.
124. Leach, "Legitimacy of Solomon, p. 251.
125. Most recently see Cuddihy, *Ordeal of Civility,* part I.

126. Claude Lévi-Strauss, *Tristes Tropiques: An Anthropological Study of Primitive Societies in Brazil* (New York: Atheneum, 1972), p. 381.

127. Ibid., p. 215.

128. Genesis Rabbah 85:1.

al loro minor fratello chiamato Onia : perche hebbe Simeone tre figliuoli, i quali (come dicemmo)hebbero il prēcipato del facerdotio, Giefu fi chiamò Jafone, Onia fu detto Menelao. Moffe adunque prima feditione Giefu prencipe de' facerdoti contro Menelao, & divifo il popolo fauoriuano a Menelao i figliuoli di Tobia ; ma la maggior parte del popolo aiutaua Iafone. La onde Menelao, & i figliuoli di Tobia oppreffi fuggirono ad Antioco, facēdogli fapere che voleano lafciare le paterne le

Rabbinic Civilization

terne le · · · · · · · · loro
d'edific · · · · · · · · ro la
circonc · · · · · · · · e la-
fciati ti · · · · · · · · Ma

fi deliberò Antioco di condurre in Egitto l'effercito per ampliare il fuo felice imperio; defiando occupar quel paefe, e fprezzado i figliuoli di Ptolomeo come deboli, & a tanta imprefa inetti. Venendo adunque con gran potere a Pelufio, ingannò Ptolomeo, & occupò l'Egitto ; & auicinato a Menfi città, la prefe, indi fi volfe verfo Aleffandria per affediarui Ptolomeo, e pigliarla. Ma fu cacciato non pure d'Aleffandria, ma di tutto Egitto anchora ; facendogli fapere i Romani, che vfciffe della prouincia, come altroue habbiamo dimoftrato. Narrerò particolarmente di quefto Re , come egli occupò la Giudea, & il tempio. Perche ne ho parlato puntualmente ne' miei primi fcritti, hora mi pare necefsario per più chiarezza di quelle cofe replicarle. Tornato adunque Antioco Re di Egitto, per timore de' Romani conduffe egli l'efsercito a Gierufalēme, oue peruenendo l'anno 143. dopò il regno di Seleuco, la 153.olimpiade, a i 25. del mefe Chisleu, detto da Macedoni Apelleo ; & la prefe fenza contrafto , perche gli aprirono le porte i fuoi partiggiani. Entrato adunque in Gierufalemme vccife molti, i quali gli erano grandemente contrarij, & vccife parimente

D   rimente

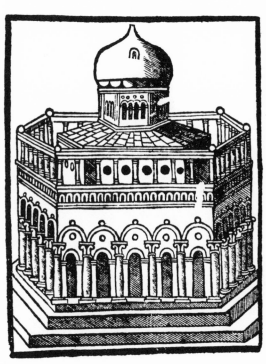

Margin notes:

I. Machi.

Antio co và in Eg itto.

Come fu rouinata Gierufalē me, e rub bato il tē pio.

דבר חכמה שמע משכיל והללו ועליו יוסיף

(בן־סירא כא: טו)

RABBINICS AND RABBINIC EDUCATION

By

RONALD A. BRAUNER

This essay addresses itself to the form, structure, and content of the Rabbinic Civilization program at the Reconstructionist Rabbinical College (RRC). It is written in the spirit of sharing a frame of reference and an approach to rabbinic education which we feel is necessary if we are to bring about the needed changes in the meaningfulness, applicability, and pertinence of the studies which are directed at preparing an individual for service to his people.

The ideal of the pursuit of knowledge for its own sake is beyond question. It seems that a basic function of the human intellect is to discover truths wherever they may exist. Such a search is valid in itself and needs no external justification. Surely, adherents of Jewish tradition understand this, such pursuit having informed a significant part of our culture since earliest times. One aspect of scholarship, in latter times, seems to be in danger of being forgotten and, in being forgotten, may well render scholarship's only contribution to humanity an aesthetic rather than an ameliorative one. Pure knowledge, pure search for truth which is not in some way mitigated by a concern for the uses to which knowledge may be put, is ultimately of limited value in improving the human condition. If, in fact, Jewish tradition is greatly concerned with improving the quality of life then that fact must, in and of itself, constitute *one* of the goals of scholarly investigation. Knowledge which facilitates understanding of self truly is knowledge with a divine component, and the liberation of that divine component is, in Jewish terms, a human imperative.

Rabbinic education, the training offered to those who will eventually minister to the emotional, spiritual, and intellectual needs of the Jewish community, must translate the accomplishments of scientific investigation into substance directed toward *helping people*. The form-critical determination, for example, of the composition of a given mishnah well serves the needs of science, but such a determination might also serve to demonstrate the dynamic nature of Jewish life and culture, the elasticity inherent in Jewish tradition, which reflects our people's ability to continue to come to grips with the vagaries of daily life.

To elucidate the dynamic nature of Jewish tradition is to suggest to contemporary Jews that their search for an accommodation between the pull of the past and the push of the present is subject to resolution. This resolution is possible because the tradition, in large measure, shows itself to be capable of innovation, adaptation, reformulation, and synthesis. The tradition of which we are a part has *itself* always responded to the needs of its adherents; this response is, in fact, the tradition itself. Rabbinic education which utilizes scholarship and enables its students to perceive and communicate this truth to others is education of the highest order because it brings scholarship to the service of the people.

It is axiomatic that there exists a positive relationship between the material studied and how that material is taught. If rabbinical students are being trained ultimately to serve the needs of the community, then an irreducible component of their training must consist of the best use of the most efficacious methods of teaching and learning for the student himself so that he, in turn, may meaningfully convey the substance of what he learns to those whom he will serve. Scholarship and pedagogic expertise are inseparable—pedagogy without substance is a vain exercise, and knowledge without effective means of communication and assimilation is arcane.

While there can be no substitute for rigorous, in-depth study of the sources, similarly there can be no substitute for enabling the student, on his own, but with benign *guidance,* to discover, formulate, interpret, and synthesize. A teacher, at his best, is a facilitator of inquiry and a partner in the common search for knowledge. A teacher must constantly work toward enabling his students to become independent thinkers and investigators —in a sense, he must work toward making himself eventually superfluous vis-à-vis his students.

Illustrative of this is the seminar practice of searching through and assembling, from primary sources, the rabbinic treatment of a student-selected theme in aggadah and one in halakhah in conjunction with the study of units 7 and 8 (described below). Each student chooses, according to his or her own interests and predilections, a subject area for investigation. All pertinent primary source material is collected and organized in such a way as to demonstrate thematic development from biblical to early medieval times. This assembled material is reproduced, distributed in advance to all seminar participants, and studied by them prior to a descriptive and analytic presentation by the student investigator. In this way, in an average year, a student will have studied a total of more than a dozen specific themes, and in the course of this study will have been trained in how and where to seek for material, and how to organize, synthesize, and ultimately communicate selected aspects of that research to others.

A brief description of the rabbinic program is in order. In addition to a full postgraduate university course of study in a discipline complementary to some aspect of Jewish civilization, students at the RRC spend eight hours per week in Rabbinic Core Studies for their second out of five years at the college. Four hours are devoted to the Rabbinic Core (the focus of this essay), two hours to Talmud text, and two hours to Midrash. Rabbinic text study may, upon specific direction or student election, be continued in any or all of the subsequent years until graduation. In what follows, attention will be given, specifically, to aspects of the work done within the framework of the Rabbinic Core. While the nature of this essay does not permit the full explication and detailing of all the major ideas and concepts which are developed over the course of the year, it does reflect, in summary fashion, some *major* points of view which constitute frames of reference for the study of Rabbinic Civilization. Indeed, one of the essential elements in the effective study of Rabbinics is the formation of such frames of reference to which text study may be related and with which the processes inherent in rabbinic life may be more clearly seen. Additionally, such frames of reference are indispensable aids in beginning to perceive the relatedness of rabbinic studies to all subsequent periods in Jewish life—a demonstration and evaluation of the organic nature of all Jewish civilization is precisely *one* of the reasons for which the RRC exists and is a major criterion in the formulation of the content of its academic program. It will be noted below that each of the eight units of the core seminar is introduced with a series of questions. These kinds of questions are proposed by the seminar students themselves, at times *before* the study of a particular unit, and occasionally *after* a cursory reading of the appropriate material has been completed. The employing of student-suggested questions is a device for insuring, as much as reasonably possible, that the content of each unit will truly address itself to the

students' needs and concerns. It has been fascinating to note, over the
past years, the great similarity in the questions different groups of students
will propose. The questions presented below are, in fact, highly representative of those for which *all* rabbinics classes have sought responses.
Following these questions is a presentation of the *basic* reading expected
of each student. This reading, as it must be, is always subject to alteration,
but what appears here is the distillation of those materials which have
remained most valuable as sources for the students' inquiry and discovery
of reasonable responses to their questions. Subsequent to the reading here
are summary treatments of some major considerations which have become part of the frames of reference spoken of above.

UNIT 1. *Nehemiah, Ezra, and the Restoration*

1. What, if any, are the changes in values between the biblical and
   early rabbinic periods? To what extent were these changes brought
   about by contact with the non-Jewish world?
2. How did the concepts of God, Torah, and Israel expand and develop in the early rabbinic period?
3. What were the nature and dynamics of authority in both the
   religious and political spheres at this time?
4. What were the social/cultural phenomena with which the Jewish
   people had to contend?
5. What was happening, developmentally, to Jewish custom and
   ritual?
6. What were the continua between the pre- and post-exilic Jewish
   communities?
7. Is it possible to speak of halakhah in this early period?
8. What were the essential characteristics of the Palestinian Jewish
   community which differentiated it from its neighbors?

H. Albeck, *Mavo Lamishna* (Jerusalem, 1967), pp. 3–39.
W. F. Albright, *From Abraham to Ezra* (New York, 1963).
S. Baron, *A Social and Religious History of the Jews* (New York, 1952–67),
   I: 134–64.
E. Bickerman, *From Ezra to the Last of the Maccabees* (New York, 1962).
Z. H. Chajes, *Student's Guide to the Talmud* (New York, 1960), pp. 44–55.
A. Guttmann, *Rabbinic Judaism in the Making* (Detroit, 1970), pp. 3–94.
J. Klausner, *Historiah shel Habayit Hasheni* (Jerusalem, 1963), I: 243–312.
K. Koch, "Ezra and the Origins of Judaism," *Journal of Semitic Studies*
   19, no. 2 (1974).

G. F. Moore, *Judaism* (New York, 1971), 1: 3–82.
J. Myers, *Ezra-Nehemiah* (Garden City, 1965).

Most of the scholarship dealing with this period in Jewish life has directed itself toward demonstrating the profound changes which were introduced into Jewish civilization as the result of both exile in an alien land and the efforts of Ezra the Scribe in national restoration. What is too frequently not understood is that the continua between pre- and post-exilic Judaism are much more numerous and profound than any changes which may have been introduced in the fifth century B.C.E. Yehezkel Kaufmann has demonstrated this most effectively in his critique of the long-accepted "axioms" of the source-composition of Scripture. Further investigation of appropriate primary and secondary sources reveals that most changes in Jewish life attributed to Ezra were, in fact, already extant or, most basically, were amenable to implementation *not* so much because of the efforts of Ezra but rather because the people were ready for them. Rather than insist that it was Ezra who was responsible for the program of the dissolution of mixed marriages, for example, it should be noted that Ezra addressed himself to a Judean populace, not a northern one—and such mixed marriages were essentially a northern problem. Ezra's success in these endeavors was the success of a man given credit by history for an achievement already a fact of history. To understand one aspect of historiosophy is to understand that biblical and post-biblical literature have a distinct tendency to incorporate a *state* of affairs in a *person* of affairs. The study of the development of Jewish civilization can never be the study of distinct personalities divorced from the environment-mass which produced them. In most cases, the historical personality is the people itself!

It was possible for Torah to become the law of the land not so much because of the willingness of the Persian monarchy or the initiative of Ezra but because the Jewish people already had a long, law-centered tradition stretching back centuries into the biblical period. What Ezra did do, if anything at all, was to *articulate* and begin to *formalize* values and characteristics that were already the property of the people. Ahad Ha'am's "Moses" is instructive here in considering the historicity of Ezra.

Aside from the moot contentions of Albright, Bickerman, Moore, Noth, and others with respect to the changes which occurred in Jewish life, it is undeniably clear that the developed biblical concepts of Covenant and Peoplehood continued even beyond the Exile and Restoration period, and informing these concepts remained the powerful orientation of historiosophy. No study of our past can be engaged in profitably without full consideration for historiography and historiosophy.

UNIT 2. *Greek, Roman, and Jew*

1. What were the characteristics of the Greco-Roman period in Jewish life which differentiated it from others?
2. What influences upon Jewish life may be traced from Greco-Roman sources? What is the validity of the methodology employed in discovering those influences?
3. What basic aspects of Greco-Roman culture seem to have been irreconcilably antagonistic to selected aspects of Jewish civilization?
4. What, if any, were the continua between the Exile-Restoration period and the Greco-Roman period?
5. To what extent may Apocrypha and Pseudepigrapha be utilized in understanding aspects of developing Jewish civilization during this period?
6. What, in this period, may one begin to speak of as normative?

M. Avi-Yonah, "Jewish Art and Architecture in the Hasmonean and Herodian Periods," in *The World History of the Jewish People* (New Brunswick, N. J., 1975), Vol. 8.
Y. Baer, *Yisrael Ba'amim* (Jerusalem, 1955).
S. Baron, *A Social and Religious History of the Jews* (New York, 1952–67), 1: 165–285.
B. Cohen, *Jewish and Roman Law* (New York, 1966), 1: 1–64.
D. Daube "Rabbinic Methods of Interpretation and Hellenistic Rhetoric," *Hebrew Union College Annual* 22 (1949).
Z. Falk, *Introduction to Jewish Law of the Second Commonwealth* (Leiden, 1972), pp. 46–92.
L. Ginzberg, *On Jewish Law and Lore* (New York, 1962), pp. 3–57.
J. Klausner, *Historiah shel Habayit Hasheni* (Jerusalem, 1963), 2:230–42.
W. L. Knox, "Pharisaism and Hellenism," in *Judaism and Christianity*, ed. H. Loewe: vol. 2, *The Contact of Pharisaism with other Cultures* (London, 1937).
S. Lieberman, *Hellenism in Jewish Palestine* (New York, 1932), pp. 47–82.
———, "Roman Legal Institutions in Early Rabbinics . . .," *Jewish Quarterly Review* 35 (1944).
Philo, *The Special Laws* (London, 1929–62), vol. 3.
V. Tcherikover, *Hellenistic Civilization and the Jews* (Philadelphia, 1959), pp. 117–74.

It is important to remember that in very large measure, the history of a given idea cannot be demonstrated. At best, one can really only speak of the chronologically organized graphic attestations to an idea, but surely its first appearance in graphic representation constitutes no proof whatsoever that an idea saw birth in its being recorded. Further, wisdom and precision teach that many of the most significant ideas in human history are common to numerous cultures which have had little or no contact with one another, and that it is entirely reasonable to assume that many significant ideas are transcultural and "float in international waters." In dealing with the kinds of questions outlined above, it is well to ponder the facts that written records reflect only an infinitesimal portion of man's endeavors, that there is no such thing as "objectivity" in the hands of any author, and that the stimuli for the composition and reasons for the preservation of some ancient document may be more instructive than the contents of the document itself!

Many have been led astray in attempting to utilize such books as Ben Sirah in describing the progress of formative Judaism, and yet, after all is said and done, that book might well be, in the main, simply a kind of handbook for the would-be city sophisticate. Surely, the wisdom of Ben Sirah far predated its composition, and such wisdom was largely universal. Essentially, the book can be seen as a collection of "good advices" for one interested in social climbing in the cosmopolitan society of which its author had become a member. The greatest Hellenic influence to be noted here is that such a book was written by a Jew, and its greatest value for us may well lie in its portrayal of the challenges and responses in attempting to live in two civilizations!

Arguments as to the origins of the various hermeneutic principles employed in Rabbinic Judaism will never be settled. Parallel principles of textual analysis can be demonstrated in diverse cultures. Even biblical literature itself reflects, in rhetorical usage, some of the very principles later attributed to Hillel et al. (Exod. 6:12 for the *qal vahomer,* for example). The greatest Greco-Roman influence in this area is to be found *not* in the genesis of the principles themselves but *rather* in their articulation and categorization.

UNIT 3. *The Roots of Religious Self-Rule*

1. What developments here can be traced to antecedents in Jewish civilization?
2. What was the nature of the authority for ritual, social, and legal traditions and enactments?

3. To what extent are "objective" historical phenomena reflected in rabbinic ritual and ethical teachings?
4. What were the processes by which personal and communal life were organized and maintained?
5. In what ways was the tension between tradition and change dealt with?
6. How did legal institutions attempt to respond to the challenge of Jewish life in two civilizations?

J. Agus, "Ancient Sanhedrin or Sanhedrin Assembly," *Judaism* 1, no. 1 (1952).
H. Englander, "The Men of the Great Synagogue," *Hebrew Union College Annual* (1925).
A. Guttmann, "Foundations of Rabbinic Judaism," *Hebrew Union College Annual* pt. 1 (1951–52).
J. Klausner, *Historiah shel Habayit Hasheni* (Jerusalem, 1963), 2:32–42.
H. Mantel, *Studies in the History of the Sanhedrin* (Cambridge, Mass., 1961).

While some will doubtless find it disturbing to contemplate, it is nonetheless possible that such institutions as *Soferim, Hakhamim,* and *Knesset Hagedolah* never really existed. Upon careful study, one notes the strong rabbinic tendency for historical retrojection, for institutionalizing a past which could only be conceived of in terms of the present. As such, one will read of Abraham's study in the yeshiva of Shem and Eber (where else would a Jew of Abraham's stature have spent his youth!) and of the Bet Din of Samuel (how else could the tacky problem of Moabite conversion have been dealt with other than in court!). It was inconceivable to the rabbinic mind that there was ever a period in Jewish history when orderly rule through halakhah did not exist and when scholars, judges, and teachers, as *organized, identifiable* groups, did not function. For the rabbis, everything had a purposeful origin, and anything positive which Jews did had its origin in the divinely momentous (*misinai*) or in the humanly procedural (Ezra and the *bet din shel shiv'im ve'ehad*). Were all of tradition, however, to be based upon the principle of *halakhah lemosheh misinai,* then surely the elasticity and adaptability necessary for coping with variable social realities would have been precluded. The "invention" of retrojective judicial and deliberative institutions guaranteed that needed change could be dealt with as part of a *process,* and that any "revolution" in Jewish life could be evolutionized just as surely as a greater, more knowledgeable court could reverse the decision of a smaller, less knowledgeable one. Such retrojection was a direct expression of a similar biblical tendency (the description of the Tabernacle influenced by the anatomy of the First Temple, for example) but was surely not conscious. This process however, endowed accepted practices in Jewish life with authority and legitimacy. Ultimately, there is less importance in determining the historicity of pre-rabbinic institutions than there is in recognizing that the Jewish people in rabbinic times conducted themselves *as if* such institutions did in fact exist.

Many sections of Mishnah and Gemara, even though they purport to deliberate over the contemporary normalization of a given practice, actually constitute post facto rationalizations of practice already extant. At times, support for a given practice was attributed to an earlier honored personage (Ezra, Simeon ben Shetah, Hillel) or honored school (Bet Hillel, Shammai), but always the "what should be" was fixed in consideration of the rational extension of the "what was," for in truth, the people, the ultimate determiners of the fabric of Jewish life, were offspring of their own past.

UNIT 4. *Judaism and Christianity*

1. At what point did Christianity become an entity separately identifiable from Judaism?
2. What were the social, cultural, and historical circumstances which ultimately led to this differentiation?
3. What are authentic Jewish elements in early Christianity and what, if any, are Christian elements in Rabbinic Judaism?
4. On what specific points did formative Christianity most differ with Rabbinic Judaism?
5. To what extent may formative Christianity be seen as an alternative response to the same phenomena which were of importance to Rabbinic Judaism?
6. What changes in rabbinic theology occurred as a result of the confrontation with early Christianity?

S. Baron, *A Social and Religious History of the Jews* (New York, 1952–67, 2: 57–88; 129–71.

L. Baeck, *Judaism and Christianity* (Philadelphia, 1958).

N. Bentwich, "Judaism in Early Christianity," *Jewish Quarterly Review* 1 (1909) : 131–38.

J. Bonsirven, *Palestinian Judaism in the Time of Jesus Christ* (New York, 1964).

G. Dalman, *Jesus-Jeshua* (New York, 1971).

D. Daube, *The New Testament and Rabbinic Judaism* (London, 1956).

M. Friedlander, "Pauline Emancipation from the Law," *Jewish Quarterly Review* 9 (1909).

L. Ginzberg, "The Religion of the Jews at the Time of Jesus," *Hebrew Union College Annual* 1 (1924).

M. Goldstein, *Jesus in the Jewish Tradition* (New York, 1950).

R. T. Herford, *Christianity in Talmud and Midrash* (Clifton, N. J., 1966).

S. Krauss, "Imprecation Against Minim in the Synagogue," *Jewish Quarterly Review* 9 (1897).

J. Lauterbach, "Jesus in the Talmud," in *Rabbinic Essays* (Cincinnati, 1951).

J. Mann, "Rabbinic Studies in the Synoptic Gospels," *Hebrew Union College Annual* 1 (1924).

R. Marcus, "Judaism and Gnosticism," *Judaism* 4, no. 4 (1955).

C. Montefiore, "Rabbinic Judaism and the Epistles of St. Paul," *Jewish Quarterly Review* 13 (1909).

C. Montefiore, *Rabbinic Literature and Gospel Teachings* (New York, 1970).

M. Smith, *Tannaitic Parallels to the Gospels* (Philadelphia, 1951).

It is clear that early Christianity never appealed to large numbers of Jews and that its greatest growth took place among Gentiles. Nevertheless, it must be remembered that the first Christians were Jews, and their thinking, as can best be reconstructed, reflected definable, albeit *minority,* viewpoints within the normative Jewish mass. Rabbinic Judaism's strongest rejection of Christianity came about only when political and social frictions had grown to difficult proportions. The period of the Jerusalem Church saw little dispute between the two, but once the shift to the Antioch Church was accomplished, and once the politicization of Christianity had obtained, profound theological responses were offered through Rabbinic Judaism. When Christianity became clearly identifiable, at least in the Jewish mind, as a Gentile phenomenon, the most vehement rejections were articulated. It is, of course, futile to attempt to make value judgments about the inferiority or superiority of given points of ideology in the early Rabbinic and Christian traditions. Similarly, it is not in the best interests of truth and scholarship to compare, as so many have done, the worst in one tradition with the best in the other. It is, however, important to recognize that some profound changes occurred in Rabbinic Judaism as a result of its confrontation with Christianity—most significant of these being the attempt to organize and clarify those theological positions for Jews of which Christianity taught differently. For the first time in Jewish history, conscious efforts were made to articulate notions of reward and punishment, salvation, life after death, and the like. Such articulations, unlike those of Philo, which were much less polemic and much less representative of the thinking of the masses, came to reflect developing normative Jewish thought and served to insure that, on a theological level, the differences between the two traditions would forever remain distinct.

The facilitating of the spread of Christianity among the Gentiles necessitated a de-emphasis, and even an elimination, of certain basic Jewish concepts and practices which, to non-Jews, would be either incomprehensible or repugnant. The practice of circumcision would be repulsive for people nurtured in the Greco-Roman tradition, which saw this as mutilation of the body. The parochial Abrahamic covenant concept would be meaningless to those who shared neither historical nor familial ties with the Jewish people, and the organization of life through halakhah (not to be confused with "law") would be too sectarian and too oppressive to be either attractive or workable in a non-Jewish culture. It is precisely these points which Pauline and later Christianity eliminated or rationalized away, and correspondingly, the selfsame notions which Rabbinic Judaism increasingly emphasized. Circumcision was now spoken of as a *sine qua non* for redemption-salvation, the Covenant concept became firmly linked to circumcision and even more parochial, and halakhah was now, for all practical purposes, regarded as a universal value and even inherent in the functioning of the natural world itself!

The more Christianity presented itself as a challenge to Judaism and the more Jews began to suffer at the hands of Christians, all the more did the concept of peoplehood grow among Jews and all the more would the development of Jewish civilization be irrevocably affected.

UNIT 5. *Sadducees, Pharisees, and other Sectaries*

1. What were the bases upon which sectarian designations were established?
2. To what extent may an ideological fragmentation of society be studied through reference to the proliferation of sectarian titles?

3. In what ways can one speak of normative Judaism during this period?
4. How reliable is the information upon which we base our knowledge of the various sects?
5. What social and historical factors seem most to have led to the increased emphasis upon apocalyptic and messianism?
6. Why did the distinctions of *havurah* and *am ha'aretz* develop during this period?
7. To what extent was sectarianism contradictory to the concept of peoplehood?

G. Allon, "The Attitude of the Pharisees Toward Roman Rule and the Herodian Dynasty," *Zion* 3 (1938).

A. Dupont-Sommer, *The Jewish Sect of Qumran and the Essenes* (London, 1954).

L. Finkelstein, *The Pharisees* (Philadelphia, 1962), 1:73–81, 101–44; 2: 570–625, 762–98.

A. Guttmann, "Pharisaism in Transition," in *Essays in Honor of Solomon B. Freehof* (Pittsburgh, 1964).

B. Heller, "Massada and the Talmud," *Tradition* 10, no. 2 (1968).

S. Hoenig, "Historic Masada and the Halakhah," *Judaism* 13, no. 2 (1972).

J. Klausner, *Historiah shel Habayit Hasheni* (Jerusalem, 1963), 3:107–40.

J. Lauterbach, "A Significant Controversy Between the Sadducees and the Pharisees," *Hebrew Union College Annual* 4 (1927).

———, "The Pharisees and Their Teachings," *Hebrew Union College Annual* 6 (1929).

H. Loewe, "The Ideas of Pharisaism," in *Judaism and Christianity*, vol. 2, *The Contact of Pharisaism with Other Cultures*, (London, 1937).

N. McEleney, "Orthodoxy in Judaism of the First Christian Century," *Journal for the Study of Judaism* 4, no. 1 (1973).

R. Marcus, "The Pharisees in the Light of Modern Scholarship," *Journal of Religion* 32 (1952).

———, "Pharisees, Essenes and Gnostics," *Journal of Biblical Literature* 73 (1954).

G. F. Moore, *Judaism* (New York, 1971), 1:56–71, 190–204.

J. Neusner, *From Politics to Piety* (Englewood Cliffs, N. J., 1973).

D. Polish, "Pharisaism and Political Sovereignty," *Judaism* 19, no. 4 (1970).

E. Rivkin, "Defining the Pharisees: The Tannaitic Sources," *Hebrew Union College Annual* 40–41 (1969–70).

C. Roth, "The Zealots: A Jewish Religious Sect," *Judaism* 8, no. 1 (1959).

S. Zeitlin, *The Rise and Fall of the Judaean State* (Philadelphia, 1964), 1:178–87.

The ultimate clarification of the nature of the Pharisees and Sadducees may never come. Available primary sources are sparse, contradictory, and unenlightening. It may very well be that such definitive, identifiable groups never really existed at all but rather are so identified as a result of the Hellenic tendency to taxonomize and label. Reading of the sources would suggest that it was eminently possible to classify all Jewish elements in rabbinic civilization either as Essene, Zealot, Pharisee, or Sadducee, but the knowledge we have gained from sociology and anthropology would lead us to doubt whether rabbinic, or any, society could ever be analyzed in such precise terms. It is significant that we do not even know with certainty the origin or denotation of these sectarian designations. It is reasonable and clear that in a vibrant, developing culture, ideological differentiations will proliferate. What is not so clear, however, is whether such a society would ever choose or be able to classify all of its constituents with meaningful and precise labels. In rabbinic sources, the terms *Pharisee* and *Sadducee* are invariably employed (except in obscure cases) in *polemic* contexts, and one does not find Pharisees, for instance, outside of such contexts, ever referring to themselves as such. Josephus, on the other hand, addressing himself to a Greco-Roman audience, understandably employed such terms as would be meaningful to people oriented toward thinking in categories and labels. Such might also be said for Christian Bible sources employing these terms in historico-polemic contexts. Undeniably, rabbinic civilization adopted this tendency to categorize, and as such, it reflects another foreign influence deeply imbedded in Jewish culture. But the fact remains that no reliable proof can be demonstrated for the authenticity and applicability of sectarian designations. We may say that all Jews were Pharisees and that those who held ideological positions divergent from the accepted norm were labeled in such a way as to differentiate them from the mass. If the minority divergences did not touch upon matters central to normative Judaism (and the people were and are the determiners of centrality and periphery), one holding them could be assigned to Bet Shammai; in the case of more significant divergence, the term Sadducee could be assigned, and so on, in degrees, depending upon the nature and severity of the difference from the normative mass— Boethusian, Epicurean, heretic, *min*. In all cases, our reliance upon these ancient designations for the recovery of history is misleading, and we may well be guilty, in a later age, of the same tendency toward institutionalization as our forebears who gave us the Bet Din of Samuel and the Men of the Great Assembly.

UNIT 6. *Rabbinic Interpretation*

1. What criteria were developed to judge the validity and appropriateness of a particular textual interpretation?
2. To what extent did contemporary social and religious exigencies demand textual reinterpretation?
3. How were the designations *pshat* and *drash* employed and to what ends?
4. How were hermeneutic principles employed to protect tradition and authority and yet allow for growth and development?
5. What is particularly Jewish about the rabbinic methods of interpretation and what may be attributed to foreign influences?

L. Ginzberg, *On Jewish Law and Lore* (New York, 1962), pp. 127–50.

M. Kadushin, *The Rabbinic Mind* (New York, 1972), pp. 97–107.

J. Lauterbach, "Allegorists in Talmud and Midrash," *Jewish Quarterly Review* 1 (1909).

J. Mielziner, *Introduction to the Talmud* (New York, 1968), pp. 117–55.

G. F. Moore, *Judaism* (New York, 1971), 1:247–50.

L. Rabinowitz, "The Talmudic Meaning of Peshat," *Tradition* 6, no. 1 (1961).

D. Weiss, "Towards a Theology of Rabbinic Exegesis," *Judaism* 10, no. 1 (1961).

I. H. Weiss, *Dor Dor Vedorshav* (Vilna, 1904), 2:49–65.

I. Wolfsberg, "On the Nature of Rabbinic Interpretation of the Bible," *Talpiot* 5, nos. 1–2 (1950).

One idea that emerges clearly from a study of this aspect of rabbinic civilization is that any mode of textual analysis and interpretation which was necessary for finding accommodation between tradition and contemporary life was developed and employed. While the articulation and categorization of such things as hermeneutic principles was a direct Hellenistic influence, the application of these principles in defining and expressing peculiarly Jewish values was decidedly rabbinic. As in so many other areas of Jewish life, the actual origins of particular conventions were either unrecognized or forgotten, and hermeneutic systems came to be seen as so distinctively and authentically Jewish that only Hillel or Rabbi Ishmael could have been their authors. However, there must have been some realization of the relatively recent development of textual hermeneutics since these principles were assigned not to Moses but rather to his successors in a much later period.

The terms *pshat* and *drash* are most difficult to deal with insofar as their precise application is concerned. A study of the employment of these terms reveals that their definitions are neither stable nor regular. But ultimately, the lack of stability and regularity may be a clue to discovering something of their nature. It seems that in rabbinic and post-rabbinic sources, a particular exegete will designate a certain understanding with which he does not choose to take exception as *pshat,* and in so defining a particular reading as beyond manipulation, may then proceed to offer original insights which he will call *drash.* The application of the term *drash* then becomes a way of outlining an area in which original thinking may be done without the danger of contradicting accepted tradition. In turn, that exegete's *drash* interpretation may well become, for his successors, a subsequent *pshat,* an understanding which is perceived as being beyond question, and newer insights and textual appreciations, offered in the spirit of embellishing but never contradicting the text, are formulated in terms of their being *drash*—in a word, *pshat* is conceived of as definitive and beyond argument whereas *drash* is the designation for an area of inquiry where open-endedness and extension are considered to be valid. One generation's *drash* becomes the next generation's *pshat!* In this respect, then, these terms can never be understood as absolute but rather must be seen as being relative to the delineation of areas of investigation outlined either consciously or unconsciously by the particular discussant. To designate a source as being *pshat* is to disavow any intention of tampering with tradition, and to designate a source as being *drash* is to employ a provision of the tradition itself for its own eventual augmentation.

UNIT 7. *Aggadah*

1. How may midrash aggadah be defined and what is its relationship to midrash halakhah?
2. What are the sources employed in aggadah and what methodology determines their utilization?
3. What are the historical and cultural roots of the aggadic genre?
4. In what circumstances are aggadic expositions employed and to what ends?
5. To what extent is aggadah a valid source for discussing normative Jewish thought?
6. What conditions and circumstances lead to the preservation of some aggadot and the disappearance of others?

7. What is the authority of an aggadah and to what extent are its teachings "binding?"
8. What are the implications inherent in aggadic literature for the subsequent development of Jewish civilization?

H. Albeck, *Mavo Latalmudim,* (Tel Aviv, 1969), pp. 79–143.
B. Bamberger, "The Dating of Aggadic Materials," *Journal of Biblical Literature* 68 (1949).
Z. H. Chajes, *The Student's Guide Through the Talmud* (New York, 1960), pp. 139–253.
L. Ginzberg, *On Jewish Law and Lore* (New York, 1962), pp. 127–50.
M. Kadushin, *A Conceptual Approach to the Mekilta* (New York, 1969).
————, *The Rabbinic Mind* (New York, 1972), pp. 97–130.
S. E. Karff, "Aggadah: The Language of Jewish 'God-Talk'," *Judaism* 19, no. 2 (1970).
K. Kohler, "The Pre-Talmudic Haggadah," *Jewish Quarterly Review* 5 (1893).
J. Lauterbach, "Allegorists in Talmud and Midrash," *Jewish Quarterly Review* 1 (1909).
A. Marmorstein, "The Background of the Haggadah," *Hebrew Union College Annual* 6 (1929).
M. Mielziner, *Introduction to the Talmud* (New York, 1968), pp. 117–55.
S. K. Mirsky, "Sources of Halakhah in Midrashic Literature" (Hebrew), *Talpioth* 6, no. 3 (1957).
G. F. Moore, *Judaism* (New York, 1971), 1:135–216.
J. Neusner, "What Is Normative in Jewish Ethics?" *Judaism* 16, no. 1 (1967).
L. Rabinovitch, "The Talmudic Meaning of Peshat," *Tradition* 6, no. 1 (1963).
B. Rosenzweig, "The Hermeneutic Principles and Their Application," *Tradition* 13, no. 1 (1972).
H. Strack, *Introduction to the Talmud and Midrash* (New York, 1965).
I. H. Weiss, *Dor Dor Vedorshav* (Vilna, 1904), 1:97–130.

When one speaks of the rabbinic mind, he speaks, ultimately, of the Jewish mind. It is too frequently unrecognized that the rabbis were not the originators of the value-concepts and perceptions which are reflected in rabbinic literature. Rather, one must understand that the rabbis were exemplars of the conduct and values of which they spoke, they were the *formulators* and *articulators* of ethics and halakhot that were already a firm part of the culture of the Jewish people at large. The rabbis themselves sprang from the people; they were of the people but perhaps differed from them in that they constituted a class whose felt obligation was to propagate those values, and whose main life-pursuit, with only a few exceptions, was to engage in study and teaching. It is wholly misleading to speak of rabbinic civilization in terms of the novel contributions of the rabbis, as if to suggest that without them, the mass of philosophy, theology, ethics, and law that is part of our national definition would never have become such. One of the most significant aspects of all Jewish civilization is the widespread, *public* domain of the values with which Jewish life has become identified. Social and religious movers succeeded when and where they did because they addressed themselves to a constituency which was sympathetic to their teachings and which *shared* their insights—most often, social movers saw success because they, more than the average person, were able to grasp more fully, in organized and organic ways, what the people were saying and doing. They, perhaps more than most others, were able to give timeless expression to the values of the culture which bore them. Masses do not lead, masses do not teach, and masses do not have the leisure to systematically study, organize, and teach those values which they somehow recognize as essential for the perfection of life and of the next Jewish generation.

Revelation at Sinai, however it might be defined, at its core speaks of the public intention to live Jewishly—biblical law, regardless of how its origin might be spoken of, was, even at such an early period, *descriptive* rather then *prescriptive*. The good and the beneficial in the law was subsequently spoken of as imperative so as to insure that the best of contemporary life would be preserved beyond the lifetimes of its source, the people. The same, in essence, may be said for the classical prophets. The divine charge they heard was the voice of the values of the society from which they had emerged. The voice they heard was the voice of the best and most timeless in the value system of the people, which the prophets, more consistently and more acutely, were attuned to and more driven to verbalize than others.

If the core and substance of Jewish values and perceptions of the world are to be found in aggadah, then we understand that at its root, aggadah is a rabbinic telling to the people what the people have always been saying but not always hearing.

UNIT 8. *Halakhah*

1. In what ways do the "traditional" and "scientific" definitions of halakhah agree and differ?

2. What is the relationship of halakhah to aggadah?
3. What social, cultural, and historical factors influence the development of halakhah?
4. What are the processes which determine the application of halakhah in given instances?
5. To what extent is halakhah a valid source for discussing normative Jewish thought?
6. What conditions and circumstances lead to the maintaining of some halakhot and the desuetude of others?
7. What is the authority of a halakhah and to what extent is a halakhah binding?
8. What are the implications inherent in halakhic literature for the subsequent development of Jewish civilization?

J. Agus, "Theoretical Evaluation of Jewish Law," *Proceedings of the Rabbinical Assembly of America* 22 (1958).

H. Albeck, *Mavo Lamishna* (Jerusalem, 1967), pp. 3–39.

———, *Mavo Latalmudim* (Tel Aviv, 1969), pp. 79–143.

Z. H. Chajes, *The Student's Guide Through the Talmud* (New York, 1960), pp. 1–135.

B. Cohen, *Law and Tradition in Judaism* (New York, 1959).

J. Cohen, "הלכה and the Life of Holiness," *Proceedings of the Rabbinical Assembly of America* 22 (1958).

S. S. Cohen, "Authority in Judaism," *Hebrew Union College Annual* 11 (1936).

Z. W. Falk, *Introduction to Jewish Law of the Second Commonwealth* (Leiden, 1972), pp. 1–43.

L. Ginzberg, *On Jewish Law and Lore* (New York, 1962), pp. 77–124, 153–84.

A. Guttmann, "Foundations of Rabbinic Judaism," *Hebrew Union College Annual* 23, pt. 1 (1950–51).

M. Kadushin, *The Rabbinic Mind* (New York, 1972), pp. 340–67.

I. Klein, "An Attitude to הלכה," *Proceedings of the Rabbinical Assembly of America* 22 (1958).

B. M. Leiser, "Custom and Law in Talmudic Jurisprudence," *Judaism* 20, no. 4 (1971).

M. Mielziner, *Introduction to the Talmud* (New York, 1968), pp. 117–87.

S. K. Mirsky, "Sources of Halakhah in Midrashic Literature" (Hebrew), *Talpioth* 3, nos. 1–2 (1947).

G. F. Moore, *Judaism* (New York, 1971), 1:83–160, 251–80.

J. Newman, *Halachic Sources* (Leiden, 1969).

J. Petuchowski, "Problems of Reform Halacha," *Judaism* 4, no. 4 (1955).

E. Rackman, "The Dialectic of the Halakhah," *Tradition* 3, no. 2 (1961).
S. Schechter, *Aspects of Rabbinic Theology* (New York, 1969), pp. 116–69.
D. S. Shapiro, "The Ideological Foundations of the Halakhah," *Tradition* 9, nos. 1–2 (1967).
I. H. Weiss, *Dor Dor Vedorshav* (Vilna, 1904), 2:173–84, 201–26.
W. S. Wurzburger, "The Oral Law and the Conservative Dilemma," *Tradition* 3, no. 1 (1960).

Closely tied to our discussion of aggadah above is the institution of halakhah. At its heart, halakhah is simply a variant expression of aggadah and is surely a midrash on life itself. Halakhah attempts to formalize and regularize those functions of life which are felt to be ameliorative and insuring of continued Jewish identity and probity. In rabbinic civilization, halakhah is applicable to all facets of life because there exist in all facets of life the valued, the timeless, the sublime. No human endeavor is outside the rule of law simply because all human endeavor contains elements for the perfection of life itself. The rabbis no more "invented" halakhot than they "invented" the value-concepts expressed in aggadah. However, the organization and systematization of halakhah was indeed a rabbinic contribution, and the assigning of validity and sanctity to meaningful parts of Jewish life was the rabbis' greatest contribution.

It is undeniable that the prescriptive nature of halakhah has its origins in the descriptive and that the dynamics of *drash* to *pshat* are applicable here too. Halakhah always consisted of the rabbinic "legalization" of the best elements of widespread Jewish practice. Reference to such rabbinic principles as עת לעשות לה' הפרו תורתך ("when times demand, even parts of Torah may be annulled"), אין גוזרין גזרה על הצבור אלא אם כן רוב הצבור יכולין לעמד בה ("only restrictions which the people will tolerate may be legislated"), and המנהג מבטל את ההלכה ("accepted practice negates legal prescription") illustrates graphically that the rabbis and the people were mutually dependent partners and that halakhah, at its very roots, was quintessentially democratic. The implications for the contemporary reconstruction of the original democracy of halakhah are clear. The nearly universal Israeli practice of purchasing flowers and delicacies on Friday in preparation for the Sabbath is as much as authentic expression of כבוד שבת and וקראת לשבת עונג as anything formulated by Hillel, Rabbi Judah, or Maimonides. It is precisely in this analysis of the descriptive nature of minhag/halakhah that we may continue to assure, as our ancestors so directed us, that all Jewish life will flourish, and that the Jewish people will continue to contribute elements for the perfection of the world and the actualizing of the godly in all mankind.

"BEYOND ALL THE SONGS AND PRAISES OF DAVID": NISHMAT KOL HAI

By

KENNETH S. COHEN

INTRODUCTION

The noble and beautiful prayer *Nishmat Kol Hai,* "The Soul of Every Living Being," is a complex and intriguing work that has been popular among Jews for centuries. It appears in the liturgy in all the Sabbath and festival morning services as the conclusion of the *Psukei de-Zimra* (introductory biblical hymns) service. The final part of *Nishmat,* the *Yishtabah,* "Praised Be Your Name," containing the benediction of the entire prayer, likewise concludes the weekday *Psukei de-Zimra* section in morning prayer. Parts of it figure impressively in the morning service for Rosh Hashanah and Yom Kippur; the המלך יושב על כסא רם ונשא —"O King, seated upon a high and exalted throne"[1] is chanted in lofty, regal tones, to underscore one of the great theological themes of the High Holidays—the kingship of God.[2] Its frequent occurrence and place of prominence in Jewish liturgy alone would demand a serious study of the *Nishmat;* the beauty of its poetry, not to mention its theological significance, is even more compelling.

This discussion of *Nishmat Kol Hai* will attempt to examine the prayer from both historical-critical and literary perspectives. In the first treatment, such questions as authorship, language, style, versions, and history will be discussed, particularly as they pertain to dating the prayer. Dating will be stressed, not because it is a question of ultimate importance for appreciating the *Nishmat,* but rather because key features of the prayer, and methodological problems in its study, converge on the question of

75

fixing its date of composition. Following this investigation will be a literary analysis of the work, dealing with nuances of style, language, and grammar in a more detailed running commentary. Thus, the first part of this paper will deal with the theoretical, objective features of the *Nishmat;* the second part, more subjective, will deal with how the poet expresses himself and what meaning or feelings he might wish to convey.

HISTORICAL-CRITICAL ANALYSIS

The beginning of the prayer *Nishmat Kol Hai* appears in T.B. *Pesahim* 118a, where R. Johanan identifies *Birkat ha-Shir,* the concluding blessing for the recitation of the *Hallel* psalms during the Passover *seder,* as *Nishmat Kol Hai.*[3] The same R. Johanan also links *Nishmat* to the thanksgiving prayer for rain, stating אילו פינו מלא שירה כים וכו' אין אנו מספיקים להודות ה' אלהנו עד תשתחוה (T.B. *Berakot* 59b; cf. *Taanit* 6b), which is found verbatim in the *Elu Finu* section of our *Nishmat* prayer. Rav Judah's version of the beginning of the thanksgiving prayer for rain, מודים אנחנו לך על כל טפה וטפה שהורדת לנו, might give a clear indication why one finds the flamboyant use of numbers in the *Elu Finu* section. "The thousand millions and ten thousands of myriads of benefits" which the poet mentions probably refer to every raindrop that God graciously bestows upon the earth. Another talmudic reference to our prayer is found in T.J. *Berakot,* where Bar Kappara, an older contemporary of R. Johanan, cites lines of *Nishmat* within the context of another prayer.[4]

An earlier and more impressive citation is found in Mishnah *Pesahim* 10:5, furnishing a phrase with the same words and order as found in the *Uvmakhalot* section of the *Nishmat:* לפיכך אנחנו חיבין להודות להלל לשבח לפאר לרומם להדר לברך לעלה ולקלס...[5] It appears from these sources that at least parts of the present *Nishmat* were used for primarily two functions: as part of the thanksgiving prayer for rain, and as the *Birkat ha-Shir,* the "Benediction of Song," required after the recitation of the *Hallel* in the *Haggadah* of the Passover *seder.*

These considerations have been scrutinized by scholars in their efforts to date various sections of the prayer. The usual scheme is to divide the *Nishmat* into three major sections. *The* first, from נשמת כל חי to לך לבדך אנחנו מודים, is said to be the original, earliest text, known by the time of the Mishnah.[6] Medieval traditions of dubious value attribute the authorship of this section to the apostle Peter, who, in a fit of remorse, wrote it to emphasize monotheism against heretical, trinitarian, or pagan views.[7] Proof of a more serious nature is offered by citing R.

Johanan's identification of *Nishmat Kol Hai* as the *Birkat ha-Shir* for the Passover *Hallel*. This section is not so neatly defined—starting from אלו פינו to either ממצרים or וכל קומה לפניך תשתחוה.[8] Because of the appearance of lines from this section in talmudic passages referring to the thanksgiving for rain, scholars have suggested either a late tannaitic or an early Amoraic date.[9] The third and remaining section is considered a later addition, dating from saboraic or geonic times, up to circa tenth century C.E.[10] However, by adhering to the method used for dating the first two sections, i.e., on the basis of quotations in rabbinic literature, at least part of this third section can claim mishnaic composition. The sequence of nine synonyms for praise occurs in this section, and this has been pointed out to be identical to that found in Mishnah *Pesahim* 10:5, probably antedating the other references.

Obviously, this whole procedure of comparing similar phrases or titles shows serious methodological problems. The coincidence of a phrase or word in a prayer and in some relatively datable text does not prove any necessary dependence of one upon the other. J. Heinemann, in his excellent work, *Prayer in the Period of the Tanna'im and the Amora'im*,[11] convincingly argues that the search for some *Ur*-text of a prayer, some original source from which derive other, similar phrases, is a futile and mistaken one. An excellent example of this methodological problem is presented by Heinemann's chart of the nine verbs of praise in Mishnah *Pesahim* and parallels in the *Nishmat* and the *Ribon Kol ha-ʿOlamim* of the *Birkot ha-Shahar* service.[12] Although extremely similar (even at times identical) in wording and order, there are still differences in terms of sentence structure and grammatical forms. A more dramatic example is shown where Heinemann compares six versions of the *G'vurot* motif, the theme of God's mighty acts.[13] Although they appear in different prayers in different contexts, they all use essentially the same phrases and have the same meaning. However, they differ widely in their order, grammatical construction, sentence structure, and in other features.[14] Instead of indicating some original text from which others borrowed and adapted, these parallels show a free, broad use of standard prayer commonplaces that were constantly on the lips of the faithful. The range of variation between these texts is so great that it is impossible to determine an orderly, direct influence of one version on another. Rather, these stock phrases freely drift in one form or another through many prayers and literary works. If literary dependence cannot be proven using these parallels, then dating on that basis is indefensible.

Moreover, even if one grants the possibility that these references indi-

cate the existence of a phrase in mishnaic or talmudic times, there is no
guarantee that the prayer mentioned in rabbinic literature is the same
one we have today. The mention of a title or a few snatches of a prayer
in classical rabbinic literature only testifies to the probability of the early
existence of some form of a *Nishmat* prayer; how much of this is reflected in our present text is difficult to determine. The general consensus
of scholars is that there must have been a shorter *Nishmat* called *Birkat
ha-Shir*, which was later enlarged. This position is supported by the fact
that the *Seder Rav Amram* (27b) gives a considerably shorter version
of *Nishmat*, indicating to some an earlier text.[15] This may be correct.
Nonetheless, there are only two or three sentences of any significant
variance in most of the Ashkenazic and Sephardic versions, which indicates a fairly early acceptance of our present text. Quotations from early
rabbinic literature or variations in prayerbook texts are helpful in establishing a broad period for date of composition, but they cannot narrow
down the time with any meaningful precision.

Dating also figures into the problem of authorship. As mentioned
above, the first section of the *Nishmat* has been attributed to the apostle
Simeon Peter, due to a supposed acrostic שמעון in the prayer. Similarly,
Simeon b. Kafia (medieval) and Simeon b. Shetah (Second Temple)
have been candidates for authorship.[16] In the Ashkenazic version, following the citation of Psalm 33:1, dealing with the upright and righteous,
certain letters are printed in large type, spelling in acrostic the name
Isaac. The different order in the Sephardic ritual leads to the acrostic
Rebecca. All this is spurious; forced acrostics like these to indicate the
author's name are not a feature of Jewish liturgical poetry before the
medieval period.[17] The numerous attempts to discover the author's name
through fanciful acrostics perhaps indicate the true anonymity of the
prayer; in any case, no one has yet been universally accepted as the
author of *Nishmat*, in part or in its entirety.

A further argument adduced for proving the relative age of the prayer
is one that relies on language and style. Excluding the homiletic ascription
(or dedication) of the prayer to Isaac or Rebecca,[18] scholars place the
writing of *Nishmat* within the greater rabbinic period—ranging from
tannaitic to geonic times. Evidence submitted for rabbinic or geonic
authorship are vocabulary or syntax that are likely or certain to be nonbiblical, and the striking repetition or verbosity of much of the prayer.
The first criteria are fairly sound; *Nishmat* contains a number of phrases
or words that are most probably rabbinic. For instance, the transitive use
of the hiphil form והמקריץ is rabbinic, not biblical. ולקלס, from the root

קלס, means "mock, scoff" in biblical Hebrew; the opposite, "to praise," is rabbinic.[19] חובת, absolute חובה, in the sense of "obligation" or "duty," is much more common to rabbinic usage. Likewise, אברים, from אבר or איבר, means "limbs, parts" in rabbinic Hebrew,[20] whereas in biblical Hebrew it means "pinions, wings." Other stylistic features, such as the insertion of direct biblical quotations introduced by words like כדבר שכתוב כאמור in poetry,[21] the sudden changes of meter,[22] and occasionally uneven parallelism[23] indicate a type of Hebrew poetry informed by, but different from, authentic biblical poetry.[24]

Nevertheless, the extent of the biblical Hebrew syntax and vocabulary in the prayer should not be underestimated. There is impressive literary and conceptual parallelism running through all its sections. The quotations or reminiscences from Scripture, especially from the Psalms or Isaiah, are overwhelming. Most of the words and their uses are solidly within biblical tradition; in the final analysis, very few forms or words in *Nishmat* are complete innovations. What is different is the way all these phrases are put together. After reading the oldest Hebrew poetry, such as the Song of Deborah, the Song of Moses, and the Song at the Sea, and then reading the psalms of praise in *Psukei de-Zimra,* one is struck, when confronting *Nishmat,* by a new form or genre. The clear observation is that *Nishmat* is a *prayer,* a direct address of praise and thanksgiving to God from the congregation of Israel. Many of the psalms are addresses or supplications to God. However, closer biblical examples to *Nishmat* can be found in the *Psukei de-Zimra,* with David's prayer in 1 Chronicles 29:10–13 or the Levites' prayer in Nehemiah 9:6–11, a poetic prose.[25] It might also be the case that *Nishmat* is a hybrid variety of Hebrew poetry, a cross-breeding of classic Hebrew תהלה, praise or hymn, and the collective song of thanksgiving, תּוֹדָה.[26]

The criterion of repetitiveness or verbosity is a different type of problem. Elbogen claims that the constant repetition of synonyms for praise points to a later redaction; he does, however, admit that such inordinate repetition already appears in the Mishnah, *Pesahim* 10:5. Nonetheless, since the version of Rav Amram is briefer, he contends that the multiplicity of synonyms is a later addition.[27] It is undeniable that there is a great deal of repetition of words of praise or thanksgiving in this prayer; indeed, from a statistical point of view, about one out of every five words in the prayer is a praise.[28] Elbogen's recognition of the mishnaic "verbosity" in praise immediately weakens his argument. Furthermore, although the poet states in the *Elu Finu* section that even were we superhuman, "we would still be unable to thank You," one gets the impression that this is only a rhetorical device, in the midst of beautifully extravagant poetry, to emphasize man's duty to thank and praise God.[29] This responsibility is later explicitly stated: "For it is the obligation of all created before You, our God . . . to give thanks, to praise, . . . beyond all the songs and praises of David . . ." It is an obligation or duty to thank and praise God *beyond* all of David's psalms! Accordingly, the whole point of *Nishmat,* when the poem is taken as a complete unit, is to go beyond David's hymns of praise; the poet clearly "pulls out all the stops," using all the Davidic praise words and more, to meet this obligation. Thus, the verbosity Elbogen observes is a conscious literary device used to get a specific point across. It might well be that some later poet or editor added parts here and there, and threw in more praises for good measure, yet the aim of the prayer, to praise God to the highest, and its use as a fitting conclusion and synopsis for the biblical psalms of praise, is remarkably achieved.

The conclusion that may be drawn thus far is that *Nishmat Kol Hai,* taken as a whole, exhibits formal features that tend to exhibit rabbinic rather than biblical composition. The particular use of stock phrases, many of which derive from the Bible, different grammatical constructions and new vocabulary, tend to indicate a rabbinic mode of expression. The overall stylistic impression is that of something different from biblical hymns of praise and thanksgiving. From a methodological viewpoint, it is questionable whether the verbatim appearances of lines of the *Nishmat* in talmudic passages or in other prayers indicates any conclusive proof of an original text that can be dated. Repetition of synonyms is seen to probably be an intentional literary device rather than evidence of a later redaction. The search for authorship in a poem like *Nishmat* is a futile effort. On the other hand, the fact that both Ashkenazic and Sephardic rites have preserved almost identical versions of the *Nishmat* points to a fairly early date, before the two traditions significantly diverged. Finally, it has been shown that the investigation of the prayer through the question of dating has been a useful one. Its usefulness has not been to set any specific date on the prayer, but rather to tease out and discuss major features of *Nishmat,* enabling one to fit it into the context of the history of Hebrew literature.

LITERARY ANALYSIS

Up to now, the focus of discussion has been on objective problems of history and language. Attention will now be directed to a more subjective evaluation of the poem, aided by literary and linguistic analysis.

The first impression one receives from reading *Nishmat* is that it seems like a number of prayers of praise loosely connected to each other. The sense of *prayer* is felt because of the element of direct address; "we," the congregation of Israel, or in the broader sense, "we creatures," address the divine You. Moreover, this worship of praise and thanksgiving is concluded with a blessing. One of the interesting features of this poem is that all living things are exhorted to join "us" in this praise, in a rather loud stage-whisper, while "we" are supposedly directly speaking to God. Images of parts of the body thanking and praising God seem somewhat bizarre, and sometimes the "we" abruptly moves into "they," losing the thread of discourse. Furthermore, it first sounds like a prayer that could easily have been said in one paragraph, and could have dispensed with the inordinate repetition of synonyms for praise.

However, further readings and recitations of the prayer change this negative first impression. It fits well within the context of both the *siddur* and the *Haggadah*. The prayer has a remarkable sense of rhythm and momentum, a sense of direction toward a climax. Somehow words or phrases create associations between sections, and a feeling of unity is achieved. How is this sense of unity elicited, and from whence does it derive its undeniable power and beauty?

The setting of the prayer within the context of the *Psukei de-Zimra* is an immediate clue. Reminiscent of the final line of the Psalter, Psalm 150:6, this prayer is called upon to sum up and conclude the "mini-Psalter" of the morning service, the *Psukei de-Zimra*. The universal import of the initial phrase, "the soul of every living being shall bless Your name . . . ," is then reinforced by the parallel of the next line, "the spirit of all flesh shall continually glorify and extol your fame." [30] This meshes well with the quotation from Zechariah 14:9 immediately preceding the *Nishmat*—"on that day the Lord shall be one and His name one." All beings shall come to recognize that there is one God alone, who is king over the universe. This universality is then given a temporal dimension, through the use of the words אלהי הראשונים והאחרונים, כל תולדות, תמיד, and the biblical use of the phrase, מן העולם ועד העולם, "from eternity to eternity." [31] The claim of exclusivity for God as our deliverer and redeemer, expressed through essentially synonymous parallelism (גואל ומושיע פודה ומציל...), is couched between two almost identical proclamations of God's uniqueness— אין לנו מלך אלא אתה and ומבלעדיך אין לנו מלך. This statement about the unity of God, and Israel's exclusive loyalty to

Him, is neatly concluded with לך לבדך אנחנו מודים. Conceptually, an interesting notion of a "particularistic universalism," as in Deutero-Isaiah, is expressed here. All creatures and all generations will thank and praise God, indicating the universality of the message. At the same time, only "our God" is recognized as existent and active. God's activities in the natural realm, manifesting his mercy to every individual creature, are expressed through the series of participles in parallel, recalling Psalms 145:14 and 146:17, 18.

Though most of the words and forms in this section are easily within biblical style,[32] there are several words of rabbinic provenance. מפרנס and והמקיץ are rabbinic words or forms. המנהג עולמו בחסד, "who guides His world with kindness," clearly illustrates the spatial, rabbinic under-standing of עולם, especially since it is in parallel to ובריותיו ברחמים, "and His creatures with mercy." ברב is a theological and linguistic problem. If one understands it in the rabbinic sense, "larger portion, majority," saying that God is praised by "*most* of the hymns of praise" becomes an insult to God. The biblical meaning, "great quantity," is far more ac-ceptable.[33] Noteworthy as well is the switch of discourse from direct address, talking to God in the second person, to a third-person description of His attributes in the passages beginning with אלהי הראשונים and concluding with והזוקף כפופים. Heinemann suggests that third-person discussion of God in a prayer is a later development, under the influence of the *Kaddish*.[34] In any case, the paragraph is neatly tied up with "to You alone we give thanks," resuming direct address.

Thanksgiving is then the central theme for the next major section, beginning with אלו פינו מלא שירה כים, "were our mouth full of song as the sea . . ." This is probably the most exquisite poetic section in the prayer, if not in the liturgy. Hyperbole is used to its best advantage here; the unusual and grand similes of our mouth full of song as the sea, our tongue with ringing praise as the roar of the waves, lips like the expanse of heaven, eyes shining like the sun and moon, all in flowing, rhythmical parallelism, are simply intoxicating! By juxtaposing parts of the human body with superlatives from the larger world of natural phenomena, an incredible sense of infinity is conveyed. This is precisely the point—it is meant to illustrate that the benefits God showers upon man are infinite, and that to reciprocate, man would have the impossible task of offering Him infinite thanks. Even if man were superhuman, with eyes like sun and moon, this effort to fully praise God would fail. The following line, "for one-thousandth part of the thousand millions and ten thousands of myriads of benefits," indicates the infinity of the debt of gratitude mankind owes God.[35] As mentioned above, the immensity that figures so largely in this section may be due to its usage as a thanksgiving for rain, for thanks is due for every single raindrop God causes to fall upon the earth.

The style and language are not foreign to biblical poetry. The image of praises roaring like the waves can be found in Psalm 93:4 and Isaiah 35:6; *Shir ha-Ma'alot,* Psalm 126:2, contains similar notions and phrases. The broad expanses of heaven proclaiming God's glory can be found in Psalm 19:2.

אלו and מספיקים, both commonly found in rabbinic Hebrew, are still found, though rarely, in the Bible.[36] Parallelism and metrical regularity are beautifully evident in this section.

The next section, beginning with ממצרים גאלתנו, "from Egypt you have delivered us," although said to be a much later addition to *Elu Finu,* blends very well with the preceding line. It contains the thread of historical perspective indicated by "our fathers and us." The shift in focus is now to the historical goodness that God has shown to Israel, beginning from the Exodus (echoing the Song at the Sea, which precedes the *Nishmat*). The image is no longer that of a transcendent God directing His creation, but rather a personal deity caring for His people. The parallelism and meter are short but flowing; note the rhyme effect with the first-person-plural pronominal suffix:

ומבית עבדים פדיתנו   ממצרים גאלתנו
ובשבע כלכלתנו   ברעב זנתנו
ומדבר מלטתנו   מחרב הצלתנו
ומחליים רעים ונאמנים דיליתנו

This retrospect is summed up by "until now Your mercy has helped us . . . ," and then the hope for the future is expressed, in the only entreaty of the prayer—"may You never forsake us, Lord our God." In terms of language, nothing here is exclusively rabbinic.[37] The tone is one of poetic address rather than descriptive poetry.

"Therefore," עַל כֵּן, because of this beneficence manifested in the past, there is good reason to praise God with our entire being. The earlier poetic image of the parts of the body in *Elu Finu* is taken up again, first in a general sense—limbs, soul, and tongue—and then in a specific sense —mouth, tongue, knee, stature, heart, inward parts. "We" are no longer doing the praising; metaphorically, "they," the parts of our body, are worshipping and praising God. This is obviously not a new idea in the

prayer; however, the abrupt, emphatic הֵן הֵם,[38] "behold, they," emphasizes the third person, along with the following string of thanking and
praising verbs in the third-person-plural imperfect. The effect is one of
jarring interruption to the rhythmical flow. The anatomical metaphor is
resumed again, in smoother fashion, leading to a direct, conscious quotation from the Bible, Psalm 35:10, furnishing a justification for all this
imagery—"all my bones [= being] shall say: Lord, who is like you . . ."
This use of direct quotation from Scripture, preceded by an introductory
word like ככתוב or כאמור, is a rabbinic or "New Hebrew" innovation,[39]
providing an אסמכתא to substantiate the poet's views or images.[40]

The poet then seizes upon the מי כמוך phrase in the psalm, and asks
the rhetorical question, "who is like You, who is equal to You, who can
be compared to You,"[41] continued with the familiar attributes of God,
"great, mighty, awesome, most high God, creator of heaven and earth."[42]
The verbs switch again, to first-person plural, returning the focus of attention from parts of the body praising God to "us"—"*we* shall praise,
laud, and glorify You." A second proof text is furnished—Psalm 103:1.
This verse, "bless the Lord, my soul, and all that is within me, His holy
name," is an apt summation (more appropriate, perhaps, than the
Psalm 35:10 passage) for the exhortation to praise the Lord with all
one's being.

The prayer continues with a midrashic exposition* of the conceptions
of divinity presented above—that the Lord is God, great, mighty, and
awe-inspiring:

> God—in the abundance of Your might
> Great—in the glory of Your name
> Mighty—forever
> Revered—for your awe-inspiring acts
> The King who sits on a high and lofty throne.[43]

The next section, שוכן עד, is thematically connected to the preceding
lines, emphasizing the transcendent kingship of God. The recognition
of God's exalted kingship is that which causes the righteous to spon-
taneously praise Him, as expressed by a third biblical quotation, psalm

---

*"Midrashic exposition" is here understood as the rabbinic technique of drawing out
the meaning or consequence of a given word in a phrase. In this instance, and in the
one that will shortly be mentioned, the exposition is one of plain and immediate
meaning or implication, and not one of flight of a creative imagination.

33:1: "Rejoice, righteous ones, in the Lord; it is fitting for the upright to praise." A second instance of a midrashic exposition immediately follows, seizing upon the words ישרים and צדיקים:

By the mouth of the upright	You are praised
By the words of the righteous	You are blessed
By the tongue of the faithful	You are exalted
In the midst of the holy	You are sanctified.[44]

Perhaps to emphasize the universality of praise for God, the poet seems to switch the subjects of these praises throughout the prayer. At first, all living things should praise and thank God; next, parts of the body are used in hyperbole to stress our inability to sufficiently praise God. Then, the praisers seem to be identified with the Israelites who were rescued from slavery in Egypt and kept alive in the desert. The anatomical metaphor then returns, and the parts of the body are themselves giving all manner of praise to God. The poet then underscores through the use of two proof texts that this unusual metaphor represents our whole being, bringing the focus back to the personal, individual unit. With the acclamation of God as great and exalted king, the praisers are specifically the righteous. The group then expands to include "the assemblies[45] of the tens of thousands of Your people, the house of Israel," throughout all generations. The crescendo moves to its peak when the poet boldly states, "for it is the obligation of all created . . . to give thanks, to praise . . ." Every created thing has a *duty* to thank and praise the Lord;[46] it is no longer a רשות, a voluntary, nonrequired act. Then follow the famous nine synonyms of praise and thanksgiving found as well in the Mishnah, extravagantly heaping praise upon praise. The final line of these remarkable passages goes so far as to say that the obligation for praise surpasses even all the hymns of praise in David's psalter, many of which had just appeared in the *Psukei de-Zimra*. In other words, one is not freed of his *halakhic* or moral duty by reciting the *Psukei de-Zimra*— using this understanding, the *Nishmat*'s function is to point out this inadequacy, and to try to fill the breach by adding praise upon praise, until the mind is saturated with all these glorious synonyms.

The ישתבח comes as the conclusion of the prayer, riding on the crest of this exultation of God, effusing praise and glorification. One is bombarded with these synonyms! God is recognized as the great and mighty one, king over heaven and earth, to whom pertain all manner of glories:

Song and praise,
hymn and psalm,
power and rulership, eminence,
greatness and might,
fame and glory,
holiness and royalty,
now and forever.

Using solidly biblical terms,[47] the poet constructs a series of parallels that stretches the language (and the mind) to its limits.[48] The חתימה, or concluding benediction of the prayer, is a fitting summary of the content and purpose of *Nishmat,* blessing God the King who is great in praises, the God of thanksgivings, Lord of wonders, who is pleased by song and psalm, the life of the universe.[49] The two basic threads of the prayer, thanksgiving and praise, are explicitly recalled and brought together in the benediction. God's great transcendent kingship is celebrated, and the suitability of psalm and hymn are underscored, reinforcing the recitation of *Psukei de-Zimra* or the *Hallel* on Passover. Finally, the last phrase, חֵי הָעוֹלָמִים, nicely recalls the beginning of the prayer, וְנִשְׁמַת כָּל־חַי, helping to bring this complex prayer toward a coherent unity. As a postscript, the *Nishmat* in the morning service is followed by the reader's *Kaddish,* a great sanctification of God's name, and then by the *Barchu,* which translates this praise and adoration into action—bowing before God the King.

Is it a coincidence that *Nishmat* fits so well as the conclusion of *Psukei de-Zimra* or *Hallel;* was it selected for those positions in the liturgy because of its content, or was it written expressly for this purpose? Is this prayer an original unity, or was it created by connecting already-existent works into a new whole? These questions are not easily answered; in the final analysis, what matters is that it *now* stands as a unity, and serves the function of concluding services of praise, and does so admirably. It is true that the logical coherence of the work weakens in places; likewise, the abrupt subject-person changes, alteration of modes of address, and eccentric rhythm or parallelism patterns might detract from its formal and aesthetic elegance. Nonetheless, it still stands as a great example of liturgical poetry. The basic themes of praise and thanksgiving carry throughout the prayer, aided by word associations, direct quotations from the Bible, and midrashic expansion. The language and style of the prayer is heavily influenced by classical Hebrew poetry, particularly the Psalms and Isaiah. Much of the prayer is in beautiful parallelism, and has a fine, flowing rhythm. What might tend to surprise the reader is the novel or unusual uses of essentially biblical language and form.

Furthermore, the poem tends to gather a momentum through the repetition of praises, building up into a tremendous climax at the end of ובמקהלות. The final section, ישתבח, nicely summarizes the major concepts, heaps the praises higher, and manages to stylistically connect the end of the prayer to its beginning. Finally, and perhaps most importantly, *Nishmat* is meant to be a prayer or hymn of praise to literally end all praises. In this it succeeds remarkably. The lavish use of language is a striking device to inundate the mind with praises, to stretch the limits of the imagination to infinity. Moreover, the impression given by this prayer is that the content or meaning of each praise is really secondary to its cumulative effect. The writer is here reminded of E. A. Poe's poetry; the meaning of the word is subservient to the overall mood that the poem seeks to convey. *Nishmat Kol Hai* creates an atmosphere of jubilant, ecstatic praise and thanksgiving, an overwhelming experience not unlike that which was sought by the Merkabah mystics when they recited their long and lavish hymns. It serves as a brilliant finale for the symphony of praises in the *Psukei de-Zimra* and the *Haggadah*. It is no wonder, then, that this great prayer is so frequently and prominently used in traditional Jewish liturgy!

NOTES

1. P. Birnbaum, *High Holiday Prayer Book* (New York: Hebrew Publishing Co., 1960), Rosh Hashanah, p. 169; Yom Kippur, p. 255.
2. For an excellent treatment of the theological meanings behind the *Nishmat,* within the context of the High Holidays, cf. M. Arzt, *Justice and Mercy: Commentary on the Liturgy of the New Year and the Day of Atonement* (New York: Holt, Rinehart & Winston, 1963), pp. 40–46.
3. Rav Judah claims that *Birkat ha-Shir,* required by the Mishnah, *Pesah.* 10:7, is *Y'hallelukha,* cf. T. B. *Pesah.* 118a. Levy explains that the "Blessing of the Song " after the Egyptian *Hallel* (Pss. 113–118) is *Y'hallelukha;* the "Blessing of the Song" after the Great *Hallel,* Ps. 136, concluding all the praises sung, is *Nishmat Kol Hai.* This is the case in the Haggadah לוי א. **יסודות התפלה,** (תל אביב, 1969).
4. לך תכרע כל ברך. Cf. I. M. Elbogen, **התפילה בישראל בהתפתחותה ההיסטורי׳** (תל אביב, 1972) 86 .p.
5. ח. אלבק, **ששה סדרי משנה,** סדר מועד (ירושלים, 1952) ע׳ 178.
6. A. Z. Idelsohn, *Jewish Liturgy and Its Development* (New York: Sacred Music Press, 1932), pp. 364–65, n. 4.
7. Elbogen, p. 86; *Encyclopedia Judaica,* S. V. "Nishmat Kol Ḥai" (vol. 9, col. 1177).
8. Idelsohn, pp. 364–65; *Encyclopedia Judaica,* Loc. cit.
9. Ibid.
10. Ibid.
11. J. Heinemann, *Prayer in the Period of the Tanna'im and the Amora'im* [Hebrew] (Jerusalem: Magnes Press, 1966).
12. Ibid., p. 41.
13. The corresponding lines in *Nishmat* are: "He awakens the sleepers and arouses the slumberers; He causes the dumb to speak and sets the captives free; He supports all who fall and raises up those who are bowed down." The others are Maimonides' version of the *Nishmat,* the second blessing of the *Amidah,* the *Hibbur Berakot* version of *Birkot ha-Shahar, Emet v'Yatziv,* and the Ashkenazic version of the piyyut *Ana Adonai Hoshia Na;* Heinemann, pp. 40–41.
14. Ibid., pp. 41–42.
15. Elbogen, p. 86, p. 414, n. 6; *Encyclopedia Judaica,* col. 1177.
16. S. Baer, 661–62 ׳ע ׳ב כרך (ניו יארק, 1945) **אוצר התפילות,** תיקון תפילה. **סדר עבודת ישראל** (תל אביב, 1957) ע׳ 206.
17. S. Lieberman, *Hellenism in Jewish Palestine* (New York: Jewish Theological Seminary, 1962), pp. 79–80, indicates that the use of acrostics to discover authorship existed in the Orient in the second mill. B.C.E. Alexandrian grammarians searched Homer for such acrostics. However, "in earlier rabbinic literature this kind of acrostic is not mentioned" (p. 80).

88

18. Baer, p. 209.
19. Perhaps coming from the Greek καλός ("beautiful"); cf. L. N. Dembitz, "Nishmat," in *Jewish Encyclopedia*, 9: 313–14; Artz, pp. 44–46.
20. This derives from the Targum Onkelos, וִיפַלֵּג יָתָהּ לְאֵיבָרָהָא (Lev. 1:6), עיין תפילה, אוצר התפילות, ע' 665.
21. Cf. n. 39.
22. E.g., the passage of הן הם יודו ויברכו abruptly switches to כי כל־פה לך יודה.
23. E.g., the insertion of נצח within a balanced sequence of attributes in ישתבח.
24. Features of biblical poetry, such as parallelism and metrical regularity, are not precisely defined, and should not be followed slavishly. Eissfeldt points out that parallelism is not the absolute hallmark of poetry, nor is metrical regularity its consistent factor. O. Eissfeldt, *The Old Testament: An Introduction* (Oxford: B. Blackwell, 1966), pp. 57–64.
25. In *Nishmat* many of the poetic parallelisms are directed or ordered into a coherent address by key prose sentences. For instance, "for this is the duty of all created," or "for to you, Lord our God and God of our fathers, pertain . . ." set up the logical sequence for the series of praise parallels that follow, and give the prayer a sense of direction.
26. Cf. Eissfeldt, pp. 105–9, 120–24. The *Nishmat* has a twofold aim, to praise and to thank God. It is interesting to note that *Nishmat* follows Exod. 15:1–18, offered by Eissfeldt as a classic example of early Hebrew תְּהִלָּה, in the *Psukei de-Zimra*, and follows Ps. 136, his example for the collective thanksgiving, in the *Haggadah*. תּוֹדָה is the classic Hebrew for thank-offering, expanded to include individual thanksgiving psalms (Eissfeldt, p. 121). 1QH, although used collectively, is written in this individual style. Here we have a collectve thanksgiving. Note that the form הוֹדָאוֹת, used twice in our prayer, is not found in the Bible.
27. Elbogen, p. 87, p. 414, n. 6.
28. There are 340 words in the Ashkenazic *Nishmat* (Dembitz, p. 313), and approximately 60–65 of them are terms for praise (about 20 synonyms). The most frequently used roots are שבח (9x), ברך (8x), ידה (7x), הלל (6x), and פאר (6x).
29. Cf. I. Abrahams, *A Companion to the Authorized Daily Prayerbook* (New York: Hermon Press, 1966), p. 142. Compare the Apocalypse of Baruch 54:8, a second century C.E. work; cf. also *Avot de Rabbi Nathan* I.25. The rabbis thought it blasphemous for man to presume to capture God's infinite greatness and beneficence in mere human words; cf. T. B. *Berakot* 33b and *Megillah* 18a. In these talmudic passages, such verbal extravagance is unmistakably denounced, and is perhaps a polemic against the Hekhalot literature using this style (cf. G. Scholem, *Major Trends in Jewish Mysticism* [New York: Schocken, 1954], p. 60). In *Elu Finu* this disclaimer is couched in the same "purple prose" the rabbis attacked.
30. Cf. Job 12:10.
31. Cf. Ps. 106:48.
32. Another instance of employing biblical phrases is הנה לא ינום ולא יישן from Ps.121:4. Its position in the series of participles jars the flow of the passage, although it does introduce the notion that not only does God not sleep, He awakens others (probably referring to resurrection and immortality).
33. The Sephardic ritual avoids the problem by offering בְּכָל instead of בְּרֹב. Cf. Baer, p. 206.
34. Heinemann, p. 43.
35. This difficult line appears in numerous variations, often with the deletion of the

confusing אלף of אֲלָפִים אֶלֶף אַלְפֵי אֶלֶף מֵאָלֶף אַחַת. Cf. Baer, p. 207. Likewise, וְרִבֵּי is often mistakenly pointed וְרוֹב.

36. אִלּוּ—Eccles. 6:6 and Esther 7:4; מַסְפִּיקִים from שׂפק (biblical) or ספק (rabbinic), cf. 1 Kings 20:10 and Ben Sira 15:8.

37. שָׂבָע, "plenty," appears in Gen. 41:29 and Prov. 3:10. דְּלִיתָנוּ a piel perfect of דלה, can similarly be found in Ps. 30:2.

38. Cf. Gen. 3:22, Num. 31:16. It could also be pointed הֵן הֵם, cf. Job 8:19.

39. In 2 Kings 14:6 (cf. 2 Chron. 25:4), a direct quotation from Deut. 24:16 is preceded by the following: ככתוב בספר תורת משה אשר צוה ה' לאמר. The concordance indicates a good number of passages using ככתוב as preceding a reminiscence from the Torah, but these are almost entirely concerned with legal passages that are paraphrased or summarized. None occurs within the context of poetry.

40. The second half of the quotation, "who delivers the poor from one stronger than he, etc.," seems oddly out of place here. The Sephardic version smooths the reading by supplying the following: שועת עניים אתה תשמע צעקת הדל תקשיב ותושיע.

41. Cf. Ps. 89:7, Isa. 9:25; similarly, see again Exod. 15:11.

42. Cf. Gen. 14:19; also the *Avot* prayer in the *Amidah*.

43. This is a rabbinic, rather than biblical, feature. עיון תפלה, in the אוצר התפילות, suggests that the four attributes are really five. אל of אל עליון is an unnecessary and forbidden repetition; he suspects that it should be מלך עליון. If this were the case, it would coincide well with the exposition—המלך—היושב על כסא רם ונשא. He admits, however, that the term מלך עליון is not found in the Bible, Mishnah, or Talmud. (אוצר, pp. 688–89). For the image of God sitting on His throne, cf. Isa. 6:1 and 57:15.

44. For the acrostics seen in this, and variations of this passage in the different rituals, see above and Baer, p. 209.

45. וּבְמַקְהֲלוֹת, plural construct of מַקְהֵל, "assembly." The Sephardic pointing is וּבְמִקְהֲלוֹת; cf. Baer, p. 209.

46. One is reminded of the injunction in the *Sh'ma,* Deut. 6:5, to love the Lord with all one's mind, soul, and might.

47. Cf. 1 Chron. 29:30, Hab. 3:3.

48. The Merkabah mystics put themselves into ecstatic trances by pronouncing praise after praise to God; cf. Scholem, pp. 59–60.

49. חֵי הָעוֹלָמִים — there is a significant question as to the use of עוֹלָם in this prayer. As mentioned earlier, המנהג עולמו clearly refers to a spatial notion of עוֹלָם. Two other instances, מן העולם ועד עולם and מעתה ועד עולם, are probably used in a biblical, temporal sense. חי העולמים could therefore mean "life of the ages" (= "eternity") or "life of the worlds." The traditional commentary, עץ יוסף, sees העולמים as "worlds," a religious polemic against heretics who would deny another world. "Universe" is a tentative solution, as in P. Birnbaum's *Daily Prayer Book* (New York: Hebrew Publishing Co., 1949), p. 336, incorporating the eternity of worlds and time.

A RABBINIC COMMENT ON EXODUS 1:10

By

SAMUEL TOBIAS LACHS

In recent years there has been an increased interest in, and more serious consideration given to, rabbinic interpretation of the Bible, not as midrashic literature but as pointing up the literal meaning of the biblical text. Talmudic and midrashic comments have generally been dismissed by scientific biblical scholars as mere far-fetched and fanciful exercises in homiletics. Today this attitude is beginning to change, and the new interest in old ideas has extended to the medieval Jewish exegetes, who have been shown to have advanced remarkable explanations and shown insights into the text of Scripture which have been substantiated today through our increased knowledge of the languages of the ancient Near East.

One interpretation of the rabbis, long considered fanciful and homiletic, is the comment on Exodus 1:10, which should be no longer ignored but taken quite seriously. It concerns the well-known charge of Pharaoh to his people: "Come, let us deal wisely with them lest they multiply, and it come to pass, that, when there befalleth us any war, they also join themselves unto our enemies and fight against us, and get them up out of the land." [1]

The major difficulty with this verse, which has been a *crux interpretum,* is the last phrase: ועלה מן הארץ —"and get them up out of the land." [2] Why was Pharaoh concerned and afraid that the Israelites might leave the land? If his fear had been that they were a subversive element of the population, not loyal to the government, which is the apparent meaning of the verse, he should have welcomed their departure. It likewise cannot be argued that he did not want them to leave because then he would have been deprived of cheap slave labor, for as yet, according to the verse, they had not been enslaved.

A recent suggestion at a solution is that of Professor Moshe Greenberg, who argues as follows:

> Our story assumes that Pharaoh claimed absolute authority over all his domain. For the Israelites to win their freedom to "go up from the land" would not have been so much a loss to Egyptian economy—for the people were not yet enslaved, whatever Gen. 47:6 implies—as a blow to that authority. What Pharoh wants, we now learn, is not to be rid of the Israelites—as we might have supposed from his first statement (verse 9)—but to keep them in his power as subjects, to do with them as he sees fit. Such power-hunger cannot bear the thought of a loss of objects to control.[3]

He then cites several examples of the Pharaoh's insatiable desire for absolute control.[4] Granting the validity of the thesis that Pharaoh was power-hungry, the explanation does not fit the text. Pharaoh was worried about a specific situation—the occasion of a war or an invasion in which the Hebrews might side with the enemy and thus aid in the conquest of the land of Egypt by the invaders. Logic demands that it is better to get rid of those who present a threat to one's position than to retain them as a constant source of fear and anxiety. We must therefore look elsewhere for a solution.

The rabbis understood ועלה מן הארץ as a euphemism meaning not that they i.e., the Israelites, will go up out of the land, but that the Egyptians themselves will have to go up out of the land. The Talmud records the following: "And fight against us and get them up out of the land"—it should have read, "and we will get us up!" Rabbi Abba b. Kahana said: "It is like a man who curses himself and hangs the curse upon somebody else."[5] For this interpretation to be taken seriously, one basic element must be established, that is, do we find any other examples of this type of euphemism in the Bible?

The Bible contains a variety of euphemistic expressions. There are those for dying,[6] sexual intercourse,[7] and for the performing of natural functions.[8] What concerns this investigation is the use of a euphemism involving avoidance of direct implication of the speaker and/or the avoidance of direct implication in an oath which carries with it dire consequences for the speaker. In these two latter categories we can cite the following as illustrations:

1. Num. 16:14: "Even if you had brought us to a land flowing with milk and honey, should you gouge out those men's eyes? We will not come." [9] "Those men's eyes" is a euphemism for "our eyes."
2. 1 Sam. 29:4: "Should it not be with the heads of these men?" [10] "These men" is a euphemism for "us."
3. Ibid. 25:22: "God do so unto the enemies of David, and more also if I leave of all that pertain to him by the morning light so much as one male." [11] "The enemies of" is a euphemism meaning David himself.
4. Ibid. 20:16: "The Lord require it at the hand of David's enemies." [12] Here again "enemies" is a euphemism for David himself.

It is our opinion, in light of the fact that the Bible does employ euphemistic expressions of this variety, that the rabbinic interpretation cited in the Talmud is most reasonable as indicating the literal meaning of the passage.

We turn now to the historical implications of this interpretation, which involves the identification of the Pharaoh who is the speaker in the passage. If the supposition that the Pharaoh of the Joseph-Jacob period was a Hyksos, then this "new king who knew not Joseph" [13] is best identified with one of the native Egyptian royalty. When the Hyksos (Rulers of Foreign Lands) invaded Egypt ca. 1720 B.C.E., they settled in the Delta area and made their capital at Avaris. This was concurrent with the latter days of the Thirteenth Dynasty at Thebes in Upper Egypt. The Hyksos were for the most part Semites who entered Egypt from the direction of Palestine. Although the records from the Hyksos period are scanty, it seems as though the Egyptian rulers were vassals to the invaders but ruled their subjects in Upper Egypt. Their political and religious center was at Thebes. What is clear, however, is that Kamose, the last Egyptian ruler of the Seventeenth Dynasty at Thebes, drove the Hyksos out of Middle Egypt and confined them to the Delta region. The complete ouster of the Hyksos from Egypt was accomplished by Ahmose (ca. 1570–1545), the first Pharaoh of the Eighteenth Dynasty, who also destroyed their capital of Avaris.

During the Ninteenth Dynasty the cultic center remained at Thebes, but by the time of Rameses, the capital was removed to the Northeastern Delta area. The Hyksos invasion and domination had a profound effect upon the Egyptian mentality. The Hyksos period was referred to as "The Great Humiliation," particularly during the Eighteenth Dynasty, and it was determined that such a national disaster would never again be permitted to happen. Having ousted the foreign invaders, but fearing another attack from the northeast, the only direction where they were vulnerable, the Egyptians fortified the Delta region. They continued, nevertheless, to harbor the fear that should another Asiatic invasion occur, the remaining Semites in Egypt, namely the Israelites, might join with them, and the *Egyptian* rulers might have to "go up out of the land," i.e., from Lower Egypt of the Delta back to Upper Egypt to Thebes, suffering the same humiliation they had endured during the Hyksos period. If this reconstruction is correct, then the Pharaoh of Exodus 1:10 is Rameses II (1290–1224) of the Nineteenth Dynasty, whose building projects were intended as defenses against any future invasion from Asia. At that time the fear was directed against the Hittites, who were a constant threat to Egyptian security.

NOTES

1. Exod. 1:10: הבה נתחכמה לו פן ירבה והיה כי תקראנה מלחמה ונוסף גם הוא על שנאינו ונלחם בנו ועלה מן הארץ.

2. *NJPS* translation, "and gain ascendancy over the land," follows M. Lambert, *Revue des Études Juives* 39 (1899): 30. NEB: "and they will become masters of the country." Ehrlich compares it with Hos. 2:2. Saadia translates "they will chase us out of the land."

3. M. Greenberg, *Understanding Exodus,* vol. 2, part. I, The Heritage of Biblical Israel (New York: Melton Research Center, 1969), p. 22.

4. Ibid.

5. T. B. *Sota* 11a: ועלה מן הארץ הארץ מיבעי ליה. א״ר אבא בר כהנא כאדם שמקלל את עצמו ותולה קללתו בחבירו וועלינו מן הארץ מיבעי ליה יגרשונו מן הארץ .Cf. Rashi *ad loc.:* מאי ועלה הלואי שיצאו שונאיהם מארצם הואיל וויראי׳ מפניהם. See, however, Rashi to Exod. 1:10: ורבותינו דרשו כאדם שמקלל עצמו ותולה קללתו באחרים והרי הוא כאלו כתב ועלינו מן הארץ והם יירשוה.

6. Cf. Gen. 5:24: ואיננו כי לקח אותו אלהים; ibid. 47:30: ;ושכבתי עם אבותי Isa. 26:19 : שוכני עפר; Dan. 12:2: ישני אדמת עפר; Gen. 37:35 : ירד שאולה ibid. 49:29: נאסף אל עמי; I Kings 2:2: הלך בדרך כל הארץ; Jer. 51:39: וישנו שנת עולם; et al.

7. Gen. 4:1: ידע (although this usage is common in Akkadian); ibid. 30:15: שכב עם; ibid. 6:4: בא אל; Exod. 19:15: נגש אל אשה; Gen. 20:4: קרב אל. Also euphemisms for menstruation: ibid. 27:11: ארח כנשים; ibid. 31:35: דרך נשים.

8. For urinating הסך את רגליו, lit., "to cover the feet;" Judg. 3:4. 1 Sam. 24:4.

9. אף לא אל ארץ זבת חלב ודבש הביאתנו ותתן לנו נחלת שדה וכרם העיני האנשים ההם תנקר לא נעלה. Rashi and Sforno take האנשים ההם as a euphemism while Ibn Ezra and Rashbam refer it to their followers.

10. הלא בראשי האנשים ההם.

11. כה יעשה אלהם לאיבי דוד וכה יסיף אם אשאיר מכל אשר לו עד אור הבקר משתין בקיר. The LXX for לאויבי דוד reads τῷ Δαυείδ. Cf. S. R. Driver, *Notes on the Hebrew Text of the Books of Samuel* (Oxford, 1890), p. 154: "the insertion of לאויבי is probably intentional, to avoid the appearance, as the threat in b was not carried out, of the imprecation recoiling upon David himself."

12. I Sam. 20:16: ויכרת יהונתן עם בית דוד ובקש ה׳ מיד איבי דוד. On this and v. 15, see Driver, op. cit., ad loc.

13. Ex. 1.8: ויקם מלך חדש על מצרים אשר לא ידע את יוסף. Cf. T. B. *Sota,* loc. cit.: ויקם מלך חדש וגו׳ רב ושמואל חד אמר חדש ממש וחד אמר שנתחדשו גזירותיו.

וְאֵלֶּה שְׁמוֹת בְּנֵי יִשְׂרָאֵל הַבָּאִים מִצְרַיְמָה אֵת יַעֲקֹב אִישׁ וּבֵיתוֹ בָּאוּ
(שמות י״ב) וְהַמַּשְׂכִּילִים יַזְהִירוּ כְּזֹהַר הָרָקִיעַ וּמַצְדִּיקֵי הָרַבִּים
כַּכּוֹכָבִים לְעוֹלָם וָעֶד • וְהַמַּשְׂכִּילִים אִלֵּין אִינּוּן דְּמִסְתַּכְּלֵי בְּרָזָא
דְּחָכְמְתָא (נ״א יַזְהִירוּ דְּנָצְצִין בְּרָזָא דְּחָכְמְתָא) • יַזְהִירוּ נָהֲרִין וְנָצְצִין
בְּזִיוָא דִּ
עֵדֶן וְדָא

Medieval Civilization

אִיהוּ רָזָא כּוֹכַּבַּיָא

זֹהַר דְּהַאי רָקִיעַ נָהִיר בְּנֵהֲרוֹ עַל גִּנְתָּא • וְאִילָנָא דְּחַיֵּי קַיְּים בְּמְצִיעוּת
גִּנְתָּא דְּעַנְפוֹי חַפְיָין (ר״ח עֲלֵיהּ) (נ״א עַל) כָּל אִינּוּן דְּיוּקְנִין וְאִילָנִין
וּבוּסְמִין דִּבְגִנְתָּא בְּמָאנִין דְּכַשְׁרָן • וּמְטַלְּלִין תְּחוֹתַיְהוּ כָּל חֵיוַת בָּרָא
וְכָל צִפְּרִין שְׁמַיָּא יְדוּרוּן תְּחוֹת אִינּוּן עַנְפִין :

זֹהַר אִיבָּא (ב) דְּאִילָנָא יָהִיב חַיִּין לְכֹלָּא • קִיּוּמָא לְעָלַם וּלְעָלְמֵי עָלְמִין
סְטְרָא אַחֲרָא לָא שַׁרְיָא בֵּיהּ אֶלָּא סְטְרָא דִּקְדוּשָׁה • זַכָּאָה
חוּלָקֵיהוֹן אִינּוּן דְּטָעֲמִין אִינּוּן קַיְּימִין לְעָלַם וּלְעָלְמֵי עָלְמִין • אִלֵּין אִקְרוּן
מַשְׂכִּילִים וְכַכָּאן חַיִּין בְּהַאי עָלְמָא וְחַיִּין בְּעָלְמָא דְּאָתֵי :

זֹהַר אִילָנָא דָּא זַקְפָּא לְעֵילָּא לְעֵילָּא חֲמֵשׁ מֵאָה פַּרְסֵי הֲלוּכֵיהּ (ג) שָׁתִּין
רִבּוֹא אִיהוּ בִּפְשִׁיטוּתֵיהּ בְּהַאי אִילָנָא קַיְּימָא חַד זָהֲרָא • (ד) (זֹהַר)
דְּכָל גּוָֹנִין קַיְּימִין בֵּיהּ וְאִינּוּן גּוָֹנִין סָלְקִין וְנָחֲתִין וְלָא מִתְיַישְּׁבֵי כְּדוּכְתָּא
אַחֲרָא בַּר בְּהַהוּא אִילָנָא • כַּד נַפְקֵי מִנֵּיהּ לְאִתְחַזָּאָה כְּגוֹ זֹהַר דְּלָא
נָהֲרָא מִתְיַישְּׁבָן וְלָא מִתְיַישְּׁבָן קַיְּימָן וְלָא קַיְּימָן בְּגִין דְּלָא מִתְיַישְּׁבָן
בְּאֲתַר אַחֲרָא • מֵאִילָנָא דָּא נַפְקֵי (ה) תְּרֵיסַר שִׁבְטִין דְּמִתְחֲמָן בֵּיהּ
וְאִינּוּן נַחֲתוּ בְּהַאי זֹהַר דְּלָא נָהֲרָא לְגוֹ גָּלוּתָא דְּמִצְרַיִם בְּכַמָּה מַשִׁירְיָין
עִלָּאִין

(א) (פי׳ יסוד • פי׳ יסוד כינס דכים חסדים וגבורות וסמכאל וסט״רא סס ז׳ון וכולוגין סס כו׳ע כילס קיומס מיסוד דכינס ועיין
במקק׳מ • תרס׳כ׳) : (כ) (סיי׳ס) : (ג) ו׳ קלויות : (ד) קלויות : פ׳ עיון ריס פ׳ לך לך מוס : (ס) פי׳ נסמח י׳כ סכעים סס מי׳כ נכולי אלכסון סכאים
מח״מ לוסיד וכ׳ הרמ׳כ כסו׳ ה׳נ חלק לו׳ סי׳ מ׳ס ה׳ל דע ׳כ כת׳מ ים י׳כ נכולי דרומית וסס נכול דרומית רומית נכול דרומית תחתית
ודרומית מזרחית ודרומית עוד נכול מערכית סס ד׳ • עוד נכול לכוגיל לכוגית רומית לכוגית תחתית לכוגית מערכית לכוגית מזרחית סס ד׳ • עוד נכול
מזרחית רומית מזרחית תחתית מזרחית עוד נכול מערכית רומית מערכית תחתית מזרחית סס י׳כ כנגד י׳כ אורות עליונים להס ד׳ סויות לסס מי־ככת
י׳כ סבעי ישראל עכ׳ל וס׳ מ׳ן מ׳ס עיון עליו כסדר י׳כ נכולי אלכסון • קר׳כ׳ן :
שֵׁמִית   א   !

תַּלְמִיד חָכָם... דִּבּוּרוֹ בְּנַחַת עִם כָּל הַבְּרִיּוֹת... מַקְדִּים שָׁלוֹם לְכָל
אָדָם... וְדָן אֶת כָּל הָאָדָם לְכַף זְכוּת... אוֹהֵב שָׁלוֹם וְרוֹדֵף שָׁלוֹם...
מִכְּלָל דְּבָרָיו בְּמִשְׁפָּט... אוֹמֵר עַל לָאו לָאו וְעַל הֵן הֵן... עָלָיו
הַכָּתוּב אוֹמֵר וַיֹּאמֶר לִי עַבְדִּי אָתָּה יִשְׂרָאֵל אֲשֶׁר בְּךָ אֶתְפָּאָר.
(מִשְׁנֵה תּוֹרָה, הִלְכוֹת דֵּעוֹת, פ״ה: הל׳ ז׳-י״ב)

Moses de Leon, *Zohar al Ha-Torah*
Livorno, 1887

THE COINCIDENCE OF CENTERS OF JEWRY
WITH CENTERS OF WESTERN CIVILIZATION

By

ARTHUR J. ZUCKERMAN

I

Is the rising generation of Jews about to experience a series of events which has occurred with startling repetition in the millennia-long history of the Jewish people—to be witness to a shift in political, economic, and cultural power from a prominent world center to a heretofore underdeveloped region? And as an unfailing accompaniment of such slippage and transfer of dominance, are the Jews to repeat the experience of the centuries whereby they have removed the center of their own communal life toward the newly ascendant focus of energy? Precisely such a convergence of vitality—Jewish and general—has taken place again and again in the past.

Portents of the Future

Will future historians view the Kennedy administration in the United States as the high-point-of-no-return of American predominance in the world; and, on the other hand, the Nixon-Ford regime, the Indo-China and Watergate disasters, and subsequent economic crises, as the signs of its incipient decline and decay? It would be premature to propose another area, such as, for example, the Middle East (which has only just begun to sap the resources of Europe and America), as the new challenger for leadership in the Western world. Yet the presence of a three-million-strong Jewish community in the State of Israel, already second only to that in the United States, and located at the crossroads of the region, suggests that a foreshadowing of such a future may be in the making. This is especially so in the light of a recurring motif in the Jewish past. That is, the center of gravity of the Western world and the center of Jewish civilization have coincided with amazing regularity, almost to the point of fascination for the perceptive observer. But are we about to witness in the case of Israel today the rarer instance when the vortex of Jewish dynamism preceded and fore-shadowed the rise and development of new environmental vigor? Or is something far more disastrous and unprecedented in the making—namely, that the present incipient decline will not be followed by a resurgence of vitality somewhere else; rather, instead, that the decay of the West is irreversible into the foreseeable future?

A Thesis of Creativity Through Transition

With remarkable frequency, the centers of Jewry have gravitated to and converged with the regions of efflorescence in the Western world;* one might even hazard the claim that on occasion the attraction between them has been mutual. Wherever in the West a domain has come to cultural and political fruition, one can expect to find there or nearby the focus of Jewish creativity and hegemony over other communities. This salient fact contributes to understanding a cause of the perennial renewal and vitality of Jewish civilization. Local exemplars of Jewish vibrancy developed in close contact with excelling cultural products of the West, always challenged and stimulated by the non-Jewish environ-ment, frequently competitive with it, occasionally shaping and in-fluencing, but rarely, if ever, completely overwhelmed by non-Jewish ascendancy. This striking fact may lead to a revaluation of the tradi-tional denigration of mobility and migration in Jewish destiny. It may also help prepare Jews emotionally for the painful dislocations which inevitably accompany the fall of mighty empires.

Persistence Despite Dispersion

The experience of migration and resettlement is as old as the Jewish people itself. From Mesopotamia to the Promised Land to servitude in Egypt and back to the Homeland, the Hebrews spent their early cen-turies in setting the pattern of wandering that was to become so promi-

---

*The term *Western* in this brief survey is used to to designate the entire stage of activity of the Jewish people during its nearly four thousand years of wandering and repose, that is, the totality of lands and continents up to the borders of India.

nent in their future. But in spite of such mobility—or perhaps because of it—they developed an amazing persistence. Forged in the crucible of adversity, and welded thereby into a people of almost indestructible caliber, their perserverance enabled them to bear witness to the rise and fall of the proud and powerful over close to four millennia.

A relative latecomer on the stage of history, the Jewish people borrowed freely from its advanced environment while imprinting the stamp of its own experience. During the intervals of its neighbors' political weakness, as in King David's long reign, the Jewish state pushed to the limits of its own political and geographic growth. But threats to national existence were endemic in periods marked by expansion of the surrounding empires. Thus, the northern kingdom of Israel fell victim to Assyrian conquest in the late eighth pre-Christian century. There followed its final submergence and disappearance in the conqueror's mighty cultural stream. But this first exile proved to be the last time that a major segment of the Jewish people succumbed in consequence of displacement. For the visible reality of subjugation and dispersion made an indelible impression on the Judean remnant back home. It meant that the prophets' warnings of punishment through conquest had translated into factual experience. The harsh actuality of the northern kingdom's obliteration sensitized the Judeans to the prophetic utterances which continued to warn that God Himself would encompass their own destruction also as penalty for transgression. These admonitions were tempered by the divine promise that exile and scattering would eventually yield to return and restoration. Toward the start of the sixth century voracious Babylonia gobbled Judea and duplicated for its inhabitants the calamity of the northern Israelites. Large numbers of Jews were forced out of their land and into close contact with the magnificent civilization of the conqueror. However, while settled on foreign soil, the Judeans retained their community life, their language, and other aspects of the ancestral heritage. They established a portable house of assembly wherein they substituted prayer for offerings and reviewed their national literature on Sabbaths and holy days. The threats of punishment which they found stored therein, as well as the promise of Return, nourished their hope and faith, as did also new leaders in a strange land. Thus, unlike their countrymen of the kingdom of Israel, despair did not overwhelm them; they successfully resisted complete cultural and ethnic inundation. Instead, they became living witness to a new, unforgettable experience, which, fortunately, occurred after only a relatively brief interval—the collapse of "invincible" Babylonia before the onslaughts of irresistible Persia. Almost immediately thereafter they fulfilled the prophets' promise of the Return, if only with a small minority of the exiles. For perhaps the first time in history, a people came back home ethnically whole from involuntary captivity.

Therein the survivors of Judea set the pattern of the future. Military defeat and dispersion were to be repeated but never again the disaster of the Lost Ten Tribes. Instead, adversity created persistence through all times and climes. Steeled by its ancient experience, in which prophetic castigation and subsequent "punishment" yielded to "divine" restoration, the Jewish people thereafter braved the fiercest torrents on native and foreign soil but never succumbed to them. Instead, they managed to outlast the mightiest empires of the West. Having witnessed their decline or collapse, each in turn, Jewry moved on, often transferring to the new scene essential requirements for vitality and growth.

Self-Governance Fosters Survival

The Jews' retention of their identity, whether on the march or at rest, cannot be thought of as an automatic aspect of their existence, one that may be taken for granted. It had to be worked for intensively in order to be achieved and sustained in each generation. In this process, belief and practice merged; myth and social institution interacted and supported each other mutually, and so produced in the end tenacious survival. Repeatedly, as will become clear, Jewish persistence at its most vigorous and creative coexisted in time and space with the major centers of Western dynamism.

As already indicated, the tribulation of exile and dispersion suffered by the northern kingdom of Israel was never forgotten. But in time the folk were taught to believe that the northern Israelites had not actually succumbed or disappeared but were confined beyond Sambatyon, certain to be restored eventually as an integral part of a united Israel. This teaching was bound up with the conviction that the Jewish people was God's special concern, whom He intended for a designated role in His plan for mankind. They were "a kingdom of priests and a holy nation"; such a "kingdom" required a distinct national existence. To Jews, it was beyond question that their folk would survive every misfortune, whether of human or superhuman origin. The divine Promise guaranteed final victory, which included also the entire nation's return to the Homeland in the Messianic Age.

The convictions of the fathers found support and longevity in the social institutions maintained by the sons who, in turn, incorporated into communal agencies the teachings of the elders. Down to modern times, every generation of Jews endeavored to make secure the foundations of their separate group existence by insisting on self-governance of their community.[1] Autonomy became the distinctive feature—in fact, the very core—of Jewish existence after the destruction of the state in 70 C.E. The Roman emperors recognized the *nasi* (prince) of the Jews as an associate king (*rex socius*) with authority over all his people in the empire. Both in Parthian Persia and in the later Islamic caliphate, the exilarch (*resh galuta*), claiming descent from King David, exercised rule over Jewish communities throughout the realm. In early medieval Europe, such chartered rights of communal autonomy were completely acceptable in a society organized on the basis of tribal and ethnic groupings, structured also according to hierarchical stratification and "estates." Therein the Jews constituted a distinct ethnic and religious "nation" ruled over by a prince (*nasi*) of their own who had functioned as a Davidic exilarch in Baghdad.[2] But long after European tribal groupings had coalesced into some form of territorial or national entity, the Jews still insisted upon and secured their traditional rights of communal governance, which now involved an active participatory electorate. The power of the Jewish community over its own members equaled, and at times even exceeded, the authority of kings and princes over their subjects in a feudal regime. Powerlessness was far from being the hallmark of medieval Jewish autonomy. But self-governance required a considerable array of social institutions: schools, academies, law courts and codes; social welfare, taxation, and law enforcement agencies; students, teachers, notaries, legal experts, judges, lay and professional functionaries; religious institutions. By means of their coercive power, the communal authorities translated the doctrines of the fathers into the daily life and activity of the individual and group. They maintained a vital, operational interaction between traditional teaching and personal-communal actuality. The effect of a functioning polity on Jewish identity, self-awareness, and continuity was pervasive. Communal, regional, and occasionally national autonomy through the ages produced the paradox that the Jewish people, a landless and stateless community until a generation ago, has in actuality experienced ongoing, functional governance unmatched in length of time by any nation in the Western world. Wherever they went, the Jewish people carried their Torah. But Torah was a portable government, an operational polity functional in all places, that animated Jews in all lands and climes beyond the power to measure.

No simple account can adequately explicate the Jews' resiliency in the face of defeat, exile, flight, dispersion, and resettlement. Only the fact of their persistence is undeniable. But already at the very beginning of their history, the Hebrews oscillated between the major foci of ancient culture located in Mesopotamia on the one hand and in the Nile Valley on the other, until they came to rest in Israel, the land bridge connecting the two. Thereafter, they have continued to be insistently and irresistibly drawn toward vibrant nuclei of power and creativity.

Centers of Western and Jewish Civilization Coincide

When the Homeland began to emerge from its own dark age following the return from Babylon, the military triumphs of Alexander the Great had already begun and prepared the way for the coming extensive expansion of Hellenistic culture. Postbiblical and early rabbinic Jewry in the Land of Israel grew to maturity in the period of dominance by Hellenistic-Roman civilization which was centered in the lands bordering on the Mediterranean. But here the Jewish people also was concentrated. One generous estimate finds that in the first century as many as seven-eighths of all Jews inhabited countries whose shores were washed by that sea, while Jewry constituted as much as one-fifth of the population of the eastern territory of the Roman Empire. The latter's incipient decline in the third century and eventual collapse, the rise of Christianity as the state religion, and the gathering clouds of the European Dark Ages finally drew the curtain on the Hellenistic-Roman period of Western civilization. Each one of these stages speeded up the emigration of Jews from the Mediterranean basin. The Land of Israel faced the prospect of becoming emptied of them even in the absence of military coercion or forced exile. Alarmed leaders tried to stem the flight, largely eastward-directed. But even the promise that burial anywhere in the soil of the Holy Land was the equivalent of being laid to rest under the altar of the Temple, and the ban against departure as long as either mate in the family elected to remain, or other efforts, did not help to halt emigration.

The flight of Jews from their Homeland in this period directs attention to the fact that just as the mobility of the Jewish people has been in the direction of eventual foci of vitality and creativity, so also with equal frequency, Jewish migration has been an escape from stagnation and decay. The steady egress from Israel and the other lands of the Mediterranean during the decline and subsequent collapse of the Roman

Empire turned out to have been a way to elude the enveloping gloom of the European Dark Ages. Instead, Jewry trekked into the far more vigorous Sassanian Persia.

Eager to fill the vacuum left by Rome, Constantinople made a bid to become the new center of the West. But Christian Byzantium had no great attraction for Jews, certainly not at all comparable to the appeal of its increasingly more successful rival, renascent neo-Persia. Before the end of the fourth century, a great nucleus of Jewish vitality attained its flowering in Iraq-Iran as evidence that the center of gravity of Jewish life had indeed slipped out of Israel and the area of the Mediterranean. Distinguished teachers and new academies had arisen that easily outrivaled the remnants left behind in the Homeland. At the same time, the institution of the exilarchate provided diaspora Jewry with a ruler recognized by the authorities, one who claimed direct descent from King David. Eventually, by the sixth century this Jewry achieved the culmination of its creative powers in the monumental Talmud of Babylonia, while its counterpart, the Palestinian Talmud, suffered permanent arrest of its growth.

Early in the seventh century the two major empires of the age, Byzantium and Parthian Persia, were locked in a life-and-death struggle during which Persian troops threatened Constantinople and succeeded in advancing as far as Egypt. In the conquest of Palestine the Jews collaborated, deeply stirred by Messianic hopes and fervor. At the fall of Jerusalem the Persians entrusted them with the control of the Holy City which they retained until 617.

When the Muslim conquerors pursued their enterprise to win the Western world for Islam and toppled the Parthian Persian Empire, they found a mature, long-established center of Jewry reaching from Syria to the borders of India. An indication of the prominence of Iranian Jewry around the middle of the seventh century is seen in the gift, by Islam's "Commander of the Faithful," of the daughter of the Persian king to the Exilarch Bustanai as his wife, while the Muslim warrior himself took her sister for his own spouse (or gave her to his son as wife).

Islam did not grow up in an intellectual and religious wasteland. Rather, it took root in soil long fertilized by Judaism and Christianity. Eventually, the Islamic Caliphate rose to dominance in a territory that had long since demonstrated its political, economic, and intellectual vibrancy. Islamic power, in fact, gravitated to the areas identified as the older Parthian Persian center, with which Jewish creativity and vigor had earlier been associated. Islam's conquest of the eastern and southern Mediterranean basin brought it finally beyond North Africa to Europe.

Jews collaborated with Arabs in the expansion of Islam into Spain and France. They became the military garrisons in some of the major European towns captured by the advancing conquerors. They initiated a westward movement of their fellow-Jews. One of these early migrants, a former exilarch of Baghdad, was warmly welcomed by the Frankish kings, who ceded to him hereditary lands in free allod for the founding of a Jewish princedom in France in the year 768 along the Mediterranean and the southern border with Spain.[3]

During the ninth and tenth centuries, Baghdad emerged as the metropolis of the Western world, its pivot of political and economic hegemony and a dynamic focus of cultural stimulation. Compared to the caliphate and its capital, Charlemagne's Aix-la-Chapelle and empire were backwoods caricatures of power eager for some slight nod of recognition, mediated by Jewish diplomats and military men, from the world ruler enthroned in the east. The exilarch, confirmed in office by the caliph, continued in his role as the reigning prince of the Jews. He lived in state as resident of a palace within his own domain, located in the vicinity of the capital. The academies of Sura and Pumbeditha, headed by geonim, shared with him control over Jewish communities throughout the empire. During the period of Saracen domination into the age of the Crusades, the major communities of the Jewish people remained in close and very fruitful interaction with the efflorescent civilization of Islam, where eighty percent of all Jews were located.

The decline of the Muslim center after the twelfth century speeded up Jewish emigration westward, stretching from the borders of Iran to the beaches of North Africa. Had Jews remained in the lands of Islam and not moved out readily, then all of Jewish civilization might have stagnated in time as did, in fact, those remnants of once-vibrant North African, Palestinian, and Iraqi Jewries which stayed behind. When, by the end of the thirteenth century, Christian Spain, France, and the Holy Roman Empire were emerging as the intellectual and economic hub of the Western world and its axis of political power, the center of gravity of Jewry had already shifted out of the Muslim sphere of influence into Europe. In turn, France, Spain, Poland, Italy, the Ottoman Empire, and Central Europe attracted Jews in the ages of their own greatest puissance, which also coincided with the periods of most vigorous local Jewish development. Eventually, in the early twentieth century Europe ruled the world. Simultaneously, almost all Jews lived within the confines of that continent, its dependencies, and its American outreaches overseas. The Europeanization of the Jew and his culture was on the way to consummation except for enclaves in Muslim lands and Eastern Europe. After World War II New York became the greatest world capital ever known. By then the largest aggregate of Jews in history had converged on its metropolitan area and within a three-hundred-mile radius, exerting concomitant influence in world Jewry. As a kind of reflection of the balance of world power at the time, the two most numerous diaspora Jewries were located in the United States and Soviet Russian territory. Then, in the 1970s, a restored and expanded but still tiny and beleaguered State of Israel overtook the vast Soviet Union in regard to Jewish population and became the unchallenged aspirant to at least second place in world Jewish concentration and sway.

Thus, the coincidence of Jewish and Western nuclei of supremacy is a prominent and fascinating aspect of the millennia-long Jewish experience.

But are Jews simply drawn into areas of ascendance and opportunity as driftwood is sucked into a whirlpool? Or is the mercurial mobility of the Jewish people related in a significant way to the repeated development of a new vortex of Western dynamism and its spiritual and economic renascence?

Shifting readily from one world focus to another as the tide of civilization ebbed and flowed, Jews on occasion performed cultural transfusion by carrying to an underdeveloped region the resources it urgently needed. At about the time that Jewish communities began to arise in early medieval Europe, Jewish scholars and scholar-merchants contributed toward the restoration to that continent of Greco-Roman science and thought, which had managed to survive in the East. From the eighth to the eleventh century, Jews were very prominent in international trade. They traversed four major trade routes by land and by sea on their journey from France and Spain to India and China and back. They served to raise the material level of European life. But they brought in cultural products as well as spices, silk, and furs. Out of a caliphate surging toward the apogee of its power, they transmitted learning in translation such as Hebrew texts (eventually to be rendered into Latin) derived from Arabic versions of Greek sources; or the Arabic translation itself. Learned Jews made original contributions in medicine, mathematics and philosophy which were carried westward.

Of no less significance was Jewry's introduction of a revolutionary form of urban governance to a Europe still trapped in the feudal system. At a time when the right to govern was restricted to the ruling aristocracy, Jewish merchant communities offered a living example of participatory self-government in small urban units. After the year 900 their own princedom, ruled by successive scions of the Davidic dynasty, collapsed in the ruins of the Carolingian Empire. They were left without a central Jewish authority recognized by the emperor and corresponding to the exilarchate in the eastern caliphate. But existence, whether as Jews or as a trading community, was inconceivable and perhaps impossible without self-governance. So Judah b. Barzilai al-Barceloni of the early twelfth century provided a legal instrument which he reports he found in an "ancient" version. Thereby a community of Jews, in time of need, were enabled to set up a local authority to which they voluntarily subjected themselves. They selected a qualified individual, conferred on him broad coercive powers, and swore to accept his judgments under threat of the ban.[4] Such autonomous Jewish entities preceded the rise of urban and suburban non-Jewish trading colonies which later grew into self-governing medieval towns. They, in time, outlived and superseded the feudal system. Eventually, these autonomous urban institutions germinated European democracy.

Now that the wheel has come full turn and Jews are on the move again toward the source of their being, they have been carrying back to a barely awakened Middle East the cultural and spiritual remains snatched from a mortally ill Europe, its scientific concepts and techniques and the democratic process in an earlier, pristine state. The role of Jews as intermediary has had to remain latent, barely activated in the environs of Israel for well over a generation. It still awaits a modus vivendi with Arab, Muslim, and African neighbors, although devoid of imperialistic designs. Israel's potential as a bridge for the nations is enhanced by its demographic composition. Over half of its Jewish population have their roots in the civilization and psychology of the peoples of the region. On the other hand, Israel's potential gifts may remain spurned and rejected for a very long while, perhaps permanently. That would entail stark consequences for its inhabitants and irretrievable loss for its surroundings.

II

The oscillation of Jewish centers from one world axis to another highlights the migratory character of world Jewry, one of the widely known features of Jewish history. On the other hand, largely over-looked has been the fact that the Jewish people's mobility is actually of a dual tendency. The role of coercion has been readily identified and underlined, and several theories have been proposed to explain the pressures leading to expulsion of Jews. For example, S. W. Baron has shown how the growth of ethnic homogeneity and the concomitant rise of national feeling have been prime movers in the forcible elimination of Jews from a territorial unit, in contrast to the far greater tolerance of the unlike in a multi-ethnic society.[5] He identifies examples of such nationalistic development, involving tragic consequences for Jews, in the expulsions from England in 1290, from France in the course of the fourteenth century, and from Spain in 1492. Others have emphasized a shrinking economy as a powerful factor contributing to the erosion of Jewish status. Whatever the cause, it is noteworthy that forced relocation was likely to propel Jews in the direction of a society experiencing relative growth and expansion and, consequently, capable of affording refuge to them and the possibility of resurgence once more.

Choice in Jewish Migration

A second aspect of Jewry's mobility has received far less notice—the role of "choice." The ambulatory nature of Jewry's centers suggests that their anchorage in a land and immersion in its culture were seldom so ponderous and so deep as to render Jews immobile. Quite the contrary. This was especially true in pre-modern times, when the distinctiveness of the Jewish community and its separateness from the environment were strongly perceived. In addition, the temporary nature of their right of residence in a given land, as defined by governmental charters, underscored their loose relationship to society. This enabled them to be responsive to invitations for resettlement somewhere else, especially in the direction of pioneer areas requiring their specialized skills and resources. Thus, when Emperor Louis le Débonnaire issued a mandate of protection to the Hebrew Abraham of Saragossa around 825, it was done with the understanding that he would immigrate and settle within the Carolingian Empire together with his entourage, who were also guaranteed rights derived from Abraham's own privileged relationship to the Crown.[6] Instances of self-propelled migration in response to an invitation of resettlement were fairly constant in pre-modern Europe, especially in an age when scant populations confronted vast, uncleared forests; in fact, relocation by choice was perhaps as frequent as the need to react to forced dislocation. However, the movement of Jews, whether in answer to proferred amity or in response to coerced expulsion, necessarily was toward a society that could afford room for them.

An example of eager welcome may be recognized in the charter of rights tendered by Bishop Rüdiger in the year 1084 out of his expressed desire to "magnify a thousandfold the distinction of our locality" by bringing in Jews for the purpose of making a town out of his village of Spires. He doubtless valued and felt a need for their special skills as traders and their widespread commercial connections. But Jews must have been in demand at the time. For Bishop Rüdiger had to offer highly attractive terms of settlement, obviously intended to be competitive with those of other princes, as is evident from his declaration: "I hereby grant to them as law whatever better [one] the Jewish people have in whatsoever city of the German realm." Presumably following other precedents and responsive to the demands of the Jews, the bishop provided them with an area of their own, protected by a stone wall. Thereon the Jews themselves could stand guard at its gates and turrets together with their own hired men. Within the walls, Spires Jewry was empowered with rather complete autonomy: their community head was to function as judge even when a non-Jew brought charges or a claim against a local Jew.[7] We may assume that Jews were badly wanted in the Rhine Valley in 1084 because they could perform highly desired functions not otherwise available locally. They were expected to set into motion the commercial development of the region. To the extent that such hoped-for revival became an actuality, Jews might find themselves before long at a burgeoning center of cultural growth. This, in fact, became a reality by the thirteenth century. Thus their resettlement, whether voluntary or not at the start, eventually exposed their own civilization to powerful stimulation and the possibility of recurrent renewal and revitalization.

Like the Jews in Spires and in the Rhineland of the eleventh century, the later emigrés from Germany, the self-motivated or involuntary, found a hearty welcome and unparalleled new opportunity in fourteenth- and fifteenth-century Poland; so also the exiles from Spain in Italy and the Ottoman Empire (including Israel) after 1492. In fact, the sultan was pleased beyond measure with the gift of such unexpected valuable bounty. And so too Russian-Polish Jewry, only weakly integrated into their milieu, victims of bloody pogroms and threatening insecurity, began scrambling out of the decadent czarist regime near the end of the nineteenth century and fled Europe in their millions, a portent of things to come but yet undreamed of. They resettled primarily in America, which became the new world center after World War II, when two intercontinental wars in a generation had exhausted Europe's strength. Those emigrés helped bring American Jewry to fruition. At the same time, another, much smaller stream from the same East European source founded the *Yishuv*, which became Israel. In this manner contemporary Jewry, abetted significantly by escapees from the Holocaust, acquired its two major foci of hegemony for today and tomorrow. One shudders at the consequences had Russian-Polish Jewry been so deeply enmeshed in their environment, economically and emotionally, that they failed to stampede across frightening distances during the decades 1881–1921, but remained behind in much larger numbers only to be hurled finally into Hitler's ovens and gas chambers. As happened with noteworthy regularity throughout the centuries, their migrations terminated at what eventually became significant centers of vigor and creativity. But just as the mobility of the Jewish people throughout the confines of the Western world has been in the direction of eventual foci of vitality and productivity, so too, with equal frequency, Jewish migration has been a flight from stagnation and backwardness.

Mobility Forges Escape from Stagnation and Decay

It is tempting to think of the Jews' mobility as a sensitive barometer to presage events still in the womb of the future. Led by their most sensitive and daring, Jews in the past withdrew from lands slipping into the mire while being attracted irresistibly to emerging centers of vibrancy and opportunity.

The determination of over 160,000 Soviet Jews in the past decade to deliberately uproot themselves from their land and strike out for a new future overseas, especially in Israel, constitutes their affirmation of identity with an indomitable Jewish people and its destiny. At the same time, it is a rejection of the Soviet enterprise, its fate and future, which once held in thrall large numbers of Jews.

Why should the cultural and scientific elite amidst Soviet Jewry, actually the privileged among them, take the lead and choose emigration despite the personal disaster which the very act of decision immediately entails?

A news item of February 1976 contrasts the reaction to Soviet society on the part of a Jew and a non-Jew of similar academic attainments. The Jew was a mathematician and computer specialist; his wife, an ethnic Russian and a geologist, was not a Jew. He was impelled to emigrate out of awareness of his Jewish identity, a longing to be at home in his own land, and aroused by some relatively mild Antisemitism. Word had just come that the two of them now had permission to leave for Israel.

"I feel my country is there [in Israel], not here," he explained.

But for his wife, Russia, not Israel, is her country.

"I like my land very much. I do not want to think that I cannot see this place again. I like this place very much."

Until she married a Jew she was apparently unaware of any serious defects in the Soviet system; emigration would hardly have occurred to her.

"As time went on I realized we could not [survive here]," she said.

She applied for a visa to Israel when her husband did. Having taken that first step, she felt that she had to take the next one and share the fate of a visa Jew, namely, joblessness. So when her husband was dismissed in consequence of his application for a visa, she resigned her post at the institute, where she served as a geologist, in order to protect her friends and colleagues. Her marriage had brought her to understand the outlook of a Jew and to identify with his fate and future. In the process she became aware of the failings in the Soviet system and realized there was no future for her, as his wife, in that land, although the separation was very painful. In the end she chose the way of emigration.[8]

Solzhenitsyn demonstrates that one does not have to be a Jew in order to react against Soviet barbarism and choose exile. But it surely helps. Jewish identity and destiny appear competent to sensitize one to social defects because even only incipient decay is likely to victimize the Jew very early, ahead of others. Thus, the Jewish condition magnifies for the Jew the poignancy of environmental rot and drives him to migration, at the same time that the relatively undisturbed non-Jew feels no such compulsion, even though similarly situated with respect to career.

Jewish eisodus and exodus into and out of a land, a region, or even a city appear so related to the rise and decline of that locality as to constitute almost a barometer of impending events. It may appear far-fetched to search for a broader relevance in the proportionately minuscule emigration of Soviet Jews from their land. Yet it may be a sign of the times that the European Communist leaders' conference of June 1976 made it clear that they would no longer accept the Soviet claim to dominance of the movement and sole guardianship of purity of the faith.

We may conclude that Jewish culture has developed and survived, not in isolation but in intimate, fruitful, stimulating contact with the dominant civilizations of the West. Ghettoization of the intellect is far from being representative of the Jewish people at its creative peaks. Many of the ascendant societies in turn offered the relatively tiny nation of Israel, or the Jewish minority in its midst, alluring solutions—economic, political, spiritual—to both perennial and transitory human problems. Contemporaneous political struggles and intellectual issues also agitated the Jewish community and its leaders, and were involved in its internal conflicts. Jewish thinkers were impelled to work out their own solutions to the same questions, to reinterpret and make relevant the traditional Jewish answers, to adapt the contributions of others, or to combine all these methods in order to retain the devotion of the people to their heritage. In the pre-modern age, the Jewish community was subjected to tremendous pressure from a society basically violent and rapacious, and little concerned for justice and equity. In such circumstances, the durability of Jewish community polity depended on the zeal and indefatigable dedication of the man in the street. Only basic integrity on the part of the community managers could be expected to elicit his fervor. At the same time the leaders had to be responsive to human needs and the demands of a participatory electorate. On the whole, they were relatively successful in maintaining their people as a distinctive entity that resisted absorption by their neighbors. In consequence, a solid core of Jews never yielded completely to the allure of Canaanite, Egyptian, Assyrian, Babylonian, Persian, and European civilizations; of Hellenism, Rome, Christianity, or Islam in the eras of their greatest power and influence. In the end, Jews bore witness to their decline and decay.

American Jewry, the leading Jewish community of our time, stands athwart the major center of the Western world. Clearly, the relocation of Jewry once more to the vortex of Western civilization has achieved its consummation in our day. Yet, in the light of the past, the primary weakness of American Jewry is the lack of all-embracing community and of any unifying polity, one that would include individual Jews and communal agencies and provide participatory direction to the whole in Mordecai Kaplan's felicitous phrase of "organic community." This failure, in spite of tentative steps toward that end, may turn out to be a fateful weakness in a period of multiplying crises. At the moment of the shift of Jewry's center from Europe to America in the early 1940s, an ineffectual community in the United States, caught unawares and fumbling in disarray, was unable to respond to the call of the hour. Its failure to secure any semblance of a halt to the Holocaust plunged contemporary Jewry to the nadir of its power and into the throes of its deepest shame. An adaptable American Jewish community, located at the chief nucleus of contemporary power and influence but alert to the needs of tomorrow, would endeavor to achieve a national polity for itself here and now.

The State of Israel appears to embody the hope of the future for Jews. A commonwealth in the ancestral Homeland has countered most dramatically the seductive appeal of other nationalisms for Jews. Its achievements illustrate the Jewish people's response to the central demands of today: the revival and free development of historic peoples and thir cultures as segments of an international, cooperative community, and democratic social control over material and intellectual resources to secure human advancement while safeguarding individual freedom. Zionism and Israel have turned Jews away from the absorption that spells disappearance into their surrounding national entities and have captured their loyalty to a revitalized Jewish people and its civilization in the social-democratic form predominant in Israel. The thrilling rescue of hijacked hostages at Entebbe, Uganda, on July 4, 1976 dramatized further Israel's role in a time of crucial need. In contrast to the refusal of any government to act in behalf of Jews exposed to unique danger, and the total paralysis of American Jewry in that moment, Israel's energetic use of the full panoply of its sovereign power with breathtaking effect is a promise for the future of the Jewish people and its destiny.

If storm clouds gather and crises grow, the need will become ever more pressing for closer collaboration between Jewry's two major communities, which today encompass 65 percent of all Jews. Nor should the rest of world Jewry be left behind. In the face of a reorientation of the United Nations in favor of partisan interests of which the Jewish people have been chief victims thus far, the possibility of new shifts of power, and the caliber of presidential leadership which the American people has been able to summon in the contest for the helm of its government—the need now becomes paramount to effect the reconstitution of the transnational Jewish people in our time.

NOTES

1. Simon Dubnow saw as evidence for the continuing vitality of the Jewish people the recurring centers of Jewish autonomy and their hegemony over other communities. However, he did not take note of the coincidence of major foci of Jewish creativity with centers of Western civilization, nor of the role of Jewish migration in effecting a convergence of these two. See Koppel S. Pinson, ed., *Nationalism and History: Essays on Old and New Judaism by Simon Dubnow* (Philadelphia, 1958), pp. 253–324, 336–53. For a full description of Jewish autonomy, see Salo W. Baron, *The Jewish Community,* 3 vols. (Philadelphia, 1945).
2. See Arthur J. Zuckerman, *A Jewish Princedom in Feudal France, 768–900* (Columbia University Press, 1972), pp. 74–101, 112 ff.
3. Ibid., chap. 4.
4. *Sefer haShetarot,* ed. S. Z. J. Halberstamm (Berlin, 1898), pp. 7–8. Evidence for the broad self-governing powers of the Spires Jewish community already in 1084 is provided below in n. 7. For the early eleventh century, B.-Z. Dinur, *Yisrael Bagolah* (1961), I, 3, p. 11.
5. S. W. Baron, *A Social and Religious History of the Jews,* Vol. 11 (1967), pp. 198–99.
6. [Ca. 825]
   Emperor Louis le Débonnaire declares that he has taken under his protection the Hebrew, Abraham of Saragossa, who has commended himself to the Emperor.
   Text: *Formulae Imperiales* ed. K. Zeumer, *Monumenta Germaniae Historica,* Legum sectio V, no. 52, p. 325. Translation: Arthur J. Zuckerman
   To all bishops, abbots, counts, governors, district officers, and other of our officers, let it be known that this Hebrew, Abraham by name, inhabitant of the city of Saragossa has come into our presence and commended himself into our hands, whereupon we have received and do retain him under our protection. [1.] Thereby we decree and order that neither you nor your subordinates nor your successors shall presume to cause disquiet to the named Jew for any illicit reasons whatsoever, nor initiate false charges; [2.] nor shall you presume to separate anything from, or diminish, his own property or his merchandise at any time at all. Nor shall you exact any toll or post horses or lodging and food for military or official purposes or tolls for transport vehicles or towpaths or portage or fees for plying a trade or dues for transport. But let it be permitted him to live quietly under our protection and defense and to serve faithfully our palace treasury without illicit contrary action on the part of anyone. [4.] Moreover let it be permitted him to live by his own law and to employ Christian servants to perform his tasks except on the Lord's day and feast days. [5.] Also, if a Christian shall have a case at law or a suit against him, let him offer in testimony three proper Christian witnesses and three likewise proper Hebrews and vindicate his cause with them. But if he shall have a case or a suit against a Christian, let him present proper Christian witnesses

in testimony on his behalf and convict him with them. But if any of them, Christian or Jew, shall wish to conceal the truth, the count of that city by a correct and just investigation shall make each one of them to tell the truth in accord with his own law. Moreover let it be permitted to him to buy foreign slaves and to sell them nowhere else except within our Empire. But if any cases at law shall arise or take place against him or his men, who have legal status through him, which cannot be decided locally without serious and unjust loss, let them be suspended or kept for our Presence where they may receive definitive sentence according to law. And so that this authorization may be believed the more truly by everybody and observed the more diligently, we have ordered it to be signed according to our custom and sealed with our seal.

7. September 13, 1084

Bishop Rüdiger of Spires grants the Jews admitted there certain liberties.

Text: Hilgard, *Urkunden zur Geschichte der Stadt Speyer* (Strassburg, 1885), no. 11. Translation: Arthur J. Zuckerman

In the name of the sacred and undivided Trinity. I, Rüdiger surnamed Huozman, Bishop of all Nemetenses, desirous of making a city out of the village of Spires, thought that I would magnify a thousand-fold the distinction of our locality if I should bring together also Jews. When they came together I settled them outside the community and habitation of the other townspeople and placed a stone wall about them so that they might not be easily disturbed by the insolent commotion of the rabble. [1.] Now the place of their residence, which I had acquired legally—first the hill, partly by purchase partly by exchange, the valley on the other hand I received by gift of the heirs—this place, I say, I have given over to them on this condition, that they pay annually three and one-half pounds of money of Spires for the common use of the friars. [2.] I have assigned to them, moreover, within the ambit of their own habitation and from the area outside (the gate) up to the harbor on the river and in the port itself, the free right to exchange gold and silver, indeed, to buy and sell everything they please. The same license I have given them too throughout the entire urban area. [3.] Moreover, I have given to them a burial place from the landed estate of the church under conditions of hereditary [tenure]. [4.] I have also added this: that if any Jew from somewhere else shall be a guest among them, let him pay no toll there. [5.] Moreover, just as the tribune of a city among the townsmen so also their own community head may judge every quarrel which arises among them or against them. But if by chance he shall not be able to make a determination, then let the case go up before the bishop of the city or his chamberlain. [6.] The watches, the guards, the fortifications around only their own area they shall provide; the guards, however, together with their servants. [7.] They may legally keep nurses and also hired servants from among our [people]. Slaughtered meats which appear to them forbidden by the sanction of their own law they may legally sell to Christians, [and] Christians may legally purchase them. In summary, as the acme of my kindness I hereby grant to them as law whatever better [one] the Jewish people have in whatsoever city of the German realm. And so that none of my successors may be able to worsen this grant and concession for them, or force them to a larger payment, as if they themselves had usurped this condition and had not received it from a bishop, I hereby turn over to them this charter of the named grant as a proper witness. And so that the memory of this same fact may continue throughout all time, I hereby corroborate it by signing with my own hand and complete it by having it sealed with the impression of my seal as can be seen below. This charter was given the Ides of September . . .

8. *New York Times*, February 6, 1976, pp. 1, 10.

Modern Civilization

אתו׃ (י) ויאמר־לו אלהים שמך יעקב לא־יקרא שמך עוד יעקב כי אם־ישראל יהיה שמך ויקרא את־שמו

זעגנעטע איהן׃ (י) שפראך נעמליך צו איהם׃ דיין נאמען איזט יעקב, מאן זאל דיך אבער ניט מעהר יעקב נעננען, זאנדערן

יהיה ממך ומלכים מחלציך יצאו׃ (יב) ואת־הארץ אשר נתתי לאברהם וליצחק לך אתננה ולזרעך אחריך אתן את־הארץ׃ (יג) ויעל מעליו אלהים במקום אשר־דבר

זייא פרוכטבאר, אונד מעהרע דיך, איין פאלק אונד איינע מעננע פעלקער ווערדען פאן דיר הערקאממען, אונד קעניגע אויס דיינע לענדען הערפאר געהען. (יב) דאס לאנד וועלכעס איך דעם אברהם אונד יצחק געשענקט האבע, וויל איך דיר געבען, נעמליך דיינעם זאמען נאך דיר וויל איך דאז לאנד איינגעבען. (יג) גאט ערהוב זיך פאן איהם, אן דעם ארטע, ווא ער מיט איהם גערעדעט האט

באור

נקרא יעקב אף על פי שהחליף שמך שרו של עשו, כי הוא לא נשתלח לך להחליף את שמך, אבל מעתה לא יקרא שמך יעקב כי אם ישראל יהיה שמך, וזה טעם ויקרא את שמו ישראל, וגו ירמוז שקרא את שמו ישראל מוסף על יעקב לא שיאסר להקרא יעקב עכ"ל׃ (יא) אני אל שדי, שאני כדאי לברך שהברכו' שלי · פרה ורבה. על שם שעדיין לא נולד בנימין ואעפ"י שכבר נתעברה ממנו · מחלציך הם המתנים, ולשון ר"ע ספורנו אכנסים הגוים למלכות ולא תצטרך לתת עליך איש נכרי כענין במלכי אדום שמלה ממשרקה שאול מרחבות הנהר וזולתם עכ"ל · את הארץ אשר נתתי לאברהם וליצחק לך אתננה, כאשר נתתי להם כן אתננה לך, ירמוז זה לשבועה כי להם נתנה לשבוע' ... וזהו שאומ' בכל מקו' אשר נשבעתי לאברהם ליצחק וליעקב, או שיהיה הכפל הנבואה לו לשבועה כאשר פירשתי ... (הרמב"ן) · לך אתננה ולזרעך אחריך אתן את הארץ ...

The Jew . . . must rediscover, reinterpret and reconstruct the civilization of his people. . . . If this be the spirit in which Jews will accept from the past the mandate to keep Judaism alive, and from the present the guidance dictated by its profoundest needs, the contemporary crisis in Jewish life will prove to be the birth-throes of a new era in the civilization of the Jewish people.

Mordecai M. Kaplan, *Judaism as a Civilization.*

Moses Mendelssohn, *Sefer Netivot Ha-Shalom*
Vienna, 1795

PALESTINE AND MOROCCO AND THE BONDS OF PEOPLEHOOD

By

JANE S. GERBER

The apprehension of the tragedy of Galut and the omnipresent hope of redemption have accompanied the Jewish people through all their lands of dispersion until the onset of the era of emancipation. Faithful to the tradition of Jewish peoplehood and the centrality of Zion in the life of the individual Jew, Moroccan Jewry did not suddenly awaken to the call of return to Zion as a result of twentieth-century nationalist formulations. Profound ties between Moroccan Jewry and the land of Israel, both psychological and tangible, preceded by centuries the modern call of Zionism. These ties often assumed an institutionalized form and provided a special coloration to Jewish communal life in the Maghreb. Precisely at the moment when Moroccan Jewry was adjusting to new challenges of integration after the Spanish expulsion of 1492, attempts began to strengthen the communal bonds with the land of Israel. It is the purpose of this study to examine some of the echoes of the Moroccan Jews' links to Zion which appear in the various communal records of the Jews of Fez. Since the period immediately prior to the advent of the French to North Africa has been treated elsewhere, we shall concentrate on an earlier period whose record is scarcely known.[1]

Beginning with the pogroms in Spain in 1391 and continuing throughout the fifteenth and sixteenth centuries, thousands of Jews from the Iberian Peninsula sought refuge in North Africa. After 1492 in particular, large numbers of Sephardim arrived in Morocco, many of them reaching the important cultural and economic center of Fez.[2] While for some Jews Fez served as simply a temporary refuge en route to more

119

favorable asylums or to Palestine, most Jews who reached the shores of Morocco at that time made a concerted effort to begin life anew.[3] Efforts at integration, however, did not obliterate the deep bonds which Moroccan and Sephardic Jewry retained with the land of Israel. Indeed, the trauma of a new exile, coupled with the endemic instability of the political situation in the Maghreb, underscored the apprehension of Galut on the part of the Jews and probably played no small part in strengthening the longing for redemption and return to Palestine.

After the Ottoman conquest of Palestine in 1516, political and economic conditions in the land favored renewed settlement of Jews.[4] Jews from all over the Diaspora began to flock back to the ancient or newly reconstituted settlements of Palestine. While, for a brief period of time in the sixteenth century, the economic and political situation in Palestine improved, the settlements still retained their ancient custom of dispatching envoys or emissaries to the Diaspora to collect funds. By the seventeenth century, the routes of the envoys were well defined, and Fez was one of the most important collection points in North Africa.[5]

The emissary from Palestine came armed with letters of introduction and often with religious books. He recorded his receipts and frequently kept notes on his adventures.[6] Upon his return to Palestine, the envoy was expected to render a detailed accounting of his collections.[7] The native Jewish communities, in turn, collected and recorded the sayings, sermons, and legal decisions of the Palestinian envoys.[8]

It was not uncommon for the Jewish settlements of Palestine to dispatch an envoy of Moroccan origin to Morocco.[9] Thus, for example, a Jew from Demnat in Morocco, who had immigrated to Palestine, was sent to the Maghreb in 1707.[10] Occasionally a Palestinian envoy remained in Morocco, teaching and disseminating the scholarship of Palestine on Moroccan soil.[11] If the Palestinian envoy died in Morocco, his tomb was carefully maintained and became the site of pilgrimage for Jews and Muslims alike.[12] Pilgrimage to such shrines was intimately linked with the local Jewish festival of Hilloula and was observed until the contemporary period.[13]

When an envoy arrived in Fez, especially one of local origin, great festivities ensued.[14] The esteemed visitor was received with honor and delivered a sermon in the great synagogue which served the entire community.[15] As early as 1603, if not before, the Jews of Fez made special provisions for receiving an envoy from Jerusalem and collecting funds on his behalf.[16] The communal leaders, Isaac ibn Zur, Judah Uzziel, and Samuel ibn Danan, decreed that every synagogue in the *Mellah* establish a special fund for Jerusalem. Contributions to this fund were to be made by each man on his wedding day, at the birth of a son, at the time of the son's circumcision, on the first day of the month of Adar, and at the holiday of Purim. A special treasurer was appointed for this purpose in each synagogue. At the end of the year, the treasurers would deposit their collections with three outstanding men in the community, Samuel ibn Danan, Solomon ha-Cohen el-Haddad, and Pinhas ha-Cohen b. Nehemiah. This ordinance (*Takkanah*) was deemed to be sufficiently important to be co-signed by more than one dozen dignitaries of the community.[17]

Throughout the seventeenth century, the Jewish community of Fez was subjected to unrelenting extortionary pressures by the rival Muslim factions in the city. In addition to the heavy fiscal exactions they had to meet, the Jews suffered from the plagues, droughts, and other natural disasters punctuating this period. The charitable instincts of the community were thus pressed to their limits when envoys from various cities of Palestine succeeded each other in rapid order.[18] The leaders of Fez were forced to regulate the flow of contributions, setting priorities on the amounts to be donated to the cities of Safed, Hebron, and Jerusalem.[19] In a *Takkanah* of 1678, the rabbis decreed that envoys from Jerusalem be given a maximum of 400 *oukiyot,* those from Hebron 300, and those from Safed 200 *oukiyot.*[20] In the 1690s, extant records indicate that seven envoys visited Morocco.[21] Between 1700 and 1707 six envoys arrived in Fez for an extended period of time.[22] Perhaps for expediency's sake or, more likely, as a result of the uncertain conditions in the countryside, a local Jew was appointed to continue the envoy's journey southward into the Sahara region or the Atlas Mountains to collect funds. Given the droughts of 1713, 1721–24, 1729, 1730, 1738, 1741, 1742, and 1744, accompanied by the exodus of Jews from Fez to other Moroccan cities, it became increasingly difficult for the local Jews to meet their desired quotas.[23] In one instance, the Jews of Fez forwarded their contribution to a treasurer in Tetouan, Rabbi Moses ibn Ezra, since they had been unable to collect sufficient funds during the envoy's sojourn in the city. Unfortunately, the boat of the envoy caught fire en route to Algiers and all the collections from Morocco were lost. The Jews of Fez, at great hardship, valiantly duplicated their contribution, and Rabbi Jacob ibn Zur, the leading eighteenth-century rabbinic scholar in Fez, even sent a letter to the rabbi of Tlemcen, Saadiah Chouraqui, explaining the plight of the envoy and suggesting that the Jews of Tlemcen emulate the behavior of the Jews of Fez.[24]

The frequency of visits of envoys to Morocco decreased in the eighteenth century, as a result of the chaotic political conditions in Morocco, and the hazards of travel and piracy in the Mediterranean.[25] The problem of piracy was not alleviated until the conquest of Malta in 1798 and the French conquest of Algeria in 1830. Perhaps the less frequent solicitations were the immediate context motivating the leaders of Fez to issue a new decree on charitable contributions to Palestine in 1728. In this ordinance, the rabbis of Fez permitted the envoys to revert to the old practice of going from house to house in the *Mellah*, soliciting each family individually in accordance with prearranged assessments.[26]

Monetary donations to Palestine never fully replaced the consistent desire of Jews to immigrate, or "ascend," to Palestine themselves. Since the eternal sanctity of the land was preserved in the hearts of the Jews in exile, reiterated daily in their prayers and infused in all their activities, it is natural that the bonds between Morocco and Palestine were strengthened by a constant trickle of migration. According to Jewish tradition, "If the husband wishes to go to Palestine but his wife refuses, she may be compelled to go; if she refuses to comply, she may be divorced and forfeits her marriage contract."[27] Similarly, if the wife wishes to go to Palestine and the husband refuses, he may be compelled to go or to divorce her and pay her marriage contract in its entirety. Despite the hazards of travel to Palestine during this period, as well as the special emigration tax levied upon Jews by the Muslim authorities,[28] Jews nonetheless continued to emigrate from Morocco to fulfill the religious duty of living in the Holy Land. Precisely because conditions were so precarious, Moroccan rabbis were called upon to adjudicate in the case of spouses who could not agree upon the desirability of *aliyah*.[29]

Redemption and resettlement in the land were intimately associated in the popular imagination with the figure of Elijah the Prophet. While Elijah has served as a symbol of Jewish hope and suffering throughout the centuries of dispersion, his seat adorned Moroccan synagogues until recent times.[30] The imminence of his appearance was coupled in the folk psyche with the yearning for return to the land.

The Jews of Fez shared their meager funds with envoys from many corners of the world. Following the Chmielnitski pogroms of 1648, Polish survivors reached as far as Fez to collect money for the ransoming of captives. Since the ransoming of captives was one of the most important charitable acts of a Jew, the inhabitants of the *Mellah* could not dismiss the requests of these envoys. It appears that numerous abuses arose in dispensing charity to individuals whom the Jews did not know and whose society was unfamiliar to them. These beggars from "Ashkenaz and Poland" arrived with officially signed letters of introduction,[31] asserting that they were collecting money to ransom captives. Later, it was discovered that many of the letters were forgeries. Therefore, in 1700, the leaders of Fez promulgated an ordinance that no envoy from "Poland, Ashkenaz, and their environs" could be given more than two *reals* by the community, regardless of the status of the individual envoy.[32] The *Takkanah* of 1678, which apportioned the amount of money to be contributed to envoys from Palestine, also stated that no envoy from Poland be awarded more than 100 *oukiyot,* a sum less than that allocated to each of the major Jewish communities in Palestine.[33] Whether it was suspicion of the Polish envoys or simply a reflection of the hierarchy of values within the community, contributions to Palestine superseded those to other Jews in dire distress.

By the nineteenth century, Moroccan sources are replete with references to Palestine. A nexus of institutions and collection agencies had developed to nurture the Yeshivot in Palestine, particularly that of Raḥel Imenu.[34] Sephardic, Ashkenazic, and specifically Maghrebi institutions all invoked the precedents of loyalty, charity, and messianic redemption in reaffirming the links between Morocco and Palestine. Life in exile in Morocco, underscored by constant reminders of Muslim disdain and animosity, was continuously tempered by the Moroccan sense of community with Jews in other lands. It was particularly the link with Palestine, the central role which it retained in the perspective of the Moroccan Jew, the intertwining of the concepts of Holy People and Holy Land, which helped to ennoble the bitter centuries of exile for Spanish and Moroccan Jew alike. It is little wonder that the creation of the State of Israel stirred fervent emotions and messianic fervor among Jews in the most remote reaches of the Atlas Mountains. As the fragmentary documents reveal, their links and contacts had been kept alive for centuries through Jewish ideology and the continuous presence of the Palestinian emissary.

NOTES

1. Eliezer Bashan, "The Attitude of 18th and 19th Century Moroccan Rabbis as to the Duty of Settling in Eretz Israel' (Hebrew), *Vatiqin* (Ramat-Gan), 1975, pp. 35–46.
2. On the population of Fez and the numerical weight of Sephardim and Toshavim (indigenous Jews), see Jane Gerber, "The Demography of the Jewish Community of Fez after 1492," *Proceedings of the Sixth World Congress of Jewish Studies,* 11 **(Jerusalem, 1975), pp. 31–44.**
3. Joseph ben Naim, *Malkhe Rabbanan* (Jerusalem, 1931), offers a massive bio-bibliography of Moroccan Jewry with important factual data on all Jews living in or passing through Morocco. See p. 118b on Solomon el-Aluf, who left Fez for Jerusalem in this period, p. 10b on Abraham Azulai II, p. 99b on Suleiman Uhnah, a Jew from Fez who became one of the leading figures in the Kabbalistic movement in sixteenth-century Safed. Further details are available in M. Ben-ayahu, "Le Toldot Kishreyhem Shel Yehude Marocco 'im Eretz Yisrael," *Sinai* 35 (1954), 317–40.
4. Uriel Heyd, *Ottoman Documents on Palestine* (Oxford: Clarendon Press, 1960); Y. Ben-Zvi, *Eretz Yisrael ve-Yishuvah be-Yimai ha-Shilton ha-Othmani* (Jerusalem: Mosad Bialik, 1965), pp. 205–64.
5. A. Ya'ari, *Sheluhe Eretz Yisrael* (Jerusalem: Mosad ha-Rav Kuk, 1951), p. 23.
6. The most famous record of adventures of an envoy from Palestine is that of Haim Joseph David Azulai in the eighteenth century. An interesting envoy's record is contained in the Ben Zvi Institute, MSS 293.
7. Ya'ari, p. 23.
8. Jacob ibn Zur. *Leshon Limudim,* Enelow Memorial Collection 884 and 0060 of the Library of the Jewish Theological Seminary of America. 884 contains letters from Safed and Jerusalem, while 0060 includes the letters of envoys arriving in Morooco betwen 1670 and 1750.
9. *Malkhe Rabbanan,* pp. 12b, 14b, 32b.
10. Ibid., p. 80b.
11. Ibid., p. 32b, on Hiyya Dayyan, an envoy from Hebron who arrived in Morocco in 1561, settling first in Sale and afterwards in Meknes.
12. Ibid., pp. 102a–b, on the veneration of the grave of Amram Diwan, an envoy from Hebron who died in the Moroccan interior in 1682.
13. Louis Voinot, *Pèlerinages Judéo-Musulmanes du Maroc* (Paris: Editions Larose, 1948). Personal experience in Marrakech in the summer of 1975, as well as in the cemetery of Sefrou, confirmed the prevalence of the belief in miraculous powers of the graves of envoys among the remnants of Moroccan Jewry today.
14. *Kerem Hemer,* 2 vols. (Leghorn, 1871), vol. 2, pp. 155, 29a.
15. Ibid. It is interesting to note that this was one of the few occasions during which the community ignored its usual polarization along communal lines. This fact

emphasizes the great communal significance attached to the arrival of an envoy. Special songs were also composed in honor of the envoy.

16. Ibid., vol. 2, pp. 48, 8b.
17. Ibid., vol. 2, pp. 48, 8b.
18. The impact of Muslim politics on Jewish life can be seen most graphically in Saadiah ibn Danan, *Dibre ha-Yamim shel Fes,* Xerox of Ben Collection, Library of the Jewish Theological Seminary of America.
19. By the middle of the seventeenth century, the city of Tiberias was sufficiently eclipsed that it no longer sent envoys to Morocco. On the other hand, Fez now received special envoys from the Maghrebi settlement in Jerusalem as well as the Ashkenazim of Jerusalem.
20. *Kerem Hemer,* vol. 2, pp. 137, 25a.
21. Ya'ari, p. 307.
22. Benayahu, op. cit., p. 328. The envoys were Rabbis Jacob ha-Levi Beruhim, Isaac Bitton (of North African origin), Solomon Emanuel Morenu, Samuel Yoakil (envoy of Hebron and of the Maghrebi Yeshivah of Jerusalem), and Solomon Waroun de Campos.
23. Mordechai Berdugo, *Dibre Mordechai* (Meknes, 1947), p. 15.
24. Benayahu, p. 326.
25. Ya'ari, p. 360, and H. Z. Hirschberg, *Toledot ha-Yehudim be-Afrika ha-Tzefonit* (Jerusalem: Mosad Bialik, 1965), 2:283–84.
26. *Kerem Hemer,* vol. 2, pp. 155, 29a.
27. *Ketubot* 110b.
28. Bashan, p. 44, where this fascinating piece of information is cited from MSS 467, pp. 28b–29a, of the Montefiore Collection.
29. Jacob ibn Zur, *Mishpat u-Sedakah be-Ya'kob,* 2 vols. (Alexandria: Chaim Mizrahi, 1894), 1:28, 44a. The Moroccan rabbis were of more than one opinion on this matter. In general, when conditions were particularly troubled in the Mediterranean in the eighteenth century, Moroccan rabbis refrained from compelling a wife to migrate with her husband to Palestine. While the duty of settling in Palestine was not ignored, the danger of travel rendered it inoperative temporarily. For further information on the diversified responses of the Moroccan rabbis, ones which reveal their keen sense of the longing for *aliyah* and its practical obstacles, see Bashan, op. cit.
30. In connection with a research project conducted under the City University Faculty Research Foundation Grant in 1975, I was able to see the remaining synagogue edifices in a number of cities of Morocco and observed the central ornamental and religious role of the carved *kisseh Eliyahu* in the Moroccan synagogue.
31. *Leshon Limudim,* p. 8b, contains a letter from a Polish envoy to Fez preserved by Rabbi Jacob ibn zur.
32. *Kerem Hemer,* vol. 2, pp. 46, 8a.
33. Ibid., vol. 2, pp. 137, 25a.
34. See, for example, Central Archives of the History of the Jewish People, #315, a receipt of collections for Jerusalem collected in Fez by R. Jacob ibn Zimra in 1882; #318, containing the receipt of funds from Fez for the Sephardim in Jerusalem; MA/F/5, a request from the rabbis of Jerusalem to the rabbis of Fez for the *Kuppah* of Raḥel Imenu in 1881; and #335, a document appointing treasurers or overseers in Fez for the *Kuppah* of Raḥel Imenu in 1881.

PENNIES AND HEAVEN

By

JUDAH GOLDIN

Revolutions fail because you can't break habits. At best you can displace one by another, just as bad: stop biting your nails and start smoking; stop smoking and start nibbling all day long, so if tobacco won't kill you, the overeating will. And so it goes. Prevent people from going to church, and they queue up for the better part of the day to have a look at Lenin in a casket. Tell people they can't have Christmas, so they mail out Hanukkah greetings. If it isn't Billy Sunday, it's Billy Graham.

Despite more than forty years of conscientious rebellion against my upbringing, I find that my exertions are futile, and I am ready to capitulate. Indeed, I have capitulated. I was about thirteen when I had a teacher (a *rebbe*, I would have said then) whom I disliked. I disliked his plump cheeks, his Prince Albert frock coat, his full and neatly trimmed black-silver beard, the yardstick he held in his hand to beat us with (occasionally) or poke in our ribs (frequently), his sarcasm tinted with biblical proof texts, his perch on a high stool, which several years later I was to discover also in illustrations of stories by Dickens. I learned nothing from him; I can't even recall what talmudic treatise we read that year; *q.e.d.* But one thing he said did impress me, and I never forgot it.

He said that God hates the arrogant. God says, "There isn't enough room in the universe for both the arrogant man and Me." The arrogant is hideous, disgusting to both God and man. There he walks, the arrogant man, head held high as though he were on stilts and could only look down from above at everybody else, if he cares to look down at all. Why was Mount Sinai chosen as the site of the revelation of the Ten Commandments? Because it was the smallest of all the mountains in the region. What was the compliment paid to Moses by the Torah? That he was the humblest of all men on the face of the earth. And mind you, the teacher added, the Torah says that Moses was the humblest of all men on the face of the earth, which means that he was only more humble than his contemporaries. He did not even attain to the humility of the Patriarchs.

Years later, of course, I found these sentiments and examples in the Midrash, but (truth must be acknowledged) I first met them in the teacher I disliked.

The teacher did not stop with those few observations but went on, for instance, that God chose to appear to Moses in a low bush and not in a lofty tree. I am not sure if the teacher quoted also the relevant verses from the second chapter of Isaiah. Or referred to Rabbi Levitas of Yavneh in *Pirke Abot* 4:4. But I do recall the punch line as it were: A modest man—by which he meant plainly, a decent man (*odom hogun*) —walks with his eyes downcast.

Probably one remembers what his powers of recollection are waiting for. At all events, I remember that moralizing session so well because I was in the middle of a piety phase those years and I immediately put the lesson into practice. That very day I walked home with my eyes to the ground, inhaling and exhilarated by my modesty. And the next day, too, to and from school, I walked looking at the ground and only surreptitiously stealing a glance at the sky overhead; but I knew that the Holy One, blessed be He, understood. In my mind I could even see Him smile tolerantly. And the days after similarly, even if I walked with a friend, I looked not up but down. I probably forgot occasionally, but I righted myself as soon as I remembered. This was surely the way Moses did it, and of course Hillel, and before them the Patriarchs; and in France, which was the strangest place for a Godfearing Jew to live, Rashi too, I was sure, walked through his vineyards in this fashion as he thought about his grapes and his commentaries. And though my *rebbe* did not walk that way, as I saw when I watched him on Henry Street, it made no difference. I had no high opinion of him anyway. There was only one proper way for a good man to walk. Ugh, how repulsive the arrogant man was with his nose up in the air. (In those days we did not suspect it might be polluted.) And then I got the bright idea that maybe God was One because that was the smallest number. God too was essentially modest, and what finer model could one have? Even as He is gracious and compassionate, so be thou; and so on and so forth. Why, on Shavuos He came all the way down from heaven to give the Torah to Israel.

So I got into the habit of looking at the ground as I walked. A year passed, then another, and though it is difficult to fix the moment when the attractiveness or persuasiveness of piety ceased to be irresistible, the habit stuck. I don't mean that I never looked at the sky as I was out walking, or turned my eyes away from all the high mountains and hills that are lifted up, like the Woolworth Building in the distance (cedars of Lebanon and ships of Tarshish were not within sight, at least in Manhattan; and the Empire State didn't come till later). I saw quite a lot from the neck up. But I found that if I wanted to think about something as I was walking, if I did not want to be distracted from my thoughts, it was best to look down. Look down, and you're an island unto yourself; look up, and there is danger you might miss the curb too.

As I say, the habit persisted, and the older I got the more I found myself looking down rather than up. Doubtless because with the years there was more and more to think about, it was also harder to think fast, and habits don't break easily. Soon I was walking pretty much as I had walked when I was thirteen and fourteen, and possibly fifteen, except that now, alas, God paid no attention to me.

Or did He? "There is no God" is what the fool says, and even he says it only in his heart. It is almost incredible how many pennies and dimes lie waiting to be picked up, and on some days quarters too, *under* your nose. The punishment of the arrogant is prompt and this-worldly. I don't know why, but nickels are rare. When they do turn up they're usually near parking meters. Quarters are not common, and the ones I come upon generally lie in the middle of the street. Once I was almost run over by a truck as I dashed heedlessly into the midst of traffic to recover that shining coin. I swerved back in time to avoid a serious accident, and there beside me was another quarter! Surely supernatural, because (to repeat) quarters are rare, even singly. To this day I'm convinced that there were more of them on that street, but I could not see too clearly after the deliverance from death and the screech of the brakes. I'm embarrassed to report the next find, but I have resolved to tell all. Well, once during a Yale alumni reunion weekend, I found a five-dollar bill on High Street, between Elm and Chapel. This happened only once (I mean on High Street), but that may be due to the decline in attendance of the rich alumni at the annual New Haven festivities in recent years. They seem to prefer to drop their loose change elsewhere.

From my experience it appears that the rich don't hold on tight to their spending money. They are careless more than they are charitable, which is only human after all: when the revolution comes, there will be neither carelessness nor charity, and one will then walk with eyes downcast for fears more proximate than the fear of God. And I can tell something about the social and economic state of a country simply by taking a stroll. I never found anything in Athens, except once a ten-drachma note on the Acropolis: but that's the haunt of tourists. Strange to say, during an extended stay in Munich, where prosperity and pornography are widespread, I found only one mark. But they keep their streetwalkers so smart and their streets so clean, how can a visitor glean anything after the reapings of the streetcleaners? Copenhagen offers only a modest harvest, as a rule in the late afternoon. (Enough of the Book of Ruth!) During the tourist season, from Passover to Passover, Jerusalem, that is, the neighborhood around the King David, is not bad: all depends on luck and the rate of the lira. England (London, Winchester, Oxford)? Here the problem is (was) that you need a sack for the pennies. Not that you'll find too many ("sack" is therefore overstatement), but you feel silly pocketing so big a coin with so little buying power. These pre–currency reform coins were useful, however, as gifts for young nephews who never saw a half-dollar in their lives. In Rome, the competition is too stiff. How about Paris? My experience is limited.

God bless America. It is still the most profitable location if you live here, even if the streets are not paved with bullion. I do not understand the newspaper headlines reporting that the American dollar is today worth less in the international market. If true, foreigners have lost their sense of values. Worth less to whom? To walk along the street aimlessly or engrossed in something like thought, and suddenly to see a dollar bill, and pocket it, and think, "This is not to be reported as income," is as delicious an experience as not being called to account for deducting expenses for improvements on a California hideaway. No fluctuations on the exchange can affect that. One time, as I was approaching the Tappan Zee Bridge, a dollar bill I held loosely in my left hand to pay the toll flew out the car window. I was very much irritated by my carelessness, but there followed a mildly pleasant afterthought, of some kindred soul finding it eventually.

Dollar bills, however, are not an everyday find, even if their purchasing power is diminished. They are a kind of Sabbath (beg your pardon) or new moon bonus. Even then it's not guaranteed. Another five-dollar bill I once found in New York City on Riverside Drive between 115th and 114th Streets was on a weekday. One Saturday, in New York City,

I was walking home from the synagogue at a leisurely pace with a pious gentleman, and when we reached the corner of the apartment house I then lived in, in the street, right at the curb, I saw a quarter. Here was a crisis, because I did not know how long it would take my companion to wish me a good sabbath and say goodbye. I could not just stand in the street right at the curb with one foot on the coin. That would be eccentric: why not move onto the sidewalk if we were there? It was out of the question scissorslike to put one foot on the sidewalk and place the other foot on the coin in the street. To move on but keep my eye on it would be ineffective if another passerby came upon it in the meantime. Something radical had to be improvised ad hoc. But I could think of nothing. So I stepped up wearily on to the sidewalk in hopes that my friend would take his leave quickly. He did, but not without these parting words: "Good Shabbos. When a man gives up a small profit, his gain is all the greater later. Good Shabbos." He walked on, and I just did not have the heart to return to the scene of my temptation.

Back to staples, however. A little bit of modesty will amply repay you with pennies and dimes. They are literally everywhere, and they can provide funds for small postage or an hour's worth of parking from time to time. What with postal rates rising too often, extra penny stamps in the wallet are a convenience. I admit I am somewhat perplexed: why are small coins scattered around so freely, lightheartedly, as though it were infra dig to keep pennies and dimes in the pocket? Is it a declaration that they are worthless? Why not nickels then? "No Pennies," reads a sign over the toll booth on the Saw Mill River Parkway, implying that Upper Westchester is no place for the lower classes? Or that pennies are too unimportant for the attention of the high-powered machines? Man has finally become the hireling of his inventions. Serves him right too for worshiping efficiency. Of all Molechs! Is it because pennies are small in size? Let alone Mount Sinai (confer above), they are not smaller than shirt buttons. I haven't seen one on the streets in years. I cannot believe there are that many men with holes in their pants pockets. Or, considering the new styles, women either.

All seasons are equally providential, but some are more interesting than others. In a puddle of rain pennies sparkle. When a coin is embedded in frozen snow, all is not yet lost. Press your heel into the ice over the coin and rotate your leg slowly right, then left, and right again and left again. Remove your foot. The coin comes loose in less time than it takes to write down these instructions, and is smooth to the touch. A new dime on a well-trimmed lawn is like a happy, winking eye. In the summer, in parks, dollar bills sometimes enjoy protective coloration. It's the same with pennies when the fallen leaves in the autumn are dry-brown and brittle. The tokens, quarter-size-and-styled, with presidential faces, distributed for a while by some gas stations when they had gas, and obviously thrown away by the customers the minute they drove off or a little later, at first added an element of challenge of recognition to the walks one took, but soon proved a nuisance. When you're in earnest, make-believe is in bad taste.

If I were pious I would say, God loves pennies because they buy so little, nothing in fact; like the saint whose ambition was to become zero and succeeded—no one remembers his name. However, there's no need to ascend to such exalted lowliness: it is extreme shortsightedness to ignore the talmudic observation that "Here a penny, there a penny, in the end a tidy sum." It works even faster with dimes. At this rate the meek may yet inherit the small change of the earth.

Nevertheless, walking with downcast eyes has its built-in penalties. Follow my quondam *rebbe*'s counsel and you will indeed be rewarded with pennies and dimes, but you will also discover that your greed has grown insatiable. There is more joy over one penny found than over a week's salary with deductions, but no contentment comes. For now you walk on wanting to find still another, and having found it you look for one more, and then more, and you're never satisfied. You are happy with what you found, but you want more than you deserve. And on those rare melancholy strolls when you do not find any coin at all (of course there are always paper clips, but they don't satisfy the basic craving), the disappointment is a blow. Even shorn of piety, you are prepared to rebel and look up, as though to say by force of onetime habit, "Supposing, then, I have sinned, what do I do to You, O watcher of men?"

On the bad days in particular, not to be forgiven are those who spit out their chewing gum on the sidewalks for others to trample down into the shapes of coins, pennies, nickles, quarters. The dark and sometimes bronze blobs are not only a disappointment to the humble man but an outrageous strain on his back. Naturally you bend to pick up a coin too. But in the latter instance you bend, you pick up, and draw up forthwith. Chewing gum keeps you bent longer because you refuse to believe that it is not the coveted coin, and so you stay head down longer just to make sure. Uncertainty is unbearable, and no scholar will be satisfied with quick impressions.

Apparently a remedy for penniless days is available, recommended to me by a sensitive colleague. He has advised me to check the coin-return receptacles of pay telephones in drugstores or the railroad terminal. He never passes a pay telephone, he says, without checking, with the index finger. However, I think that's undignified. I don't mind doing it when I am at the station, but I will not make a special trip there just to inspect telephones. And to enter a drugstore in your own neighborhood, make your way to the telephone booths and explore, then leave without buying something, creates suspicion. This can't be done more than once or twice. Moreover, the teenagers are so long on the phone, you're worn out waiting. Besides, when the coin finally drops, they themselves check to see if by chance it has been returned.

Real consolation comes from getting the wrong change in your favor after a purchase. However, (a) it doesn't happen often enough, now that the new math is taught in all consolidated schools, and (b) sometimes you are likely to be seized by a spasm of virtue and you return the surplus to the clerk. The smugness during the rest of the day is most unattractive. It's more or less the same with paying your fare on a crowded double-decker bus in London, as you get off before the attendant has had time to confront you.

Humility, therefore, is not without its drawbacks. But is there any conduct which is exempt from disadvantages? I cannot say that my *rebbe* or teacher had in mind some of the tangible rewards I've enjoyed, but I remain indebted to him, for quite a sum, I suppose, though I disliked him. Come to think of it, it was the second chapter of the treatise *Baba Metzia* that he taught me; it's called "Finders Keepers." Take a look at it. But this too may be no more than fantasy.

FROM TRADITION TO MODERNITY: AHAD HA-AM'S QUEST FOR A SPIRITUAL ZIONISM

By

ALFRED GOTTSCHALK

Ahad Ha-Am had a great reverence for the Bible since he considered it the bedrock out of which Judaism was built. Fully schooled in its contents and in the commentaries and master commentaries which comprised traditional Jewish biblical scholarship, he was at ease in its complex thought-molds and its exegesis. His veneration for the Holy Scriptures, upon which he drew so heavily in the development of his own philosophy of "Spiritual Zionism," did not preclude a critical approach to biblical materials, however, as well as to the highly selective use of the researches of the biblical scholarship of his day.

When it is taken into account that Ahad Ha-Am was a confirmed agnostic, it becomes clear that his attitude toward the Bible and its exegesis flows from other than traditional religious considerations. He regarded reverence for the past and its religious heritage as a vital psychological attitude, even when its vast body of belief is no longer deemed tenable in the modern world. Criticism of the Bible meant, for Ahad Ha-Am, the constructive use of those aspects of biblical thought which would enable modern Judaism to survive its spiritual crisis and which would assure it of its historical continuity.

The attitudes of reverence for tradition and of criticism of tradition abide in tension in Ahad Ha-Am's thought and are held together by the mortar of Spiritual Zionism. The founder of the philosophy of Spiritual Zionism entertained the belief that the literary creations of the Jewish people were the product of the Jewish National Spirit, brought into being to assure the national survival of the Jewish people. With this notion as a premise for the investigation of the Jewish past, the Bible and tradition must be viewed both as inevitable consequences of the creativity of the National Spirit and as its objects of reverence.

It would be a mistake to explain Ahad Ha-Am's deferential attitude toward the *kle kodesh* (sancta) of Jewish life on the basis of his hasidic upbringing alone. The ideas developed in his mature years were undoubtedly affected by early childhood attitudes and the learning of his formative period. We must probe and understand these and other influences and relate them to the system of thought that he later evolved. The final product of his life's cogitation, the program of cultural, spiritual, secularist Judaism, is a composite so complex that it betrays self-consciousness in its construction. Ahad Ha-Am's philosophy is as much a program of action as a system of thought. As such, it has a pragmatic motivation without which Spiritual Zionism cannot be understood.

In his *Reminiscences,* Ahad Ha-Am reveals that he had successfully mastered the Bible to the satisfaction of his teachers by the age of eleven. His father then removed him from primary school (*heder*) and provided him with a private tutor with whom he studied Talmud and the Responsa literature. After the age of fifteen, he pursued his studies without benefit of a tutor and became an acknowledged authority on the most complex legal literature, the Rabbinic Codes.[1] Like so many other talmudists, Ahad- Ha-Am must have constantly rediscovered the Bible, particularly as it was understood in the Talmud, since talmudic law bases itself upon scriptural texts.

Ahad Ha-Am's use of the Bible as the basis for his ideological structure cannot be reduced to subjective motivations alone. He held it to be a basic characteristic of Judaism to value abstract ideas free of subjective reference.[2] To him, appreciation of the Bible must flow from objective awareness; ideas relative to the Bible must be justified by their conforming to abstract and objective principles. The attempt at objectivity by Ahad Ha-Am, the development of an authentic *Hokhmat Yisrael* (or its German equivalent, *Die Wissenschaft des Judenthums*) can never be separated, however, from the ongoing flow of Jewish life and existence. Ahad Ha-Am asserts that the Bible is a product of Hebrew objective culture. It is observed that the degree of culture a nation has achieved can be viewed from two aspects. One aspect would deal with what the culture has produced and the other with the state of cultural life at any given moment. The former aspect is an objective measuring rod of a nation's culture, while the latter is dependent upon subjective evaluation. Objectively,

> a nation's culture is something which has a reality of its own: it is the concrete expression of the best minds of the nation in every period of its existence. The nation expresses itself in certain definite forms, which remain for all time, and are no longer dependent on those who created them, any more than a fallen apple is dependent upon the tree from which it fell.[3]

Objective and subjective aspects of culture do not necessarily attain the same degree of development at the same time. In the history of a nation, there may be periods in which "a few exceptionally gifted minds" represent the reservoir of its spiritual strength. It is these minds which produce "an original culture" dependent upon "the state of culture" at that particular moment which may not be fully comprehensible to the masses of people. The England of the seventeenth and eighteenth centuries, which produced men such as Shakespeare, Bacon, Locke, Hume, as well as other brilliant writers, exemplifies this particular point. These gifted minds created new intellectual avenues in literature and philosophy which are relevant even to the present day.[4]

Turning to Hebrew culture, Ahad Ha-Am holds that "so long as the Bible is extant, the creative power of the Jewish mind will remain undeniable."[5] The Hebrew Scriptures, then, represent for Ahad Ha-Am proof positive that, at least in that period of creativity, objective culture existed. Furthermore, Ahad Ha-Am disagrees with ideas current during his time that there was no authentic Hebrew culture outside of the Scriptures and that the literature that had been produced in the Diaspora was not expressive of true Hebrew genius. To the contrary, Ahad Ha-Am asserts that the Jewish spirit has undergone no change in its essential characteristics.[6] He finds no basis for the fashionable tendency among non-Jewish scholars and most Jewish scholars to underscore the fundamental difference between prophetic teachings and the ritually oriented Judaism which evolved during the period of the Second Temple and received its final form after the destruction of the Temple. The prophetic teachings are held by these scholars to be exclusively moral, directed toward a lofty spiritual level, whereas the Judaism concerning itself with external regulation, which came later, impoverished its strength by the creation of "innumerable trivial ordinances" which were lacking in moral values. Upon close inspection, Ahad Ha-Am notes, these two aspects of Judaism, while they differ considerably in content, are nevertheless the extension and the product of one spirit of which both are a true expression.[7]

Since the Bible is the prototype of Hebrew objective culture, it occupies a primary place in Jewish literature. It follows, in Ahad Ha-Am's mind, that Hebrew has been the language of the Jewish people ever since it came into existence. Ahad Ha-Am does not consider the prehistory of the Jewish people (that is, accounts of its possible existence outside the chronicled history of the Bible) as having any relevance whatsoever. Consequently, his conclusion that Hebrew alone "was, is and will be our national language always,"[8] follows as a natural sequence. Hebrew literature for Ahad Ha-Am includes the Aramaic portions of the Bible, the Targumim, Midrashim, as well as the Palestinian and Babylonian Talmudim, because for a time Aramaic was the language of the Jewish people. The Babylonian Talmud was not created on Jewish soil and would, by strict interpretation, have to be excluded from the "true national literature." However, since it falls under the broad canopy of the creation of the Jewish National Spirit, Ahad Ha-Am sees fit to include it, but without resolving the conflict with his restricted definition of Hebrew literature. What Jews wrote in other languages, whether or not it was linked to the matrix of Jewish religious thought, was considered by Ahad Ha-Am as part of the national literature of the host people or host nation with whom the Jews lived.[9] While attributing positive elements to the modern Haskalah movement, the negative factors and aberrations which resulted from it are traced by Ahad Ha-Am to Moses Mendelssohn's German translation of the Bible.[10]

That the Jews were called "the people of the book" from the time of Mohammed is common knowledge. The book, of course, refers to Scripture, and cojoining the people to the book was accomplished by observers of the religious and cultural life of the Jew and his intimate relationship to the Bible. Ahad Ha-Am maintains that the relation between a people and its literature is one of parallel development and mutual interaction when the people is a normal one.[11] Literature has as its function the propagation of new ideas, and the life of the people attends to the rest. A new idea thus propagated becomes an integral part of consciousness and an independent dynamic force emancipated from its literary origin. Such, undoubtedly, was the atmosphere in which the Bible was created. However, if a "people of the book" has become a "slave to the book," and if the book has become a crutch, the freshness that comes with spontaneity of action and emotion evaporates. This leads to a petrification of both people and book. Little changes in such periods of stagnation; the people wither and the book stagnates because there is no longer any living confrontation between the two.[12]

Ahad Ha-Am concludes that Jews have been a "people of the book" for two thousand years but were not always so. The Hebrews were not a "people of the book" in the age of the prophets or even in the period of the Second Temple. The spontaneity necessary for a fresh and self-reliant reaction to life was not absent, as witness the famous teaching of Hillel: "What is hateful to you, do not to your neighbor, that is the whole law." [13]

As an example of this fluidity Ahad Ha-Am also points out that the biblical law of *lex talionis,* "an eye for an eye,"[14] was considered too savage for a civilized nation, and the rabbinic tradition (i.e., the Oral Law) understood the meaning of Scripture in this passage to mean "the value of an eye for an eye, compensation in money and not retaliation in kind."[15] Side by side with the written law, then, there was an oral law which Ahad Ha-Am interpreted to be the "inner law, the law of the moral sense," which acted as a corrective upon the written law, often fundamentally changing its intent. However, when this was reduced to writing, it also became congealed and, according to Ahad Ha-Am, this moral sense was left with only one clear and firm conviction—that it was spent and that it was to be subservient to the written word forever.[16]

The book, rather than one's conscience, became the arbiter in situations of conflict. Reflecting to a great extent the orthodox climate in which he was reared and against which he revolted, Ahad Ha-Am observed that "the heart had no longer the right even to approve of what the written word ordained." [17] The right to question the tenets of the written word was abrogated and authority had to be blindly accepted. To make his point Ahad Ha-Am cites the commentators on Hillel's statement who throw the caveat at Hillel's moral interpretation of the law by explaining away the saying, which is the crown jewel of the Talmud, that what is meant by "your neighbor" really is God. This, claim the commentators, was clearly Hillel's intention—underscoring that you are not to go against God's will because you would not like your neighbor to go against your will. Similarly, if instead of the Bible the Babylonian Talmud had laid down the principle of "an eye for an eye," and the talmudic commentators rather than the early sages had been given the right to interpret it, they would have insisted upon its literal meaning.[18] Ahad Ha-Am's depreciation of the talmudic commentators stands really in sharp contrast to the actual nature of the talmudic commentaries, since one could hardly draw a generalization about them spanning several centuries and covering the multifarious schools which they represent. However, to make his point, Ahad Ha-Am categorically insists upon this differentiation, extolling thereby the nature of the biblical text and of the early commentators and sages who were the originators of the oral law.[19]

While the word Torah technically is equated with the Pentateuch, it has acquired a greatly expanded meaning in Jewish tradition and is used with reference to the totality of Jewish religious teaching. As such it embraces the ethical, the ceremonial, social mores, legal materials, as well as theological concepts. Consequently, Ahad Ha-Am's attitude toward the Bible, in terms of his general critique and approach, is applicable to these other areas as well. While Ahad Ha-Am conceived of all these facets of Torah as emanating from the Jewish National Spirit, or the lack of it, he was within the basic premises of his suppositions when he rendered a critique of the adoring, uneducated, gullible religionists who still clung to superstitious beliefs, outlandish laws and practices which were bequeathed by previous generations. In modern times, such credulous religious beliefs have been ferociously attacked through logical and scientific investigation. Despite this, many religionists, including educated people, adhere to inherited beliefs without giving them a second thought. Iconoclastic attack on such beliefs resulted only in a redoubled defense and sentiment of reverence for the past, akin to what had at one time manifested itself in worship of the dead.

The concept of evolution, which revolutionized previous methodologies and can now be applied to researches into the development of human ideas and institutions, is too formidable for the pat answers of the past. The historian is primarily interested in treating the history of civilization as a natural phenomenon, applying categories of investigation such as those we find in biology, and using such descriptive terms as *birth* and *process of growth,* with the primary obligation to understand how things develop, what conditions are requisite for their existence and development, and how change takes place. The historian, therefore, is not interested in condemning or praising one or another system. His primary concern is understanding by penetrating the workings of the human spirit. "The human spirit abides by eternal laws, and its fruits at any given time are dependent upon its stage of development and the nature of its environment at that time."[20] The historian appreciates that we apprehend reality differently from our ancestors because our world is dissimilar to theirs and our apprehension of reality is structured differently than theirs. Thus, what was a hallowed truth in one generation might be considered an absurdity in a subsequent generation.[21] Ahad Ha-Am laments that, while the historical method had an impact upon and has developed new attitudes toward the past in the world generally, no comparable development has taken place in Jewish thought. This is accounted for, in part, by the inability of some Jews, because of orthodox or nationalist presuppositions, to pass a negative judgment on a particular practice.

In Western countries the picture is somewhat different in that Jewish thinkers regarded Judaism solely as a religion, and the more liberal of them attempted to reform religion and religious practice through logical criticism, which Ahad Ha-Am considers a dated method. According to Ahad Ha-Am, the fallacy of logical criticism lies in its applying the standards of reasonability, prevalent in our own age, to ancient ideas and customs in preference to studying in an objective way the circumstances of their evolution and development within the context from which they emanate.[22] The essential task, then, is one of *verstehen,* not of judging or of culling from the tradition, by logical criteria alone, those elements which seem relevant and have contemporaneous significance. Ahad Ha-Am felt, "Basically, religion is a matter of feeling, and not of beliefs. Beliefs may change drastically, but feeling remains."[23]

Ahad Ha-Am clarifies this point in this discussion of Rabbi E. Lolli's attack on the *Shulhan Arukh*[24] (published in *Hashiloah*) demanding the abolition of those laws within it which are no longer relevant and asking that it be concluded "this is not our Torah." Ahad Ha-Am notes, "There is no doubt that basically he is right."[25] Ahad Ha-Am agrees with Rabbi Lolli that no modern Jew with education can subscribe to that which the rabbi wished to expunge from having authority for contemporary Jewry. However, Ahad Ha-Am takes serious issue with Lolli's conclusion that to say "this is not our Torah" would be wrong. It is "our Torah" in the guise that it developed at an earlier time. The same is true of the Talmud and the Bible.

> These three together (Bible, Talmud, *Shulhan Arukh*) are simply three different steps in the process of the development of one essence—the Jewish national spirit—in accordance with the circumstances and the requirements of different epochs in history.[26]

Rabbi Lolli, quoting Samuel David Luzzatto (1800–1865), a defender of tradition, thought that the Mishnah and the Talmud were not originally designed as codes. The latter, nevertheless, came to be regarded as such, and the decisions arrived at became binding upon observant Jewry. The subsequent code of Maimonides, the *Mishneh Torah*, made no attempt to distinguish religious laws on the basis of their intrinsic value or contemporary relevance. The tradition was revealed by God and one was not free to tamper with it. Despite many of the religious laws, customs, and traditions of the Bible and the entirety of what is called Torah, one must not, as Reform Jewish scholars did, select one over another on the basis of its logical compatibility with our thought, but must show reverence for the past and summon adequate sentiment to appreciate the position of these reservoirs of the Jewish spirit within their historical context.[27] The difference between Lolli and Ahad Ha-Am seems, however, more pointedly to be that Lolli still believed in the divine authority of the *Shulhan Arukh* as such and wished to select from it that which continued to remain religiously relevant in order to keep the authority and binding nature of the *Shulhan Arukh*. Ahad Ha-Am, who believed not a whit in the binding nature of the precepts of the Bible and the codes as such, looked upon this vast body of literature as having its mooring in a particular aspect of time and therefore relevant only to it. He was capable intellectually and emotionally of revering the totality of it, even those aspects which remained repugnant to him.[28]

The historian of Jewish religious thought, Dr. Yehezkel Kaufmann, recognized that Ahad Ha-Am's views on the evaluation of the Jewish people and its literary productivity represent a "psychological and historical entity."[29] Ahad Ha-Am projected a "national ego on the analogy of the individual self" in which past, future, memories, impressions, hopes, and desires are all intertwined as the common heritage of the nation.[30] Every national enterprise, and Ahad Ha-Am would consider biblical scholarship such an enterprise, can be evaluated by the manner in which it fully grasps this basic truth. The Jewish people possess a *volksgeist* which permeates all of their existence. Suffusing every aspect of life, this spirit represents the creative force of the people and is a manifestation of its will to live.[31] The national organism, which in Spencerian terms is made analogous to any other physical organism, is governed by a natural basic drive which Ahad Ha-Am calls *Ha-kium Ha-leumi*.[32] This "instinct of self-preservation" works on the subconscious level.[33] It illuminates the evolution of the Jewish religion and, in the case of the Jewish people, it explains its belief in monotheism and the purpose of the religious commandments and institutions as protective coloration against the animus of the hostile societies in which Jews have been condemned to live since their dispersion. The "instinct of self-preservation" of the Jewish people created this organic Jewish culture as a means to this end, and their present-day existence is a testimony to its staying power.[34]

As severely critical as he was of Jewish scholarship, which denied its inherent linkage to the Jewish national past, and as consistent as he was in denouncing this approach as being characteristic of the science of Judaism, Ahad Ha-Am was equally incisive when it came to the analysis of the development of the religious emphases of Judaism. His own logical deductions relating to the origins of Judaism were no less a departure from the orthodox tradition upon which Ahad Ha-Am was weaned than that of West European Jewry's "reformers" and researchers into the Jewish past. Ahad Ha-Am broke radically with the Jewish tradition, and with the Jewish commentators upon whose thinking he drew liberally, in his denial of the existence of a transcendent and supernatural God, and in his substituting the national will to live and the inspirational propensities of the Jewish National Spirit. Jewish ethics, clearly reflected in the Bible, as demands made upon man by God, are translated into the nation's innate perception of the moral sense which comes to take the place of divine inspiration.[35] "He that keepeth Israel shall neither slumber nor sleep" (Ps. 121:4) equated with the "national will to live."

In his appendix to the *Protokol Derekh Ha-Hayim,* which was written to serve as a set of bylaws for the Bene Moshe (the society which spearheaded the Hoveve Zion movement and served as a fraternal order), Ahad Ha-Am enumerates, early in his career as a polemicist, those indispensable factors which comprise "the national possessions" of the Jewish people. These are: Palestine and its settlement; *Torat Yisrael,* its language and wisdom; the memory of our forefathers and their history; the customs of our ancestors and their way of life from generation to generation. By these the people were to be welded together in a strong, spiritual bond, awakening the national spirit in the hearts of all the living.[36] These ideas, which were present at the outset of Ahad Ha-Am's literary and scholarly career, permeated his philosophy throughout, to the very last essay that he was to write— "Summa Summarum."[37] It was incumbent upon the nationalist Jew to have a positive attitude toward the national traits of Judaism. This does not, however, impose belief in the ideas of religious Judaism but merely a deferential attitude toward them. Once having stated this, Ahad Ha-Am could very well say: "I, at least, can speak out concerning the beliefs and opinions my ancestors have bequeathed me without my fearing to snap the bond that unites me to my people."[38]

As illustrative of this statement of "spiritual freedom," showing how Ahad Ha-Am felt about the Bible and Jewish practice, evidence may be brought from a number of internal ideological conflicts within the Zionist movement. In 1911 *Hapoel Hazair* (The Young Workman) printed an article by the Socialists' spokesman, Hayyim Brenner (1881–1921), which unequivocally stated that Hebrew nationalism was not tied to traditional Judaism, and that young Jews were in no way obligated to show reverence for the belief of their ancestors or to humiliate themselves before "some sort of heavenly father." Further, they were free of the "hypnos" of Scriptures in that they had a closer affinity to many secular books. What, then, Ahad Ha-Am asks, is left of their national heritage from the past? To which he replies, "Nothing, neither obligation nor even negation!" [39] Ahad Ha-Am further points out that those who want to free themselves from the yoke of Judaism by rejecting the teaching of its past can be compared to one who wishes to "liberate" a tree by cutting off its roots. Jewish national roots go deep into the ground of the past, and from this tree modern nationalism draws its nurture. Consequently Ahad Ha-Am concludes that

> a nationalist Jew even though he be a total unbeliever cannot say: I have no portion in the God of Israel, in that historic force which has kept our people alive and has abundantly enriched its spirit and way of life in the course of thousands of years. He who in truth has no portion in the God of Israel, no feeling of relationship to that "exalted world" in which our forefathers absorbed their minds and their hearts in every generation and from which they drew their moral strength—such a one though he be a proper man is not a nationalist Jew, even though he lives in the land of Israel and speaks the holy tongue.[40]

Ahad Ha-Am underscores his belief that a nationalist Jew, though he be a complete atheist, is to be accepted as a Jew in the same manner as an ultra-traditionalist Jew, the difference being that the one says "I believe" and the other says "I feel." However, when one is not tied to the national past either through faith or through feeling, what remains for him that he should be obliged to call himself a Jewish nationalist? The Hebrew language? "Remove from it the 'hypnos' of the past, what is left for us and of it? . . . Why should we then not turn our backs on it, if we find, and indeed it is possible to find, another more beautiful than it?" [41] God, the Bible, Hebrew without the "hypnos" of the past, would have no unique place in the thinking of the present.

Ahad Ha-Am, who was known to belong to the nonreligious wing of the Hoveve Zion, was subject to attacks by the orthodox for being a heretic and an enemy of religion. In the midst of a controversy which was threatening to split the Hoveve Zion, he received a letter from Rabbi Jonathan Eliasberg, son of Rabbi Mordechai Eliasberg, a famous orthodox scholar, who expressed concern over the seeming advocacy of religious reform contained in Ahad Ha-Am's essay, "Torah She-Balev." This is the essay in which Ahad Ha-Am attacked the notion of the "people of the book" and of the congealed state of the oral law, rendering an instantaneous response to life impossible. Ahad Ha-Am replied in *Hamelitz,* under the title "Divre Shalom" (Words of Peace), setting forth again his objections to reform in religion, and reinforcing his view of the Jewish past in terms of evolutionary principles. Since attempts at reform of the Jewish past are ill-fated, he has no inclination to mix into matters of religion or its reforms as such. In addition, he has no inclination to confuse the problems of religion with those of *Hibbat Zion* (The Love of Zion).[42] Reforming Judaism is like trying to freeze fire. It takes place only when men find it impossible to believe any more in the existence of God. Religion is religion only as long as its believers believe in the existence of God. When this belief is undermined, reforms are advocated.[43]

Baruch Kurtzweil sees "something of that quiet demonism" in Ahad Ha-Am's attempts here at "diplomatic blurring of the differences which exist between the two worlds—between the world of religious faith and of atheism . . ." Even while reiterating his belief that the ideal of *Hibbat Zion* could liberate Judaism both from its subservience to a code which no longer had relevance and from religious practices which were no longer meaningful, Ahad Ha-Am seems to smooth the ruffled feathers of Rabbi Eliasberg by using, in the course of his essay, such expressions as "until the merciful God will clarify matters."[44] He closes on a conciliatory note since, in line with his views, he felt it necessary to show proper deference to Rabbi Eliasberg while thoroughly disagreeing with his religious convictions. Kurtzweil is undoubtedly correct, although somewhat harsh, in stating that "on the basic principles of religious faith, even the Reformers are closer to traditional Judaism than the author of *Words of Peace.*"[45]

In line with the arguments laid down in *Torah Mi-Zion,* Ahad Ha-Am opposed a prominent French Jew, Salomon Reinach, who advocated the religious emancipation of East European Jewry from orthodoxy and, particularly, from the ceremonial law relating to the observance of the Sabbath and the dietary regulations,[46] both of which are clearly and unmistakably proclaimed in the Hebrew Scriptures.[47] In these articles Salomon Reinach argues that the dietary laws make meat dear and prevent Jews from having healthy and cheap forms of food, such as swine's flesh, available to them. The Sabbath involves financial loss to businessmen and is a disadvantage for the poor, who cannot obtain work in factories if they are Sabbath observers. Reinach proceeded to point out that during the Hasmonean period Mattathias permitted the desecration of the Sabbath for the purpose of self-defense. Ergo, Reinach reasons, since survival is at stake for the Jewish community, violation of the Sabbath is permitted.[48]

Ahad Ha-Am, in a biting criticism, counters these ideas by pointing out that what Mattathias did was to make it possible for Judaism to survive. For this reason he allowed his men to desecrate the Sabbath by defending themselves against the enemy. The Sabbath, Ahad Ha-Am maintains, "has been sanctified by the blood of our people and has shielded it for thousands of years from spiritual degeneration . . ."[49] He is well aware, without Reinach's instruction, that the Sabbath and other religious observances evolved out of crude beliefs and the emotions of primitive man and did not come into being full grown in their present form. Nevertheless, modern people can still find the Sabbath a delight and observe the dietary laws in their homes for the simple reason that they do not seek the opprobrium of other Jewish people who would otherwise consider their table profane.[50] In a final rejoinder to Reinach, he quotes Mattathias: "Our holy things, our pride, and our glory have been laid waste; why then should we live?"[51]

Similarly, when Max Nordau,[52] co-worker of Theodor Herzl, in the forefront of political Zionism, maintained that he saw no national values in the observance of the Sabbath, Ahad Ha-Am wrote a brilliant defense of the Sabbath entitled "Shabbat V'Zionut" (Sabbath and Zionism), in which he defended the Sabbath as a fundamental and historic institution of the Jewish people. He wrote,

> Whomsoever feels in his heart a true bond with the life of the nation throughout the generations, . . . even though he denies the "world to come" or a Jewish state—cannot visualize the existence of the Jewish people without "Queen Sabbath." . . . More than the Jew has kept the Sabbath, the Sabbath has preserved the Jew.[53]

It is clear that Ahad Ha-Am's issue with Reinach and Nordau is really not intellectual but emotional.[54] Ahad Ha-Am is no less a reformer in principle than either of these men appears to be. Yet, when it came to the practical aspects and implications of reform, he casts these to the wind since they would sunder the organic unity of the Jewish people. He condemns as vehemently as any reformer the petrification which Judaism has undergone. What is at stake is not theological speculation but *tehiat Ha-ruah,* the revivification of the spirit.

There are bold assertions in the writings of Ahad Ha-Am in which he negates that criticism which, based on the Jewish past, justified the assimilationist tendencies of European Jewry. Ahad Ha-Am was greatly intolerant of those whom he accused of using biblical criticism to further and accelerate a program of acclimatizing Jews to Western civilization and of justifying their bid for civil emancipation and civil liberties. He pictured as the end result of this process the total absorption of Jewry into Christian civilization.[55] He had seen evidence of this in Germany, France, and particularly England, where Oswald John Simon, a scion of one of the prominent Anglo-Jewish families, had proposed a new Jewish church whose moorings were to be totally cut loose from the national elements of Jewish tradition and which was to confine itself to the established verities of Judaism which were universally acceptable.[56]

A certain Zionist who published an article in the *Oesterreichisch Wochenschrift* in which intermarriage is condoned, is severely taken to task by Ahad Ha-Am.[57] Ahad Ha-Am, whose own daughter had intermarried, takes this opportunity to oppose intermarriage in unequivocal terms. He reacts similarly in his essay "The National Ethic," in which he discusses Max Nordau's *Dr. Kohn.* Nordau states in this work that there is within the Zionist position no logical cause for opposition to intermarriage. Ahad Ha-Am feels that since intermarriage is a danger to the preservation of the people, it is then a moral duty for the nationalist Jew to sacrifice his individual happiness for the sake of the preservation of his people.[58] Ahad Ha-Am, in his opposition to intermarriage, clearly echoes Ezra's alarm when the latter, in surveying the religious life of Palestine upon his return to it from exile in Persia, interdicted intermarriage and insisted that intermarried couples sever their matrimonial ties for the sake of the purity of the Israelite cultus. "Now therefore give not your daughters unto their sons, neither take their daughters unto your sons."[59] He continues,

We have broken faith with our God, and have married foreign women of the peoples of the land; yet there is hope for Israel concerning this thing. Now let us make a covenant with our God to put away all the wives, and such as are born of them, according to the counsel of the Lord.[60]

Ahad Ha-Am, like Ezra, feared that the physical loss of an Israelite contributed to the weakening of the solidarity of the Jewish people, and that the entry within it of foreign elements would militate against the full flowering of the Jewish National Spirit.

His biological approach is to be contrasted with the great theoretical leeway he is willing to give to anyone who, though a free-thinker, nevertheless considers himself a Jew. In response to the article "Speech and Silence," a member of the Hoveve Zion addressed a letter to Ahad Ha-Am which raises the following question: How would Ahad Ha-Am classify a Jew who loves his people, its literature, its spiritual possessions, who wants the revival of the people in the land of its fathers, longs for its liberation, but at the same time is a freethinker, with everything that this implies—who believes in nature and nature's law but does not recognize the Creator, providence, and certainly not divine revelation with all of its subsequent ramifications? Is such a Jew ours, or does he belong to our enemies? Can we separate him from the people and say to him: "Leave the camp!"[61] Ahad Ha-Am responds to this question that this Jew belongs to "us." He is a son faithful to his people and to its spirit, as much as are the masses of believers and, in a certain sense, even more so.

Ahad Ha-Am develops the viewpoint that pantheistic nationalism is a position with which he is in full accord as compared with monotheists who see nature only as a function and manifestation of the deity.[62] Ahad Ha-Am believed in the functioning of the natural law, which, to him, is a higher expression of logical truth than is monotheism. Monotheism, however, in biblical times, represented the highest expression of the Jewish spirit; it attributed to the deity ethics which Ahad Ha-Am believes to be the substratum of religion and from which religion draws its greatest strength. In a letter to Dr. Solomon Schechter, Ahad Ha-Am states:

I do not agree with you as regards the subordination of ethics to religion in Judaism; on the contrary, as I have suggested in various essays, I think that religious development has followed moral development . . .[63]

For Ahad Ha-Am, the apex of Jewish creativity and the exemplars of ethics were the Hebrew prophets. Although Ahad Ha-Am deals in detail only with Moses, who is the father of the prophets,[64] he applies his deductions and generalizations concerning Moses to the rest of the prophetic movement.[65] With a striking lack of critical insight, he distinguishes neither between the pre-exilic and post-exilic prophets nor between the universalist and particularist positions within the prophetic writings as such.[66] This constitutes the major weakness in Ahad Ha-Am's biblical criticism. Here again, in accordance with his nationalist presuppositions, he adopts a reverent attitude and interprets prophetic teaching in terms of the moral philosophy of his day, particularly in the use of such terms as the categorical imperative and absolutistic ethics.[67]

Ahad Ha-Am's view of the Bible and Jewish tradition, then, represents an admixture of nationalism, skepticism, and what Dr. Joseph Heller calls his hasidic inclinations.[68] According to this writer, the latter were always present in Ahad Ha-Am and led him to enthrone feeling, rather than reason, as the primary prerequisite for an empathetic viewpoint toward religious beliefs and the literature in which these beliefs are embedded.

NOTES

1. *Kol Kitve Ahad Ha-Am* (Tel Aviv: Dvir, 1956), pp. 466, 486, 492 ff.
2. Particularly was this the case with the idea of justice, which was viewed in an entirely objective sense. Aryeh Simon and Joseph Heller, *Ahad Ha-Am, Ha-ish, Po'alo Ve-torato* (Jerusalem: Magnes Press, 1955), pp. 192–95.
3. Ahad Ha-Am, *Selected Essays,* trans. L. Simon (Philadelphia: Jewish Publication Society, 1912), p. 259.
4. Ibid., p. 260.
5. Ibid., p. 261. For a full discussion of Ahad Ha-Am's conception of culture, note Aryeh Rubinstein, "Tefisat Ha-'kultura' Be-mishnat Ahad Ha-Am," *Melilah* (Manchester) 3–4 (1950): 289–310.
6. Ahad Ha-Am, *Selected Essays,* p. 263.
7. Ibid.
8. *Kol Kitve,* p. 180.
9. Ibid., p. 179. Stated positively, "ki ha-'am 'azmo roeh sifruto ha-leumit rak ba-meh she-katuv bilshonenu . . . " ("For the people itself recognizes as its national literature only that which is written in Hebrew"). Writers such as Lev Levanda, although superior to Perez Smolenskin, have virtually been forgotten, for the former wrote in Russian and the latter in Hebrew.
10. Ibid., p. 77.
11. Ibid., pp. 51 f. The article is entitled, "Torah She-ba-lev" ("The Torah within"). Ahad Ha-Am contrasts *'am sifruti,* "a literary people," with *'am ha-sefer,* "people of the book," denoting the congealing of the spontaneous Torah of the heart.
12. Ibid., pp. 52 f.
13. Ibid., p. 52. Hillel the Elder (ca. 70 B.C.E.), born in Babylon, went to study at the academies in Jerusalem and became a foremost sage around whom a school came to group itself. His teaching appears in *Shab.* 31a.
14. Exod. 21:24.
15. *Kol Kitve,* p. 52. Cf. T.B. *Baba Kama* 83b.
16. *Kol Kitve,* p. 52. "The voice of God in the heart of man" no longer had any authority on its own. Whenever problems of life requiring solutions occurred, they were to be found in a book. The slogan for this approach came to be characterized as *nete sefer we-neheze* ("Let's get a book and see"). Ibid., p. 52.
17. Ibid. As Professor Shaoul Hareli pointed out in "Ahad Ha-Am and Jewish Destiny" (unpublished lecture, Hebrew Union College, 1956), p. 11, Ahad Ha-Am distinguished between a "people of the book" and *'am ha-sifrut* ("a literary people"). The latter implies creativity and the rejection of outdated forms; "it means to grow spiritually."
18. *Kol Kitve,* p. 52.
19. Ahad Ha-Am then develops the position that the exaltation of the written word came to be accepted in Judaism with rabbis and people unable to revolt against

150

its authority. Only *Hibbat Zion,* the free and spontaneous "love of Zion," is an antidote for this petrification of the spirit. *Kol Kitve,* pp. 52 ff.

20. Ibid., p. 271.
21. Ibid., p. 272.
22. Ibid.
23. Letter of Ahad Ha-Am to M. K. (Moses Kalischer?), April 12, 1899, in Ahad Ha-Am, *Iggerot* (Tel Aviv: Dvir, 1956), 2:275. Note also the discussion by Moshe Dubshani, *Mishnat Ahad Ha-Am* (Tel Aviv: Dvir, n.d.), pp. 71–80.
24. A compendium of laws edited by Joseph Karo (1488–1575).
25. *Kol Kitve,* p. 272.
26. Ibid.
27. Ibid., pp. 272 f.
28. In correspondence with Rabbi Lolli, Ahad Ha-Am presses his point "that religion alone does not account for our survival, and that the western Jews, who assert that it does, tie themselves up in a hopeless tangle of paradoxes and sophistries, thereby proving that they may lose their civil rights if they admit that the Jews are a separate nation . . . " Quoted in Ahad Ha-Am, *Essays, Letters, and Memoirs,* p. 261. The full letter is to be found in *Iggerot,* 2: 62–63.
29. Yehezkel Kaufmann, " 'Ikare De'otav shel Ahad Ha-Am," *Ha-Tekufah* (Berlin) 24 (1928): 424.
30. *Kol Kitve,* p. 81. Ahad Ha-Am here acknowledges his indebtedness to John Stuart Mill and Renan, who stressed that the national self or ego is in its essence the commingling of past and present.
31. Ahad Ha-Am defines this by the expression *hefez ha-kium ve-ha-osher,* "desire for life and happiness." *Kol Kitve,* p. 61. Elsewhere, *hush ha-kium,* "instinct for survival." Ibid., p. 421.
32. "The national instinct for self-preservation." Ibid., p. 421.
33. Ibid.
34. Ibid., pp. 78–80.
35. Ibid., p. 162.
36. *Derek Ha-hayyim,* ed. Abraham Lubarsky and Eliyahu Zeeb Halevi Lewin-Epstein (New York: Maslansky Publishers, 1905), p. 12.
37. "Sak Ha-kol" was written in 1910, and the essay appeared in *Hashiloah* in late spring of 1912. Leon Simon, *Ahad Ha-Am: A Biography,* p. 242.
38. *Kol Kitve,* pp. 68 f.
39. Ibid., p. 407.
40. Ibid., p. 408.
41. Ibid. The term "hypnos" came into vogue in Ahad Ha-Am's day. It was believed that ideas of the past could be brought through hypnosis into the present. Dr. Schiller observes that for Ahad Ha-Am, "Die Gesellschaft, die Lehrer, die ganze Umgebung sind die Hypnotiseure, die uns ihre Gedanken einimpfen. Und nicht nur Zeitgenossen! Es gibt Hypnotiseure in der fernsten Vergangenheit, und ihre Ideen wirken noch immer auf uns suggerierend—wir glauben selbst zu denken, und wir denken die Gedanken jener." Salomon Schiller, "Achad-Haam," *Heimkehr, Essays Juedischer Denker* (Berlin: Verlag Louis Lamm, 1912), p. 82.
42. *Kol Kitve,* p. 57. Leon Simon points out that Ahad Ha-Am's skillful reply to Rabbi Eliasberg was carefully couched so as not to risk the splitting off of those who were religious from the Hibbat Zion movement. Hence, the title of the article, "Words of Peace." He did not, however, compromise his view that Hibbat Zion could "liberate the Jewish heart from subservience to the petrified code and ended with a plea for mutual tolerance . . ." Simon, *Ahad Ha-Am: A Biography,* p. 114.

43. *Kol Kitve,* p. 58. "Kol ha-omer letaken et ha-dat hare hu be-eynai k-ilu omer l'-karer et ha-esh. . . . Ha-dat hee dat kol zeman she-ba-'aleha ma-aminim bimkorah ha-elohi."

44. Ibid., p. 60.

45. Baruch Kurzweil, "Judaism—the Group Will-to-Survive? A Critique of Achad Ha-Amism," *Judaism* 4 (Summer 1955): 210. Mordecai Kaplan takes strong exception to Kurzweil's critique, making such statements as, "Ahad Ha-Am never denied the existence of God. On the contrary, he expressed himself in terms that definitely implied a belief in God." Mordecai Kaplan, "Anti-Maimunism in Modern Dress," *Judaism* 4 (Fall 1955): 305. Kaplan's slashing attack against Kurzweil falls short of proving Kurzweil in error, and in parts of the article actually reinforces the vital points of Kurzweil's thesis.

46. Reinach expounded his views in an article, "L'émancipation intérieure du judaisme" (*L'Univers Israélite,* nos. 6, 8, 12), footnoted in *Kol Kitve,* p. 301.

47. The proclamation of the Sabbath is found in Gen. 2:1–3; Exod. 31:13–17. Laws relating to Sabbath observance are delineated in Exod. 20:8–11, 31:14, 15, 35:2–3; Lev. 23:3, 24:8; Num. 15:32–36; Deut. 5:12--15. The dietary laws are enjoined in Gen. 9:4; Lev. 11:1–47, 17:11; Deut, 14:3–20. The law prohibiting the seething of a kid in its mother's milk, Exod. 23:19, 34:26; Deut. 14:21, is explained by the rabbis "as referring to three distinct prohibitions: cooking meat and milk together, eating such mixture; deriving any benefit from such a mixture" (Hul. 115b). Kaufman Kohler, "The Dietary Laws," *Jewish Encyclopedia* (New York: Funk & Wagnalls Co., 1903), 4: 596–600.

48. *Kol Kitve,* pp. 301–2.

49. Ibid., p. 302. Ahad Ha-Am's reverence for the Sabbath was profound despite his unbelief in its divine ordination. He felt its presence. He could write: "Even now when Sabbath is over, from the time of the setting of the sun until the candle is lit, I love to sit in my corner and sink into the very depth of my feelings. I feel then, as if my soul was uplifted to the very heights . . . and various memories of my youth would come to consciousness, memories stirring up laughter, pleasant, pleasant to me indeed. . . . Sometimes my lips would almost automatically break into a familiar Aramaic chant, the familiar melody too would distinctly slip out of my mouth in a still, small voice, and tears would well up and stream from my eyes; I don't know why or how." Quoted in the Hebrew by Joseph Heller, "Ledmuto Ha-nafshit Ve-haruhanit shel Ahad Ha-Am," *Melilah* (Manchester) (1955): 257.

50. *Kol Kitve,* p. 302. The Sabbath, dietary laws, and other customs, ceremonies, and observances, Ahad Ha-Am considered as historical instruments, "L'kadshe Ha-umah," for the sanctification of the nation, and were to be regarded as sacred even if one could no longer believe in them. Ahad Ha-Am the "rationalist" and "atheist" ("ha-kofer") was always to be found at the side of the defenders of the tradition whenever it was in peril. Simon and Heller, *Ahad Ha-Am, Ha-ish, Po'alo Ve-torato,* p. 89.

51. *Kol Kitve,* p. 302.

52. Max Nordau was a remarkable and versatile man. While practicing medicine and psychiatry, he was also a ranking newspaperman, poet, dramatist, and fiction writer. Allied with Herzl, he developed a "three-dimensional Zionism." The first dimension is personal, communal, or national; the second, international or global; the third, transglobal or "cosmic Zionism." Nordau conceived of Zionism in both Jewish and universal terms. It was a philosophy which for him "was not a retreat from the ancient Jewish ideal of human brotherhood; it merely sought to ensure Jewish survival in the interim between nationalism and brother-

hood." Meir Ben-Horin, "Reconsidering Max Nordau," *Herzl Year Book*, vol. 2, ed. Raphael Patai (New York: Herzl Press, 1959), p. 169. Nordau had brought to Zionism a universal dimension whereby Zionism would be the instrument leading mankind to the goal of brotherhood and love. Meir Ben-Horin, *Herzl Year Book*, 2:170.

53. *Kol Kitve*, p. 286. The phrase, "Ki yoter mi-she-yisrael shomru et ha-Shabbat, shamrah ha-Shabbat otam" ("For, more than Israel observed the Sabbath, the Sabbath preserved them") has become so well known that it has been included, among other liturgies, in that of the Reform movement's *Union Prayer Book I* (New York: CCAR, 1957), p. 31. Of interest on this subject is Leon Simon's essay, "Ahad Ha-Am and Traditional Judaism," *The Brandeis Avukah Annual,* ed. Joseph S. Shubow (Boston: Stratford Co., 1932), pp. 128–34.

54. Simon notes that for Ahad Ha-Am, "the theological basis is gone, but the superstructure remains." Consequently, Ahad Ha-Am could say, "The Sabbath is a characteristic manifestation of the national spirit of Israel, therefore it is holy." Simon, *Brandeis Avukah Annual.* Ahad Ha-Am would say, "ani margish" ("I feel"), where the traditionalist would say, "ani ma-amin" ("I believe"). He considered someone as being a "ba'al dat amiti" ("a truly religious person") even though he was not a "ba'al emunah" ("a man of faith"), on the view that the former was a "ba'al regesh dati" ("a person of religious feeling"). Ahad Ha-Am notes that in his time there were among many peoples individuals in this category who sustained religion. Joseph Heller, "Ahad Ha-Am We-ha-masorah," *Mezudah* (London: Ararat Publishing Society, 1943), pp. 148 f. A detailed discussion of Ahad Ha-Am's analysis of the question of the survival of Judaism and its practice is found in Yehezkel Kaufmann, *Golah Ve-nekhar* (Tel Aviv: Dvir, 1932), 2:425 ff., and M. Z. Lewinson-Levy, "Yesod Ha-regesh Be-massekhet Ahad Ha-Am," *Hadoar,* March 26, 1937, pp. 326 f.

55. *Kol Kitve*, pp. 1 f.

56. Ibid., p. 262; also in Simon, *Ahad Ha-Am: A Biography*, p. 239.

57. *Kol Kitve*, pp. 290 f. In his essay "Dibbur U-shetika" ("Speech and Silence"), Ahad Ha-Am refers to the incident recorded in the newspaper where a well-known Jewish writer in Vienna married a non-Jewess, adopted Christianity, but still considered himself a Zionist.

58. *Kol Kitve,* pp. 162 f.

59. Ezra 9:12.

60. Ezra 10:2–3.

61. *Kol Kitve,* pp. 291 f.

62. Ibid., p. 292. In whose view is nature more exalted, Ahad Ha-Am asks—in that of the monotheist or the pantheist? He concludes, in the pantheist, for in monotheism nature is a creation of God and a difference exists between *El* and *'olam* ("God" and "the world"). In pantheism all is subsumed in nature and this difference does not exist. "And the 'spirit of God' which is discernible to him [the pantheist] in the depth of the foundation of existence, is not in his view something above nature, but both are identical." *Kol Kitve,* p. 292. The "nationalist pantheist" sees the strength of the creation of the spirit of the people from within, as opposed to the monotheist, who believes it to be without, that is, in God. The "national pantheist," by contrast, recognizes that the "national spirit" proceeds of its own inner force. Both the nationalist who retains a belief in the super-natural and the pantheistic nationalist feel honor and love for "le-kinyane ha-'am ha-ruhaniyyim" ("the spiritual treasures of the people") and desire the existence of the national on the basis of the historic nexus between "kudsha berikh hu, ve-orayyta ve-yisrael" ("God, Torah and Israel"). *Kol Kitve,* p. 292.

63. Letter to Dr. S. Schechter (Florence), London, March 29, 1911. Quoted in Ahad Ha-Am, *Essays, Letters, Memoirs,* p. 270.

64. Moses as "Av ha-neviim" ("Father of the Prophets"), possessed of extraordinary powers, is widely attested to in the rabbinic tradition; e.g., T.B. *Megilla* 13a speaks of him as "av ba-torah, av be-hokhmah, av ha-neviiut" ("father of the law, wisdom and prophecy"). Cf. T.B. *Sotah* 12a and *Exodus Rabbah* 1:20. Compare also J. D. Eisenstein, *Ozar Israel* (New York: J. D. Eisenstein, 1911), 6:299–302.

65. *Kol Kitve,* pp. 90–92.

66. Ibid., pp. 138 ff., 156 f., 275 ff.

67. Ibid., pp. 281 ff., 343 ff.

68. Simon and Heller, *Ahad Ha-Am, Ha-ish, Po'alo Ve-torato,* p. 130.

JOHN MILTON'S PSALM TRANSLATIONS
AND PARAPHRASES

By

CAROLE KESSNER

It is little more than a literary truism to remark that the Book of Psalms had a pervasive influence on seventeenth-century English religious poetry. Yet the nature and extent of that influence is greatly in need of study, for it is a debt more acknowledged than fully understood. The Hebrew psalms permeated the imagination of the entire range of religious poets from the Anglican dean of St. Paul's, John Donne, to the country parson George Herbert, from the mystical Henry Vaughan to the political Andrew Marvell. But as fundamental as the psalms were for all these, they were perhaps even more so the matrix of the religious imagination of the great Puritan poet John Milton.

Although the psalms were central to congregational and private worship throughout the history of Christianity, they were especially significant to the Protestant reformers, who had many reasons for loving them. First, the reformers of the sixteenth and seventeenth centuries were intent upon reviving the practices and authority of the Primitive Church, and Israel's psalms were known to have played a significant role in the life of the early Church. Not only are there hymns in Luke 1:46–55, 1:68–79, 2:29–32, which are modeled after the Hebrew psalms, but also, ninety-three passages from the Book of Psalms are quoted in the Christian Bible, some of them several times.[1] Hence, it is not surprising to read in *The Sweet Psalmist of Israel* (Boston, 1722) that for the true Puritan, David was the divine Poet, for he "derived his *Inspiration* not from Parnassus, but from *Zion,* the Mount of God."[2] Secondly, since many reformers, particularly the Puritans, rejected formal communal worship and emphasized, instead, individual meditation, they found the psalms particularly useful as paradigms of meditation. As Calvin himself had pointed out in his *Commentary on the Book of Psalms:*

> The varied and resplendent riches which are contained in this treasury it is no easy matter to express in words. . . . I have been accustomed to call this book, I think not inappropriately, "An Anatomy of all the Parts of the Soul"; for there is not an emotion of which any one can be conscious that is not here represented as a mirror.[3]

Thus, because of their rich content, because they provided the spiritual continuity between the Hebrew Bible and the Christian Bible, and further, because their language is simple and concrete, without extravagant expression, the psalms became *the* prayerbook of the Puritan Christians— a point that is demonstrated in part by the proliferation of English psalters in the seventeenth century, confirmed by the fact that the first book published in America was *The Bay Psalm Book* of 1640, and substantiated by the famous prayer meeting of the Independent Army at Windsor in 1647, in which psalms played the preeminent role.[4]

John Milton, it is safe to assume, was nourished from infancy on psalmody, for he was born into a pious and very musical Protestant family, and, as one critic writes, "the psalms were not only patterns of meditation and devotion, but also an important part of his intellectual and theological milieu."[5] These ancient lyrics, in fact, did provide John Milton with a great well of resources for the mark of their influence upon him can be found everywhere in his poetry and prose. Not only did he translate and paraphrase nineteen different psalms; not only did he quote from these Hebrew lyrics in his prose and poetry; not only did he borrow images and poetic structures from them, but, more important, they nourished his political and religious imagination. Milton, like the Israelites, firmly stood his ground on earth, but always with eyes upturned to the splendor and majesty of the Throne of God.

Psalmodic image and idea, however, are far too ubiquitous and complex in Milton's work for comprehensive analysis in this essay; hence this study will be solely limited to the poet's three efforts at psalm translation and paraphrase. Conveniently, critical consideration of Milton and the psalms begins with the very first of his published works—the two psalms, 114 and 136, which he paraphrased in 1624 at the age of fifteen. Nothing very significant can be said about these youthful exercises, though a few observations are in order. They are, as William Riley Parker (Milton's most recent biographer) says, a "very free rendering" of the Hebrew, "more Milton than Psalmist."[6] Undoubtedly, Milton was yet too full of youthful audacity and spirit to have concluded, as the compilers of *The Bay Psalm Book* later did, that "God's Altar needs not our pollishing."[7] Not until his psalm translations twenty-nine years later do we sense so humble an attitude. These psalms of 1624 were written in Milton's last year at St. Paul's, when, Parker informs us, the young poet had begun studying Hebrew grammar and the Psalter. Parker suggests that they may have been written as school exercises or at the suggestion of his father, who, as a fairly accomplished musician and as a Puritan, certainly would have had considerable interest in English versions of the psalms that might be set to music. Milton's rendering of these two psalms is ornate and pretentious: Psalm 114 is set in nine pentameter couplets—a choice which necessarily led him into difficulty, for the original Hebrew is in unrhymed bi-cola of a basically 3+3 meter, grouped into four strophes, verses 1 and 2, 3 and 4, 5 and 6, 7 and 8. Here, the Hebrew with accentual markings of the first strophe of Psalm 114, a literal translation of the Hebrew, followed by Milton's version of the same, will demonstrate just how free, both metrically and stylistically, Milton was with his paraphrase.

בְּצֵאת יִשְׂרָאֵל מִמִּצְרָיִם
בֵּית יַעֲקֹב מֵעַם לֹעֵז
הָיְתָה יְהוּדָה לְקָדְשׁוֹ
יִשְׂרָאֵל מַמְשְׁלוֹתָיו

After Israel went out of Egypt
  The house of Jacob from a barbaric people
Judah became his sanctuary
  Israel his dominion.

When the blest seed of *Terah's* faithful Son,
After long toil their liberty had won,
And past from *Pharian* fields to *Canaan* land,
Led by the strength of the Almighty's hand,
Jehovah's wonders were in *Israel* shown
His praise and glory was in *Israel* shown.

This first attempt at psalm paraphrase is grandiloquent and undoubtedly influenced by familiarity with Sylvester, Sternhold and Hopkins, and other translators; but as William Riley Parker notes, at least one of the excesses deserves comment: the change at the opening of the Hebrew parallelism "Israel . . . the house of Jacob" to "the blest seed of Terah's faithful son" may appear to be a "mere genealogical flourish, until we reflect that Abraham's father, Terah, like the poet's grandfather Milton [a Roman Catholic], was an 'idolator,' whereas Terah's devout son, like the poet's own father [a Protestant], had the faith to obey when called to go out into a place which he was to receive for an inheritance." [8] About the reason for Milton's choosing to translate this particular psalm, there can be only speculation. Perhaps the choice was dictated merely by personal taste—and this, for a fifteen-year-old, would indicate superb discrimination, for the psalm is, from the poetic point of view, an extraordinary lyric. In structure and in language it is one of the most beautiful in the Psalter; and, perhaps, the sheer beauty of this poem is what caused Milton to return to it ten years later in 1634 to paraphrase it in Greek. But if we cannot speculate with any certainty about the reason for choosing 114, we can make the case for 136 with much less difficulty; for although it heretofore has gone completely unnoticed in Milton criticism, these two psalms are closely linked by tradition. Psalm 114 is the second in the group known as the "Egyptian Hallel," the whole cluster of psalms, 113–118, taking its name from the mention of the exodus in line 1 of 114. The Talmud considers these to be a single composition, and they are recited as a unit in the synagogue during the important festivals and during the Passover Seder Service. It is traditionally held, moreover, that these are the hymns recited by the disciples of Jesus after the Last Supper: "After reciting a hymn, they went out to the Mount of Olives" (Mark 14:26, Matt. 26:30). [9]

Psalm 136 is known in Jewish tradition as "The Great Hallel" because of the twenty-six repetitions of the refrain "For His mercy endureth forever." Its two major themes are God as Creator and God as author of history, the guide of Israel from its beginning, at the Exodus, and from that time forward. This psalm, too, is recited after the Passover meal directly following the Egyptian Hallel. Perhaps Milton did both these paraphrases for the Easter season. Nevertheless, whatever his motivation may have been, Milton's rendering of Psalm 136 has quite the same features as 114—although this time he uses tetrameter. Once again he employs ornate images, such as "golden tressed sun," and erudite epithets, such as "large-limbed Og"; and clearly the demands of his iambic tetrameter line force him into such absurdly overblown embellishments as:

The horned Moon to shine by night
Amongst her spangled sisters bright.

The direct translation of the Hebrew is simply: "The moon and stars to rule by night."

Milton next turned to English psalm paraphrase in 1648, when he rendered into meter the nine psalms, 80–88. These psalms have long been the subject of much critical speculation, some of it quite perceptive and valuable, some of it not very illuminating. In 1920, E. C. Baldwin asserted that these early works reveal Milton's slight command of Hebrew;[10] but to this Marion Studley rightly responded that while the translations may not be good evidence of his knowledge of Hebrew, they are, in fact, excellent evidence of his familiarity with the Psalters popular in England at that time.[11] And this is essentially where the scholarship remained on Psalms 80–88 for over thirty-five years until William B. Hunter picked up the idea and not only elaborated on the influence of the contemporary psalters upon Milton's translations, but also suggested that the poet may have been involved in preparations for the Revised Scottish Psalter of 1650.[12] Margaret Boddy, however, then proposed that Milton's translations of 1648 were linked to the prayer meeting of the Independent Army at Windsor, which took place at the end of April 1648.[13] But all of these studies, however suggestive they may be, miss the obvious point that psalms were read always for meditation and comfort. And this very point actually had been made long before by one of Milton's early critics—his biographer, Masson, who put it quite simply: "Their mood fitted him."[14] And it is this suggestion that is returned to in the studies by William Parker, Michael Fixler, and Carolyn Collette.[15] Collette insists that with regard to Psalms 80–88 and the later translations of 1–8, one must look at the events of Milton's life and the events of English history, in the light of the content of the psalms he chose to translate. For, as Collette correctly points out,

> such representative men as Calvin, Donne, and the members of the Westminster Assembly urged the psalms as private prayers, and . . . theologians like Beza explicated them as prefigurations of events in Christian history. We know that Milton was aware of such traditions and interpretations from evidence in his own works. It seems inevitable that in those times when external events were pressing upon his private life he should express his grief and distress in these traditional sources of comfort.[16]

What, then, were the pressing events of the time? Personally and politically, the spring of 1648 was ominous for the anti-royalist Puritan

Milton. Not only was the threat of civil war hovering over the nation, but restoration of Charles I seemed a very likely probability, and the specter of enforced intellectual and religious conformity rose up once more. By April of 1648, the Scots had raised an army of nearly forty thousand, which was to unite with the Presbyterians to invade England against the Independents. Moreover, on April 24 Parliament was convened, and this time over three hundred representatives, more than double the number of the preceding winter's session, answered the call, shifting the balance against the radicals as three critical bills were passed. The first was a bill stating that the monarchic system was not to be changed; the second was a resolution to shelve the no-address Resolution, which would have prohibited approaches to Charles I. Both of these were meant to thwart the Independents' resolve to break completely with the king. Finally, the Presbyterians managed to push through a bill calling for the "Suppression of Blasphemies and Heresies," an act which once again enforced conformity, and which once again proved to Milton that "New Presbyter is but Old Priest writ Large." Hence, in a frame of mind at once angry, fearful, and desperate, Milton very well might have turned for consolation and inspiration to a group of psalms which echoed his own emotions. These pslams, 80–88, are both personal and national; and just as inextricably bound as the individual and the nation were for the Hebrews, so were they tied together for Milton, for whom Israel was the type of England. In Milton's mind nothing could be clearer than the fact that Israel's chosenness, her true religious vocation in ethical nationhood, as a "light unto the nations," was to be resumed and fulfilled by a reformed English nation. In *Areopagitica,* England's destiny is explicitly outlined. "Why else was this nation chosen before any other, that out of her as out of Sion should be proclaimed and sounded forth the first tidings and trumpet of reformation to all Europe?" [17] And in *Of Reformation,* complaining of England's failure to meet the challenge of her role as world leader, Milton asks,

> . . . how should it come to passe that *England* (having had this *grace* and *honour* from GOD to be the first that should set up a Standard for the recovery of *lost Truth,* and blow the first *Evangelick Trumpet* to the *Nations,* holding up, as from a Hill, the new Lampe of *saving light* to all Christendome) should now be last, and most unsettl'd in the enjoyment of that *Peace,* whereof she taught the way to others . . . [18]

Because Milton made the identification between Israel and England, he naturally found a great deal of meaning in the political psalms—the one group that Anglicans like George Herbert almost completely neglected. For the Anglicans, salvation was individual, temporal history of little consequence because redemption was not bound to the spiritual world. Salvation was only to occur in the spiritual, noncorporeal world at the remote end of world history—whatever its linear course might be—though certainly that marvelous event could be experienced during the lifetime of an individual inwardly in his soul, which would thus transform his soul into a saintliness that did not need to correspond to any situation in the external world. Hence, the political psalms would have little meaning. Milton's view, however, was decidedly more Hebraic; for although he never repudiated the Christian idea of spiritual and heavenly redemption (and at different times in his life that conception took on more or less significance), he also adopted the stance of the biblical prophets who envisioned a perfected community here on earth—an End of Days which could break into history at any moment in the immediate future.

Like the Hebraic messianic conception, Milton's vision was at the same time both backward-looking and forward-looking. Here it is quite useful to refer to Gershom Scholem's descripton of the "restorative" and "utopian" elements in Jewish messianism. Scholem writes:

> The restorative forces are directed to the return and recreation of a past condition which comes to be felt as ideal. More precisely, they are directed to a condition pictured by the historical fantasy and the memory of the nation as circumstances of an ideal past. Here hope is turned backwards to the re-establishment of an original state of things and to a "life with the ancestors."[19]

For Milton, the restorative element is present as the desire to reconstitute the biblical idea of covenant-community; that is, the idea of the nation chosen by God and freely accepting the responsibility for leading the entire human race to ultimate redemption. It is the impulse toward the reestablishment of an idealized Davidic political entity in which not a particular church or specific sect demands loyalty and devotion, but rather, in which the nation itself, conceived of as a divinely consecrated community, becomes the object of love and fidelity. This, then, is the fundamental content of Milton's "restorative" vision, which, of course, was the impelling force behind his religious patriotism.

But Scholem writes that there was yet another force which operated in Jewish messianism: the utopian. The utopian element consists of forces which press forward and renew; they are nourished by a vision of the future and receive utopian inspiration. They aim at a state of things which has never yet existed. The problem of Messianism in historical Judaism appears within the field of influences of these forces. . . . Both tendencies [the restorative and the utopian] are deeply intertwined and yet at the same time of a contradictory nature; the Messianic idea crystallizes only out of the two of them together. Neither is entirely absent in the historical and ideological manifestations of Messianism. Only the proportion between them is subject to the widest fluctuations. . . . The restorative tendency, per se, even when it understands itself as such . . . is nourished to no small degree by a utopian impulse which now appears as projection upon the past instead of projection on the future.[20]

Moreover, Scholem explains that this utopianism itself falls into two categories: on the one hand, it is a "radical form of the vision of a new content which is to be realized in the future"[21] but which is really a restoration of the lost ideal past; on the other hand, however, there are some new elements which slip into the restorative type of utopianism, which have nothing to do with bringing back past content and which arise out of a vision of an entirely new order. "The completely new order has elements of the completely old, but even this old order does not consist of the actual past; rather, it is a past transformed and transfigured in a dream brightened by the rays of utopianism."[22] Hence, Scholem concludes,

the dialectically linked tension between the utopian and restorative factors provides us also with deep tensions in the form of Messianism crystallized in rabbinic Judaism, to say nothing of the interiorization of these impulses in Jewish mysticism.[23]

Finally, with regard to the tension of these two forces, Scholem points out that the stronger the loss of historical reality, that is, the less the political or actual restoration of the Davidic kingdom became possible (such as during the destruction of the Second Temple, or when the reality of exile became clear), the more intense "the consciousness of the cryptic character and mystery of the Messianic message" became—the more elaborate the content of the eschatological vision.[24] This analysis of the dialectic of Jewish messianism is a very useful analogue for the understanding of Milton's career and his Messianic projections. Though both the restorative and utopian elements are present in him, it seems apparent that when the political climate favored the Cause, Milton's messianic vision was more restorative; when the Cause seemed, and then was, lost, he was more utopian and his visions were more colored by apocalyptic mysticism. Hence, in the period roughly between 1641 and 1656 Milton's messianism was, using Scholem's terms, more restorative, for then political reform seemed very possible. After the Restoration it became more and more utopian.

One further point that must be made here is that it is the realm of conservative forces in Judaism that prevents us from completely identifying Milton with the ancient Hebrews and that colors Milton's thinking with regard to Judaism and Jews in general. As Gershom Scholem defines it,

> the conservative forces are directed toward the preservation of that which exists and which, in the historical environment of Judaism, was always in danger. . . . They have established themselves most effectively in the world of *Halakhah*, in the construction and continuing preservation and development of religious law.[25]

This, of course, is precisely the area that Milton vehemently rejects. We need only remember his vivid but conventional remarks on "Jewish beggary"[26] in *Of Reformation* (the very treatise in which he sees England as a type of Israel), or his argument against ceremonial law in *Reason of Church Government*, in which he regards the law as "the old pompe and glory of the flesh,"[27] to remind ourselves that Milton was no Judeophile. Milton's views regarding the Hebrew Bible and the Jewish people were both inconsistent and complex. On the one hand, he could write about Jewish ceremonial law:

> O but the innocence of these ceremonies! O rather the sottish absurdity of this excuse! What could be more innocent than the washing of a cup, a glasse, or hands before meat, and that under the Law when so many washings were commanded, and by long tradition, yet our Saviour detested their customes, though never so seeming harmlesse, and charges them severely that they had transgrest the Commandments of God by their traditions and worshipt him in vain.[28]

And he could speak in *Christian Doctrine* of the abrogation of the Mosaic Law: "On the introduction of the gospel, or new covenant through faith in Christ, the whole preceding covenant, in other words the entire Mosaic law was abolished." And after offering seven reasons for the abolition of the law he adds:

To these considerations we may add, that the law which not only cannot justify, but is the source of trouble and subversion to believers; which even tempts God if we endeavor to perform its requisitions; which has no promise attached to it, or, to speak more properly, which takes away and frustrates all promises, whether of inheritance, or adoption, or grace, or of the Spirit itself; nay, which even subjects us to a curse; must necessarily have been abolished.[29]

Yet he could, on the other hand, invoke the Mosaic Law in his *Doctrine and Discipline of Divorce:*

This therefore shall be the task and period of this discourse to prove, first, that other reasons of divorse besides adultery were by the *law of Moses* [Deut. XXIV] and are yet to be allowed by the Christian magistrate as a piece of justice, and that the words of Christ are not hereby contraried.[30] [italics added]

And in *Of Reformation* and *Areopagitica,* he summons the image of the nation Israel as a type of the nation England. Yet when the question of the readmission of the Jews into England arose in the 1650s, Milton's voice was not to be heard. Later, in *Christian Doctrine,* he writes that the dispersion of the Jews throughout the world proves the existence of God because He had "forewarned them [that it] would happen on account of their sins." And, as Samuel Stollman points out, in the *Doctrine and Discipline of Divorce* Milton makes a similar reference to the contemporary Jews: "and surely such a nation seems not to be under the illuminating guidance of God's Law, but under the horrible doom rather of such as despise the Gospel . . ."[31]

Milton's ambivalence on the subject of the authority of the Hebrew Bible and his silence on the subject of the readmission of the Jews is, as Samuel Stollman suggests, a distinction between Hebrew and Jew. "Milton," he says, "dichotomizes the Old Testament into 'Judaism and Hebraism'."[32] Don M. Wolfe concludes that:

Milton's failure to speak for the Jews sprang from a tolerationist psyche unique among his contemporaries, informed by a vast learning, untouched by superstition, influenced by a reluctance yet to be unravelled. Though like his fellows Milton separated the Jew Jesus from the Christian Jesus, he never fell into the habit of separating as two species the Jew of the Bible from the Jews of his own time. He was an Old Testament Christian, more at home with the fire of the prophets than with the revolutionary love of the New Testament. He could not portray the meek and loving

Christ in *Paradise Regained* even as the Puritans could not glean their battle cries from the Gospels. But even a prolonged preoccupation with Old Testament Judaism did not induce Milton to take his stand with Richard Overton and Roger Williams for liberty of Jewish conscience.[33]

And thus, it is not surprising that during the question of the readmission of the Jews into England in the 1650s, Milton's voice was not heard. Nevertheless, in the 1640s, although the political situation in England was certainly ominous, Milton's restorative vision was active. Whereas for the moment it looked more than hopeful for the Royalists, there still was the outside possibility of an Independent counterattack, particularly since the Puritans were convinced that God was on their side. Thus, for the depressed Milton, gloom was sometimes edged with the light of trust; and so the troubled poet turned, in his time of sorrow, to the words of his ancient counterparts, the poets of Israel who, also disconsolate and fearful of enemy attacks, turned their voices to the God in whom they trusted and who they knew would ultimately restore them to favor. The political situations and the human emotions described in Psalms 80–88 were, as both Parker and Collette suggest, extraordinarily analogous to Milton's own position in the spring of 1648; hence there need be no more explanation of why he rendered these psalms into English at this time in his life other than Masson's "their mood fitted him."

As Milton himself tells us, these psalms are cast in common meter, and "wherein all but what is in a different character are the very words of the text, translated from the original." That Milton referred to the Hebrew text as well as the available Psalters is confirmed by his marginal transliterations of a number of difficult Hebrew words. These marginal notes, moreover, show him to have considerable skill in Hebrew, rather than "slight" as Baldwin suggests: for if we look at the very first of the transliterations, we see that the Hebrew עוֹרְרָה (Milton's rendering is the Sephardic "gnorera") certainly does carry the connotation of awakening—precisely as Milton has translated it. In fact, the note to verse 3 in the Jewish Publication Society edition of Psalms, acknowledging the difficulty of this very word, reads *"stir up,* lit. 'arouse, awaken' as though God's might had been dormant." [34] Milton has translated the line "Awaken thy strength, come, and *be seen."* In verse 4, Milton transliterates עָשַׁנְתָּ (gnashanta) and renders the line "Thy smoking wrath *and angry brow."* Once again, the Jewish Publication Society edition affirms Milton's concern for the precise translation. (The JPS note reads, *"be angry,* lit. 'smoke' as in lxxiv.1.") [35] We can account for extreme textual deviations quite simply by recognizing that the necessities of meter and rhyme forced Milton to embellish his text; but, in turn, embellishment frequently afforded him the opportunity to insert contemporary references and personal feelings.

Psalm 80 is Israel's lament for her devastation and prayer that God will deliver her from her enemies. The time seems to be the last days of the northern kingdom of Judea, just before the captivity; the mood is remarkably analogous to Milton's in 1648, and doubtless he saw in this psalm of Israel's peril an equivalent to the perils facing England—particularly those which threatened the Independent reformers. In fact, the parallel between the two situations is very sharply emphasized by Milton's interpolation in verse 6 (verse 7 of the JPS edition) of his paraphrase. Here Milton freely translates:

> A strife thou mak'st us *and a prey*
> To every neighbor foe
> Among themselves they *laugh, they *play,
> And *flouts at us they throw
> .   .   .

In Hebrew, the phrase "and a prey" does not appear; and the starred words "laugh," "play," and "flouts" are extrapolations (for the demands of meter) from the Hebrew יִלְעֲגוּ (jilgnagu). With regard to these lines, William Riley Parker suggests that Milton "can hardly avoid thinking of his personal unhappiness." But Parker is using this as evidence for his theory that at the same time Milton was writing *Samson Agonistes.* He says, "the spirit of *Samson Agonistes* is everywhere in these psalms" (as the spirit of the psalms is everywhere in *Samson Agonistes*).[36] Of course, Parker is correct in seeing the influence of psalms on *Samson,* though not especially these psalms. After all, Milton had been reading psalms all his life (translating them as early as his fifteenth year), and undoubtedly he went on doing so for the rest of his life; and just as psalms are to be found in his very earliest work, there is surely no reason to believe that they would not be present in his last. But the group 80–88, and particularly 80, does not seem to be linked to *Samson.* Rather, it appears much closer in content to the political prose tract *Of Reformation,* which was published in 1641. In this work, Milton renders the poetry of verses 7–14 of Psalm 80 into prose:

> One Tri-personall GODHEAD! Looke upon this thy poore and almost spent, and expiring *Church,* leave her not thus a *prey* to these importu-

nate *wolves* that wait and think long till they devour thy tender *Flock* these wild Boars that have broke into *thy Vineyard,* and left the print of their polluting hoofs on the Soules of thy Servants. [italics added]

The Psalm translation reads:

   7. Cause thou thy face on us to shine
      And then we shall be safe
      A Vine from Egypt thou has brought

    .   .   .   .

12. Why hast thou laid her Hedges low
      And broken down her Fence,
    That all may pluck her, as they go
      With rudest violence?
    The *tusked* Boar out of the wood
      Upturns it by the roots,
    Wild Beasts there browse, and make their food
      Her Grapes and tender shoots . . .

This is not a reflection of Samsonian inward personal unhappiness, as Parker would have it, but rather the unhappy voice of the prophet speaking for the nation. Moreover, as Carolyn Collette explains, Theodore Beza, whose psalm commentaries were "certainly orthodox by seventeenth century Protestant standards," and whom we know Milton regarded as authoritative, pointed out the analogy between the Protestant Church and Israel in Psalms 80, 82, 83, and 85. Beza regarded them as prophetic statements of "the persecutions the Reformation would have to face." [37]

Collette, however, goes on to say that Beza interpreted Psalms 81, 84, 86, 87, and 88 as "the personal lamentations of godly men caught in the turmoil of such persecutions." She concludes that:

> while we will never know what Milton's opinions about Beza's interpretations were in 1648, it seems a reasonable conclusion from his mention of Beza in his prose during the 1640's that he knew Beza's work and his theological position and had not rejected them. [38]

Collette then proceeds to illustrate the many similarities between Beza's interpretations and Milton's political writings. Yet it is hard to believe that Milton regarded Psalm 81 as a "personal" lamentation. Certainly he saw that this is a composite psalm—verses 1–8 are praise (which Jewish tradition has always associated with the Harvest Festival because of the reference to the blowing of the ram's horn at the new moon), and 9–17 are divine oracles in which God reminds Israel that he brought them out of Egypt, freed them from bondage and fed them in the wilderness, and commanded them not to worship strange gods; but the people did not heed his words and so he "let them go" and punished them. If now they will only obey, he will "subdue their enemies" and cause them to prosper—"with honey out of a rock would I satisfy thee." Undoubtedly, Milton regarded this as a most timely text, as once more God refuses to rescue his people, England, because they do not obey God's word. Again, this is not a personal lamentation, but a prophetic message about national political redemption. It is Milton in the "restorative" cast of mind.

Psalm 82 also is applicable to the political situation of the spring of 1648. It is, says Parker, "a vision of divine judgment against the high spiritual powers whose rule 'in darkness' is responsible for the wickedness of the world." This psalm translation is especially interesting because of the additions Milton makes to the original. He expands the Hebrew parallel bi-colon "God standeth in the congregation of the mighty; He judgeth among the gods." to:

> God in the great assembly stands
> *Of kings and lordly states*
> Among the gods on both his hands
> He judges and debates.

This interpolation seems an obvious reference to Milton's contemporary political scene. What could Milton have meant other than that which Carolyn Collette suggests: "Charles cannot act willfully without expecting to be judged"? Moreover, Collette points out that "the additions to the second verse seem to refer to Charles's unrestrained use of his prerogatives and indulgence of his favorites who were the first target of the Protestant reformers": [39]

> How long will ye pervert the right
> With judgment false and wrong
> Favoring the wicked *by your might,*
> *Who thence grow bold and strong?*

Psalm 83 is yet another political psalm—a lament of the besieged community. It describes the nation as surrounded by enemies bent on her annihilation; and in this Milton had little need to embellish the ancient complaint—the meaning is patently clear.

> For lo thy *furious* foes *now* swell
>   And storm outrageously,
> And they that hate thee *proud and fell*
>   Exalt their heads full high
> Against thy people they contrive
>   Their Plots and Counsels deep,
> Them to ensnare they chiefly strive
>   Whom thou dost hide and keep.

Psalm 84, however, moves out of the purely political realm to the personal—but it is a joyous song, not a lament. Like Psalm 81, the superscription says that it is to be sung according to the Gittith (which is believed by some to be a popular melody); but unlike Psalm 81, it is not broken in the middle by God's admonishing words and reminder of history. Instead, Psalm 84 is an unbroken, intense, and beautiful paean to joy in God's sanctuary: "How lovely are Thy dwellings fair!" It records the psalmist's intense yearning for the communion with God that he has experienced in the sanctuary. Surely in this inspired lyric Milton could find consolation, inspiration, and new hope:

> No good from them shall be withheld
>   Whose ways are just and right.

It is this very message that we find once more at the conclusion of the Sabbath hymn in Book VII of *Paradise Lost* (ll. 631–32)—a passage taken directly from Psalm 92.

With Psalm 85 we return again to the political, for this is a prayer of the returned captives of Babylon that the divine anger, which had permitted the national disaster of exile and devastation, will turn again to favor, so that the people can once more face the future with optimism and trust. Here, Milton makes an interesting addition to the last verse:

> Before him Righteousness shall go
>   *His Royal Harbinger,*
> Then will he come, and not be slow,
>   His footsteps cannot err.[40]

In this and Psalm 83, it was easy for Milton to see prefigurations of the seventeenth-century English political scene; and expanding on Beza's commentary that the psalm refers not to the Babylonian captivity but

> to the beginning of the kingdom of David, so that by the name of captivitie, not the carrying away of them from their habitation is to be understood, but the miserable servitude of the people under the Palestines which had overcome them after the death of Saul . . .[41]

Carolyn Collette suggests that in terms of types and symbols,

> it is but a short step to an interpretation of [Psalms 83 and 85] in light of the events of 1648. In such an interpretation Cromwell becomes the fulfillment of the type of David. Having just come to power, he is threatened by dangerous enemies. If the Presbyterians and Royalists succeed in restoring a king to the throne, the Independents will be returned to servitude.[42]

But, in fact, in 1648 it may not have been Cromwell at all whom Milton had in mind. It very possibly may have been Lord Fairfax whom he saw as the much-needed spiritual and political leader; perhaps the virtuous Fairfax was to be Righteousness, the *Royal Harbinger* of peace and salvation. In the prophetic words of Milton's translation of Psalm 85:

> Mercy and Truth *that long were missed*
> > Now *joyfully* are met;
> *Sweet* Peace and Righteousness have kissed
> > *And hand and hand are set.*

In his sonnet to Fairfax, written in 1648, the same year in which he translated Psalm 85, Milton says:

> O yet a nobler task awaits thy hand;
> > For what can War, but endless war still breed,
> > Till Truth and Right from Violence be freed.

As Parker wistfully puts it, "Milton's sonnet was one which might have changed the history of England, and of the world—had its plea been heeded, had Fairfax accepted the role of leadership that Cromwell finally played." [43]

Psalm 86 once more is a personal cry for help. A pastiche of quotations from the Psalter and other parts of the Bible, it is a powerful appeal to God in time of trouble; and undoubtedly Milton found comfort and relief in the process of translation:

Thy *gracious* ear, O Lord, incline
O hear me, *I thee pray*
For I am poor, and almost pine
With need *and sad decay.* . . .

I in the day of my distress
Will call on thee *for aid;*
For thou wilt *grant* me *free access*
And answer, *what I pray'd.*

The brief Psalm 87 is a song of Zion as the center of the world; and if Zion was the type of England, the prophetic, patriotic meaning is clear. That Milton was thinking of England is suggested by his expansion of verses 6 and 7. The biblical verses read:

The Lord shall count in the registers of the peoples:
"This one was born there." Selah.
And whether they sing or dance
All my springs are in thee.

Here is Milton's rendering:

The Lord shall write it in a Scroll
That ne'er shall be outworn
When he the Nations doth enroll
That this man there was born.

Both they who sing and they who dance
With Sacred Songs are there,
In thee *fresh brooks and soft streams glance,*
And all my fountains *clear.*

Milton's translation of the last line quite clearly derives from his understanding of the original, for in the Hebrew the word מַעְיָן means "fountain" or "source"; but the addition of "fresh brooks and soft streams," admittedly interpolated for metrical purposes, nevertheless evokes a touching picture of the English countryside.

The last of this group of translations, Psalm 88, is the most personal of the entire group and it must have had profound significance for Milton. It is a dark and gloomy psalm which describes the bitterness of the poet. And though there are many other psalms of personal lament and suffering, this one is *sui generis* in that at no point is there a touch of light or an edge of hope. It is an extraordinarily hopeless *cri du coeur*, accented by numerous references to the dark nether world; and, as Parker remarks, since the psalmist expresses a fear of "lifelong severance from human intercourse as the result of some incurable affliction,"[44] Milton must have felt the personal significance of this poem, for, by the spring of 1648, his health was quite poor and he was gradually going blind. He had put aside his poetry for political prose, but his words were largely ignored; thus, surely he must have felt estranged from society and perhaps cast out by God himself. One cannot avoid coming to the same conclusion as Parker that

> it was some comfort perhaps, for a man in such personal misery, to realize that another poet walked through the same shadows. It was some comfort, for a man who saw in his country's troubles the rebuke of an angry God, to reflect that it had happened before. In making his translations he allowed himself but little freedom, for the original was more pertinent than a paraphrase.[45]

What words could express more precisely Milton's mood than these of the afflicted ancient psalmist:

> Lord God that dost me save and keep
>   All day to thee I cry;
> And all night long before thee *weep*
>   Before thee prostrate lie. . . .

> Reck'n'd I am with them that pass
>   Down to the dismal pit;
> I am a man,* but weak alas
>   And for that name unfit. . . .

> Thou in the lowest pit *profound*
>   Hast set me *all forlorn*
> Where thickest darkness *hovers round,*
>   In horrid deeps to *mourn.* . . .

> Through sorrow and affliction great
>   Mine eye grows dim and dead,

Lord all the day I thee entreat
   My hands to thee I spread. . . .

Why wilt thou Lord my soul forsake,
   And hide thy face from me,
That am already bruis'd, and shake
   With terror sent from thee. . . .

Lover and friend thou hast remov'd
   And sever'd from me far.
They *fly me now* whom I have lov'd
   And as in darkness are.

These nine psalm translations beg to be read as a chiaroscuro of Milton's personal and political situation as against his religious faith. To fault these lyrics for their lack of fidelity to the original or for metrical and stylistic mediocrity is to ignore their personal value to the poet. "Their mood fitted him"—and that, for the moment, was enough. Read as spiritual exercises in solace, their poetic faults gradually diminish as the voice of human outrage swells to an existential cry.

In 1653 Milton returned to psalm translation, and we may conjecture that once more he turned to it for comfort and hope. This time he chose to translate Psalms 1–8, a group which has a slightly different spirit from those of the earlier translations. Psalms 80–88 give voice to the spokesman for the suffering nation in times of dire political circumstances; Psalms 1–8 are, for the most part, far more personal prayers of lament.

It is true, of course, that in 1653 the political situation was not yet at rest; although Charles I had been beheaded in 1649, the army now held political power, with Cromwell at its head moving toward dictatorship. On April 20, 1653 Cromwell dissolved the ostensibly representative Rump Parliament, and on July 4 he replaced it with the Barebones Parliament of only 139 persons chosen by the Lord-General. Moreover, the Anglo-Dutch War, which had erupted in the summer of 1652, continued to rumble. Although Milton had been retained by the Barebones Parliament as Secretary for Foreign Languages, he could hardly have been pleased by these turns of events. After all, in *The First Defense of the English People,* which he had written in 1651 as a reply to Salmasius (the French scholar who had been commissioned by the exiled Charles II to attack those who were responsible for Charles I's beheading), Milton made it quite clear that he had supported representative government over monarchy because it promised deliverance from tyranny. Indeed, that entire work ended, not with a final attack on Salmasius, but with words of warning to the English people:

> After so glorious a deed, you ought to think, you ought to do, nothing that is so mean and petty, nothing but what is great and sublime. To attain such praise there is only one way: as you have subdued your enemies in the field, so shall you prove that unarmed and surrounded by peace you of all mankind have highest courage to subdue what conquers other nations of men—faction, avarice, the temptations of wealth and the corruptions that wait upon prosperity.[46]

These words of caution reverberate in the 1652 sonnet to the heroic Cromwell, when Milton warns him:

> . . . yet much remains
> To conquer still; peace hath her victories
> No less renown'd than war, new foes arise
> Threat'ning to bind our souls with secular chains.

Yet it probably was not these events alone which cast Milton into profound despair in the summer of 1653. More likely it was the staggering combination of private tragedies and personal attacks; by this time Milton had become totally blind; in May of 1652 his wife died after childbirth; in June 1652 his infant son died; and waiting patiently all this time for a reply from Salmasius to the *Defense,* he found himself the object of numerous attacks from others—especially disturbing was the vicious, abusive *Regii Sanguinis Clamor ad Coelum adversus,* attributed to Alexander More, but actually written by Dr. Peter du Moulin. In this miserable tirade, Parker writes, the author calls Milton a

> starving grammarian with a venal pen—one who had been expelled from Cambridge for profligacy, had fled to Italy in disgrace, and had returned to England as a fomentor of rebellion and licence. . . . The author of the infamous *Defensio* was an ignoble cur, a blotch, an ulcer, an inexecrable villain, a wretch more vile than Cromwell, a pest more despicable than a louse.[47]

To this vicious diatribe, Milton replied with a vigorous and equally abusive counterattack, *The Second Defense of the English People,* which appeared in May 1654. Milton was now involved in a pamphlet war.

Under the agonizing pressures of such terrible circumstances, is it so surprising that Milton would once more turn to the Psalms? During the week of August 8–14, he translated Psalms 2–8 at the rate of almost one a day. Only Thursday, August 11, is omitted and, as Parker points out, Psalm 1 had been translated earlier in 1653.

Of this group of psalms, only the second is national or political, for it describes the vain actions of nations who plot against God's anointed. Psalm 1, however, is as fitting a prologue for this cluster of psalms, as it is for the entire Psalter. A didactic, ethical psalm, it describes the nature of, and happy consequences for, the man who will truly understand the message of the Psalter—the pious, righteous man. And to this godly man it contrasts the behavior and fate of the wicked or ungodly. The entire message is summed up in Milton's couplet rendering of verse 6:

> For the Lord knows th' upright way of the just,
> And the way of bad men to ruin must.

Although Psalm 2 refers to the national sphere, it nevertheless can be regarded as an extension of the first psalm, for if the first is a delineation of the two paths for individuals, the second is a delineation of the two paths for nations. It is the content of Psalm 1 extended and applied to the realm of the community. The deep meaning of this psalm for Milton becomes obvious when we realize that it appears in his work from the earliest to the latest. In 1626, in *In Quintum Novembris,* he writes:

> Meanwhile the Lord, who turns the heavens in their wide revolutions and hurls the lightning from his skyey citadel, laugh at the vain undertakings of the degenerate mob and is willing to take upon himself the defence of his peoples' cause.

Milton's 1653 translation of verses 4 and 5 of Psalm 2, from which this derives, is:

> . . . he who in Heaven doth dwell,
> Shall laugh, the Lord shall scoff them, then severe
> Speak to them in his wrath, and in his fell
> And fierce ire trouble them;

Reference to this psalm, however, appears at least nine times: in Books I, l. 10; II, 173, 191; V, 602–605, 718, 736, 846, 886; VIII, 77; XII, 52 of *Paradise Lost;* Book II, l. 44 of *Paradise Regained,* and Book I, chap. V of *Christian Doctrine.*[48] It should be noted, however, that some of these references are not to verses 4 and 5, but rather to the typologically charged verses 7 and 8, which Milton translates as

> ... but I, saith hee,
> Anointed have my King (though ye rebel)
> On Sion my holi' hill. A firm decree
>   I will declare; the Lord to me hath said,
>   Thou are my Son. I have begotten thee
> This day; ....

This is the source of the passage in Book V of *Paradise Lost* in which the War in Heaven is set in motion with a dramatization of the revelation of Christ to the Angels:

> This day I have begot whom I declare
> My only Son, and on this holy Hill
> Him have anointed. . . . [603–605]

And this is the critical passage for Milton's statement in *Christian Doctrine* regarding the generation of the Son. He writes at the beginning of chapter V:

> It is evident upon a careful comparison and examination of all these passages, and particularly from the whole of the second Psalm, that however the generation of the Son may have taken place, it arose from no natural necessity, as is generally contended, but was no less owing to the decree and will of the Father than his priesthood or kingly power, or his resuscitation from the dead.

However doctrinally significant verses 6 and 7 were for Milton in *Paradise Lost* and *Christian Doctrine,* in 1653 it undoubtedly was the first few verses which attracted him.

> Why do the Gentiles tumult, and the Nations
>   Muse a vain thing, the Kings of th'earth upstand
>   With power, and Princes in their Congregations
> Lay deep their plots together through each Land,
>   Against the Lord and his Messiah dear?
>   Let us break off, say they, by strength of hand
> Their bonds, and cast from us, no more to wear,
>   Their twisted cords: ....

Is it not possible that Milton read and translated these words and reflected upon the hostile behavior of the foreign nations to England?

But with Psalm 3 an entirely different mood is set, for this psalm initiates a group of five which are the distinctly private prayers of a distressed soul, besieged by illness and vindictive enemies. Surely, Milton's emotions were aroused when he translated:

> Lord, how many are my foes!
>   How many those
> That in arms against me rise!
>   Many are they
>   That of my life distrustfully thus say,
>   "No help for him in God there lies."

In Psalm 4, he pleads:

> Answer me when I call,
> God of my righteousness;
> In straits and in distress
> Thou didst me disenthrall
> And set at large; now spare,
>   Now pity me, and hear my earnest pray'r.

Yet despite the severity of the circumstances described, both psalms end on a note of trust and hope. The last verse of Psalm 4, sometimes called "An Evening Prayer in Relief," says:

> In peace at once will I
> Both lay me down and sleep,
> For thou alone dost keep
> Me safe where'er I lie:
> As in a rocky Cell
>   Thou Lord alone in safety mak'st me dwell.

Psalm 5 is sometimes referred to as a "Morning Prayer" because of verse 4, which Milton translates as follows:

> Jehovah thou my early voice
>   Shalt in the morning hear,
> I' th' morning I to thee with choice
> Will rank my Prayers, and watch till thou appear.

This psalm, however, echoes 3 and 4 in circumstances: once again the speaker is the object of evil actions and words. And in this psalm Milton could see the connection and the appropriateness of verses 9 and 10 to his own situation in the pamphlet war:

> For in his falt'ring mouth unstable
>> No word is firm or sooth:
> Their inside troubles miserable:
> And open grave their throat, their tongue they smooth.
>> God, find them guilty, let them fall
>>> By their own counsels quell'd;
>> Push them in their rebellions all
> Still on; for against thee they have rebell'd.

Psalm 6 is perhaps the most personal of the whole group. It is the poignant prayer of a tormented man whose body is afflicted and whose mind is tortured by the words of ill-wishers:

> Lord in thine anger do not reprehend me,
>> Nor in thy hot displeasure me correct;
> Pity me, Lord, for I am much deject,
>> Am very weak and faint; . . . .
> Wearied I am with sighing out my days,
>> Nightly my Couch I make a kind of Sea;
> My Bed I water with my tears; mine Eye
>> Through grief consumes, is waxen old and dark.

With his Hebrew counterpart, Milton, too, turns his heart with trust to God first for relief and not the least for vindication.

>> The Lord hath heard, the Lord hath heard my pray'r
> My supplication with acceptance fair
>> The Lord will own, and have me in his keeping.
> Mine enemies shall all be blank and dash't
>> With much confusion; then grow red with shame;
> They shall return in haste the way they came
>> And in a moment shall be quite abash't.

With regard to the next psalm in the sequence, William Riley Parker perceptively suggests that "thinking of how his character had been defamed by More in the *Clamor*, Milton might have found relief in translating Psalm 7." [49] Parker's point is extremely well taken once one notes that this psalm is rather unique insofar as it singles out one particular individual as the enemy. But oddly, Parker then says that Milton "dictated an explanatory note 'Upon the words of Chush the Benjamite against him.' " This remark is a bit misleading, for what Milton did was merely to include a translation of the actual words of the superscription to the psalm—precisely as he did for Psalm 3, which begins: *"When he fled from Absalom."* Of course, the superscription may have held special significance for Milton, who undoubtedly recalled the implied historical context: Cush, of the tribe of Benjamin, which was Saul's tribe, probably took an active part in Saul's jealous pursuit of David by defaming him. Hence, this psalm, more than any of the others, implies the tragedy of personal enmity within the community caused by political and religious contention. In Psalm 7 the poet prays for God to judge this malevolent enemy and to punish him accordingly; but he suggests that this evil slanderer will bring about his own ruin:

He digg'd a pit, and delv'd it deep,
And fell into the pit he made;
His mischief that due course doth keep,
Turns on his head, and his ill trade
Of violence will undelay'd
Fall on his crown with ruin steep.

Psalm 8 rings a new sound. Gone are the fervent pleas for deliverance from affliction and slanderous enemies; instead, the psalmist sings a hymn to the majesty of God and his manifestation in the grandeur of heaven, and he reflects on the paradoxical nature of man:

When I behold thy Heavens, thy Fingers' art,
     The Moon and Stars which thou so bright hast set
In the pure firmament, then saith my heart,
     O what is man that thou rememb'rest yet,
And think'st upon him? or of man begot
     That thou him visit'st and of him art found?
Scarce to be less than Gods, thou mad'st his lot,
     With honor and with state thou hast him crown'd.

With this psalm, Milton concluded his translations. But quite different from the dark and pessimistic Psalm 88 with which the first group of translations ended, this sublime praise of God's majesty, man's dignity, and nature's grandeur ends with an harmonic resonance of joy and humanity. It is suggestive to note that much of this psalm echoes the first chapter of Genesis. Surely, Milton heard these reverberations, for this very psalm is alluded to in Book VII (620–28) of *Paradise Lost* in the Angelic hymn to God's six days' work, and then immediately following in Book VIII (15–38) in Adam's question to Raphael concerning the importance of "this Earth, a spot, a grain, an Atom" compared with the grand and elaborate universe.

Although Milton was motivated by very similar emotional needs in his translations of 1648 and 1653, there are some interesting differences between the two groups which should be mentioned. The most obvious difference is that Psalms 80–88 are "done in meter," whereas 1–8 are "done into verse." Each psalm of the 1648 group uses common meter of eights and sixes, although instead of rhyming only the second and fourth lines, Milton rhymes the first and third as well. Each psalm of the 1653 group is set in a special metrical form of its own. Milton only specifies the meter for Psalm 2—*Terzetti*—but E. C. Baldwin has analyzed prosodically the remaining seven. He tells us that:

> Ps. 1 is in heroic couplets; Ps. 2 is in "terzette" or Italian tercets; 3 is in a peculiar six-line stanza or iambic quatrains and trimeters; 4 a different six-line stanza; 5 a four-line stanza of iambic tetrameter, trimeter, and pentameter; 6 an iambic pentameter quatrain; 7, a six-line stanza of iambic tetrameter riming ababba; 8, an eight-line stanza riming ababcdcd.[50]

Moreover, in the superscription to the 1648 psalm, Milton specifies that he is translating from the original. In these translations, he also italicizes the English words for which there are no Hebrew equivalents, and he gives marginal transliterations for problematic Hebrew words. For the 1653 group, he gives no written indication of direct translation. Yet the striking fact here is that the very group which Milton tells us is a direct translation from the original, is far less faithful to the Hebrew than the other. The explanation for this is not far to seek; the limitations and demands of common meter forced Milton into all kinds of ornamentation and embellishment; but when he was free to choose from among a variety of metrical schemata he could avoid rhetorical flourish. But faithful to the *sense* of the original as these may be, we must concur with Merritt Hughes, who finds that Psalms 1–8 still fail "to give the effect of their models."[51] Hughes observes that "already Milton was laying the stress on 'the sense variously drawn out from one verse into another' as he was to do in *Paradise Lost*."[52]

For all the technical differences between the psalm translations of 1648 and 1653, which superficially can be explained as different stylistic experiments, the deeper significance of the two sets of translations is most fully appreciated in the light of three considerations: first, the centrality of psalms in seventeenth-century Protestant worship; second, the political and personal circumstances of Milton's life in 1648 and 1653; and third, the content of the psalms Milton chose to translate—both in their original Hebrew meaning and in the later Christian context. Awareness of the interrelationship of all three of these points weakens any theory that Milton had intended to versify the entire Book of Psalms but for some unknown reason abandoned the project, obviates the notion that he was merely engaging in stylistic exercise, and sharply underscores the fact that these psalm translations were profoundly meaningful to the great English poet and patriot.

NOTES

1. A. F. Kirkpatrick, ed., *The Book of Psalms* (Cambridge, 1902), pp. 838–40.
2. Quoted in Perry Miller, *The Puritans* (New York, 1963), p. 78.
3. John Calvin, *Commentary on the Book of Psalms,* trans. James Anderson (Michigan, 1949), 1: xxxvi.
4. Margaret Boddy, "Milton's Translations of the Psalms: 80–88," *Modern Philology* 64, no. 1 (1966) : 3.
5. Carolyn Collette, "Milton's Psalm Translations: Petition and Praise," *English Literary Renaissance,* 196, 247.
6. William Riley Parker, *Milton: A Biography* (Oxford, 1968), 1:19.
7. Miller, p. 77.
8. Parker, p. 19.
9. *The Bible Reader: An Interfaith Interpretation,* ed. Walter M. Abbott, S. J., et al. (New York and London, 1969), pp. 369, 376.
10. E. C. Baldwin, "Milton and the Psalms," *Modern Philology,* 17 (1920) : 457–63.
11. Marion Studley, "Milton and His Paraphrases of the Psalms," *Philosophical Quarterly* 4 (1925) : 364–72.
12. William B. Hunter, "Milton Translates the Psalms," *Philosophical Quarterly,* 40 (1961) : 485–94.
13. Boddy, p. 3.
14. David Masson, *Life of Milton* (London, 1859).
15. Michael Fixler, *Milton and the Kingdoms of God* (London, 1964).
16. Collette, p. 259.
17. *John Milton: Complete Poems and Major Prose,* ed. Merritt Hughes (New York, 1957), p. 743 (hereafter cited as Hughes).
18. *Complete Prose Works of John Milton,* ed. Don Wolfe et al. (New York, 1959), I:525 (hereafter cited as YP).
19. Gershom Scholem, *The Messianic Idea in Judaism* (New York, 1972), p. 3.
20. Scholem, pp. 3–4.
21. Ibid.
22. Ibid.
23. Ibid.
24. Ibid., p. 7.
25. Ibid., p. 3.
26. YP, 1:520.
27. Ibid., p. 766.
28. Ibid., p. 829.
29. Hughes, p. 1009.
30. Ibid., p. 704.
31. YP, 2:290.
32. Samuel Stollman, "Milton's Dichotomy of 'Judaism' and 'Hebraism'," *PMLA* 89 (January, 1974) : 108.

33. Don M. Wolfe, "Limits of Miltonic Toleration," *Journal of English and Germanic Philology*, 60 (1961): 846.
34. *The Book of Psalms,* ed. A. Cohen (London, 1945), p. 263. The Authorized Version translates it as "stir up thy strength."
35. Ibid., p. 264. The Authorized Version reads, "O Lord God of hosts, how long wilt thou be angry against the prayer of thy people?"
36. Parker, 1:322.
37. Collette, p. 249.
38. Ibid., p. 250.
39 Ibid., p. 252.
40. Here the word "royal" means that Righteousness will herald the coming of Christ the King. Milton's allusion to Psalm 85 in *On Time* indicates that at this time he read these psalmodic lines in a Messianic context.
41. Collette, p. 253.
42. Ibid.
43. Parker, p. 336.
44. Ibid., p. 324.
45. Ibid.
46. YP, 2:552.
47. Parker, p. 422.
48. Hughes, p. 933.
49. Parker, p. 430.
50. Baldwin, p. 47.
51. Hughes, p. 161.
52. Ibid.

THE THEORY AND PRACTICE OF GERMAN-JEWISH EMANCIPATION

By

STEPHEN M. POPPEL

Theories about the nature of Jewish emancipation can be divided generally into two groups—those that stress the decisive influence of developments in the context surrounding the Jewish community, and those that emphasize the significance of undertakings within the Jewish community itself.

To the student of general European history, the theory of the interdependence of Jewish emancipation and general progress that is most familiar is that of Marx, as articulated in his essay "On the Jewish Question." If one overlooks the specifically anti-Jewish animus and polemical excess of this essay, then what remains is a theory of Jewish emancipation that ties any improvement in the Jewish condition to a general improvement in all of society—specifically, the emancipation of civil society from the trammels of capitalism, typified for Marx by the Jew.

By contrast, the student of Jewish history will be familiar as well with a second theory linking Jewish emancipation to external developments, one that is far more sympathetic to its subject than Marx's—namely that of Professor Baron. Beginning with his early and highly influential revisionist article "Ghetto and Emancipation," Baron has argued that Jewish emancipation was simply a necessary and inevitable aspect of general political modernization—a process in which the modern, secular state emerged in association with an individuated citizenry, freed of any mediating political allegiances such as had characterized the medieval "society of estates." Baron argued that "when the modern State came

185

into being and set out to destroy the medieval corporations and estates and to build a new citizenship, it could no longer suffer the existence of an autonomous Jewish corporation. Sooner or later it had to give to the Jews equal rights in civil and public law. . . . Emancipation was a necessity even more for the modern State than for Jewry; the Jew's medieval status was anachronistic and had to go." [1]

In the context of the eighteenth century, Baron's thesis is best illustrated by the example that seems to have inspired it, namely, the emancipation of the Jews of France by the Revolutionary National Assembly. At least in terms of the rhetoric of emancipation, Baron's view is corroborated by the celebrated declaration of the delegate Clermont-Tonnerre, that "to the Jews as a nation everything must be refused; as individuals, everything must be given them. They must be citizens. . . . There cannot be a nation within a nation." [2]

Despite this substantiation, there is some basis for questioning such a straightforward explanation of emancipation. One must consider as well the delays in legal enactment, the different treatment of Sephardi and Ashkenazi Jewry, and the evident setback dealt by the so-called Infamous Decrees of 1808, which once again singled out the Jews as a group as the objects of special legislation. Nevertheless, the fact is that as long as the liberal political theory of the Revolution prevailed, Jewish emancipation in France seemed in the long run to be necessary, secure, and irreversible.

What of the other cases, to which any general theory, such as Baron's, should be applicable?

The German case, to which I shall direct my attention, seems considerably clarified by reference to Baron's theory of dependence. This is so even in view of what must be the most striking feature of German-Jewish emancipation, namely, its halting and sometimes retrograde progress. Just as France's leading position in Jewish emancipation can be explained in terms of her advanced political development, so can the more retarded situation in Germany be explained in terms of that country's relative political backwardness. Thus, the emancipation of the Jews of Prussia, ultimately the dominant state in Germany, came only with the establishment of constitutional, representative government in the North German Confederation of 1867, later extended directly to the newly unified Reich of 1871. The comparable moment in French history —in which political modernization and Jewish emancipation were likewise combined—had already come eight decades earlier in the Revolution. This association of political modernization and Jewish emancipation seems to be confirmed in Germany even by its various fleeting, abortive appearances—in the general movement for reform in Prussia following her defeat by France in 1806, and again in the resolutions of the short-lived national assembly of 1848 in Frankfurt.

Thus Reinhard Ruerup, of the Free University in Berlin, has argued—in apparent support of Baron's position—that Jewish Emancipation was simply a precipitate of the advent of bourgeois society in Germany. "The condition of the Jews and their position in the state were felt to be unbearable: unbearable not only, not even primarily, for the Jews, but for the state and the Christian population." To be sure, the debate over the Jewish question lasted for over a half-century, but once the "technical-industrial" base of "bourgeois-liberal society" had been established, Jewish emancipation could no longer be deferred. "The technical-industrial advances," Ruerup wrote, "the prolonged economic boom, and the rise to ascendancy of liberal ideas effected a fundamental transformation of the whole pattern of social relations. . . . Jewish emancipation became an integral part of the comprehensive new structure." Indeed, Ruerup explains the delay in Jewish emancipation in terms of the inherent difficulties involved in "the attempt to emancipate the Jews in a society that was not itself, or only in part, emancipated." [3]

All told, the result is to confirm Baron's theory with regard both to the timing of emancipation and to its final motivation. But what of the long delay? What of the period of debate and striving before the attainment of legal emancipation, before the putative "necessity" of emancipation became so overwhelming as to be realized in its achievement? Furthermore, if emancipation had finally become such an absolute necessity, how can one explain the subsequent lively debate about its possible revocation? How can one explain the tenacious resistance both to the full elaboration of legal emancipation, at least until the period of the Weimar Republic, as well as to the translation of legal emancipation into full social integration? Here, too, Ruerup argues, the contrast with France was decisive, the contrast between the French liberal-revolutionary model of emancipation and the German "enlightened," state-oriented approach.

Whereas in France action had been confined to one single act of emancipation leaving social integration to the unfettered interplay of social forces, opinion in Germany continued to look upon the state as an educational as well as legal institution. . . . Here emancipation was conceived . . . as a prolonged process of social integration, and full equality was visualised only as the crowning achievement at the end of that road. Accordingly Jewish emancipation became . . . largely the business of the bureaucracy, of that progressive civil service that was stamped with the die of enlightenment.[4]

Perhaps the best example of this approach can be found in that much-cited champion of Jewish emancipation, Christian Wilhelm von Dohm, who was, it should be recalled, precisely one such reform-minded, enlightened bureaucrat. To be sure, Dohm argued in abstract terms for the creation of a secular polity in which "the Christian and the Jew, more than all that" would be simply "citizen[s]." But he also assumed that the improvement in the Jew's civil status would be justified retroactively by strenuous efforts at self-improvement.[5] Ruerup's contention is further corroborated by the evidence that Jacob Toury has amassed in his own work on this subject, which depicts what was almost a preoccupation of German authorities with what Toury calls the "productivization" of the Jews—that is, their vocational reorientation away from peddling, petty trade, and finance toward crafts, manufactures, and agriculture—as a precondition for emancipation.[6] The stress on agriculture, reflecting the physiocratic notion of the primacy of this sector, was only one example of the retrograde and anachronistic nature of this supposed reform in an age of nascent industrialization and urbanization. Here too the character of policy toward the Jews seems at odds with any general explanation in terms of an abstract commitment to modernization.

Given the tentative and conditional aspects of state policy regarding emancipation, the Jews in Germany may be excused if the ultimate historical necessity of emancipation escaped them, and if they continued to struggle to deserve emancipation and to hasten its achievement. To some extent, Baron's position must be understood as a refutation of precisely this assumption that the Jews were the suppliants in the process of emancipation. Quite the contrary. "Left to themselves," Baron insisted, "the Jews might for long have clung to their corporate existence. For Emancipation meant losses as well as gains."[7] Here, perhaps, is the real polemical animus of Baron's thesis. Not only was emancipation imposed on the Jews, but they even lost by it. Nevertheless, though Baron's theory of emancipation is partly confirmed in retrospect, it was not—as I have already suggested—the one operating in the minds of German Jewry. To understand what was, it is necessary to turn to our second class of theories, those that stress the significance of undertakings within the Jewish community itself, and the autonomy of Jewish actions.

Here the key lies in the analysis of the term *assimilation,* which came to be used loosely by German Jews in two altogether divergent senses. On the one hand, as a synonym for what we might more accurately call acculturation, it referred to the extent to which the Jew had assimilated himself to the culture of the surrounding milieu. But at the same time it described a process whose *object* was the Jew, namely, the assimilation of the Jew *by* his surrounding society—that is, his social integration. Though these two processes are in theory quite separate, throughout the modern period most German Jews assumed that there was in fact a functional link between acculturation and integration of every kind— social, political, and economic. On this premise rested the whole ideology of assimilationism, which assumed that an acceptable degree of acculturation, short of the complete abandonment of any Jewish identity at all, would secure the integration of Jews as Jews. Typically, the measures contemplated by this strategy involved the redefinition of Judaism in exclusively confessional terms, and the stress on the political integrability of the Jew thus defined. The ideology was neatly summed up in the familiar phrase, "German citizen of the Jewish faith"—later incorporated in the very title of the leading Jewish organization during the period of the Empire.

The situation in Germany proved, however, to be more intractable than the Jews at first imagined, and the fact that the processes of acculturation and integration were not directly linked produced a considerable measure of frustration and cognitive dissonance. In this regard the quip that the history of the Jews in Germany was one long tale of unrequited love seems especially accurate. Here as elsewhere, Mendelssohn himself had set the pattern early on by his counsel to his coreligionists in 1782 that they needed only to love and they would be loved in return.[8] What resulted was essentially a dialectic of frustration: The Jews' very assumption that it was in their own power to hasten progress could make it appear that the lack of progress could be attributed to some failing of their own, which spurred them, in turn, to ever-renewed and more strenuous efforts at self-improvement and acculturation.

Although in one sense these efforts at reform were a matter of the Jews' own undertaking, they were at the same time wholly conditioned by the implicit goal of acceptability in Christian society. The consequence was that Jewish aspirations were shaped by what Jews adjudged the governing principle of society to be at any given moment—with the intention of exploiting that principle to the advantage of their own integration. Accordingly, Jews tended to envision the external reality that

most favored their own aspirations. The perception was not always accurate, and at times it could be woefully overoptimistic or sorrowfully
out of phase with actual developments. Thus the Haskalah, itself a
product of social and intellectual modernization, imagined that it would
benefit from similar changes supposedly wrought in German society at
large. But as attractive as the notion of a religiously neutral society was
in theory, in practice it fell short of the dimensions necessary to sustain
large-scale integration.[9] Furthermore, apparent enlightened toleration on
the part of Christians could serve merely as a guise for conversionist
sentiment—as was evident both in the famed Mendelssohn-Lavater
confrontation and in the reforms for Jewish education proposed by "enlightened" bureaucratic reformers.[10] Moreover, even well after Romanticism had displaced *Aufklaerung* as the reigning ideology in Germany,
Jewish reformers continued to operate on the basis of notions of enlightened universalism. Likewise, the efforts of young intellectuals like
Immanuel Wolf or Leopold Zunz to substitute the "bond of *Wissenschaft*"
as a universal principle were no more realistic.[11] Similarly, in a later
phase of their history German Jews sought to secure their acceptance as
Germans by way of identifying with what they thought best in German
culture—with Kant, Goethe, and even Heine—without realizing, however, either that their refined tastes might not be widely shared or—more
importantly —that their subjective cultural inclinations carried no necessary implication for their standing in Christian society.[12]

At the same time that Jewish aspirations for integration were conditioned by the Jews' evaluation of the ideological context, they were
equally formed by the way Jews imagined that they appeared to Christians. Here a glance at the educational reforms undertaken by the
Haskalah itself—as opposed to those advanced by Christian reformers—
is most revealing. In the programmatic proposals of Wessely, as well as
the actual curricula of the modernized schools established by the
Haskalah, there is a revealing stress on deportment.[13] Public behavior
and public appearance had suddenly become an issue of the first importance. One *Maskil,* for example, writing in *Hameassef,* urged greater
order in both school and synagogue lest Jews appear ridiculous and become objects of derision.[14] The matter of Yiddish was also raised in this
context of how the Jews appeared to the outside world. Yiddish was
condemned not only as being corrupt itself but as aesthetically and even
morally corrupting.[15] "Pure German or pure Hebrew," Mendelssohn
urged, only not Yiddish, which, he feared had "contributed not a little to
the immorality" of his brethren.[16]

These concerns with public appearance and respectability prevailed for as long as there were Jews in Germany, and they surface time and again in matters as divergent as the motivations for religious reform and the treatment of Jewish immigrants from Eastern Europe.[17] That this was so should not, however, be cause for astonishment. Certainly it was consistent with the entire strategy of assimilationism. Moreover, it can well be understood in terms of what we know about the changes in Jewish consciousness produced by modernization—specifically its reorientation to the world outside Judaism.[18] For modernization brought an end not only to the legal and political autonomy of the medieval Jewish community, but also to the relative autonomy of the values that had characterized traditional Jewry. Indeed, this reorientation of values can be taken as one of the defining features of the modern period in Jewish history. Put simply, Jews began to see themselves through Christian eyes. The negative evaluation of themselves and their own religion that they consequently came to internalize could serve as the basis for attitudes of self-criticism and even of self-disdain and self-hatred. Emancipation did not—as some German Jews discovered to their dismay—necessarily mean liberation.

It was precisely in response to this situation, as much as to the putative ineradicability of anti-Semitism, that Zionism developed in Germany. To its adherents it offered the psychological benefit that derived from the liberating affirmation of a comprehensive Jewish identity: now, German citizens of the Jewish *Volk*. What was striking about Zionism, however, was the extent that it, too, was conditioned by its German context, despite its claim of an autonomous perspective. This was true not only in such formal aspects as the dueling and drinking of the Zionist university fraternities, or the countryside rambling of the Zionist youth movement, or the stress on order and discipline for their own sakes within the movement as a whole —but in more essential regards as well.[19]

Even in the matter of nationalism itself, specifically concerning the problem of Zionist-Arab relations, where the German Zionists sought to stake out a position free of the chauvinistic expansionism of German nationalism, they reacted in a very German way, and slipped into a typically German unpolitical stance, which imagined that difficult conflicts of a political nature could be transposed to the realm of the ethical, and resolved by impartial reference to abstract principles.

Thus, on closer analysis, it appears that the Zionists and the assimilationists were nearer to one another than either would have liked to think. Both shared the assumption that had characterized Jewish efforts for acceptance in Germany from the time of the Haskalah—namely, that German resistance to the Jews could be traced to some objective defect in the Jews themselves, and that self-improvement would have to precede, but would assuredly bring, emancipation and subsequent integration. While the assimilationists sought their remedy in an increased measure of acculturation, the Zionists imagined that the enhancement of Jewish pride and self-respect would induce respect and acceptance from others.

In sum, whatever the differences in detail, both groups subscribed to a theory of emancipation—in the Zionist case, to a theory of self-emancipation—that assumed the autonomy and effectiveness of independent Jewish action. At the same time, however, both groups reveal the overwhelming influence of their German context—both in defining their aspirations and in circumscribing the range of their achievement. Therefore, to do justice to the historical reality the historian must refer to both theories of emancipation that I mentioned at the outset: those that stress the decisive importance of context, and those that focus on undertakings within the Jewish community itself.

NOTES

1. Salo Baron, "Ghetto and Emancipation: Shall We Revise the Traditional View?" *Menorah Journal* 14, no. 6 (June, 1928) : 524.
2. Meeting of the National Assembly, 23 December 1789, in *Réimpression de L'Ancien Moniteur* (Gazette Nationale ou le Moniteur Universel) (Paris: Henri Plon, 1859), 2:456.
3. Reinhard Ruerup, "Jewish Emancipation and Bourgeois Society," *Leo Baeck Institute Year Book* 14 (1969) : 70, 84, 85, 86, 89.
4. Ibid., pp. 73–74.
5. Christian Wilhelm [von] Dohm, *Ueber die buergerliche Verbesserung der Juden,* 2 vols. (Berlin: Friedrich Nicolai, 1781–83), 1:26. See also Jacob Katz, "The Term 'Jewish Emancipation': Its Origin and Historical Impact," in *Studies in Nineteenth-Century Jewish Intellectual History,* ed. Alexander Altmann (Cambridge: Harvard University Press, 1964), pp. 1–25.
6. See Jacob Toury, *Prolegomena to the Entrance of Jews into German Citizenry* (Hebrew) (Tel-Aviv: University of Tel-Aviv, 1972), and idem, *Der Eintritt der Juden ins deutsche buergertum: Eine Dokumentation* (Tel-Aviv: University of Tel-Aviv, 1972).
7. Baron, "Ghetto and Emancipation," p. 524.
8. Statement made at the end of Mendelssohn's preface to the German translation of Manasseh ben Israel's *Vindiciae Judaeorum,* printed in Moses Mendelssohn, *Gesammelte Schriften* (Leipzig, 1843–45), 3:202.
9. See Jacob Katz, *Out of the Ghetto: The Social Background of Jewish Emancipation, 1770–1870* (Cambridge: Harvard University Press, 1973), esp. chap. 4, "The Semineutral Society"; and idem, "The German-Jewish Utopia of Social Emancipation," in idem, *Emancipation and Assimilation: Studies in Modern Jewish History* (Westmead: Gregg International, 1972).
10. See Toury, *Der Eintritt,* chaps. IIb and IIc.
11. Immanuel Wolf, "On the Concept of a Science of Judaism," in *Ideas of Jewish History* ed. Michael A. Meyer, (New York: Behrman House, 1974), p. 143; and Leopold Zunz, "**Vorrede**" to *Die gottesdienstlichen Vortraege der Juden* (Berlin, 1832).
12. See Sidney M. Bolkosky, *The Distorted Image: German-Jewish Perceptions* of *Germans and Germany, 1918–1935* (New York: Elsevier, 1975).
13. Naphtali Herz Wessely, *Divre Shalom ve-Emet,* 4 pts. (Berlin, 1782–85), esp. pt. 1. On the educational program of the Haskalah, see Mordechai Eliav, *Jewish Education in Germany in the Period of Enlightenment and Emancipation* (Hebrew) (Jerusalem: Jewish Agency, 1960).
14. Elijah Morpurgo, in *Hameassef* 3 (Shevat 5546) : 66–78.
15. See Wessely, *Divre Shalom ve-Emet,* pt. 1, esp. chap. 7, and passim.
16. Letter from Mendelssohn to Assistenzrath Klein, 29 August 1782, printed in *Gesammelte Schriften,* 5:605.

17. One revealing example of this attitude in the Reform movement is contained in the address of Israel Jacobson at the dedication of the Reform temple at Seesen in 1810, reprinted in W. Gunther Plaut, ed., *The Rise of Reform Judaism* (New York: World Union for Progressive Judaism, 1963), pp. 29–31. See also Michael A. Meyer, "Christian Influence on Early German Reform Judaism," in *Studies in Jewish Bibliography, History and Literature in Honor of I. Edward Kiev*, ed. Charles Berlin (New York: KTAV, 1971), pp. 289–303. On immigrants from Eastern Europe, see S. Adler-Rudel, *Ostjuden in Deutschland, 1880–1940* (Tuebingen: Mohr, 1959).

18. See Katz, "The Term 'Jewish Emancipation' "; p. 15, and idem, *Tradition and Crisis: Jewish Society at the End of the Middle Ages* (New York: Free Press, 1961), Chap. 23, "The Emergence of the Neutral Society."

19. For a more extensive discussion, see my forthcoming *Zionism in Germany, 1897–1933: The Shaping of a Jewish Identity* (Philadelphia: Jewish Publication Society, 1976).

Contemporary Civilization

. . . whether we succeed or fail in our immediate objectives, we shall not feel that our life has been wasted. We shall know, not inferentially and by persuasion, but at first hand and by experience, that there is a Power that makes for human salvation. We shall know God.

Mordecai M. Kaplan, *The Future of the American Jew.*

Declaration of the Establishment of the State of Israel

EDUCATION AS RELIGION

By

MEIR BEN-HORIN

Close to one hundred percent of those who practice education start out, I venture to suggest, with the conviction that the school, fundamentally, belongs to the category of instrumentality, of maidservant, of *ancilla theologiae or religionis*, of *ancilla rei publicae, ancilla factionis, ancilla moris,* or *ancilla philosophiae*. Aristotle held that "the citizen should be molded to suit the form of government under which he lives" and "that which most contributes to the permanence of constitutions is the adaptation of education to the form of government." [1]

I also am quite sure that nearly one hundred percent of all who engage in teaching live out their teaching lives without changing this article of faith about education. Moreover, it is not likely that they ever have occasion to view it as an object of doubt. In all generations, in all societies, in all religious, political, and cultural traditions, this Aristotelian persuasion has sustained and satisfied teachers, who were wont to see themselves as servants or agents of whatever authority functioned as sponsor. For schoolmen and laymen alike, this is the first principle: School is at bottom a service agency. School is created by society as its servant, as its—may I say—societizing agent par excellence.

Over the years, doubts have attacked my own belief in this axiom, and the doubts have conquered. I have abandoned the dogma of educational ancillarity. Instead, I now assert that *education is a religion.*

I

If the term *civilization* points to the sum total of the ways in which human beings relate themselves to the nonhuman environment and to each other, it will be appropriate to apply the terms *religion* and *education* to two aspects of civilization—to two distinct and distinguishable aspects at that. Other aspects or basic elements or segments of human civilizations or cultures are "science" and "art." These latter two are distinct phases of civilization as well, distinct though related ways whereby we respond to all that the words *nature* or *world* or *universe* or *reality* or Dewey's term *experience* conjure up in our minds.

Proceeding to develop the anti-ancillarist position, I now assert that religion and education are "created equal," along with "all men" who are "created equal." Religion and education are created equal in the sense that they are, along with science and art, man's distinctive, speculative, as well as transactive ways of adjusting himself to the inner and outer conditions or processes or energies which touch his existence and of which he is a part on a level all his own. Such adjustment is often achieved by creative intervention and transformation of both self and conditions, a transformation impelled by needs and guided by goals and the perception or intuition of conditions more desirable and ideal.

While thus claiming, first, distinctiveness and, second, equality under the aspect of civilization, I recognize that religion implies an education. We are not—shades of Locke—born with our religion as part of the organic equipment; education brings it to us. Ideas are not innate; they are inbred. The late Professor Horace M. Kallen, the father of the idea of cultural pluralism in America, was fond of saying: "Jews are not born. Jewish values, or the values of any other culture-group, are not a biological inheritance. They are not carried by the genes. . . . Education makes Jews." [2] In more radical and more universal language, he wrote: "A baby is only the potentiality of a human being. It is not born human. It is educated into humanity . . . by folkways and mores which constitute culture." [3] This, of course, includes the schools. Education makes human beings, and education makes religious human beings.

Thus far this is quite conventional and, perhaps, part of our basic conviction that education is a tool in the hands of something larger—namely, the making of human beings, of beings who *are* human and who are not, say, "Aryan" Eichmanns or their latter-day disciples in genocidal or Judaeocidal intent among the "Semitic" anti-Semites.

To be sure, religion implies an education. But my much more unconventional view is also that *education may be understood as a religion.*

James Kern Feibleman, who perhaps more than anybody else has taught Americans to appreciate the importance of Charles S. Peirce as a philosopher, noted this in his autobiography: "Tulane University is the name for a collection of bits of matter, including land, buildings, and even people, devoted to what for me at least is a religious purpose: namely education." [4]

What kind of argument may be made on behalf of the idea?

Rabbi Mordecai M. Kaplan, surely the twentieth century's most revolutionary American thinker in Jewish religion, has described "the essence of religion" as

> the effort to discover what makes life worthwhile, and to bring life into conformity with those laws on which the achievement of a worthwhile life depends. . . . A religion is man's quest for self-fulfillment or salvation, and *the need of self fulfillment presupposes that Reality is so patterned as to contain the means of satisfying it.*[5]

Now, according to Kaplan, different religions result from the fact that civilizations identify as *sancta,* or media of salvation-attaining, the important elements in their particular life such as institutions, places, historic events, heroes, objects of reverence. Judaism's *sancta,* for example, are Torah, the synagogue, *Eretz Yisrael* or the Land of Israel, Sabbaths and holy days, the Hebrew language, Moses and the patriarchs. At this point Kaplan speaks of the *sancta* of American civilization, namely, "the Constitution, the Declaration of Independence, Thanksgiving Day, the Fourth of July and other national holidays, the Stars and Stripes. They and what they imply will in time be identified as American religion." American Jews, according to Professor Kaplan, see no contradition between American religion's *sancta* and Judaism's,

> any more than American Christians see any contradiction in reverencing these American *sancta* as well as the Cross, the New Testament, the Church, and its sacraments and sacred days, which are among the *sancta* of Christian civilization. Religions are not necessarily mutually exclusive; they are so only when their *sancta* are interpreted as denunciatory of other religions.[6]

I cite this passage to suggest that the term *religion* is not confined to the religions which arose in ancient Judaea or Palestine. Nor does the term necessarily imply the existential reality of, and the faith in, a God who is either Person or Power or Process, Creator at will, First Actor or Principle. One is reminded of the Zionist farmer and thinker Aaron David Gordon (1856–1922), who preached and lived what he called "the religion of labor," i.e., physical labor on the soil of Palestine whereby to restore one's soul as a Jew, achieve fulfillment or salvation of the individual self and the national collectivity of the Jewish people or Judaism as a civilization.[7] Or one may reread Avraham Shlonsky (1900–1973), the iconoclastic innovator among Hebrew poets whom Moshe Shamir has named "the godfather of the new Erets-Yisraelian poetry." In Shlonsky, laboring on Zion's earth becomes worship because it permits him to join mornings—

My earth wrapping herself in light as in a Tallith.
Houses standing forth like the frontlets.
And roads descending like Tefillin's straps,
       paved by our hands.

Here a handsome town offering morn's prayers unto her creator.
And among the creators
Your son Avraham,
Poet blazing trails in Israel.[8]

The point is that if communism, nazism, nationalism,[9] democracy,[10] and labor may be regarded as religions, if Americanism may be felt to be a religion, engaging the loyalties and ultimate concerns of man and woman "unto life and unto death," then it ought to be quite legitimate to speak of education as religion, and possibly with greater justification.

Einstein has been quoted as saying that "real religion is above petty dogmas, cathechisms, solemn prayers and antagonisms. True religion is real living—living with all one's soul, with all one's goodness and righteousness."

But as a teacher I must comment that such living is living one's education, is the life of education, is—to paraphrase Dewey—ongoing reconstruction of experience so as to ensure more intelligent experience, more loving experience, more fulfilling or meaningful experience.

To Whitehead, religion was "what man does with his own solitariness." But what he does with his solitariness is, I must interpose again, what he does with his education. Responding to Whitehead's famous line, I wrote that "civilization is what man does with his humanity, enhancing it, bringing it to fuller fruition." [11] But this, too, I must now interpolate, is true for education. Education is what man does with his solitariness and with his human solidarity, with his grief and his elation, with his loneliness and the ecstasy, his emptiness and his radiance, with his discontent and his sense of self-realization. Education is what we do with our religion and our idolatry, our sciences and our arts, our reason and our irrationalities. Education is our glory and our shame, like religion. Education is our destiny.

In his *Theology of Culture,* the late Paul Tillich wrote that religion "is at home everywhere, namely, in the depth of all functions of man's spiritual life. Religion is the dimension of depth in all of them. Religion is the aspect of depth in the totality of the human spirit." [12] Considering this from the side of education, must we not maintain that education is the aspect of depth in religion? While "depth" meant to Tillich, in his words, "that which is ultimate, infinite, unconditional in man's spiritual life" or "ultimate concern," education, I insist, signifies the introduction of meaning into the ultimate, infinite, and unconditional. Only such introduction can save these terms from the status of mere sound and mere arbitrariness, mere *fiat,* nakedly fanatical tenacity in the face of relevant evidence, thick mystery wrapped in enigma and surrounded by those who police the secret or—the secret police.

My position as an educator is that the school, by its very nature, can never be the secret policeman's ally; it can only be his victim or his foe.

We have been taught that school is a social institution. It undoubtedly is. But its mission does not end when it "socializes" the learner or when it inducts him or her effectively, smoothly, and forever into the culture around him/her. School always implies transmission *and* transcendence, continuity *and* creativity, loyalty *and* critique, allegiance to past and present *and* to an intuited or envisioned better future. Ivan Illich wrote in 1972 that "we must disestablish school," because "the escalation of the schools is as destructive as the escalation of weapons but less visibly so." [13] He was convinced that "school has become the world religion of a modernized proletariat, and makes future promises of salvation to the poor of the technological age." [14] "School," he thought, "is a ritual of initiation which introduces the neophyte to the sacred race of progressive consumption, a ritual of propitiation whose academic priests mediate between the faithful and the gods of privilege and power, a ritual of expiration which sacrifices its dropouts, branding them as scapegoats of underdevelopment." [15]

In the face of this I am trying to defend the proposition that education is not world idolatry but a world religion. *Far from deschooling society, I advocate desocietizing the school.* By this turn-around of Illich's phrase I mean that if education is a religion of, by, and for mankind, it should claim the status and the freedoms as well as the mission often accorded religions. I mean that if education is understood as an authentic mode of salvation-seeking, then it may and must revere as one of its *sancta* the entirely uncircumscribed privilege of teaching and learning, of seeking and following the honest, relevant, and warranted evidence, of testing the unprecedented hypothesis which is not a clear and present crime against human bodies and minds, of forecasting in speculation and in art and science the more perfect union of the true, the good, the beautiful, and the holy. Among the geographical *sancta* of education as religion are those schools which actually function as agencies for the transmission of the given and for the transcendence of the given and the inherited. Among its saints and heroes are the men and women whose lives were actually lived for education as religion and who chose martyrdom when the occasion arose. As a recent example of such martyrdom I cite Janusz Korczak, M.D., who on August 5, 1942 sanctified the Holy Name and at the head of some two hundred Jewish orphans, boys and girls in his orphanage in Warsaw's Jewish Ghetto, walked into the Nazi death, the children walking with him on Nazi orders, their banner flying in the hot sunshine, their faces scrubbed, Korczak carrying some of the smallest, one after the other, and consoling them for a lost dolly.[16] In the whole history of education this is one of the saddest sights and one of the darkest and finest hours of the Jewish career in the world. How many monuments have been erected by the world's teaching profession for him and for the children whom he decided not to leave as the Nazi stole their young lives?

Education as religion always ordains transformation, the effort to step beyond the current sinfulness of the particular moment in history in which it has its being. Education is a religion of wrestling with the incomplete, the senseless, the demonic, the callous, the inhuman.

In *Theology of Culture* already cited, Tillich included a chapter on "A Theology of Education." In it he favors education as "initiation into the mystery of human existence,"[17] the kind of religious education which "opens up the subconscious levels of the children for the ultimate mystery of being."[18] Keeping in mind Korczak and the children, I fear ultimate mysteries. What is to me the religion of education opposes mystery with free inquiry. After all, reality on all levels may be held to be mysterious. All is mystery, from atoms to constellations of galaxies. The religion of education does not stop with mystery. It starts with it. From it, it goes on to say that we need to discover how to apply one mystery to another and elicit from their interaction such results as better medicines, better transportation, better means of communication, securer knowledge about natural events, finer architecture, safer cities and countries, longer and happier lives, more men and women who are as intelligent as they are compassionate and selfless.[19]

This is quite remote from Tillich's mystery and ultimacy. Yet my own theology of education gladly accepts Tillich's requirement in his essay where he refers to the "humanistic question," which is radical, going "to the roots and . . . not accept[ing] anything whatsoever as being beyond questioning." Tillich insisted that "The inducting education of the Church School can and must include the principle of humanist education, the correlation between question and answer, the radicalism of the question, the opening up of all human possibilities, and the providing of opportunities where the pupil may develop in freedom." [20] Nonetheless, what I call education as religion moves in a different direction, concerned as it is with education as such and not merely with education as offered by institutions of religion.

Here Professor Sterling P. Lamprecht's conclusion, in his important essay on "Naturalism and Religion" (1944), is instructive. Recognizing "danger in a too-intense religious zeal," he holds that "religion ought to be the ornament of a rich life, not the driving passion of a fixed commitment." In fact,

> Religious commitments ought never to be drilled into men; they ought never be made too early in life. If a youth adopts a definite religious point of view, he may, of course, lead a life of singleness of aim and powerful persistence of effort. But the odds are against any fine achievement by such means. The chances are that he will either become intolerant, biased, and insensitive to all possibilities of development that lie beyond the range of his youthful mind of rebel against religion and become a secularized person with scorn for earnest moral endeavor.

Lamprecht recommends the middle way, which is "to take religion with a sense of humor, a light touch, and a sensitive appreciation for what has, at least for the time being, no apparent religious import." Usually bigotry is the result of conversion: "Hence one should seek to postpone religious commitment and to accept it, not as authoritative over the whole of life, but as experimental over only certain parts of life. In that way a religious way of life might coexist, as it has too seldom coexisted, with the emancipated mind." [21]

At this point the thesis interposes itself that such coexistence may be achieved and made secure when education is brought into the fellowship of religions.

II

Education as religion implies the demand for equal dignity with other religions and equality of noninterference with its freedom—extraterritorial status, as it were, or "diplomatic immunity"—because it performs a function which is uniquely its own. None of its partners in the civilizational alliance, namely, science, art, and religion, are competent to perform education's distinctive mission.

This mission defines the meaning of education as a history-wide, global force and function on behalf of human life on earth.

The mission and the meaning may be stated as follows: *Education is the liberation and cultivation of man's two distinctive powers—the power to think and the power to love.*

The educational commandment is not, *laissez faire* or *laissez croire*. The educational commandment is *laissez penser* and *laissez aimer,* "let them think" and "let them be loving."

The terms *to think* and *to love* need to be defined clearly, cleanly, and keenly. They require operational meaning. And the appropriate methodologies for the liberation/cultivation must be worked out by those in education who deal not with its philosophy but its tactics and strategies. The appropriate materials need to be created and assembled. All forms and manifestations of human civilizations are, in fact, potential means in the hands of education. But the commandment of the religion which is education is clear: Design programs, courses, activities, experiences, projects, intra- and extra-mural events, individual works, group work, the entire life, atmosphere, administration, furniture, walls or open spaces in such a way as to liberate and cultivate mind and compassion. All activities designated educational must integrate these powers which are the principal powers whereby to achieve what, after the First World War, Walther Rathenau called "an organic self-determining and self-regenerating order of society . . . the order of culture, resting upon spirit, character, and education." [22]

But, again, only the "desocietized" school is competent to perform this specific function of liberating, cultivating, and integrating mind-love in human personality.

Clausewitz made popular the proposition that war is an act of violence, pushed to its utmost bounds, and "a mere continuation of policy by other means." Education, I propose, is *the art of intelligence, pushed to its compassionate bounds. Education is the discontinuity of war by the most enduring means.* This "art of education," as we have learnt from Whitehead, "is never easy. To surmount its difficulties, especially those of elementary education, is a task worthy of the highest genius. It is the training of human souls." [23]

III

Education as religion may come into conflict with other forms of religiosity. In the days of Socrates it did, and in the days of Korczak. Tragedy may follow from education understood as trans-gression, as aggression against all attempts at a priori confinement of mind-love's conquering and creative power.

Education as religion cannot concede the absolute rights of parents, children, the state, the party, the movement, the denomination, the economy, the convention, the tradition, the current state of science, scholarship, and art. For education, the only sovereign rights are those of the inquiring mind and the empathic, thou-tuned soul.

Education is not action. For education, the unexamined action is not worth enacting.

When he considered Jewish education, Kaplan, in *Judaism as a Civilization,* remarked that "the mind is normally motor-active rather than contemplative" and that "activity and participation in actual life" are "of primary importance in the educative process." Yet these "must not be permitted to crowd out the element of ideation. If action is the body of Jewish life, thought is the soul." [24] Nor is education "the total process of living, the complete interaction of man with man and of man with his environment." [25] The identification of the school, anywhere on earth, with the responsibility for the blossoming of the mind-love continuum contrasts sharply with the idea that "the total society" [26] can educate and that a "total educational network" is needed which

> will be a virtual spider web imposed upon the environment. It will encompass all—young and old. Home, university, factory, police precinct, law court, museum, each institution will become in part an educational one, and each member of it, a part-time teacher. The banker, the doctor, the engineer, the shop foreman will be encouraged to devote part of his work week to this form of teaching. . . . For the student, it will, in fact, be a continuum: education, re-education, possibly another type of employment; education and living becoming one continuous, intergrated process.[27]

Education as religion does not countenance the "withering away" of the school. The conception of education as environmental management,

as ecosystem control,[28] may actually be its idolatrous counterpart. Idolatry
is likely to be present where mind is separated from love and love from
mind. Of the love factor the ecosystematizer is strangely silent. For education, transformative intelligence is one with redemptive loving, and redemptive loving is in unison with being reconstructively intelligent.

Hence the educational question is not, say, "What is Judaism and how
can I best teach it?" The Jewish educational question is: "What is
school and how must I deal with Judaism in a manner appropriate for
school as the mind-love releasing and extending institution of the Jewish
people?" The same kind of questioning holds for all manner of teaching
anything and anywhere under the sun, whether in the realm of the secular or in the realm of the religious.

From the standpoint of education as religion, the question always
addresses the requirement of releasing, cultivating, enlarging, and re-
fining the activity that is mind and is "habit of truth" [29] and judgment,[30]
while uniting it with altruistic love and its habits of patience, tenderness,
grace, and peace.

Rousseau makes this point with admirable simplicity and captivating
charm:

> So Emile loves peace. He is delighted at the sight of happiness, and if he
> can help to bring it about, this is an additional reason for sharing it. I do
> not assume that when he sees the unhappy he will merely feel for them
> that barren and cruel pity which is content to pity the ills it can heal. His
> kindness is active and teaches him much he would have learnt far more
> slowly, or he would never have learnt at all, if his heart had been harder.
> If he finds his comrades at strife, he tries to reconcile them; if he sees
> them afflicted, he inquires as to the cause of their sufferings; . . . if he
> finds one who is down-trodden, groaning under the oppression of the rich
> and powerful, he tries to discover by what means he can counteract this
> oppression, and in the interest he takes with regard to all these unhappy
> persons, the means of removing their sufferings are never out of his
> sight.[31]

For the development of mind and love, that is, for education, all
elements of civilization are means. This is why education is never "for"
this or that purpose. Rather, all of civilization is for *its* supreme purpose.
Thus education is its own end, like man himself. Kant's categorical
imperative applies to both with equal force. And if, in Bronowski's
words, science "has outlasted the empires of Louis XIV and the Kaiser"
and has survived "because it is less brittle than the rage of tyrants," [32]

education, which has outlasted all empires and survived all tyrannies, will obey its religious imperative: of engaging man's mind to his love.

IV

For them which say they are teachers, conflicts of loyalty are possible and likely to occur. But if their faith is firm, their work will be consecrated to the development of open minds and loving hearts.

Teachers so educated and so dedicated will recognize, with Professor William Ray Dennes of the University of California, that

> the truth of a belief about the fission of uranium or plutonium may satisfy our curiosity, but beyond that it is every bit as compatible with our using it to make our planet wholly uninhabitable as it is with a very limited use of it to produce power in regions of the earth where power is needed to give a humane amplitude to life.[33]

They will agree with him on the factors of knowledge and of love:

> Knowledge that a pattern of living satisfies basic human needs and develops a minimum of hostile aggression, is probable knowledge of fact and is morally neutral. Until the factor of love, of approval, of commendation supervenes we have still no judgment of the goodness of a civilization or of the rightness of the moral choices that may tend to support it or damage it.[34]

Such teachers' schools will serve nothing less than the more defensible truth, the more generous and enduring good, the more delicately revelatory beauty, the deeper meaning of the holy.

Their schools' grounds will be lands of the free searching out the promise of selfhood and ethical collectivity. They will be "extraterritorial" homes of those who are brave in intelligently reconstructing whatever gains their quest may have secured.

And their schools will be—*schools*.

NOTES

1. *Politics* 5. 9, 1310a. For a critical discussion, see I. B. Berkson, *Preface to an Educational Philosophy* (New York: Columbia University Press, 1940), pp. 189, 195 ff.
2. Horace M. Kallen, *Of Them Which Say They Are Jews,* ed. Judah Pilch (New York: Bloch, 1954), p. 226.
3. Ibid., p. 189.
4. James Kern Feibleman, *The Way of a Man* (New York: Horizon Press, 1969), p. 310.
5. Mordecai M. Kaplan, *The Greater Judaism in the Making* (New York: Reconstructionist Press, 1960), pp. 458 f.
6. Ibid., p. 460.
7. On Gordon's current and future influence, see Herbert Weiner, *The Wild Goats of Ein Gedi: A Journal of Religious Encounters in the Holy Land* (New York: Meridian Books, 1963), pp. 186–215.
8. Avraham Shlonsky, *Shirim* [Poems], 2d ed. (Merhavia: Sifriyat Po'alim, 1958), **p. 165 (my translation, MBH); Moshe Shamir, "Ha-Tsa'ir Ha-Nitzhi"** [The Eternally Young], *Ma'ariv,* May 20, 1973; see also *The Modern Hebrew Poem Itself,* ed. Stanley Burnshaw, T. Carmi, and Ezra Spicehandler (New York: Holt, Rinehart & Winston, 1965), pp. 74 ff.
9. Cf. Carlton J. H. Hayes, *Nationalism: A Religion* (New York: Macmillan, 1960), esp. chap. 12, "Reflections on the Religion of Nationalism." With nazism and communism as religions he deals in chap 10, "Totalitarian Nationalism and World War II." I note his comment on education: "The school system of the national state is held to strict account for any lapse from the official theology or for any slur upon the popular mythology." " . . . there is a constant fear among heated patriots lest the masses lose their nationalist faith, and determination, therefore, that only such information should be imparted to them as will strengthen that faith and promote popular devotion to it" (pp. 170 f.). In *The Dynamics of Nationalism,* ed. Louis L. Snyder (Princeton: D. Van Nostrand, 1964), apears this passage from Jules Michelet's book *Le Peuple,* written in 1846: "The day when France, remembering that she was, and must be, the salvation of mankind, will place her children around her, and teach them France, as faith and as religion, she will find herself living, and firm as the globe" (p. 116).
10. See Ira Eisenstein, "Toward a Religion of Democracy in America," in his *Judaism under Freedom* (New York: Reconstructionist Press, 1956), pp. 245–58. *See also* Kaplan, "Judaism's Contribution to Education for Democracy," in *The Future of the American Jew* (New York: Macmillan, 1948), chap. 25, where he writes: " . . . democracy is a faith; its validity is not scientifically demonstrable. It demands *a priori* acceptance of ideals which can be proved

valid only by our committing ourselves to their realization. It is a scheme of salvation that implies belief in a Power that makes for salvation" (p. 511). In fact, *"the American religion of democracy has room for Judaism, and Jewish religion has room for American democracy.* They serve the same God, and can serve Him in cooperation. . . . There can, and should, develop in this country an American Jewish religion, which is as American as it is Jewish, and as Jewish as it is American" (p. 522). Cf. Eisenstein, "Is the U.S. Ready for a Civil Religion," *Religious Education,* no. 3 (May–June 1976): 227–29, and in the same issue the papers by Robert N. Bellah, Michael Novak, Marie L. Schneider, and Dorothy Dohen.

11. Meir Ben-Horin, *Common Faith—Uncommon People* (New York: Reconstructionist Press, 1970), pp. 47 f.

12. Paul Tillich, *Theology of Culture* (New York: Oxford University Press, 1959), p. 7.

13. Ivan Illich, *Deschooling Society* (New York: Harrow Books, 1972), p. 14. For a rebuttal, see Fred M. Hechinger, "The Challenge: De-bureaucratizing without De-schooling," *Perspectives on Education* 5, no. 1 (Fall 1971).

14. Illich, *Deschooling Society,* p. 15.

15. Ibid., pp. 63 f.

16. See Hanna Olczak, *Mister Doctor: The Life of Janusz Korczak* (London: Peter Davies, 1965). Cf. Zvi E. Kurzweil, "Korczak's Educational Writings," *Jewish Education* 38, no. 1 (January 1968), and idem, *Mishnato ha-Hinnukhit shel Dr. Janusz Korczak* [Dr. Janusz Korczak's educational system] (Tel-Aviv: Mif'aley Tarbut ve-Hinnukh, 1968).

17. Tillich, *Theology of Culture,* p. 151.

18. Ibid., p. 156.

19. Ben-Horin, *Common Faith—Uncommon People,* pp. 68 f. See also idem, "Re-Schooling American Jewry," *Journal of Jewish Communal Service* 52, no. 3 (Spring 1976): 287 f. In *Judaism as a Civilization,* Kaplan aligned himself with the tendency of modernism *"to adopt the scientific approach as the most reliable method of ascertaining the truth concerning all matters of human interest."* Hence, "the function of modern education is not to indoctrinate the mind and accustom it to defer to authority, as was the practice in traditional education, but to train the mind to think for itself, and to form opinions on the basis of sufficient evidence" (p. 36). "Education," he wrote in *Not So Random Thoughts* (New York: Reconstructionist Press, 1966), p. 52, "by means of pre-fabricated ideas is propaganda." On education vs. propaganda ("in the last analysis nothing but sublimated violence"), see Martin Buber's memorable essay, "Elements of the Interhuman," in *The Knowledge of Man,* ed. Maurice Friedman (New York: Harper & Row, 1965), pp. 72–88.

20. Tillich, *Theology of Culture,* pp. 154 f. Interestingly, in *The Eternal Now* (1956; reprint ed., New York: Charles Scribner's Sons, 1963), p. 164, Tillich quotes Prov. 8:29 and Job 28:26, noting that "the meaning of these words is that God explores Wisdom which is like an independent power beside Him." Elsewhere in the same collection of sermons he extols resistance to conformity: Non-conformity ultimately is "the resistance to idolatry, to making ultimates of ourselves and our world, our civilization and our church. And this resistance is the most difficult thing demanded of man. . . . It is not too difficult to become a critic and a rebel. But it is hard not to be conformed to anything, not even to oneself" (p. 144).

21. Lamprecht, *The Metaphysics of Naturalism* (New York: Appleton-Century-Crofts, 1967), p. 183.

22. Walther Rathenau, *The New Society* (New York: Harcourt, Brace Co., 1921), p. 139.
23. Alfred North Whitehead, *The Aims of Education* (1929; reprint ed., New York: Mentor Books, 1949), p. 62.
24. Kaplan, *Judaism as a Civilization* (1934; reprint ed., New York: Schocken Books, 1967), p. 36.
25. Shelley Umans, *The Management of Education: A Systematic Design for Educational Revolution* (Garden City, N. Y.: Doubleday & Co., 1971), p. 167. The author is director of the Center for Innovation for the Board of Education of the City of New York.
26. Ibid., p. 34.
27. Ibid., p. 185.
28. Ibid., pp. 166 ff.
29. J. Bronowski, *Science and Human Values* (1956; rev. ed., New York: Perennial Library, 1965), chap. 2, "The Habit of Truth."
30. Cf. Robert P. Pearson, "Religious vs. Secular Education in the Middle East: A Discussion of the Conflict in Middle-Eastern Literature," *Religious Education* 70, no. 4 (July–August 1975) : 398–405.
31. Jean-Jacques Rousseau, *Emile* (New York: E. P. Dutton & Co., 1950), pp. 213 f.
32. Bronowski, *Science and Human Values,* p. 67.
33. William Ray Dennes, *Some Dilemmas of Naturalism* (New York: Columbia University Press, 1960), pp. 137 f.
34. Ibid., pp. 146 f. A summary by Dennes of his empiricist philosophy of religion appears, together with a critical discussion from the panentheistic standpoint, in Charles Hartshorne and William L. Reese, eds., *Philosophers Speak of God* (Chicago: University of Chicago Press, 1953), pp. 486–95.

THE PRINCIPLES OF JEWISH FEDERATIONS

By

PHILIP BERNSTEIN

The Jewish Federations of North America represent a fusion of fundamental Jewish purposes and principles with the American environment and society. From the first two federations established by Boston and Cincinnati in 1896, the number has multiplied until there are now over 215 federations embracing 800 communities in the United States and Canada, with 95 percent of the Jewish population of the two countries. They are associated in the network that comprises the Council of Jewish Federations and Welfare Funds.

They obtain and administer over $450 million annually in their own fundraising. In addition, they receive funds from United Way general community campaigns, and have accumulated $186 million in endowment funds.

The total expenditures of the agencies they help support, including income from payments by the users of the services, from government, and from other sources, total at least $2 billion per year.

They have become the central Jewish community organizations in virtually all cities with one thousand or more Jewish people. They are increasingly the "central communal address," to which people come with needs and aspirations which they believe should have the attention of the Jewish community.

They are developing models with a potential of replication in other countries, as is apparent from the structures in France and the beginnings in England patterned after the federations here.

The following are the major principles on which they are based:

1. *Social Justice.* The purposes and motivations of Jewish Federations are rooted in the central Jewish religious maxims, principles, and precepts of the Bible, defining the requirements of a just society, and the centrality of that requirement in the Jewish way of life.

The motivations are found especially in the magnificent nineteenth chapter of Leviticus, the Ten Commandments, the Prophets, such as Isaiah and Micah, the levels of charity defined by Maimonides, and the requirements of Judaism not only for learning and prayer, but for acts of loving-kindness.

The federations are evolving expressions of those precepts.

2. *Community.* Federations are based on the concept of community—the Jewish concept of community. Social justice is understood as a community responsibility, requiring community action—not individual acts alone. Each person's destiny and fulfillment are tied to the well-being of his community. He has basic obligations to the community.

"Seek the welfare of the community in which you live and pray for it, for in its welfare shall be your peace," proclaimed Jeremiah.

"Separate thyself not from thy community," Jews have been taught from the beginnings of their identity.

The 10 percent tithe was an early expression of that obligation. The community rather than the individual has administered charity from earliest days. Federations have carried that into modern times, with structures and procedures to fit current needs and conditions.

3. *Unity.* Federations are rooted in the conviction that far more can be achieved by working together than separately; that Jews have far more elements and areas of agreements than disagreement; and that within the areas of their agreement, they can address themselves most effectively to the most important Jewish purposes and needs.

They are seeking to fulfill the precept of the Psalmist: "Behold how good and beautiful it is for brethren to dwell together in unity."

4. *Unity —Not Uniformity.* The federations make a fundamental distinction between unity and uniformity. They are based upon the former; they reject the latter. They are committed to the values of diversity and pluralism in Jewish life. They recognize the indispensability of independence of thought, creative initiatives of action, and competition of ideas.

They understand that a monolithic, uniform community is a community that cannot survive, and would be a vanishing community.

They affirm that strength and vitality in communal life must come through differences impacting on each other. They seek to bring together the widest variety of philosophies and aspirations, to identify areas of agreement, and then to mobilize the full community strength behind them.

5. *Inclusive—Not Exclusive.* Federations embrace all elements of the community—Orthodox, Conservative, Reform, and secular; capital and labor; young and old. All of these find a common meeting ground in federation. It is the only instrument in Jewish life where they do.

6. *Do Not Do Everything.* But federations do not carry all responsibilities, do not do everything in the Jewish community. Rather, they carry the responsibilities which are commonly recognized as the responsibilities of all Jews, affecting the well-being of all Jews.

They do not embrace the interests, aspirations, responsibilities of limited segments of the community. Such groups are free to carry out their own special interests.

7. *Maximum Creativity.* Federations are committed to encourage the fullest creativity, initiatives, and flexibility among their associated agencies, not to stifle them. They recognize that each agency needs leaders passionately devoted to the particular purposes of their organizations. Federation leaders, for their part, must have an equally passionate commitment to the total community, embracing the well-being of all.

Each community federation is itself autonomous, governed by the Jews of that community. No federation is directed by any national body.

8. *Quality and Excellence.* Federations place quality and excellence at the highest level of their values. It is a requirement for their own performance, and for the operation of the services they make possible. It is the standard by which they assess what they plan, and what they do.

9. *Consensus.* Federations are governed by consensus. There is no power of compulsion. The only force, fundamentally, is the force of persuasion.

Thus major decisions are not made by 51–49 votes, or even by 60–40 divisions. On critical issues there must be very substantial agreement for federation to act. Until such substantial agreement is achieved, the process of discussion, interaction, and persuasion goes forward. This deliberative process is to make possible the fullest input of views. While it may be time-consuming in the formulation of actions, it assures the quickest and most productive results of action, once initiated.

But federations are not the captives of unanimity or of a very tiny minority. A substantial majority does act, and can act effectively.

10. *Central Fundraising, Budgeting, Planning.* Federations represent

the interrelationship of unified fundraising, central budgeting, and community planning. They raise funds in one united campaign for a number of agencies and organizations, which thereby forgo their own separate campaigns. They have demonstrated that more funds can be raised jointly than separately, and at smaller costs. A greater proportion of the income, therefore, goes for the services intended, rather than for fundraising expenses. Thus, unified fundraising represents enlightened self-interest for the participating agencies, which receive greater income and can do more as a result.

A central fund must be distributed to the beneficiary agencies. An inherent requirement is central budgeting. A group representing a cross-section of the contributors' interests and values, assessing the relative needs of the agencies, makes the decisions.

Central allocation of funds is based upon a body of facts regarding the needs, services, and expenditures of the participating agencies. It is associated with a process of community planning of growing sophistication, which involves not only reacting to pressures, but initiatives in defining goals which the community seeks to achieve. It is moving beyond improvisations, to thoughtful formulations of social goals and programs.

11. *Involvement and Participation.* Federations are seeking increasingly to become the instrument of the many rather than the province of the few. Acting on behalf of the community to meet community responsibilities, they are moving to be the community's federation in the fullest sense.

They are involving more persons, with a greater diversity of interests and backgrounds, in their governing boards, in their committees, and as volunteers in their services.

They have made changes in their constitutions and by-laws to require the limitation of terms of office and board membership, to assure the infusion of new people —in decision-making, in policy determination, in their programs.

12. *Accountability—Trusteeship.* Inherent in federations is accountability. The federation's governing board is accountable to the contributing members, who generally constitute the great bulk of the Jewish families of the city. The various committees and staff are accountable to the board.

Federations are also accountable to their associated agencies, and the agencies are accountable to the federations, and to their own members.

13. *Planning With—Not For.* So, too, the planning and decision-making relationship to their agencies is based upon involvement of the leaders

and staffs of the associated agencies from the earliest stages of the process. The guiding principle is to plan with the agencies, not for them.

14. *Lay and Professional Partnership.* Federations represent a collaboration of lay leadership and professional staffs. The lay leaders are expected to be representative of a cross-section of the community. They must meeet the requirements of having earned the highest respect and regard of the elements of the community from which they come, having demonstrated outstanding qualities of leadership; are expected to understand Jewish purposes and principles, community needs and programs; and possess the skills for community service. The professional staffs are professionally trained, and must meet the test of being Jewishly knowledgeable and committed.

While the lay leaders determine policies and programs, the staffs are expected to help them in making those decisions, with their special professional experience and qualifications. The staffs have a primary role of carrying out the decisions and programs with professional expertness.

There is an inherent interdependence between the lay leaders and professional staffs. Communities which have the ablest leaders have the best qualified professionals; and where there are the ablest professionals, there are developed the most qualified lay leaders.

15. *People-Centered.* The primary concern of federations is the well-being of the people of the community, and of those outside the local community to whose needs federations are committed. The agencies serving them are the means to the end—not the end in themselves.

A major responsibility of federations is to assure the required cooperation and coordination of agencies, because no one agency today meets all the needs of a person, a family, a community. Just as the needs are interrelated, the agencies are interdependent. Each must relate what it does to what others do in order to succeed in carrying out its own sector of responsibility.

16. *Well-Being of the Total Community.* Federations understand that the well-being of the Jewish community depends on the well-being of the total community of which they are a part. It has been well said that Jewish communities cannot be islands of strength in seas of weakness. It has always been Jewish doctrine that social justice cannot be limited to Jews alone; Jews are dedicated to social justice for all mankind. "Love the stranger as thyself," the Bible taught.

17. *Interdependence of World Jewry.* Federations are committed to the responsibility that "We are our brother's keeper," wherever Jews are.

They seek to overcome degradation, persecution, poverty, and social needs suffered by Jews in any country of the world, to prevent and overcome second-class status of Jews anywhere. They understand, in an interdependent world, that there cannot be dignity for Jews in any country if there is indignity in other countries; that there cannot be security for Jews here if there is insecurity anywhere.

18. *Fulfillment—Not Only Survival.* The purpose of federations is not limited to overcoming Jewish pathologies and problems, nor even to assuring Jewish survival alone; rather, it is to press for the fullfillment of Jews and Judaism through achieving a more learned community, a more cultured community, a more ethical community.

Federations seek to build a community that will be a more noble model for the total community of which it is a part, for other Jewish communities in the world, for their children, and for future generations.

PEOPLEHOOD AND DEMOGRAPHY

By

JUDAH CAHN

The "Peoplehood of Israel" has been both a belief and goal of the Reconstructionist movement. The difficulty of achieving this goal in the Diaspora has always been evident. Varieties of national experience, pressures for accommodation to different cultural patterns, the need for political expediency, made Peoplehood a dream. But to Mordecai Kaplan, the greatest "religious statesman" of our times, it was not a fantasy. All problems were capable of solution if only there were unanimity of will. But this seemed as distant as the ultimate goal. However, even had the Jewish world achieved unanimity of will, it would have proved to be a necessary but not sufficient factor for the ultimate goal of Peoplehood. Zionism, the establishment of a Jewish state, was the essential element needed to achieve the social and cultural unity of the Jewish people. This unity would in no way diffuse or weaken the political loyalty of the Diaspora to their native countries. Judaism is a religious civilization, and would not impair political loyalty to one's country more than any other religion. Peoplehood is an element of Judaism even as evangelical activity is an element of other religions.

In 1948, for the first time in two thousand years, the establishment of the State of Israel gave the Jewish people an opportunity to weld all the components of Peoplehood and create a religious civilization strengthened by political independence. In Israel a common nationality, absence of counter-cultural pressures, and political independence to the greatest degree possible within an interdependent political world, would turn the dream of Peoplehood into a reality. To some degree this has taken place, but obstacles exist which impede rapid progress.

The problems of demography must be solved before the Peoplehood of Israel can become a viable entity. Jewish unity had previously been given its greatest impetus by the non-Jewish world. Jews were accepted, rejected, expelled, persecuted, and finally sentenced to genocide on the basis of so-called racial affinity or simply nomenclature. Only the Jews themselves recognized intrareligious differences. Cultural, religious, and philosophical conflicts were matters of importance only to the Jewish community. The Nazi machine of destruction did not differentiate between the Bundist and the Rebbe as it ploughed Jews into the ground. In many tragic instances it was only the Jews who maintained their own differences until the last tragic moment, when they realized that their common fate made internal differences completely and belatedly irrelevant.

The founders of the State of Israel were necessarily concerned with a multitude of serious problems. They had to establish an order of priorities. Sometimes, as in the case of Arab attacks, the priorities were established for them; sometimes, as with the problem of demography, the immediacy of the problem could not have been foretold. Whatever the reason, the enormity of this problem was not expected, and therefore its solution is more difficult.

The Halutzim, who constituted the bulk of the first settlers in Palestine, were, for the most part, a homogeneous group. Of course there were differences in philosophy. But these were doctrinaire differences and did not affect the basic motivation of Aliyah. There was a common religion; they were for and against the same religious tradition. There was the bond of language. Yiddish was the mother-tongue for almost everyone, Russian and Polish were also commonplace, and of course Hebrew was the most precious jewel in the linguistic diadem. The glorification of labor, the belief in the need for a reunification of Jews with the soil, and finally the belief in political and social equality as expressed in the establishment and life of the Kibbutzim, created a homogeneity which made total communication possible. This did not necessarily lead to agreement, but it did mean that everyone understood the basis of disagreement.

In the years before the Holocaust, settlers came to Palestine from other parts of the world—the United States, South Africa, Central and Western Europe. These people were absorbed quite easily into the social environment of Palestine. First, many had been born in the parts of Europe from which the majority of the early settlers came. Second, there were strong cultural bonds which again made communication easier. Shakespeare, Mozart, Pushkin, Rembrandt did not need explanation, they were merely the basis for differing value judgments. Of course a university was essential, a symphony orchestra very desirable, books as necessary as oxygen and soil. Is it any wonder that the Palestinian Jews of that time saw little if any need to create solutions for the problems of heterogeneity?

But the Holocaust produced a profound change. Jews who had never possessed a love of Zion or a desire to settle in Palestine, found refuge in that land. All attempts by England, the mandatory power, to stem the tide of refugees merely made the process more difficult, but did not stop it. For the first time the original Halutzim, who had found the Balfour Declaration a convenience rather than a reason for settlement, had to deal with nonvoluntary settlers. Many of the newcomers, who came from countries overridden by the Nazis, fell under the spell of the land and became as one with the older settlers. Perhaps it would be more accurate to say almost as one, because the differences between voluntary and nonvoluntary settlers never quite disappeared. Cultural differences, too, were an obstacle. Although German and Yiddish are related enough to make communication possible, use of either language was the tool of last resort. Yiddish was considered a rival of Hebrew and therefore was looked upon unfavorably by a people striving to broaden the cultural horizons of Hebrew. To German-speaking people, Yiddish was a jargon of East European Jews and therefore abrasive to the sensitivities of German Jews, who had been conditioned to think of East European Jews as a lesser breed. Finally, German itself was a language with such horrible connotations that it wasn't included in the language departments of Israeli schools. In addition, many of the newcomers had never attained more than a reading knowledge of Hebrew, if even that, and found it most difficult to develop a fluency in Hebrew. All these reasons, as well as others, made participation in public life extremely difficult. To make a political speech, engage in debate, or join in public forums of any kind was a practical impossibility for most of the newcomers.

Is it any wonder that these newly arrived settlers tended to remain within their own social groups, thus putting the means of integration even further out of reach? In addition, there was the problem of occupational preference. Tilling the soil and life on a Kibbutz held little interest for German Jews. They had been trained for commerce and the role of middlemen. The paper-filled briefcase became almost part of their dress. Despite all these problems and differences, both groups had many characteristics in common. This was especially true in the cultural world. The Philharmonic Orchestra was enriched by excellent German instrumentalists and conductors. Artists could communicate in their own medium without concern for verb forms or vocabulary. Artisans in both groups found common ground in areas of tailoring, styling, production, each contributing his expertise. Many Germans, because of having lived in more cosmopolitan European centers, knew more than a smattering of English, a very important asset to a land with such close and frequently dependent relations with the United States and Britain. Thus, although there were many barriers between the two groups, their common ground facilitated integration and differences became less substantive. The leaders of Palestine considered *absorptive capacity* a term related to geographic rather than cultural problems.

All this underwent a profound change in 1948. The establishment of the State of Israel, one of the greatest events in the history of the Jewish people, created changes not only in the political life of the Israelis, but in the social life, using the word *social* in its deepest and most extensive sense. The War of Independence created a military and political struggle between the Israeli and Arab world that has caused anguish and enmity which remain unabated to this moment. Through the open doors of Israel came the Yemenite Jews. These were people not merely of another culture, but of a different historical age. They had lived servile and depressed lives in Yemen, and they came to the civilization of Israel utterly bewildered and grateful. They fit into the social framework of Israel, first, because their language was not completely alien to Hebrew, and therefore before long, language communication became possible. A second reason was the fact that under Islamic feudalism the Yemenites had been a deprived people for so many centuries that they were overcome with happiness and gratitude for their new freedom. Many were superb artisans in crafts unfamiliar to the West. In fact, most Israelis looked upon the Yemenites with the special love we give to children. They served and worked with little complaint. The Yemenites added a kind of spice to Israeli life. Their crafts, their dances, songs, and poetry, all from another age, gave Israel a special flavor making it unlike any other Jewish community in the world. Again this was evidence that the magic of the land of Israel could weld cultural differences into a new and wonderful entity.

But the Israeli-Arab enmity brought to Israel other Arabs of a different stripe. Egyptians, Syrians, Iraqis, Tunisians, Algerians, of every social and educational level, fled to the safety of Israel in the face of rising Arab persecution of Jews. Thousands came from the slums of these countries, having no means at all either to sustain themselves or to adjust to the Western standard in Israel. These were not culturally educated Germans or complacent Yemenites. Thousands and thousands of these new arrivals were merely street-wise and had lived by their wits in their countries of origin. Violence was not unknown to them. The conditions under which many had lived before made slum-dwelling in Israel familiar.

It is both dangerous and untrue to generalize about any group of people. It must be stated that many of the refugees from the Arab world were men of means, culture, and great ability. Their problems were fewer and less complex during the period of adjustment. But even as these people had little to do with the slum-dwellers before they came to Israel, they wished little to do with them now. One of the social phenomena which can be seen by Western travelers in the Islamic world is the absence of anything which might be termed an "Islamic United Appeal." Whatever the reason, Islamic people do not practice organized charity. In Iran, for example, it is difficult to convince the Jews of long Iranian background rather than European origin to contribute to organized charity. As Islamic people they seem to believe that each should take care of his own immediate family, and philanthropy should be limited to "baksheesh," small handouts.

Thus in Israel the care of disadvantaged refugees from Arab countries was left almost entirely in the hands of the government. I think it would be true to say that the numbers of people and problems created by this exodus from the Arab world were overwhelming.

The land failed to work its magic. The government had to face mores dealings with family life, marriage, religion, never before experienced. In addition these were people who were quite familiar with affluence and political pressure even if they lacked these assets themselves. The Israeli government hoped that service in the armed forces would help the adjustment process for some, and undoubtedly it did. Many could not serve in the armed forces, and those who did returned to the same environment which they had left. There was one difference. A large number had been good soldiers, loyal, brave, but also observant. They realized that there were few of their group serving as officers. The fact that they were not prepared for this role was of little importance, for it was also true that very few could hope to reach the educational level which would make them eligible for these posts. This created a degree of dissatisfaction and resentment which has taken many forms. Crime, poverty, and social deprivation are interwoven wherever they exist. Israel is no exception. The crime rate there has risen, the nature of crime has become more violent, political demagoguery has manifested itself. "Protectzia," formerly limited to social and political areas of life, has been altered to include the "protection racket" so familiar in our own country.

The problems have not yet reached the proportions which exist in the United States, but if the trend is to be stopped, it must be done quickly. Social struggle is not endemic to one group. If one deprived group seems to ease the situation by anti-social activity, other groups will decide to utilize the same tactics. Adding to the difficulty are those people who believe that anti-social behavior is excusable if caused by poverty. This has proved to be a tragic even if well-meaning error.

Happily the State of Israel is confronting the situation, and despite the multitude of demands on the economy, has started to eradicate the causes. Schools, not prisons, are being created for delinquent children. Disadvantages must be removed not by rhetoric, but by actions which remove the root causes of the problem. Israel feels obligated to expand this program not only as a humanitarian act, but in order to fulfill the hope of Jewish Peoplehood. In the lexicon of Reconstructionism, this is a religious obligation as well as a social consideration.

The latest demographic problem facing Israel is the arrival of Russian Jews. If this great group of Jews had arrived twenty-eight years ago, there would have been fewer problems. The number of Russian-speaking Jews in Israel would have made communication easier. The system of the kibbutz and the general emphasis on social equality so prevalent during the earliest days of the state would have found echoes in the hearts of Russian Jews. The only reason for mentioning this fact is not to dwell on a past which cannot be relived, but rather to find some small hint which will enable the State to solve the problem of adjustment which is trying the hearts of us all.

Soviet Jewry is not finding its home in Israel to the extent we hoped for. Thousands are going to the United States, Canada, Australia, and other countries. Many who go to Israel find the difficulties so great that they leave. Certainly we all recognize that the problems faced by Israel are so overwhelming that adding to its burden seems to be unreasonable. But the ache for Peoplehood persists. The challenge cannot go unmet or the situation untreated. For example, why do we feel that Soviet Jews who opt for countries other than Israel should be prepared at schools in Rome for the linguistic and social difficulties they will face? Perhaps those who are Israel-bound should be equally or even better prepared. Soviet Jews have been culturally bombarded throughout their lives with anti-Western and anti-religious propaganda. They come from a country which is militarily secure, culturally advanced in many areas, and, for the most part, economically stable. Despite these advantages, thousands of Soviet Jews are willing to sacrifice everything for freedom and Peoplehood, which persist in spite of the Soviets' attempt to destroy them. Should these people be sent directly to Israel, where hearts are full but larder empty, or should they too be given a longer period of training, acquainting them with the language, history, and problems of Israel? There would be little difference between the cost for such a program and the need to support them in Israel. Even if the cost in dollars was great, the profit in terms of spiritual adjustment would be even greater. This longer period of training might ease the culture shock brought on by the change in climate, language, social values, and economic problems.

We, who believe in the Peoplehood of Israel, look to the small State of Israel as the fulcrum on which the Jewish world can elevate itself. For two thousand years we have awaited this opportunity. We cannot allow it to slip through our fingers. We must recognize that Israel is not the homogeneous land which was our age-long dream. History has decreed that it become a heterogeneous land, beset by all the problems implicit in such development.

My appeal for understanding this fact is not directed to the leaders and people of Israel; they are already aware of the condition. The appeal must be made to the Jewish people outside the land, who must realize that Israel is not simply a place of Horas and happy farmers always ready to burst into song. Israel is now a land beset by demographic differences which cannot be brushed aside or ignored. In the face of all difficulties Peoplehood remains the ever-present and ever-nearer goal. To paraphrase the *Ethics of Our Fathers,* it is not for us to reach the goal, but neither are we free to turn from the road which will reach it.

RELIGION WITHOUT SUPERNATURALISM

By

STEVEN M. CAHN

Reconstructionist Judaism rests on two fundamental theses. The first is that Judaism is a religious civilization, not merely a religion. The second is that Judaism should reject supernaturalism, the belief that there exists some power (or powers) not subject to the laws of nature.

Critics of the Reconstructionist movement have on occasion charged that these two theses are, in fact, incompatible, since, it has been argued, Judaism without supernaturalism would be a variety of secularism, and there can be no such thing as a secularist religious civilization.

My aim in this essay is to expose the error in this line of criticism, demonstrating how it involves a basic misunderstanding of the nature of religion. I intend to show that nothing in the theory or practice of religion—not ritual, not prayer, not metaphysical belief, not moral commitment—necessitates a supernaturalistic framework.

Let us begin with the concept of ritual. A ritual is a prescribed symbolic action. In the case of religion, the ritual is prescribed by the religious organization, and the act symbolizes some aspect of religious belief. Those who find the beliefs of supernaturalistic religion unreasonable or the activities of the organization unacceptable may come to consider any ritual irrational. But, although particular rituals may be based on irrational beliefs, there is nothing inherently irrational about ritual.

Consider the simple act of two men shaking hands when they meet. This act is a ritual, prescribed by our society and symbolic of the individuals' mutual respect. There is nothing irrational about this act. Of course, if men shook hands in order to ward off evil demons, then shaking hands would be irrational. But that is not the reason men shake hands. The ritual has no connection with God or demons but indicates the attitude one man has toward another.

It might be assumed that the ritual of handshaking escapes irrationality only because the ritual is not prescribed by any specific organization and is not part of an elaborate ceremony. But to see that this assumption is false, consider the graduation ceremony at a college. The graduates and faculty all wear peculiar hats and robes, and the participants stand and sit at appropriate times throughout the ceremony. However, there is nothing irrational about this ceremony. Indeed, the ceremonies of graduation day, far from being irrational, are symbolic of commitment to the process of education and the life of reason.

At first glance it may appear that rituals are comparatively insignificant features of our lives, but the more one considers the matter, the more it becomes apparent that rituals are a pervasive and treasured aspect of human experience. Who would want to eliminate the festivities associated with holidays such as Independence Day or Thanksgiving? What would college football be without songs, cheers, flags, and the innumerable other symbolic features surrounding the game? And even society's dropouts, who disdain popular rituals, proceed to establish their own distinctive rituals, ranging from characteristic habits of dress to the widespread use of drugs, all symbolic of the rejection of traditional society and its values.

The religious person, like all others, searches for an appropriate means of emphasizing his commitment to a group or its values. Rituals provide him with such a means. It is true that supernaturalistic religion has often infused its rituals with superstition, but nonreligious rituals can be equally as superstitious as religious ones. For example, most Americans view the Fourth of July as an occasion on which they can express pride in their country's heritage. With this purpose in mind, the holiday is one of great significance. However, if it were thought that the singing of the fourth verse of "The Star-Spangled Banner" four times on the Fourth of July would protect our country against future disasters, then the original meaning of the holiday would soon be lost in a maze of superstition.

A naturalistic religion need not utilize ritual in such a superstitious manner, for it does not employ rituals in order to please a benevolent deity or appease an angry one. Rather, naturalistic religion views ritual, as Jack Cohen has put it, as "the enhancement of life through the dramatization of great ideals." [1] If a group places great stress on justice or freedom, why should it not utilize ritual in order to emphasize these goals? Such a use of ritual serves to solidify the group and to strengthen its devotion to its expressed purposes. And these purposes are strengthened all the more if the ritual in question has the force of tradition, having been performed by many generations who have belonged to the same group and have struggled to achieve the same goals. Ritual so conceived is not a form of superstition; rather, it is a reasonable means of strengthening religious commitment and is as useful to naturalistic religion as it is to supernaturalistic religion.

Having considered the role of ritual in a naturalistic religion, let us next turn to the concept of prayer. It might be thought that naturalistic religion could have no use for prayer, since prayer is supposedly addressed to a supernatural being, and proponents of naturalistic religion do not believe in the existence of such a being. But this objection oversimplifies the concept of prayer, focusing attention on one type of prayer while neglecting an equally important but different sort of prayer.

Supernaturalistic religion makes extensive use of petitionary prayer, prayer that petitions a supernatural being for various favors. These may range all the way from the personal happiness of the petitioner to the general welfare of all society. But since petitionary prayer rests upon the assumption that a supernatural being exists, it is clear that such prayer has no place in a naturalistic religion.

However, not all prayers are prayers of petition. There are also prayers of meditation. These prayers are not directed to any supernatural being and are not requests for the granting of favors. Rather, these prayers provide the opportunity for persons to rethink their ultimate commitments and rededicate themselves to live up to their ideals. Such prayers may take the form of silent devotion or may involve oral repetition of certain central texts. Just as Americans repeat the Pledge of Allegiance and reread the Gettysburg Address, so adherents of naturalistic religion repeat the statements of their ideals and reread the documents that embody their traditional beliefs.

It is true that supernaturalistic religions, to the extent that they utilize prayers of meditation, tend to treat these prayers irrationally, by supposing that if the prayers are not uttered a precise number of times under certain specified conditions, then the prayers lose all value. But there is no need to view prayer in this way. Rather, as Julian Huxley wrote, prayer "permits the bringing before the mind of a world of thought which in most people must inevitably be absent during the occupations of ordinary life: . . . it is the means by which the mind may fix itself upon this or that noble or beautiful or awe-inspiring idea, and so grow to it and come to realize it more fully." [2]

Such a use of prayer may be enhanced by song, instrumental music, and various types of symbolism. These elements, fused together, provide the means for adherents of naturalistic religion to engage in religious services akin to those engaged in by adherents of supernaturalistic religion. The difference between the two services is that those who attend the latter come to relate themselves to God, while those who attend the former come to relate themselves to their fellow man and to the world in which we live.

We have so far discussed how ritual and prayer can be utilized in naturalistic religion, but to adopt a religious perspective also involves metaphysical beliefs and moral commitments. Can these be maintained without recourse to supernaturalism?

If we use the term *metaphysics* in its usual sense, to refer to the systematic study of the most basic features of existence, then it is clear that a metaphysical system may be either supernaturalistic or naturalistic. The views of Plato, Descartes, and Leibniz are representative of a supernaturalistic theory; the views of Aristotle, Spinoza, and Dewey are representative of a naturalistic theory.

Spinoza's *Ethics,* for example, one of the greatest metaphysical works ever written, explicitly rejects the view that there exists any being apart from Nature itself. Spinoza identifies God with Nature as a whole, and urges that the good life consists in coming to understand Nature. In his words, "our salvation, or blessedness, or freedom consists in a constant and eternal love toward God . . ." [3] Spinoza's concept of God, however, is explicitly not the supernaturalistic concept of God, and Spinoza's metaphysical system thus exemplifies not only a naturalistic metaphysics but also the possibility of reinterpreting the concept of God within a naturalistic framework.

But can those who do not believe in a supernaturalistic God commit themselves to moral principles, or is the acceptance of moral principles dependent upon acceptance of supernaturalism? It is sometimes assumed that those who reject a supernaturalistic God are necessarily immoral, for their denial of the existence of such a God leaves them free to act without fear of Divine punishment. This assumption, however, is seriously in error.

The refutation of the view that morality must rest upon belief in a supernatural God was provided more than two thousand years ago by Socrates in Plato's *Euthyphro* dialogue. Socrates asked the following question: Are actions right because God says they are right, or does God say actions are right because they are right? This question is not a verbal trick; on the contrary, it poses a serious dilemma for those who believe in a supernatural deity. Socrates was inquiring whether actions are right due to God's fiat or whether God is Himself subject to moral standards. If actions are right due to God's command, then anything God commands is right, even if He should command torture or murder. But if one accepts this view, then it makes no sense to say that God Himself is good, for since the good is whatever God commands, to say that God commands rightly is simply to say that He commands as He commands, which is a tautology. This approach makes a mockery of morality, for might does not make right, even if the might is the infinite might of God. To act morally is not to act out of fear of punishment; it is not to act as one is commanded to act. Rather, it is to act as one ought to act. And how one ought to act is not dependent upon anyone's power, even if the power be Divine.

Thus, actions are not right because God commands them; on the contrary, God comands them because they are right. But in that case, what is right is independent of what God commands, for what He commands must conform with an independent standard in order to be right. Since one could act in accordance with this independent standard without believing in the existence of a supernatural God, it follows that morality does not rest upon supernaturalism. Consequently, naturalists can be highly moral (as well as immoral) persons, and supernaturalists can be highly immoral (as well as moral) persons. This conclusion should come as no surprise to anyone who has contrasted the life of Buddha, an atheist, with the life of the monk Torquemada.

We have now seen that naturalistic religion is a genuine possibility, since it is reasonable for an individual to perform rituals, utter prayers, accept metaphysical beliefs, and commit himself to moral principles without believing in supernaturalism. And this insight provides a key to understanding Reconstructionist Judaism, for its proposal that Judaism reject supernaturalism is not a suggestion that Judaism become a variety of secularism but a call for Judaism to adopt a naturalistic religious perspective. And, considering the well-known intellectual pitfalls of supernaturalism, if Judaism is to remain a vibrant civilization in the modern world, it must come to recognize the wisdom of the Reconstructionist viewpoint.

NOTES

1. Jack Cohen, *The Case for Reigious Naturalism* (New York: Reconstructionist Press, 1958), p. 150.
2. Julian Huxley, *Religion Without Revelation* (New York: New American Library, 1957), p. 141.
3. Spinoza, *Ethics,* ed. James Gutmann (New York: Hafner Publishing Co., 1957), pt. V, prop. XXXVI, note.

TENSIONS IN THE MUSIC OF
JEWISH WORSHIP

By

JUDITH K. EISENSTEIN

There is no *motu proprio*[1] for the Jewish synagogue which dictates the selection or the performance-practice of music for its worship. Some earnest cantors and serious scholars might wish that such an edict could be issued and enforced. Perhaps they would cease to lament its lack if they remembered that the pope's rules and regulations have been honored more in the breach than in the observance, in the rank and file of Catholic churches, so much more unified and uniform in their liturgy than the synagogue can ever hope or care to be. It would be well to note that the one attempt to dictate uniform musical standards and practices was made in France in the nineteenth century, when a powerful Consistoire issued its own musical *motu proprio*.[2] How well it was observed is hard to tell, now that the communities of that country, Sephardic, Provençal, and Ashkenazic, are severely reduced in numbers and vitality.

Nevertheless, the malaise of those cantors and scholars and musicians is legitimate, and grows out of the total confusion which reigns in all of the synagogue denominations, certainly in the United States if not elsewhere. Tensions have developed between various segments of the leadership, and equally between segments of the congregations themselves. Often, to be sure, they are the outcome of power struggles or competitions for popularity. However, they are equally present among disinterested but conflicting antagonists, who are sincerely and seriously concerned with the ultimate values of worship, of Jewish life, and of music itself. Their concerns are valid, and their conflicts could conceivably be resolved by a systematic approach which would be twofold: first, and most obvious, would be the consultation of precedent; second, and seldom pursued in depth, would be an examination of the psychological impulses and effects of music in general, and in relation to worship in particular.

This essay proposes to outline the twofold approach as a preliminary to discussing a basis for selection and practice in Jewish worship. As a first step it offers a summary of the most prevalent tensions in the area. Taken at random they might be described as follows: (1) rabbi vs. cantor: this must be taken immediately out of the context of age-old jokes and regarded as the honest clash of honest opinions; (2) congregational singing vs. cantorial solo and choral art music; (3) lay choristers vs. professional singers; (4) instrumental accompaniment vs. *a capella* singing (this conflict obtains even where *halakhah* is not the determining factor; it is compounded by the choice of instruments, such as organ vs. other classical instruments); (5) contemporary art music vs. traditional art music; (6) pop music (and pop instruments) vs. what is commonly called "classical" music.

There are broad headings under which these tensions can be subsumed, which would make it apparent that they have precedents in the long history of the synagogue. One might use Curt Sachs' classification of music as either logogenic (word or idea oriented) or pathogenic (body and feeling oriented). One might establish the elitist (priestly, "high church") as against the popular (rabbinic, "low church"). Broadly speaking, there is the traditional vs. the innovative. Strangely enough, there is no correlation between the religious views of the protagonists and their musical preferences. The most radical of theologians are likely to defend the most rigidly traditional chant, and the most orthodox will promote the current popular styles, jazz or rock. The word *tradition* itself is variously defined when applied to music. To some it means the *Mi-Sinai* tunes of the Middle Ages; to others, the English and Dutch tunes of the Spanish and Portuguese synagogue, to others, the *niggunim* of the eighteenth-century Hasidim and their twentieth-century imitators, and to yet others, the Schubertian sweetness of Solomon Sulzer in the mid-nineteenth century.

Until the nineteenth century there was no systematic study of the materials and history of synagogue music. The medieval philosophers who theorized about music, from Saadiah on, were writing in the light of the *ethos* doctrine,[3] which for centuries was accepted by most of the ancient world, and later by the West, a doctrine which held that certain modes, melodic or rhythmic, and certain instruments had a direct influence on the temperaments, and thus could affect character. Also, they speculated about the music of the spheres.[4] Their writings had no relationship to a real set of sounds, and indeed, no application whatever to the "mundane" music of street, court, or synagogue. It is only by culling a phrase here, a paragraph there, from general texts dealing with other subjects, that one can gain an idea of the historic tensions concerning synagogue music. And then, we are likely to learn mainly the rabbinic side of the story. The *hazzanim* were not writers, and we learn of their practices and standards largely from the utterances of their opponents. One striking exception to this generalization is the brief but eloquent defense of choral music, written as a responsum by Rabbi Leon da Modena in 1605, succeeded by his preface to the first printed edition of the Psalms of Salomone de Rossi, eighteen years later. In the former, R. Leon (true Renaissance man that he was) defended not only choral music in the synagogue, but the need to study music and to rehearse it outside the synagogue. In the latter, we find his answer to those critics (like many in our own day) who found de Rossi's music non-Jewish. Said Leon, "Offering his powers to God, he took from the profane that he might add to the holy, honoring his Divine Benefactor with the gift He had bestowed upon him."[5]

Elsewhere, the Talmud and post-talmudic sources can be cited for and against music. A Babylonian *gaon* (Yehudai) appears as the champion of *hazzanut* and *piyyut,* and even advocates a specific song form. On the other hand, Yehudah ha-Levi, the greatest of the *payetanim,* expressed himself in the *Kuzari* as opposed to the use of metrical music in the synagogue, preferring the improvised chant.[6] There are infinite numbers of strictures by later writers against the borrowing of foreign melodies, against the practice by *hazzanim* of repeating words, against the prolonging of a prayer in song.[7] On the other hand, the Besht, Chabad, and Nahum of Bratzlav have the highest regard for melody, independent of words, as the surest vehicle for elevating the soul. They also regarded (in less sophisticated terms than those of Leon) as the greatest gift, the raising of a lowly drinking tune or shepherd-pipe melody to the rank of religious song. (This, of course, is a parallel to Martin Luther's advocacy of making the profane into the holy, borrowing from German folklore to create the chorales of the Protestant Church.)

Perhaps the prototype of tension comes quite early in our history. In the Talmud we find the following passages: "He who multiplies the praise of God to excess shall be torn from the world" (T.B. *Megillah* 18a). And again, "In the presence of R. Haninah, one went to the prayer desk to say the prayer. He said 'God, Thou great, strong, terrible, mighty, feared powerful, real, and adorable!' He waited till the other had finished, then he said to him, 'Have you ended with the praise of your God? What is the meaning of all this? It is as if one were to praise a king of the world, who has millions of pieces of gold, for the possession of a piece of silver' " (T.B. *Berakhot* 33b).[8]

Gershom Scholem believes that this criticism was aimed at the rising practice among gnostics and *Merkavah* mystics of singing hymns, which were not, to be sure, collated until the fifth or sixth century, and which are found in the *Heikhalot Rabati*. Scholem describes these hymns in the following words: "[they] reveal a mechanism comparable to the motion of an enormous fly-wheel. In cyclical rhythm the hymns succeed each other, and within them the adjurations of God follow in a crescendo of glittering and majestic attributes, each stressing and reinforcing the sonorous power of the world. The monotony of their rhythm—almost all consist of verses of four words —and the progressively sonorous incantations induce in those who are praying a state of mind bordering on ecstasy." [9]

One can heap precedent upon precedent, but what does one learn from it? A few *merkavah* hymns survived in the liturgy (e.g., *ha-aderet ve-ha-emunah*) in spite of rabbinic objection. The piyyut persisted, went in and out of favor in various periods. The words of Leon of Modena fell on deaf ears, and the music of de Rossi lay on musty library shelves for two hundred years. Rabbis inveighed, and cantors continued to repeat words and stretch out their songs. Solomon Sulzer despised the Hasidim, yet they sang tunes taken from his choral compositions with a *bim-bom-bom,* with hand-clapping and foot-stamping. In fact, precedent is there for accommodation, for compromise almost by accident.

Accidental compromise and accommodation were able to serve in a period of musical illiteracy. Not only rabbis and teachers lacked exposure to the music of the outside world, with its notation, its history, its forms, but even the cantors themselves had only a primitive notion (many even after the Enlightenment) of Western music, and a mere smattering of technical knowledge. In only two instances was there a conscious and sophisticated effort at effecting such compromise: first, the work of Samuel Naumbourg in France, cooperating with the aforementioned Consistoire, essaying the uniting of the Sephardic and Ashkenazic communities by including elements of their two widely different traditions; second, the collaboration of Solomon Sulzer with Rabbi Noah Mannheimer, attempting to preserve and purify the tradition and to blend it with the prevailing Viennese style of their time. The latter has remained the standard for "establishment" synagogues ever since—nineteenth-century Romanticism combined with German *hazzanut.*

Today, compromise and accommodation can be similarly accomplished with the application of a modicum of common sense and a large supply of good will. It is easy enough to take a little of this and a little of that, to divide a two-hour worship service equitably between preaching and singing, between congregational singing and cantorial or choral performance, between old and new music. Budgets, too, can be arranged by negotiation, to allow for instrumental music or professional singers, again in alternation with *a capella* music or volunteer choir.

However, sheer negotiation can easily produce the proverbial "camel—a horse created by a committee." In the process, the very purpose and nature of music in worship can easily be lost, if not completely negated. Therefore, the solution by precedent must be complemented by the second approach, namely, the consideration of the psychological and aesthetic aspects of the problem. Here precedent fails us. In ancient times music was presumed to have an apotropaic function (a magical effect). It could heal and it could hurt. In the writings of Saadiah Gaon we come upon the *ethos* doctrine of music (see above, n. 3). Certain rhythmic modes had, in his opinion, their particular effect on the temperaments, and in combination with each other, yet other effects.[10] This doctrine he took from the Arabic scholar Al-Kindi, who was, in turn, influenced by late Greek theorists.

In our time we do not expect such immediate effects of music. Today we speak of the power of music to engender mood or even emotion. In religious exercises there are certain moods and emotions which are broadly accepted as desiderata: transcendence of self, self-renewal, joy, hope, peace. These represent values which may be perceived intellectually, but need to be reinforced through the affect. Superficially, no one disputes this claim for music. However, the claims become mere pious platitudes unless one studies the actual processes by which affect is produced. Such study has long been carried on outside the area of Jewish worship by psychologists and aestheticists. Investigations have been made into the effect upon feeling of chromaticism in Western music. Popular assumptions about the sadness of the minor modes and the gladness of the major mode have been checked and reassessed. The shape of music has been related to the sensations of rise and fall, of incompleteness and resolution. Distinctions are carefully drawn between music for its own sake and *gebrauchsmusik,* or music intended for a specific purpose or occasion.

These investigations now need to be consulted, and their conclusions applied, where possible, to the effects of music in worship. This suggests a very full agenda for discussions among rabbis, cantors, musicians, and psychologists. Within the limited scope of this essay, the basis for discussion can be merely suggested.

Certain applications are immediately apparent without technical study. The nostalgic effect of music is an experience common to every level of music, and every level of person. The obvious concomitant of such a statement is that nostalgia has to refer to some previous experience, and if music is to arouse nostalgia it must refer to some previous musical experience. The Jew of an earlier generation remembered the awesome descending triad of the Great *Alenu* of Rosh ha-Shanah. It prepared him to fall to his knees at *Va-anahnu Kor'im* as he and his father and his grandfather had done over the years back to the dread days of the Crusades. But what is the nostalgia of the young contemporary, who has not heard the *Mi-Sinai* tune, who has never knelt or seen the kneeling? The nostalgia of today's young congregation, for the most part, extends to the tunes of the Yiddish theater disguised as Hasidic songs and transmitted by dance orchestras at Bar Mitzvah and marriage celebrations, or by latter-day descendants of the same theater —such shows as *Fiddler on the Roof* or *Milk and Honey*. Either the worshiper must be prepared, deliberately, through education, to recognize and respond to the ancient music, or that music must fulfil some other function than mere eliciting of nostalgia.

Another acknowledged method by which music produces affect is that of catharsis, by the release of pent-up feeling. This is often confused with "letting off steam," a process which is more likely to dissipate emotion than to produce it. Historically, our people has always sensed that one can achieve catharsis by listening to music as well as by making it. Our own ancestors in Eastern Europe could be reduced to sobs by the poignancy of a tenor cantor's chant. In his very thoughtful book *Emotion and Meaning in Music*. Leonard B. Meyer makes the following statement: "Emotion-felt or affect is most intense precisely in those cases where feeling does not result in or take the form of overt behavior." [11] And again later: "Emotion or affect is aroused when a tendency to respond is arrested or inhibited." [12] So much for the matinee lady at the symphony who bobs her head or taps her foot in time to the music! So much, equally, for the enthusiastic congregant who must sing along with the cantor at all times. "*Barekhu*," he sings, unable to restrain himself until the response "*Barukh . . . ,*" or the folk who consider it particularly pious to clap hands, as they follow the Torah scroll in joyous procession. Indeed, one wonders whether John Dewey could have foreseen a synagogue service of the 1970s when he made the statement: "Impulsion forever boosted on its forward way would run its course thoughtless and *dead to emotion* [italics added]. The only way it can become aware of its nature and its goal is by obstacles surmounted . . ." [13]

Emotion is also engendered by the balancing of predictability with surprise or deviation. A rise needs to be followed by a fall. A certain amount of repetition in a melody, either exact or at different pitches (in sequences), is grasped by the ear with ease, and produces the pleasure of recognition. But carried too far it becomes tedious or absurd, like the song of Beckmesser in *Die Meistersinger*. A change of key, a dissonance, a sharp deviation from the opening melodic line, arouses the attention and creates tension which seeks resolution, return, easing.

These are only a few of many generalizations that have been made about the emotional experience through music. They, and others, can be applied to practically any one of the problems set forth at the beginning of this essay. They apply to performance practices as well as to choice of materials in almost all situations. The need for nostalgic indulgence demands a proportion of material from various traditions, reinforced by prior initiation into those traditions through straightforward instruction. The alternation of inhibition and release can be achieved by the simplest devices of responsorial and antiphonal singing, by speech alternated with song, by reserving the activity of hand-clapping or finger-snapping or other bodily movements for selected sections of specific songs. On a more advanced level, it can be achieved by the use of choral compositions which must be listened to, into which congregational music has been inserted, as Bach inserted the chorale into his cantatas, and even into his great *Matthew Passion*. Every item of music in the service—a choral composition, a cantorial solo, an instrumental interlude, or a congregational song—can be judged for its balance of the predictable and the unpredictable. When nineteenth-century music is chosen, the blandest and most completely predictable can be avoided, and music can be found which contains an occasional dissonance, a surprising modulation. Twentieth-century spikiness and harshness can be tempered by the presence in the music of some recognizable elements, some touch of ancient chant, some familiar reference. A pop tune can be similarly judged. The song that can be accompanied by two chords on the guitar lacks the element of surprise. The persistent beat, unchanged and unmodified, has the same failing.

It is possible to seek out even pop tunes which contain harmonic surprises, rhythmic deviations.

This brings us to yet another consideration for the agenda of the discussion proposed above: the all-important aesthetic question of appropriateness. Little analysis is needed to perceive that the same pop song—even meeting all the requirements mentioned above—may be appropriate in a teen-age camp or a coffee house for young people, and fairly preposterous in a staid old synagogue building peopled by middle-aged men and women. But there are more subtle questions of appropriateness. They come up with the individual item in the service, and with the conduct of the service as a whole. "Is this music appropriate to the text?" we might ask. We can laugh now at the phenomenon of an *El Melekh Elyon* set to a tune marked *tempo de menuetto*, in the baroque style adopted by the Jews of southern Germany at the start of the nineteenth century. That was long ago, and it died a quiet, natural death. But what of the words *berit olam*—"an eternal covenant between Me and the children of Israel, an everlasting symbol," etc., set to the very latest variety of country-rock-blues? What of the *hashkivenu*—"May we lie down in peace . . ." set to a rousing foot-jiggling piece of jazz? (We do not discuss here the appropriateness of some of the texts which are now included in worship services, though they do enter into the domain of the musician when young composers are commissioned to set them to music.)

Similarly, we ask: Is the music appropriate to the architecture? Just as people prefer to hear popular music in a cafe setting, chamber music in an intimate recital hall, symphonic music in a large auditorium, so they might properly expect the music of worship, like the form of worship itself, to be suited to its physical environment. The small informal meeting house is a comfortable setting for congregational singing and guitar playing, and even occasional hand-clapping and other bodily movement. The large "cathedral" type of synagogue dwarfs that kind of activity, and makes it seem petty and foolish. Architecturally it demands the large chorus, the more classic instrumental background (if any), the virtuoso cantor (using *virtuoso* in no perjorative sense, but in the sense of skilled, trained vocalism and educated musicianship).

Finally, still applying the general psychological and aesthetic principles thus far suggested, judgments can be made in the light of the new functions which the worship service is called on to perform in our time. On the one hand, the synagogue is becoming an extension of the home. Gone are the large family gatherings at a Friday evening or at a Sabbath noon meal, or at the *se'udah shelishit,* when grandparents and parents and children sang *zemirot* late into the night, or through the afternoon until the time for *havdalah.* The *zemirot* are transferred into the synagogue service, where, again, each text and each tune must meet standards of style and appropriateness. The informality and warmth of the home are more easily obtained in the small meetinghouse kind of service. On the other hand, the concert hall has failed as a setting for larger forms of composition—for cantatas, oratorios, or dramatico-musical works of Jewish content. The Jewish audience for these works is in the synagogue, and could enjoy all the values of worship while hearing them in the large, imposing structures which abound in this country. They would, of course, be performed only on special occasions. In an open atmosphere, where the religious leaders and the laymen have the opportunity to think through musical problems, such a larger work could substitute for a sermon or a period of instruction—sometimes for the entire ritual. The well-composed piece of music may offer a new and emotional commentary on a biblical text, or on a set of poems by Ibn Gabirol or perhaps by Hayyim Nahman Bialik. For example, Aaron Copland's (*a capella*) cantata *In the Beginning* would be a stirring addition to the observance of *Shabbat Bereshit.* Lukas Foss's *Song of Songs* could restore the reading of that lovely text to the Pesah service, and the often neglected reading of Ecclesiastes might be revitalized by the performance of Robert Starer's oratorio based on the Hebrew text. These are random examples, but others could be found, and many more could be commissioned from talented young composers.

Of one thing we may be assured. The prospect for uniformity is poor, and probably undesirable. Just as we speak of diversity in other aspects of Jewish life, we speak of diversity in the music of Jewish life, but within what unity? Are we going to lose entirely the joyous experience of hundreds of Jewish travelers who, on visiting a strange or foreign synagogue, are able to join the congregation in song? There is an emotional value in that experience too precious to give up. By assuring some reference to tradition in every musical service, and by including at least one or two commonly known congregational hymns, the loss can be avoided. At the moment, alas, the most familiar melodies are not the noblest examples of the repertoire, but they could be replaced gradually, perhaps even one at a time, by a consensus of the planners, thinkers, and musicians who join in a serious effort to consult precedent and psychology, to resolve the tensions that now beset the world of synagogue music.

NOTES

1. This refers specifically to the decree issued by Pope Pius X in 1903, containing regulations for the music in the Roman Catholic service. For a resumé of the most important points, see Willi Apel, *"Motu Proprio,"* in *Harvard Dictionary of Music,* 2d ed. (Boston, 1974), p. 546.
2. Eric Werner, *A Voice Still Heard: The Music of Ashkenazic Jewry* (University Park, Pa., 1976), chap. 11. The regulations of the Consistoire are cited here in full.
3. For more about the *ethos* doctrine in music, see Curt Sachs, *The Rise of Music in the Ancient World* (New York, 1943), pp. 248 ff. Also, Gustave Reese, *Music in the Middle Ages* (New York, 1940), pp. 44 ff.
4. For texts of the medieval writers with translations into English, see Eric Werner-Isaiah Sonne, "The Philosophy and Theory of Music in Judaeo-Arabic Literature," *Hebrew Union College Annual* 16 (1940–41); 17 (1942–43).
5. Both responsum and preface may be found in English translation in Salomone Rossi, *Ha-Shirim asher Lish'lomo,* ed., Fritz Rikko (New York, 1967–73), 3:17 ff., 23 ff.
6. Judah Halevi, *The Kuzari,* trans. Hartwig Hirschfeld (New York, 1964), p. 125, pars, 69, 70.
7. Much of the written controversy is quoted in Israel Adler, *La Pratique musical-savante dans quelques communautés Juives en Europe aux XVII et XVIII siècles* (Paris, 1966), vol. I. Some of the same material, plus additional citations, may be read in English in Werner, *A Voice Still Heard,* chap. 7.
8. Cited in Gershom Scholem, *Major Trends in Jewish Mysticism* (New York and Jerusalem, 1941), p. 60.
9. Ibid., p. 59.
10. Saadia Gaon, *The Book of Beliefs and Opinions,* trans. Samuel Rosenblatt (New Haven, 1948), treatise 10, chap. 18, p. 402.
11. Leonard B. Meyer, *Emotion and Meaning in Music* (Chicago, 1956), p. 9.
12. Ibid., p. 14.
13. John Dewey, *Art as Experience* (New York, 1934), p. 59. Cited in Meyer, cit. *Emotion and Meaning in Music.*

THE RABBI AS PASTORAL COUNSELOR

By

HARRIET A. FEINER

Although the counseling role of the rabbi has some antecedents in the past, its modern development is to a large extent a response to American Jewish life. Traditionally the main functions of the rabbi were those of scholar, teacher, and judge. His authority was based on his knowledge of Jewish law, lore, and history as well as on the extent of his piety. His sanction came from the community and was acknowledged by members of the community, who both accepted and respected the way of life, code of law, and behavior which the rabbi represented and interpreted. However, since membership in the Jewish community involved a more total and integrated way of life than the modern Jew lives today, the seeds of counseling did inhere in the rabbinic role. In fact, both interpretation of the law and judging included elements of counseling. All of us are familiar with the stories of rabbis who did not look too carefully when asked to make a judgment about the Kashruth of a poor family's Shabbat chicken. Was this not, after all, counseling or pastoral care? In the chassidic community, the role of the rebbe or tzaddik further approached the modern counseling function, as more emphasis was placed on emotional attachment to Jewish life and to the rebbe himself, as problem-solver and as holder of some mystical powers.

Nevertheless, it is important to note that the tradition, both mitnagdic and chassidic, put the major responsibility for the care of the sick, the aging, the needy, and the bereaved on the entire community, not just on the rabbi. The injunction to visit the sick, clothe the naked, etc., was a commandment to be followed by all, not only by the rabbi as a representative of the ethical and moral sensibilities of the community.

In addition, special organizational structures were developed within the community to meet special needs, for instance the Hevrah Kadisha to ensure proper burial, etc. Perhaps the social agencies of American Jewish Federations of Philanthropies can be seen as the modern counterparts of these structures.

Currently in the United States, with the exception of the small, self-contained, ultra-Orthodox communities, the functional role of the rabbi has shifted considerably in response to the fact that for the American Jew, the Jewish community is no longer the only or even the major reference group. Several factors in American life have combined to influence the further development of the counseling function. To some extent the Jew began to define Judaism as parallel to Christianity. Inevitably, then, expectations of the rabbi reflected those of the Protestant minister. For the Protestant minister, sometimes even called a "pastor," the pastoral function is a major one. He, like Jesus, is seen as the "shepherd of his flock," the preacher and the healer, and he, with Jesus as his model, seriously tries to heal.[1]

In addition, the complexity, the anonymity, and the economic pressures of modern urban life have produced an alienating and isolating society in which the individual finds himself faced by myriads of tensions and problems with minimal community support. For the Jew, the rabbi, the synagogue, and the Jewish community, though no longer the carirers of an integrated life style, sometimes serve to dispel some of the experiences of rootlessness. They may provide comforting relationships, a sense of belonging, and many elements of a support system. To do this effectively, needs for comfort and counseling must be met.

Lastly, the counseling function of the rabbi has been stimulated by the rapidly developing mental health movement. This movement, in turn, has developed not only because of advances in knowledge of the psychology of human development and behavior but also because of the aforementioned alienating qualities of modern society and the resultant human needs. Prior to the turn of the century and the thinking of Freud, modern concepts of counseling did not exist; neither, of course, did popular demands for mental health, constant happiness, instant euphoria, peace of mind, and a generally problem-free existence. Whereas in the past, rabbinic counseling consisted largely of judging and advising, today the rabbi's pastoral work is influenced by concepts derived from knowledge of the dynamics of human development and behavior as well as by growing mental health norms and values.

In light of these influences, it seems appropriate to consider whether this development of the pastoral role will enhance Jewish life and should therefore be encouraged or whether it is a role better carried by others. It seems to me that the synagogue and the rabbi have a role to play, albeit a role that can and should be differentiated from that of the professional helper. The effective performance of this role will put the Jewish community in a position of greater strength as it will ensure the provision of services which are valued because they meet needs. The community will thus again have greater impact on more aspects of living rather than confine itself to a narrowly defined religious function.

As an attempt is made to delineate the appropriate role more sharply, it is helpful to look back at traditional community functions and the manner in which they were carried out in order to see whether we can learn anything that will be of use to us today. Earlier in this paper, note was taken of the fact that in the past, not only the rabbi but the entire community was expected to be involved in providing social services. Clearly this is a useful approach for several reasons. Social isolation is an important predisposing factor to problems in functioning. In addition, those involved in giving care reap major benefits for themselves. Service to others provides a sense of the purpose and meaning of life, thereby enhancing feelings of well-being and relatedness. Hence, a significant service can be rendered by the rabbi who sees his pastoral role as including the organization of the laity to provide effective support systems.

In the past these supports were built into living patterns. Nuclear families lived with or at least near the extended family. Kinship ties were strong, and family roles were much more clearly drawn. Consequently, the family itself was the source of a great deal of effective preventive help. Currently, social, economic, and geographical mobility means that nuclear families frequently live far from other relatives. Thus, neither the young family nor the aging one can depend on the other for assistance.

Since crisis[2] is intrinsic to life, and since close relationships can help to prevent crisis from becoming overwhelming, the kind of help that the rabbi can stimulate his congregation to provide is particularly necessary now. The rabbi can provide the kind of leadership that helps a congregation to function as a surrogate extended family. If such a network operates effectively, an unemployed member may receive assistance in relocating himself. A widow may receive the kind of support that enables her to remain a part of the group rather than withdraw and isolate herself from the company of couples, as so often happens. An older person may be welcomed and enabled to feel that he continues to have a contribution to make to the life of the congregation. A congregational community can function more effectively to provide support to people experiencing extraordinary crisis situations if it is already an integral part of its member's lives and is involved in marking the normal developmental crises of the life cycle.

Traditional Judaism provided community acknowledgment of life-cycle events through specific prescribed rituals. Thus birth, the assumption of adult responsibilities, marriage, and death were all marked by the community as well as by the individual. These events carry such major significance that at the present time they continue to be given some attention by the congregation. Nevertheless, the quality and extent of the attention as well as the Jewish meaning have been attenuated. So important an experience as the birth of a child may not be Jewishly noted at all. There is frequently a circumcision rather than a B'rith. Even Bar Mitzvah, currently the most clearly congregationally oriented occurrence in the life cycle, is often a private family celebration with little congregational participation.

Rabbinical leadership, including outreach to individual members and groups of members, could help to bring families back to the congregation to share these experiences. There are some beginning developments in this realm as young rabbis have begun to think about developing new rituals—some to mark the birth of girls and of first-born children and others to mark later events in the life cycle.[3] However, the assumption of this role has many implications for the total organization of the synagogue. Certainly massive institutions composed of five hundred families or more, mainly focused on financially supporting a building, cannot perform this function. To grasp this opportunity to serve, new ways must be found—perhaps the development of chavurot within a large synagogue or perhaps some other, totally new approach.

The development of lay participation is only one aspect of the rabbinic pastoral or counseling role. There is also a place for the provision of direct services when requested by a congregant as well as on an outreach basis when need is evident. The definition of pastoral functions that I shall use is a broad one. It includes all activities related to extending comfort or enhancing the social functioning of members of the Jewish community. To a large extent, however, the development of this rabbinic role is related to the interest of the rabbi. Although most rabbis are called upon to perform some of these duties, there is generally a good deal of choice about the extent and depth of the involvement. The rabbi who is particularly interested in this role can provide a valuable service. The rabbi who is not interested should at least develop sufficient skill to make appropriate and effective referrals.

The rabbi who seriously involves himself in developing community supports, as well as in providing direct services, must carefully consider the tension between a congregant's right to privacy and confidentiality and the help that can be offered by lay members of the congregation. He must differentiate between situations in which it is appropriate to inform congregants so that they can extend a helping hand and other situations which should not be mentioned at all without permission from the involved person. Respect for the individual dictates that this very complex matter be given thorough attention. Privacy can sometimes encourage alienation and isolation, and yet its violation can lead to disregard and disrespect for the dignity and rights of people.

Most rabbis visit sick or bereaved members of a congregation, yet the character of the visits can vary greatly. A visit can be a perfunctory social call or a source of immeasurable comfort, depending largely on the rabbi's capacity to assess and meet the needs in an individual situation. In some instances, a visit which conveys the friendship and concern of the rabbi is all that is appropriate or required. At other times, a family may desperately need assistance in coping with a crisis in its life. The only way to learn about the nature of the need is to observe carefully and listen attentively.

Thus, it is important to choose a time for the visit when it is possible to spend some time alone with the family. Rather than distract the congregant and attempt to "cheer him up," the rabbi should encourage discussion of any anxieties and concerns that are present. He may find the expression of a wide variety of feelings. Initially some of these may surprise him. Not only grief and sadness, but anger, fear, and relief may be expressed. He may, at first, feel confused by ambivalence, the almost simultaneous expression of contradictory emotions. Rather than judge these feelings, he needs to accept them as a natural and normal response. Comfort does not come from knowing that others may have worse problems, but from empathetic acceptance of the particular difficulty being experienced.

This does not mean that a helping person suspends his critical and evaluative judgment. However, it is not exercised in determining responsibility or in moralizing. It is used to assess whether the individual is able to cope with his feelings and with the reality demands of the particular situation. The crucial question relates to whether comfort, support, help in looking at realistic alternatives, and time will enable the individual or family to reorganize and continue to function effectively.

If the answer is in the affirmative, then the rabbi, together with the congregation, can meet these needs, though an extended period of time may be required. For instance, a widow or widower may need attention far more after the week of *shiva* than during it when the house is full. Continued expressions of friendship and encouragement may be necessary to enable full participation in the community to resume. If the answer is in the negative or if other professional expertise is needed to define alternatives, then a referral for more intensive help is probably needed.

In addition to the more usual work with the sick and the bereaved, the rabbi has an excellent opportunity to enhance social functioning. He may observe that a youngster in the Hebrew school is behaving in an unusual way. Perhaps the child appears lonely and without friends or is suddenly disruptive and hostile. Expressing interest in such a youngster, listening to him, encouraging him to express his feelings may help the child over a rough spot and permit growth to proceed; it may develop into an opportunity to help a child express his need for more intensive help to parents who are unaware that a problem exists; it may be an opportunity for an older child, who needs to move further away from the family, to identify with a warm, caring adult who can serve as a constructive ego ideal; or it may be one of many other possibilities.

Work with adolescent members of the community is another important area for pastoral work. As the noted psychoanalyst Erik Erikson points out,[4] young people, during the high school years, are in the process of establishing and consolidating their values and identities as separate individuals. This is a period of high energy and rapid growth. Influences outside the home are of major significance as the emerging individual separates himself from the family and readies himself for independent functioning. Though the youngster moves away from the influence of the family at this time, he or she, nevertheless, frequently feels uncertain and confused about many crucial developmental issues— sexuality, the use of drugs or alcohol, developing a balance between hedonism and altruism, among others. If the rabbi is seen as an accessible person who is willing to listen and talk openly about these issues, he has an opportunity to be an important influence in the lives of the youngsters in the community.

Currently, because of the rising intermarriage rate, almost all rabbis have the experience of being asked by parents to intervene in order to prevent an intermarriage. Though such requests continue to be made, it is doubtful that such intervention lowers the intermarriage rate. However, these situations do present an urgent need for skilled counseling, and the rabbi is uniquely qualified to provide this service. He has been sought out specifically because of his commitment to the continuity of Jewish life. To be effective in this role, he must accomplish the difficult task of maintaining this commitment while simultaneously listening to the young couple's thoughts and feelings in an open and flexible way. Breaking up the relationship may be neither possible nor wise. However, helping the couple to move toward Judaism rather than away from it and helping the parents to cope with their feelings in a way that enables them to maintain a relationship with their children rather than alienate them are both valuable, though clearly not traditional, goals.

Moreover, the rabbi's counseling role at the time of marriage should not be limited to situations in which intermarriage is being considered. An opportunity to strengthen the family and prevent malfunction is presented whenever the rabbi is asked to perform a wedding ceremony. This is a natural and appropriate time to involve the couple, or even a group of couples, in a discussion about the experience of marriage. This too can be either a perfunctory or a deeply meaningful interaction, depending upon the seriousness and skill with which it is undertaken. In our society, little formal preparation for marriage is considered necessary, yet in view of the rising divorce rate, perhaps this approach needs to be reconsidered.

In addition to situations related to the developmental aspects of life, the rabbi is often asked for help in resolving conflict situations—internal, between spouses, between parents and children, etc. Often the rabbi, rather than a member of another helping discipline, is selected because of certain unique characteristics of the relationship with the rabbi. These features, sometimes advantageous and sometimes disadvantageous, must be understood. Some people who experience serious stress nevertheless find it difficult to ask for help. It seems less threatening to discuss a problem with the rabbi. There is less formal structure; there is no requirement to clearly and unequivocably say: "I need help, I cannot solve my problems by myself." Often the discussion is initiated in an informal and unrelated context, perhaps over coffee after a service or while waiting for a meeting to begin. Whether the rabbi chooses to pick up on these tentative and frequently disguised requests for help, depends upon both his interest and his perceptiveness. Sometimes it is difficult to understand what is being asked for; however, an offer to continue the discussion at another time may bring greater clarity. On the other hand, there are also people who do not wish to relate to a rabbi in this way. They may feel self-conscious and embarrassed. They may wish to maintain their privacy and may prefer that the rabbi not know about the difficulties they face. Generally, their right to privacy should be respected.

Others may seek help from the rabbi because of the authority that inheres in the rabbinic role. They may feel a need to be told what to do by someone they regard as an appropriate authority figure or they may wish to enlist this authority to direct another person's behavior. It is in such situations that care must be exercised to avoid abuse of power. It is tempting to assume an omnipotent role, particularly when that role is assigned by members of the community. However, the use of authority is rarely helpful. It encourages dependency rather than autonomy and the capacity for self-direction. In addition, magic answers are generally unavailable. Self-understanding and considerable skill are needed to work effectively with people who come with requests for direct advice.

The range of pastoral work is great; nevertheless, the rabbinic counselor must continuously assess the situations in which he functions to determine whether he is competent to proceed, whether he needs consultation with another discipline, or whether he should work towards a referral. The decision will to some extent be based on the knowledge and experience of the rabbi. Due to the proliferation of theories and knowledge, we live in a world of specialization. The rabbi's major expertise must continue to be in those matters which relate to the Jewish experience; its history, current status, and future. He cannot be expected to possess the specialized knowledge or skill of the helping professional. Yet in order to perform pastoral functions, he should have a basic understanding of developmental psychology, of the nature of the helping process, and of the values which support this process.

For the most part, the value system of Judaism is in harmony with the value system that informs most useful theories of helping. Consequently, the rabbi can and should draw on his Jewish expertise. In fact, his congregants expect that he will. The basic framework of knowledge should help to differentiate those situations in which a person's capacity to cope with problems in living is increased by discussion of conscious reality factors from situations which present major deviations, frequently based on unconscious intrapsychic factors. In the former, the rabbi can probably be of help, though even here he may wish to make a referral. In the latter, consultation or referral are essential.

Making a referral is not a simple matter and does not mean just suggesting professional help. Too frequently such a suggestion is felt as threat or a rejection and is ignored. Not only is no further assistance sought but the possibility of talking to the rabbi is also closed off. Consequently, when a referral is made, an opportunity to discuss the feelings engendered must be provided. Even after thorough discussion, it is important to follow up and maintain contact until an appointment has been made, particularly if there is a waiting period before an appointment is available. It is difficult to acknowledge the need for help and to request it. However, support and understanding can frequently enable a person to move toward the help he needs. I do not mean to suggest, however, that the rabbi can assume the responsibility for seeing to it that help is sought. He can facilitate, he can leave his door open for further discussion—though at times this may not be helpful—but in the final analysis, the decision and responsibility lie with the person who needs help.

In this paper, I have tried to examine some aspects of the rabbinic pastoral role, its potentialities and its limitations. Within the range of possibilities, each rabbi will need to determine for himself, on the basis of his own interests and the needs of the community, what his role and function should be.

NOTES

1. Howard J. Clinebell, Jr., *Basic Types of Pastoral Counseling* (Nashville and New York: Abingdon Press, 1966) pp. 47–48.
2. The term *crisis* is used in this paper as Erik H. Erikson uses it. "Crisis is used here in a developmental sense to connote not a threat of catastrophe, but a turning point, a crucial period, of increased vulnerability and heightened potential." Erik H. Erikson, *Identity, Youth, and Crisis* (New York: W. W. Norton Co., 1968), p. 96.
3. Rabbis Sandy and Dennis Sasso have written a covenantal birth ceremony for the birth of a girl as well as a ceremony to replace the *Pidyon Ha-Ben,* while still noting the importance of a firstborn child. Dennis Sasso and Sandy Sasso, "A Covenant for the Daughters of Israel," *Moment,* May–June 1975. Also see Rabbi Steven Stroiman's article on the need to develop a ritual for the separation from family and congregation that takes place at the end of high school. Steven Stroiman, "A Rationale and Conceptualization for a New Rite of Passage," *Reconstructionist,* June 1976.
4. Erikson, *Identity, Youth, and Crisis.*

THE VALUES AND USES OF HISTORY

By
OSCAR I. JANOWSKY

The crisis of the 1960s has run its course. Turbulence had gripped college and university campuses throughout the land, challenging educational assumptions, disparaging curricular guidelines, and flouting authority based on knowledge and experience. Agitation has since abated and tumult has subsided; college youth is again quiescent and possibly acquiescent as well. But one wonders what it is that youth approves today or accepts, at least in the liberal arts which bore the brunt of the attack. In many colleges, the havoc wrought by "non-negotiable" demands, strikes, sit-ins and teach-ins, even vandalism, reduced to fragments what had been left of the old, structured liberal arts curriculum, with its "basic" courses, and these were overlaid with hastily contrived new studies which neither complemented the old nor absorbed them in a new conception of purpose or direction. The wreckage has not as yet been sorted out, but certain it is that the study of history has been a casualty.

History had long served as a unifying element in the liberal arts curriculum, even after its splintering by extravagant permissiveness. History was the chronological frame of reference, the trail through the thicket of the past. It furnished the thread of continuity in the evolution of civilization, the record of change in the development of ideas, institutions, and ideals, the cumulative effects of the struggle for human betterment, and the residue of poverty, injustice, oppression, and international strife which remained to plague humanity. But the study of this record of human achievements and failures was scorned during the turbulent 1960s as unworthy of the central place it had long occupied in college and school curricula.

Because some of the documents of the past were discredited as forgeries, or because annals and chronicles had credited unproved or naive assumptions, all of structured history was spurned as the record of errors and imbecilities. Since in the nature of things complete knowledge of the past is unattainable, and historical judgments must rest on partial evidence preserved by the contingencies of time and circumstance, the entire record was flawed as devoid of truth. Moreover, the historian was challenged, indeed ridiculed, on his basic claim to veracity and credibility, that is, his vaunted "objectivity." That, scoffed the historian's detractors, was an empty boast, a cloak of deception or at best self-deception, because the historian himself was a creature of his times, conditioned by his beliefs and desires. As such, he was not custodian of the past or its dispenser, but the creator and purveyor of his own brand of history, a warped reconstruction of the past.

The imperfections of history waxed prodigiously as they percolated down to youthful people of limited knowledge and experience, especially the self-styled "revolutionaries," who saw nothing but evil in the present "Establishment," and longed to demolish it to clear the ground for a new and glorious society of the future. These people were purists who envisaged the future as well as the past and present in absolute terms. Just as "liberation" was a farce if it did not eliminate all evil, so history that did not constitute absolute truth was adjudged rank falsehood. Similarly, if total objectivity was unattainable, the very attempt to approximate it was a delusion, indeed a snare to entrap the guileless. Since it could not present *all* the evidence of the past, it was consciously or unconsciously selective, and hence no better than a record deliberately contrived or falsified. In a word, history as written and taught was made by the historians, and their product was a "subjective" and distorted concoction no more worthy of credence than the effusions of crass propagandists.

Nay more; so-called objective history was branded as the worst kind of propaganda, because it palmed off as the record of civilization ideas formulated by the learned and institutions dominated by the rich and well-born. Such a record, it was argued, was tainted by "elitism" and "meritocracy," and had no relevance to our times. Even worse; the historian diverted the innocent from the path of progress by turning their attention to the past instead of concentrating on the evils of the present. He tallied and analyzed views and opinions as if they were of equal merit, and thus, instead of condemning the wicked past and present, he was contributing to their perpetuation.

Demands were advanced that old priorities in historical studies yield to new objectives and motivations: the slogan "relevance" was trumpeted as the measure of educative value, and "sophistication," a misty and arrogant concept, took priority over unaffected understanding. The demands could not be ignored, and some respectable institutions of higher education were obliged no longer to require basic studies in the evolution of civilization, the history of ideas, or even the roots of present problems. These must compete in the collegiate marketplace with "innovative" courses like "Marxism and Feminism," "Fear of Women," and "How to Make a Revolution," the latter a truly functional subject in futuristic shop-work.

The attack upon history is really a quixotic attempt to repudiate and deny the past. And one understands the compulsion to do so. The established order, the legacy of the past, is always imperfect; indeed it is shot through with injustice, cruelty, and hypocrisy. Idealistic youth want the evils eradicated outright and instantaneously. They yearn for a world of justice, equality, decency, and sincerity, and the past is a halter on speed. If one is in a hurry, one is loath to look back. The road traversed is often full of potholes, sharp and dangerous curves, wrong turnings which compelled redirection. Furthermore, perplexities abound when one stops to consider the past. Reflection intrudes, retarding action. When one knows what ought to be, one feels shackled by what has been. If one is obsessed with the desirable, one is impatient with caution, which counsels the possible. Hence the past, the record of history, is repudiated and concern with it disavowed. Present evils and their eradication claim all attention, with little or no concern about continuity or consequences. Action and rapid change become the order of the day, and if a panacea fails, one is certain that other means can be contrived.

Yet human life and human institutions are not toys which may be manipulated or botched. The wreckage left by hasty and ill-considered tinkering can obstruct and bedevil further attempts to set things right. The reach for the desirable, for the optimum in government and society, is praiseworthy. But reach must have some relationship to grasp, grasp of the complexities of a problem, the ramifications and consequences of a proffered solution. When the certain is slight, the probable assumed, and the possible a product of the imagination, knowledge of the past is indispensable, because imagination is a projection of the past. When the reach for what ought to be is severed from the grasp of what has been, the goal is a will-o'-the-wisp.

The assumption of our self-styled prophets and revolutionaries that their achievements would be the greater and more durable because uninhibited by the caution of knowledge of the past has proved a delusion. Their massed ranks have broken to fragments, their non-negotiable demands blown off as so much chaff. The anger and confrontations stand revealed as little more than froth—bubbly, effervescent, and overflowing, but charged with wind, and the foam has evaporated. The debris left by the hectic years of the 1960s no doubt contains grains of value, but these will have to be sorted out and evaluated in the light of history by less impatient minds.

In essence, our latter-day revolutionaries were not even suppressed. They disintegrated and faded away for lack of roots in the past. That is a pity, for they meant so well. But change that ignores history cannot endure.

The assumption that one can live solely in the present is an illusion and an obsession; the past cannot be renounced or ignored. It is neither dead nor distant. It is last year, yesterday, this morning. Every person lives in the past as well as the present; he ever stands astride the two, and there is no dividing line. The memories of yesteryear are part of the present, often no less vivid and poignant, and no less real, than the event of the moment. The past is a stream that laps at one's heels, a wave that has carried one aft, as the revolutionaries of the recent past must have learned. If you repudiate the past, it creeps up on you and overtakes you. Some of the detractors of the past must have learned to their chagrin that at thirty years of age they were themselves of the past and no longer acceptable to their followers as protagonists of present causes or architects of the future. You forfeit the present as it recedes, and your usefulness for the future is at an end.

The past is not irrelevant. It is immanent and mirrored in the present, and it enables us to understand the present by revealing the origins and development of the existing state of things. Without it we are unsure where we are because we know not where we have been. To leap out of the past is not to be liberated from it, but to plunge from a charted path, with hazards marked, into the unknown. Only self-indulgent fantasy can visualize or improvise a ready-made terrestrial paradise in the thickets of the future.

The record of the past, conceived as secular history, is not revelation of the workings of a divine plan or the unraveling of the play of inexorable fate. It is the reconstructed record of humankind—the actions, ideas, and strivings of men and women with their imperfections, cruelties, and stupidities, as well as their benevolent efforts, hopes, and aspirations. The record is never complete, but it does trace the evolution of mankind and the development of ideas and institutions. It can and does make evident the human ideas which have sought to endow the course of events with meaning and purpose. It unveils the complexities of the problems facing mankind through the ages, and the plurality of choices in the fashioning of means to resolve the problems. It attempts to ascertain why one alternative was chosen rather than another, and notes the consequences of such action. The study of this record can contribute to a realization that the present is not an "Establishment" determined for all time or maintained by diabolical interests which must be destroyed at one fell swoop. The present emerges as a stage in a process of change and development, produced by competing desires, passions, and pressures; that the process of development continues and is open to alternative choices as in the past.

The historian, too, is neither deceiver nor dupe, and his "objectivity" is not pose or pretense. He is aware of the limitations and pitfalls of his craft: that he cannot attain complete and absolute knowledge of the past; that his evidence is often no more than the "tracks" of human activities or the results of human efforts; that evidence is frequently remembrance subject to error or illusion; that testimony may be partial, even fraudulent. In a word, historical evidence is not necessarily conclusive; it may be more or less reliable, and reliability must be established.

For these reasons, the historian seeks to track down every shred of available evidence bearing on a subject. He does not just enumerate and tally but scrutinizes and weighs the evidence to determine its authenticity and credibility. He is ever on guard against tainted evidence, tainted not by its source but in its credibility. His pursuit of deception and misrepresentation is relentless. It is in the quest for and scrutiny of evidence that the historian's objectivity is most strikingly manifested; there and in the effort to determine the relevance of the evidence, and hence its applicability to the question at issue.

The historian also has a sustained passion for verification, verification of his method of using his evidence. Has he been objective in the selection of sources; that is, rigorous enough in evaluating authenticity and relevance? Has he excluded or ignored material germane to his subject? Is his grasp of the evidence incomplete because of unawareness of sources appropriate to the situation? The historian is also aware that he may err because of his preconceptions and predilections, because he knows that he may be conditioned by prevailing ideas and prejudices.

With all this probing and testing, the historian still does not claim that his conclusions constitute the absolute truth. It is the fundamentalist in religion and the doctrinaire in ideology who assert certainty or the indisputable truth of their pronouncements. The fundamentalist and doctrinaire are certain that they possess the means of ascertaining the Truth: revelation is the source of Truth for the fundamentalist; for the doctrinaire it is what is popularly known as Marxism or Marxism-Leninism-Stalinism, or Maoism, or a mystical "new consciousness" or superior intuition for the dictators of the extreme right.

It is the fetish of the single cause in historical interpretation that produces a single thesis, subordinates data to that thesis, and molds facts into the preconceived pattern. And once the single thesis is equated with Truth, it must be valid for all, and admits of no dissent. A historical judgment, therefore, becomes a judicial decision handed down from above and requiring compliance from below. And those who persist in dissenting are either dupes who must be enlightened and compelled to confess their errors, preferably in public, or they are sinners and criminals who must be punished and prevented from diverting the innocent from the path of Truth. It is this intolerance of dissent which fed the flames of the *auto-da-fé* in the past and caused incarceration as psychologically disturbed or mentally unbalanced in the Russia of today.

The historian knows that historical developments are too complex, and the impulses behind them too variable, to be reduced to a single cause. He does not lay claim to a monopoly of the Truth. He knows that absolute truth is unattainable, and he does not strive for finality but for verisimilitude or the appearance of truth, which means probability. His conclusions are, therefore, tentative and provisional. New evidence may be discovered or new insights advanced which may modify or qualify his conclusions. He welcomes criticism of his views, eagerly studies the evidence or insights adduced in contradiction to his conclusions, and stands ready to modify them if warranted. Dissent is, therefore, not only permissible; it is necessary and desirable in free inquiry to attain probable truth. This, too, is part of the objectivity of the historian.

Is this a misreading of history and an idealization of the historian? Let us examine briefly the recent past. The Russian Revolution repudiated the past and set about building a future of justice and equality. Means did not matter to Lenin, Stalin, or their successors. They drove headlong on an uncharted course, and when a stone wall was encountered, they tried another path, another means, with equal haste and ruthlessness. That millions died of hunger because of unworkable policies was dismissed with a crude metaphor: "You cannot make an omelet without breaking eggs." The metaphor is revealing: human lives are eggshells. That the method of dictatorship and intolerance of dissent produced a Stalin, a monster who devoured even his own kind, was explained by a slogan—"the cult of personality." But the method remains, because dictatorship centers in a personality or, at best, in a small coterie wielding absolute power.

George Santayana said that those who cannot remember the past are condemned to repeat it. I would add that they are doomed also to rewrite it, to fabricate false history. One simply cannot discard the past. The Russians have had to resort to a fictitious and cynical reconstruction of the past. They have repeatedly rewritten their history in accord with the meandering needs of dictatorship. And they have employed indoctrination and terror to induce acceptance of, or acquiescence in, untruth.

What has the method of the Russians achieved? It has proved effective in industrializing their country and raising it to the rank of a superpower. But we are talking about justice, equality, and humanity. Has the method of ignoring or deliberately manipulating history advanced these ideals? Hardly, for the past has caught up with the Russian dictatorship. A ruling class again dominates as in the days of the Tsars; a new ruling class, but the substance of domination and privilege still prevails. Imperialism—mastery and exploitation of weaker peoples—is again rampant, and the goals, if more ambitious, are not dissimilar to those of the Tsars. Antisemitism, the symbol and unimpeachable witness of bigotry, is again government policy, as under the Tsars. And the suppression and punishment of dissent has been even more thorough and savage under the dictatorship. The old regime of Tsarism was neither tolerant nor humane toward political dissent, but it often stopped short of the diabolical means contrived by Stalin and his henchmen to brutalize and degrade political nonconformists. Karl Marx is reputed to have said that history does repeat itself, the first time as tragedy, the second time as farce. His disciples in Russia have indeed repeated Tsarist methods as farce in the sense of mockery of their own pretensions.

Finally, neither history nor the historian is a dead-weight on progress or change for the better. The historian does not venerate the past; he studies it to understand the present. He is not blind to the faults, follies, and deficiencies of the past, but these, too, are part of the record which sheds light on the present.

Nor is history the record of unmitigated evil. History sparkles with strivings for human betterment, and the cumulative effect has been the curbing of injustice, the alleviation of poverty, the challenge to oppression. The record of history does show that progress has been painfully slow and halting. The pace needs to be accelerated, but this cannot be done by denying all past progress, by denigrating past achievements, or by angrily tearing the fabric of society to shreds. History proves that gradualness in reform has yielded more lasting effects than violent disruption. The alternative to gradualness, the attempt to encompass the millennium in one fell swoop, has multiplied human suffering without attaining the justice and decency so ardently desired.

The uses and values of history remain highly significant, and especially so for youth ripening toward rational adulthood. History promotes the spirit of free inquiry and respect for evidence. It demonstrates that there have been and are alternatives in the solution of problems; that no one has a monopoly on the truth; that dissent and difference of opinion must be respected or at least tolerated; that flamboyant assertions and reckless demands for instantaneous and total solutions, especially when accompanied by intolerance of dissent and violence, have always caused suffering and grief; that there are problems which yield only to proximate rather than total solutions. Such insights can contribute to the development of balanced, judicious, and mature minds. Above all, history can deepen understanding of the present, not as a contrivance of evil men but as the product of evolution of the past. It can quicken realization that it is fanciful and foolhardy to assume that the foundations of a better future must be the wreckage of the present. The lesson of history is that such a future can be fashioned only by painstaking and purposeful modifications of the present. History still has a basic function in education.

A CHRISTIAN MEDITATION ON
JEWISH PEOPLEHOOD

By

FRANKLIN H. LITTELL

For his doctoral dissertation at Columbia University, Rabbi Ira Eisenstein seized upon a religious problem which has grown in importance year by year: How can the pluralism of religions in America be a constructive rather than a destructive force? How can different communities and heritage interact creatively with each other? How can the majority society be led to avoid the triumphalist homogenization of the weaker by the stronger? How can the smaller community avoid both dissolution and spiritual isolation?

By 1940 scholars were no longer contemplating a triumph of the "melting pot" in matters religious, even though some leaders of the Protestant establishment—for example, the editor of *Christian Century* —continued to attack Roman Catholics as well as Jews for their stubborn refusal to blend into the once dominant tradition. The intellectual problem, as Rabbi Eisenstein saw it, was how to validate polarities that were not necessarily antithetical. His solution was to define a polarity in equilibrium, in which the poles become fruitful to each other, in which neither tends to destroy the other. This, so he wrote, provides the basis for a theory of toleration as a virtue.[1]

Leaders of the Protestant liberal establishment considered themselves the most tolerant of men, for they neither exercised strong internal discipline nor built and defended clear boundaries between the church and the world. The Jews they condemned as intolerant and particularistic, for they perversely affirmed religious separation while claiming political equality. With a keen eye, Rabbi Eisenstein perceived what many writers miss even today: that the drive for homogeneity alone, even if dressed up as "universalism," ends in totalitarianism.[2]

Although he repudiated supernaturalist arguments,[3] Rabbi Eisenstein was not prepared to abandon the continuing historical validity and usefulness of a Jewish people that had discarded some *impedimenta* which could no longer be defended against the assaults of the modern, scientific, and critical mind. In this he followed his mentor, Rabbi Mordecai M. Kaplan, whose classic *Judaism as a Civilization* (1934) had provided the primary theoretical base for the Reconstructionist movement. Rabbi Kaplan was vigorously opposed to any revelatory references or supernatural claims to substantiate Jewish chosenness or uniqueness,[4] and yet he affirmed the validity of a continuing Jewish peoplehood and even wrote of "the Jews as a pattern people."[5]

The civilizational approach did not imply any submission to gentile *Gleichschaltung,* subtle or compulsory, even though the traditional ground for resistance and separation had been abandoned. Similarly, for Rabbi Eisenstein tolerance has not been misconstrued as an easy road to assimilation: on the contrary, tolerance is termed a "virtue" which helps to facilitate a creative tension between polarities. His earliest book thus anticipates the intellectual progress made in the leading interfaith organization, the National Conference of Christians and Jews (f. 1928), which in its early years sometimes slid into an easy harmonism but in its maturity has developed and propagated clearheaded principles of interreligious dialogue. These principles of interreligious dialogue honor the dignity and integrity of the several faith communities while affirming that in bona fide interaction they may learn from each other.

The Problem of Christian Assimilationism

Whether Jewish peoplehood be defended in traditional revelatory terms or in the Reconstructionist language ("ethical nationhood," based upon the essentials of the Torah), the Jews exist. As the Holocaust proved, the Jew is known to the Adversary even if sometimes he is an enigma to himself. Although the Adversary is, of course, unable to comprehend the majesty of Jewish peoplehood in history, and must therefore define "Jewishness" in its most vulgar—i.e., racial—terms, he knows by base instinct something that the careless Jew and the slovenly gentile may have suppressed: that Jewry is a people standing alone and not numbered among the nations of the earth (Num. 23:9).

Whether the Jew is atheist or *hasid,* royalist or Marxist, scholar or farmer, his very existence is an offense to those philosophers and ideo-logues and genocidal politicians who are in rebellion against the God of Abraham, Isaac, and Jacob, and against the holy history which is in-terpreted and proclaimed in His Name.

However much is left a mystery—and two of the greatest religious mysteries since the Exodus, the Holocaust and a restored Israel, tower over our own lifetimes, however much or little a community of Jews may profess, by their very existence (and nothing else) the Jews are a sign and an affirmation (*Bekenntnis*). In this sense at least, leaving aside more difficult philosophical questions, Jewish survival is a profoundly religious matter; since the Holocaust it has become what Rabbi Emil Fackenheim has called an additional Commandment.[6]

The Christian problem is far more subtle and acute. In the specific situation, the question whether Christianity can regain credibility after the wholesale apostasy which accompanied and enabled the Holocaust, is yet unresolved.[7] In the general situation, with the rise of individual religious choice and with the emergence of post-Christian ideological options, gentiles of the North Atlantic societies are no longer automatically "Christians." A conscious choice is involved, and the evidence is over-whelming that under temptation and pressure great masses of once Christian peoples will in fact revert to heathenism and opt out of holy history. Rather than suffer, tens of millions will apostatize; rather than hold to minimal standards of Christian behavior, tens of millions will embrace, with whatever degree of enthusiasm they are capable of, the pan-Slavism, pan-Germanism, pan-Arabism, Nazism, Marxism, romantic, or "scientific" ideologies which Christendom in collapse can no longer defeat in the forum nor even prevent from penetrating the congregations.

The commandment of Jewish survival has reached a high level of religious importance because for the first time the obliteration of the Jewish people is technically possible and powerful necrophiliac machines are committed to that goal. The extraordinary importance of Christian internal discipline has been forced to the fore precisely because millions of the baptized have had to choose in the twentieth century between apostasy or suffering, and the overwhelming majority have taken the easy way.

In America, where until recently there was no clear and open conflict between national values and Christian principles, there has been as yet little attention paid by the churches and their seminaries to the lessons of the German Church Struggle and the Holocaust. Even the church publishing houses, so ignorant and/or indifferent to the meaning of the Holocaust,[8] have ignored the lessons of the Age of Apostasy almost as fully as America as a whole.

Strange as it may seem to a Jewish reader, in the Sunday Schools and adult education classes of the American churches, the names of Alfred Delp and Dietrich Bonhoeffer, Christian martyrs to Nazism, are as foreign and strange as the names of Hanna Senesh and William Ringelblum, Jewish martyrs. American Protestantism, the last solid bloc of relatively undisturbed nineteenth-century culture-religion (*Kulturreligion*) in the world, is still largely oblivious to what has happened to Christendom in the twentieth century. And the American churches, legally "free," have by social assimilation and establishment reached a degree of accommodation to the general social mores little different from that which characterized the German Protestant *Landeskirchen* at the advent of the Third Reich.

The study of Christian accommodation to Nazi totalitarianism is a pathological study of the apostasy of Christendom.[9] And the study of the nineteeenth-century process of Christian assimilation to the German romantic nationalism which preceded Nazism raises the most serious questions about religious culture and counter-culture elsewhere. The German Faith Movement—which was a neoheathen cult, the German Christians (*Deutsche Christen*)—a party of Christian collaborators who harmonized an abridged edition of the Gospel with the Nazi "Myth of the Twentieth Century," the Nazi cultus itself—which was a substitute religion for the most zealous, all three were possible only in a situation where Christian churchmen had ceased to tend boundaries.[10]

The open betrayal of the faith was preceded by secret betrayal. The way of apostasy was prepared by spiritualizers who removed the offense of the Gospel, tore down the fence between the church and the world (between Christian faithfulness and "the spirit of the times"), melded "religious" principles with cultural claims and pretensions. Nineteenth-century German Protestantism was typically comprehensive, moderate, and harmonizing. The biblical discontinuity between the highest human endeavors and the demands of the Law was muted and finally denied altogether: the German nation became a church, locus of a "realized eschatology," its actions self-validating and self-justifying.

It is a common but serious mistake to suppose that Nazism was prepared by a spirit of "secularism," that during the Third Reich there was a decline of "religious experience" and "spirituality." On the contrary, "the religion of inwardness" flourished, and a religion which had lost contact with biblical authority and truth flourished to a phenomenal degree. The idea of Christian life as a counter-culture was virtually abandoned: Christian assimilationism triumphed with the victory of Teutonic tribalism.

The Christian teachers made their substantial contribution to the dissolution of any residual notions of Christian separation from *voelkisch* ways and means. "God," "providence," "fellowship," "community," "peoplehood," and other concepts which in earlier Pietism had still retained definitely biblical content became cloudy and uncertain. The great national preacher Schleiermacher, both Pietist and liberal, was typical: we have evidence that he had personal "faith," and supreme confidence in "experience," even when his belief in God and the life to come had become most uncertain.[11] At the same time that he stressed the intensity of subjective experience, he weakened the tie to creeds and confessions that carried particularity and historicity and sacramental concreteness.

> The visible religious society can only be brought nearer the universal freedom and majestic unity of the true Church by becoming a mobile mass, having no distinct outlines, but each part being now here, now there, and all peacefully mingling together.[12]

From Christian community to *Volksgemeinschaft* was an easy step, once the liberal scholars had let down the barriers and the latter-day Pietist preachers and teachers had infused the body politic with the same emotion they once directed toward the *corpus Christi*. And Adolf Hitler claimed that *Volksgemeinschaft* would be his major contribution to the German race.

If the Old Testament was only a library of Jewish folklore and fable, as some said, why should the German man of the twentieth century hesitate to stand on the ground of his own racial memories? If intensity of religious experience and devotion were the test, and not "outward" creeds and laws, why should not that devotion be directed as well to *Volk und Staat* as *Volk und Kirche?* Why indeed! The consequence of the shift was the emergence of a fanatical devotion to the Nazi state, itself become one of the ultimate values. But the foundations of this "political pantheism,"[13] and the urgent drive toward it, were all there in German Pietism and theological liberalism. The nineteenth-century liberal theology, which began by domesticating God to the claims of culture and nation, ended by denying Him to His face.

This is the negative side of the picture, of course. No contemporary scholar can be unaware of how much is owed to those who broke the way for critical and historical methods in the study of religions. But the men of the nineteenth century looked at the world of early Christianity and the ancient Hebrews as men of the Enlightenment, and they dealt in "religions" and "founders of religions." They projected their own pre-suppositions upon the past and applied them uncritically to their own present.[14]

A good example of the breakdown of the theoretical approach of the theologians who prepared the way and finally accommodated to Nazism is a pamphlet by Georg Wobbermin.[15] Written by a patriotic professor in the midst of the developing Church Struggle, the pamphlet is extremely critical of the radical discontinuity stressed by Karl Barth and his associates in the Confessing Church. Wobbermin goes on to present with high praise the harmony of national ideals and inward piety proclaimed by that first great patriotic preacher and theologian, Friedrich Daniel Ernst Schleiermacher. Without revealing, of course, that he is distorting Schleiermacher's ethical method and purpose, he praises him for his insistence on the right of each people (*Volk*) to develop its own genius. In contrast to the point of view of the opponents of the Hitler regime, who persist in maintaining fraternal relations with sister churches in other countries, Schleiermacher is praised for his never-failing devotion to the German way of life. Instead of dividing the nation (*Volk*) by harsh creedal statements and ecumenical loyalties, the churches would do well—according to Wobbermin—to save their energies to build up the German state. Let their "positive Christianity" (the *positives Christentum* of Article 24 of the Nazi Party Platform) show itself by non-sectarian devotion to the common weal! In the divine destiny of the nation, the immanent purposes of the divine purpose are being progressively revealed, and the highest religious and political loyalty is to serve selflessly that destiny.

The particularism of a genuine Christian counter-culture is thus denied, philosophically, theologically, and politically. Eschatology shifts from church to nation (*Volk*). *Gemeinschaft* ceases to be defined in the context of the community of faithful people: it is transferred in theory and practice to the *Volk*.[16] The situation is reached which Rousseau considered the desirable political condition, which was enforced against the recalcitrant by the state homogenizing policy (*Gleichschaltung*): "The general will achieves its purest expression when all citizens confront the state as individuals and are not bound together in lesser associations."[17]

Rousseau, to be sure, had a small Swiss canton as his model. But it is not without significance that two philosophers of the Romantic school apparently as far apart as Schleiermacher and Rousseau should, as enemies of independent subpolitical centers of leadership and initiative (primary groups), be critical also of both Christian and Jewish counter-culture. For both of them, "conscience" was a function of one's awareness of his true social identity: the apparent independence of the individual was in fact limited to the framework of the state. Once it had been held that true liberty lay in obedience to God; according to the new prophets, true freedom lay in obedience to the State.[18]

Behind the face of the state apparatus, however, is a *Volk*—an entity defended religiously and politically as an ultimate—which has absorbed into itself all "lesser" loyalties and classes and groupings. The Christians blend, with few exceptions (smeared as "sectarians"). Many of the Jews refuse to blend, and they are the object of attack first from cultural antisemites and then from political antisemites.

Jewish Counter-Culture and Christian Counter-Culture

In my 1946 argument about Jewish peoplehood with Rabbi Kaplan, I had not yet given sufficient weight to one very essential fact: that the Jewish people is not defined by acceptance of certain ideas or beliefs ("Judaism"). Rather, there is a quality of *givenness* which is lacking for Christians: Christians are volunteers. Even if initially they have been "volunteered" by their parents and/or sponsors, they are volunteers: they can desert. The Jewish people has been tormented by renegades and deserters from time to time, particularly since "post-Christian" ideologies have become widely available options.[19] But a *renegade* Jew is still a renegade *Jew*. The Christian movement has been cursed from time to time by apostates, and in the twentieth century there have been mass movements of apostasy. But *an apostate Christian is no longer a Christian at all:* he has betrayed his baptism, deserted the *milites Christi,* become a prehistorical heathen (gentile) again.

And here we come upon a profound difference between the Jewish situation and the Christian situation, one that makes doctrinal and disciplinary boundary-tending far more important for the Christian church than it is for the Jewish people. It takes at least two generations for a Jew to desert, while a Christian can go bad over night. When a Jew abandons his people for a speculative "humanity," he is simply a Jew who is ignoring boundaries. When a Christian breaks discipline and assimilates to chauvinism or racism or some nonbiblical *Weltanschauung,* he no longer lives in holy history: he has retreated out of history, into his natural prehistorical condition.

These reflections have very practical import, as well as theoretical weight. A gentile who has chosen to be counted a Christian has to work at his religious vocation, for he is swimming against the current, and the life he is called to live does not come easily and naturally. In a society with some sense of pluralism, a Jew is expected to be different and may even be respected for it; a gentile who joins others in professing Christ and maintaining a style of life appropriate to that profession is considered odd, perhaps even un-American. For in recent decades America has passed beyond the happy harmonies of "Christendom," even if assimilated Christians have been slow to notice it.

It may sound strange in this day and age to put it so, but in one sense it is both easier and more free for a Jew to be a Jew in America than for a gentile to be a Christian. And it is far easier for a Christian to go bad, to go over to the legions of evil, than it is for a Jew to become a renegade.

Jewish peoplehood is a given historical fact and force, revitalized and renewed in the last half century by passing through death to resurrection. Christian peoplehood is only found rarely, and only where a company of faithful people has determined to separate itself out from the spirit of the times and deliberately to live the life of a counter-culture. The Jewish people stands alone, not numbered among the heathen, as a given fact. A Christian people, when and where such is found, comes into being by *dis*-continuity, by circumstances so unusual that the observer turns instinctively to the language of miracles to express the surprise and wonder he feels at what he sees.

After the Holocaust, Jewish survival and renewal seem miracles. And the discovery of Christians with some measure of credibility of life also inspires wonder. Perhaps my hope is that discontinuity, wonder, and miracles may be among the "polarities" which Rabbi Eisenstein will reckon with in his undergirding tensions which are creative, mutually appreciative, tolerant. In the recent generations we Christians, at least, have had quite enough of ethnic and cultural and political and religious continuities: only a radical break, a restitution of basic truths (such as the essential Jewishness of Christianity) to their central place, a recovery of a Christian style of life will suffice to reconstruct a credible Christianity.

NOTES

1. Ira Eisenstein. *The Ethics of Tolerance* (New York: King's Crown Press, 1941), pp. 23–27.
2. Ibid., p. 35, with particular attention to editorials in *Christian Century.*
3. A decade ago he translated "God is dead!" into the assertion that God is meaningless as associated with traditional supernaturalism; see his essay in *Varieties of Jewish Belief* (New York: Reconstructionist Press, 1966), p. 63.
4. See his argument with the present writer in *Reconstructionist* 13 (1947), 4:10–16, 5:16–22, 6:14–19, and also the discussion in his *Questions Jews Ask* (New York: Reconstructionist Press, 1956), chap. 8.
5. Cf. Rabbi Kaplan's essay in *Varieties of Jewish Belief,* p. 142.
6. Emil Fackenheim, "Jewish Faith and the Holocaust," *Commentary* 46 (1968): 32: ". . . in the age of Auschwitz a Jewish commitment to Jewish survival is in itself a monumental act of faithfulness."
7. See the argument in "Christendom, Holocaust and Israel: The Importance for Christians of Recent Major Events in Jewish History," *Journal of Ecumenical Studies* 10, no. 3 (1973): 483–97 and "Christians and Jews in the Historical Process," *Judaism* 22, no. 3 (1973): 263–77.
8. See Gerald S. Strober, *Portrait of the Elder Brother: Jews and Judaism in Protestant Teaching Materials* (New York: NCCJ/AJC, 1972), a decade-long follow-up to the classic by Bernhard E. Olson, *Faith and Prejudice* (New Haven: Yale University Press, 1963).
9. See the writer's *The German Phoenix* (New York: Doubleday & Co., 1960), chaps. 2 and 3; *The Crucifixion of the Jews* (New York: Harper & Row, 1975), chaps. 3 and 4; and in *Wild Tongues* (New York: Macmillan & Co., 1969), pp. 69 f.
10. For a study of these three most important religious aspects of the Nazi adventure, see Hans Buchheim, *Glaubenskrise im Dritten Reich* (Stuttgart: Deutsche Verlags-Anstalt, 1953).
11. F. D. E. Schleiermacher, *Soliloquies* (Chicago: Open Court Publishing Co., 1926), p. xviii.
12. F. D. E. Schleiermacher, *On Religion* (London: Kegan Paul, Trench, Trübner & Co., 1893), p. 175.
13. Jacques, Maritain, *Three Reformers* (New York: Charles Scribner's Sons, 1932), p. 134.
14. On the beginnings of that school of scholarship which has made us most aware of the dangers of such projection upon the past, see James M. Robinson's Introduction to Hans Jonas, *Augustin und das paulinische Freiheits-problem,* 2d ed. (Göttingen: Vandenhoeck & Ruprecht, 1965), pp. 13–14.
15. Georg Wobbermin, *Deutscher Staat und evangelische Kirche* (Berlin: Verlag A. Callignon, 1936), passim.

16. See the important study by Koppel S. Pinson, *Pietism as a Factor in the Rise of German Nationalism* (New York: Columbia University Press, 1934); that a cloudy subjectivism and ill-defined boundaries can lead as well to totalitarian politics of the Left has been proven by Karl Kupisch, *Vom Pietismus zum Kommunismus* (Berlin: Lettner-Verlag, 1953).

17. Quoted in R. H. Bowen, *German Theories of the Corporative State* (New York: McGraw-Hill Book Co., 1947), p. 25.

18. See Dorothy Fosdick, *What is Liberty?* (New York: Harper Bros., 1939), p. 55, on the Protean disguises of freedom.

19. See "The Age of Personal Decision" in the present writer's *Atlas History of Christianity* (New York: Macmillan Co., 1976), pp. 116 f.

MORDECAI KAPLAN'S CRITICISMS OF MAIMONIDES' REINTERPRETATIONS

By

HENRY MORRIS

Mordecai Kaplan has gone to great lengths to defend the enterprise of reinterpretation. Yet, surprisingly, Kaplan objects to the reinterpretations of Maimonides. He seems to think that Maimonides' and Philo's reinterpretations are completely arbitrary and hence unacceptable. He claims that Philo "read into the statements of the Torah the kind of Hellenic philosophy which was entirely alien to the Torah."[1] Philo's conception of God is found to be particularly objectionable. "When it came, for example, to the idea of God, he arrived at an idea of his own which was neither Scriptural, on the one hand, nor in keeping with the spirit of the dominant philosophy of his day, on the other."[2]

There are two points being made here. First, Philo misinterprets the Torah. Second, his conception of God is not at all traditional. These two points are also made against Maimonides in the following attack by Kaplan: "Exalted as is Maimonides' conception of God, it has manifestly more in common with the metaphysics of Aristotle than with the God-idea of the prophets and sages of ancient Israel. Not a single one of the biblical passages quoted by Maimonides means what he reads into it."[3]

There is an irony in these objections. Kaplan, who vehemently defends the program of reinterpretation, is criticizing Jewish theologians for straying from traditional interpretations. Does Kaplan apply a different standard to others than he would apply to himself?

Kaplan is justified in his criticisms of Maimonides and Philo if he is considering these theologians to be attempting to provide specifications of the original meaning of a traditional religious sentence. If so, *he surely*

269

is right in protesting that the interpretations of Philo and Maimonides are *incorrect*—i.e., they do not specify the original meanings of the biblical sentences. In addition, their concepts of God are fundamentally different from the concept that was held in the biblical period.

However, a problem remains if the interpretations of Philo and Maimonides are understood to be reinterpretations, intentional changes of meaning designed to adopt the faith to changing social and intellectual conditions. Kaplan maintains a historical perspective concerning Judaism, emphasizing the evolutionary development of religious traditions. Kaplan recognizes the need for continuity in Judaism. Thus he believes that whenever it is feasible, one should maintain the traditional religious language. "Indeed, when a word has been fraught with meaning for generations and even for ages, it is absurd to abandon it as meaningless for our day, without at least analyzing those human experiences that gave it meaning in the past."[4]

A similar thought is expressed in Kaplan's *Judaism as a Civilization.*

> Only pedantic literalists would insist that the God-idea can have meaning only in religion based on the acceptance of supernaturalism and other-worldliness. They forget that we are so constituted that we have to keep on using old words and operate with traditional ideas, though with each generation experience is enriched, and the language in which that experience is expressed necessarily acquires new meaning.[5]

He also recognizes the need for consistency in the beliefs we hold to in religion and in other areas like science. "Our conception of God must be self-consistent and consistent with whatever we hold to be true."[6]

To maintain consistency with our other beliefs sometimes necessitates reinterpretation, the intentional formulation of new concepts. If both Kaplan *and* Maimonides are understood to be reinterpreting traditional terms and expressions of Judaism, how can Kaplan with any consistency propose his own untraditional interpretations and still criticize Maimonides for proposing untraditional interpretations?

The only way Kaplan can make his criticism with any consistency is to provide *standards for reinterpretations.* For example, he could require the new interpretation to be continuous with the traditional interpretation, to preserve essential features of the traditional interpretation. Then Maimonides' reinterpretations could be criticized as not meeting the standards (discontinuous), and Kaplan could defend his own reinterpretations as meeting the standards (continuous).

These standards must be different than the standards for specifying the earliest interpretation or meaning. If a theologian tries to determine the earliest meaning of a biblical sentence or term, then his interpretation should be judged as correct or incorrect. He has entered into the field of biblical scholarship. His interpretations will be judged correct if they are in accord with our knowledge of the syntactics and semantics of biblical Hebrew. They are correct if they accurately reflect the linguistic usage of the period.

But reinterpretations cannot be judged as correct or incorrect. These standards do not apply. A theologian presenting a reinterpretation is proposing or recommending a *new* usage. It makes no sense to ask whether this new interpretation agrees with earlier usages. However, reinterpretations can be criticized. One ought not to be able to propose any interpretation at random as a reinterpretation of a biblical sentence. That would be completely arbitrary. Arbitrariness or nonarbitrariness is clearly a standard. There are others as well, such as meaninglessness, relevance, and pragmatic acceptability.[7]

Does Kaplan have any such standards? Kaplan makes the following explicit statement. He distinguishes between *transvaluation* (unacceptable or inappropriate reinterpretation) and *revaluation* (acceptable and appropriate reinterpretation). Kaplan criticizes Philo's allegorical reinterpretations as transvaluations[8] and apparently would be willing to apply the same label to Maimonides.[9] "*Transvaluation* consists in ascribing meanings to the traditional content of a religion or social heritage, which could neither have been contemplated nor implied by the authors of that content."[10]

But Kaplan's pragmatic interpretations, as well as Maimonides' Aristotelian interpretations, could not have been contemplated by the Hebrews of the biblical period. Kaplan must, therefore, rest the defense of his reinterpretations on the claim that his reinterpretations were *implied* by the biblical authors, whereas Maimonides' were not.

This statement is unfortunate. Kaplan wants the reinterpretation to be implied by the authors of the sentence. He is placing a priority, therefore, on the earliest interpretation. All appropriate reinterpretations would have to be derived from or implied by the original or earliest interpretation. But as Kaplan so often points out, Judaism has gone through several major stages in its evolutionary development. Why could not a reinterpretation be derived from a traditional rabbinic interpretation or a traditional medieval interpretation of the Bible? Why must there be such priority given to the original meaning? For example, new linguistic data have indicated the need for a different formulation of the original meaning of Genesis 1:1. But does "In the beginning God created the heavens and the earth" lose its validity as a traditional interpretation from which appropriate reinterpretations can be derived? Kaplan could avoid these problems and formulate a better standard by considering any traditional interpretation (not just the earliest one) as a proper basis for deriving a reinterpretation.

However, the standard would even then only be acceptable if one knew what Kaplan meant by "implied by the authors of that content." Then we could add "or by other traditionally recognized expounders of the passage." But this whole notion is problematical. What sense of "implied" is Kaplan referring to? Surely, he is not referring to logical implication. The criterion as it stands is too vague to apply. Perhaps Kaplan's explanation of revaluation, i.e., appropriate reinterpretation, will help.

Kaplan suggests entering into the thought-world of the authors to understand what a religious idea or institution "meant to them in the light of their experience and world outlook."[11] One may decide that the concept is obsolete and must be discarded, (as Kaplan does with the Chosen People idea). However, a reinterpretation may be in order. Kaplan says that it should be along the following lines: "But it is more likely that some modification of the original idea will suggest itself that might be related to the new situation and world-outlook in a way *similar* to that in which the original thought related itself to what was then the situation and world-outlook."[12]

How can one tell whether a particular reinterpretation has the requisite similarity? Kaplan mentions satisfying the same psychological needs in men. In *Judaism as a Civilization* he says the following about the psychological dimension:

> If we approach the Jewish civilization with the purpose of understanding its psychological—not its logical—reality, its conception of God should interest us not for what it seeks to tell concerning the metaphysical nature of the Deity, but for the difference it made in the behavior of the Jew. We should analyze the Jewish conception of God in order to learn how it functioned in the life of the Jewish people.[13]

Kaplan also wants the prayers and all Jewish observances to function in our time in a way analogous to the way they functioned in previous times.

If then we can discover just what wants these observances seem to satisfy, if we can analyze what they have meant to the Jewish people in the past, and can work out the implication of these meanings in terms of aspirations and desires appropriate for our day, we have a method of approach to the formulation of Jewish belief that is far superior to the discredited scholastic method of systematic theology.[14]

Basically, then, Kaplan's standards for reinterpretation seem to reduce to the following two necessary conditions. First, the reinterpretation must preserve the psychological and emotional associations of the statements under the traditional interpretation. Second, the reinterpreted sentence and its accompanying religious institution must function in the same way in the life of the religious community. Reinterpretations meeting these two standards are acceptable even if not identical with Kaplan's own interpretations. He says: "Reconstructionism is a *method,* rather than a series of affirmations or conclusions concerning Jewish life or thought."[15] Thus there is a tolerance of future reinterpretations and a future evolution of the tradition. This is a true advance from the medieval position, where a theologian would claim that only his interpretations were legitimate.

Is this standard workable? Will it serve to eliminate unacceptable, arbitrary interpretations? How do Kaplan's own interpretations measure up?

Let us take as a significant test case: Kaplan's conception of God. Kaplan defines "God" perhaps most often as "the power that makes for salvation."[16] There are other definitions, however. In fact in the index to Kaplan's *The Meaning of God in Modern Jewish Religion* there are twenty-four separate page references under "definitions of God." At other places in this work "God" is defined as "that aspect of reality we react to with a sense of life's unity, creativity and worthwhileness."[17] He also says that "God is that aspect that confers meaning and value on life."[18] A more cosmological definition conceives of God as the "organizing force of the cosmos."[19] Definitions centering on ethics describe God as "the power that makes for righteousness"[20] and "the power that endorses what we believe ought to be and that guarantees that it will be." [21] It is problematic to call all these statements "definitions." If they were all truly definitions, Kaplan could be charged with being inconsistent in his beliefs. However, it appears that most of these "definitions" serve to list characteristic features traditionally ascribed to God. Kaplan then reinterprets these traditional divine features.

A case in point is Kaplan's claim that God is omnipotent. Spelled out precisely (reinterpreted), it comes down to the following claim: "Belief in God must mean for us, even though we no longer believe in miracles, that nothing is too difficult for God, that whatever ought to be can and will be."[22]

Let us concentrate, then, on his major definition of "God" as "the power that makes for salvation." Salvation, Kaplan admits, is understood in a different way. Salvation is identified with "this-worldly self-fulfillment or realization."[23] For the individual this consists of the satisfaction of three basic needs: physical needs, love (interpersonal relations), and creativity. Society's goal should be to enable every individual to meet these needs. A belief in God, for Kaplan, entails at least in part the optimistic hope that men working together can achieve these goals. In this way salvation for all can be achieved.

Does the definition of "God" as "the power that makes for salvation" meet Kaplan's criteria for appropriate reinterpretation? First of all, Kaplan shows how these needs are always present in man. Moreover, seeking to satisfy these has always been a basic element in man's belief in God. Thus his reinterpretation meets his first standard, preserving the psychological and emotional associations of the concept. The second standard demands that the new concept serve the same function in the community as the traditional concept. Sometimes belief in God as the bringer of salvation served to cause Jews to be passive, waiting for God to act on their behalf. But there are elements of the tradition pointing to the necessity of Jews acting for themselves "with the help of God" to achieve their goals. This would function in the same way as Kaplan's belief—to provide the confidence and the strength for men in society to work to achieve moral ends.

Thus Kaplan's criteria have been met. However, it is likely that many other interpretations will meet these standards as well. There is no requirement by Kaplan for *semantic* continuity. Thus the new concept could have nothing in common with the meaning of the earlier concept, yet still preserve the same phychological associations and be functionally equivalent in the life of the community. The standard I would propose emphasizes the preservation of semantic features. "A reinterpretation of term 'X' is not arbitrary only if the reinterpretation of 'X' has in common with the standard interpretation of 'X' from which it was derived a sufficient number of semantically relevant features."[24] Kaplan, by defining "God" as "the power that makes for salvation," has preserved a crucial semantic feature of a more traditional concept of God. Even though the salvation he refers to is *this-worldly*, Kaplan can be seen as reviving an older sense of *yeshuah* which did not have eschatological implications. For example, David in 2 Samuel 22:51 thanks God for providing a "tower of victories" or "great victories" (*migdol yeshuot* or *magdil yeshuot*). These refer to this-worldly military victories, those David won on the battlefield, rather than some reward in a future life.

A later reinterpretation represents *yeshuot* as referring to eschatological triumphs. When this verse is placed in a new context, in the *Birkat Hamazon,* it seems to refer to other-worldly salvation. In this new context, the verse is preceded by the following nonbiblical verse: "May the merciful one enable us to reach the days of the Messiah and the life of the world to come." In this next context *yeshuot* is seen naturally to refer to salvation in the world to come rather than victories in this world.

However, Kaplan's concept of God preserves an important feature of a traditional concept of God: the bringer of this-worldly triumphs. By preserving this important semantic feature, Kaplan could claim with some justification that his reinterpretation of "God" is nonarbitrary.

By recognizing a semantic test of arbitrariness, we seem to capture the force of Kaplan's objection to Maimonides' reinterpretations. He criticized Maimonides' concept of God, claiming that Scripture does not mean "what he [Maimonides] reads into it". Kaplan could be taken to object that Scripture *does not mean and has never traditionally been taken to mean anything like what Maimonides reads into it.* He would then be right to insist that some of the meaning should be preserved. He could insist that some essential features of the meaning of a traditional verse or expression be preserved when one is reinterpreting to adapt traditional concepts to the contemporary period.

This clarification would not involve Kaplan in imposing a double standard—one for his own reinterpretations, and one for Maimonides' reinterpretations. Kaplan could claim that his reinterpretations are revaluations, i.e., they preserve semantic continuity. He would then have grounds to claim that by the same standard, Maimonides' reinterpretations are transvaluations, lacking semantic continuity.

This would have to be demonstrated carefully. But it would not be acceptable for Kaplan, who realizes the importance of reinterpretation in the development of Judaism, to criticize Maimonides simply because he reinterprets.

NOTES

1. Kaplan, *The Purpose and Meaning of Jewish Existence*, p. 22.
2. Ibid., p. 24.
3. Ibid., p. 30.
4. Kaplan, *The Meaning of God in Modern Jewish Religion*, p. 150.
5. Kaplan, *Judaism as a Civilization*, p. 150.
6. Kaplan, *Meaning of God*, p. 150.
7. See Henry Morris, *Standards for Reinterpretation* (Ph.D. diss., University Microfilms, 1974), chap. 5.
8. Kaplan, *Meaning of God* pp. 5–6.
9. Kaplan, *Purpose and Meaning of Jewish Existence*, p. 30.
10. Kaplan, *Meaning of God*, p. 3.
11. Ibid., p. 7.
12. Ibid., p. 7.
13. Kaplan, *Judaism as a Civilization*, p. 391.
14. Kaplan, *Meaning of God*, p. 3.
15. Kaplan, *Questions Jews Ask*, p. 80.
16. See, for example, Kaplan, *The Future of the American Jew*, p. 202.
17. Kaplan, *Meaning of God*, pp. 160–61.
18. Ibid., p. 165.
19. Ibid., p. 76.
20. Ibid., p. 309.
21. Ibid., p. 323–24.
22. Kaplan, *Future of the American Jew*, p. 202.
23. Ibid., p. 30.
24. Morris, *Standards for Reinterpretation*, p. 121.

THE CONVERT IN JUDAISM

By

MAX J. ROUTTENBERG

After a year of receiving instruction and of intensive study on her own, Carole informed me that she had reached the decision not to convert to Judaism. She did not give long and elaborate explanations for her decision. She stated simply, "I have become convinced that the Jewish people do not welcome converts, and I would always be a stranger among them."

I did not argue with Carole. On the contrary, I agreed with her. Fresh in my memory was an encounter with a fine lady in Scottsdale, Arizona, who took exception to my view that a Jew who did not regard a sincere convert as a complete Jew was, by that very fact, a racist. "My son married a Catholic girl and she converted to Judaism. She is a sincere convert, goes to temple every Friday night, lights the candles, and conducts herself as a Jew in every way. But every time I look at her, I know, deep in my heart, that she is not Jewish—and I am not a racist!"

This is an attitude that exists among Jews of varying types, religious and secularist, well-informed and illiterate, traditionalist and modernist. It is sufficiently prevalent to convince any objective observer that deeply rooted in the Jewish psyche is the belief that the Jews are, in their essential nature and character, different from all other peoples, and that converts to Judaism, however sincere and committed they be, could never acquire that essence and character by the process of conversion.

This belief has its roots in the genesis of the Jewish people. The biblical record is very precise on this point. It emphasizes the specialness and uniqueness of Israel. Israel was selected by God from among all the nations of the world for His very own. God entered into a covenant with

277

Israel which affirmed this special relationship. "If you will obey Me faithfully and keep My covenant, you shall be My treasured possession among all the peoples. Indeed, all the earth is Mine, but you shall be to Me a kingdom of priests and a holy nation" (Exod. 19:5–6).

Israel was assigned a dual role in this covenant with God. As a "kingdom of priests" its mission was universal, to teach God's word to all mankind. As a "holy nation" it was subject to rigorous regulations and disciplines. It could fulfill this role only in the land selected by God, and it could worship Him only in one special place in that land. "Do not worship God in like manner, but look only to the site that the Lord your God will choose . . . as His habitation to establish His name there" (Deut. 12:4–5). Thus, Israel was bound in an eternal covenant to the God of Israel and to the land of Israel.

How, then, could it function as a "kingdom of priests"? How could it spread the teachings of the Torah to the four corners of the earth? The answer was formulated by Isaiah (2:3): "For out of Zion shall the Torah emanate, and the word of the Lord from Jerusalem."

Thus, in its earliest development, Judaism was a universal religion with a universal God, but with a particular people in a particular land selected to fulfill His universal purpose. Israel was assigned a mission, but it was not to become a missionizing people. It was not to send missionaries to the gentiles, to convert them to the belief in the God of Israel. Israel was glued to its land, and its native-born citizens would fulfill its role as a kingdom of priests. The nations of the world would come to the land of Israel. "And all the nations shall flow to it, and many peoples shall come and say: 'Come, let us go up to the mountain of the Lord, to the house of the God of Jacob; that He may teach us His ways and that we may walk in His paths' " (Isa. 2:3).

There is no record of a "mission to the gentiles" to convert them to Judaism during the entire period of the First Temple. Until the Babylonian exile, there is no record of any converts to Judaism in the Bible. The rabbis of the Talmud read back into the texts views and practices which existed in their own times but not in biblical days. They speak of Abraham and Sarah as busily engaged in proselytizing the heathens. They base their interpretation on the text, "and the persons they acquired in Haran" (Gen. 12:5). The literal meaning refers to the acquisition of slaves, but the rabbis interpreted it as an act of conversion, thereby establishing the antiquity of a practice which had developed in their day of admitting religious converts into Judaism. They engaged in the same process of interpretation to validate many of the mixed marriages of the heroes of Israel: Abraham and Keturah, Joseph and Osenath, Moses and Zipporah (and the Ethiopian woman), David and Bathsheba, and many more.

A careful reading of the Bible indicates that the term *ger,* which has come to mean a religious convert to Judaism, was used primarily to refer to a resident alien in the land of Israel. According to Yehezkel Kaufmann, the resident alien became absorbed and assimilated into the life of the people among whom he dwelled over the course of several generations.[1] It was primarily an ethnic absorption of the stranger, and there was no religious ceremony or ritual marking his passage from one status to another. This process of assimilation was primarily social and cultural in nature and usually included acceptance of the God of Israel. Because of the tribal structure of ancient Israel, with the division of the land to each tribe as an ancestral inheritance, it was not possible for the *ger* ever to achieve full citizenship in the land of Israel. He could never share in the ownership of the land, which was jealously guarded by the tribes as a sacred patrimony. It was even difficult for an Israelite to "expatriate" himself from his native tribe and join another tribe.

The *ger,* because he was not of the seed of Israel, remained in a special status, and the Torah carefully regulated the relationship between the native-born and the resident aliens. The *ger* is in many matters placed in the category of the slave, the poor, the hired help. Most of the resident aliens lived in a depressed economic condition and were a socially inferior class. The laws of the Torah humanely warn against oppressing and mistreating them, "for you were resident aliens in the land of Egypt."

If the resident alien wished to participate in certain rituals of Jewish observance, especially the feast of the Paschal lamb, he had to undergo circumcision in order to qualify. It did not, however, change his status as a resident alien. Only time might eradicate the memory of his alien origin and ease his entry into the congregation of the Lord.

It was during the Babylonian exile that the exclusiveness of the people of Israel in the land of Israel was shattered. For a time, the exiles could not conceive how they themselves might worship God on foreign soil. Removed from the holy land and the holy sanctuary, they cried: "How can we sing the Lord's song in a foreign land?" (Ps. 137:4). Their prophets and teachers not only kept alive the hope of the return but expanded their spiritual horizons. The God of Israel was a universal God and could be worshiped anywhere. "Heaven is my throne and the earth my footstool: where is the house you would build for me? Where is my resting place?" (Isa. 66:1). Sacrifices on the altar were not the only means of worship. "Make thanksgiving your sacrifice to God, pay your vows to the Most High, and call upon Me in the day of trouble" (Ps. 50:14–15).

Many Babylonians were attracted to the religious views propounded by the exilic prophets and attached themselves to the people of Israel. These were not converts to Judaism, in the later sense of the term, but believers in the God of Israel. They were designated as *yirei adonai*, those who fear the Lord (see Pss. 115:11, 118:4). It is evident from the context that these worshipers of the Lord were welcome and respected, but never officially converted as members of the congregation of Israel.

This fact—that there was no religious conversion to Judaism in the days of the First Temple—may well explain the attitude of Ezra and Nehemiah to foreign wives and their children. The violent removal of the wives and children from the Israelite husbands and fathers could have been avoided by converting all of them to Judaism. That it did not take place was not because of cruelty but because conversion, as a ritual for bringing non-Israelites into the congregation, was not yet an accepted practice. There is some indication that there was a contrary view in certain circles. The Book of Ruth is taken to be a subtle protest against the events described in the Book of Ezra. Ruth, the Moabitess, was welcomed into the household of Israel. She made a marriage with one of the leading citizens of Bethlehem and ultimately became the progenitress of David, king of Israel. There is nothing in the text to suggest that Ruth was formally converted to the religion of Israel. But it does point up clearly the attitude of openness and hospitality to aliens and foreigners who wished to cast their lot with Israel. The rabbis held Ruth to be a model of the sincere convert who accepted the yoke of the commandments of the Lord and observed them faithfully throughout her life.

It is not till we reach the talmudic age that conversion as a religious ceremony emerges as a reality in the Jewish religion. The rabbis, as indicated, did not invent a new ceremony or ritual. They believed that it was an ancient practice beginning with the first Jew, Abraham. They distinguish in their reading of the biblical text between the *ger toshab* the resident alien, and the *ger tzedek*, the sincere proselyte. The resident alien is one who has accepted the obligation of certain *mitzvot*, especially the seven Noahide commandments, thereby making it permissible for him to dwell among the children of Israel in the land of Israel. The *ger tzedek* is one who has obligated himself to observe all the commandments incumbent upon a Jew and thereby enters the fold of Israel completely. The rabbis went so far as to say that God's covenant with Israel included all future converts, as it is written, "I make this covenant not with you alone, but with those who are standing here with us this day before the Lord our God, and with those who are not with us here this day" (Deut. 29:13–14; see T.B. *Shabuot* 39a).

The rabbis' view of conversion and their attitude to the sincere convert is not of one piece. It is made up of a multiplicity of views that oscillate between such extremes as unqualified opposition and outright welcome. Many of the views are conditioned by a specific historical context. Rabbi Helbo, a third-century Palestinian amora, living under the rule of the Roman Empire, could declare, probably from bitter experience, "Converts are as obnoxious to Israel as leprosy" (T.B. *Yebamot* 47b). On the other hand, Rav, the Babylonian amora of the second and third centuries, was quite positive in his view that Judaism should welcome converts: "Whoever comes to be converted should be accepted. Do not inquire into the motives of would-be converts. We may assume that they come for the sake of Heaven."

It is not possible to extract from the mass of conflicting statements either the proposition that Rabbinic Judaism welcomed converts and was busily engaged in missionary activities, or that it was essentially opposed to conversion, that it frowned upon proselytizing, and only reluctantly and after the most careful examination would admit a sincere convert to the Jewish fold. One thing, however, does emerge clearly: under Jewish law, as interpreted by the rabbis, the convert never lost his status as a convert and was not on an equal footing with the native-born Jew. According to the Halakhah there were certain disabilities that a *ger* must forever carry. He could never become king of Israel, chief of staff of the army, or even an officer. A female convert could not marry a Kohen (though her daughter was permitted to). A convert could not be a judge in criminal cases, and in civil cases only if the litigants were converts (T.B. *Yebamot* 102a). There were communities which prohibited the convert from holding public office. His status is perhaps best seen from the rule governing the redemption of captives. The order of priority is: Kohen, Levi, legitimate Jew, illegitimate Jew, *ger,* free female slave of Jewish birth. Whether one sees in these discriminations racial bias or not, the talmudic ruling that a convert may marry a *mamzer* does seem to carry such an implication.

The procedure for the reception of converts as detailed in the Talmud (T.B. *Yebamot* 47b) would indicate that extreme caution was exercised in probing the sincerity and especially the motivation of the applicants. Nothing less than incontrovertible evidence that the convert was moved by love of God and a desire to fulfill all the commandments of the Torah was acceptable to the rabbis. We may note their declaring that all those who had become Jews in the days of Mordecai and Esther were not genuine converts because they had done so *mipnei pahad hayehudim*— "because of fear of the Jews." Despite the statements of teachers like Rav and many others who proclaimed how beloved converts were in the eyes of God, the attitude of suspicion and extreme caution was the prevailing one.

In the medieval period, the so-called Dark Ages of Jewish history, conversion to Judaism was a rarity. Yet there were sufficient instances of such conversions to require the rabbinic authorities to take a position. In general, the attitude of the rabbis in this period was much harsher than that of the talmudic age. Persecution, segregation, and alienation deepened the suspicion of gentile motives, as well as heightened the hostility to those who came from the ranks of the oppressors. The tosaphist Rabbi Isaac (T.B. *Kiddushin* 70b) explained Rabbi Helbo's statement that converts were as obnoxious as leprosy to mean that by assimilating into the Jewish community, converts thereby defiled the purity of the Jewish people. There were more lenient and tolerant views expressed, and the fact is that the door was always more or less open to sincere converts; but there remained a constant fear of the danger involved, as well as resistance to the admission of "outsiders."

This attitude is expressed by one of the leading rabbinic authorities of the sixteenth century, Rabbi Solomon Luria (Maharshal), in his commentary *Yam Shel Shelomo* (M. *Yebamot* 4:49). In commenting on the passage in T.B. *Yebamot* 47b, "evil after evil comes upon those who accept proselytes," Rabbi Solomon states:

> . . . now that we are in a county not our own, like slaves beneath the hands of their owners, should one of Israel accept him [a proselyte], he is a rebel and responsible for his own death. . . . Here I give warning that anyone who is a participant in such acceptance today, when the gentile kingdom is stringent in its attitude, let his blood be upon his own head.[2]

The belief that there was a basic difference between Jews and gentiles persisted in Jewish circles. Yehuda Halevi, in explaining the doctrine of the election of Israel, stated that Israel is God's people by reason of its peculiar religious disposition, that it possesses a specific religious faculty lacking in all other nations.[3] He is followed in this view by Rabbi Judah Loew of Prague (Maharal), who emphasized that the difference between Jews and gentiles was fundamentally not one of creed and faith, but one of inner essence. The difference between the Jewish way of life and destiny and that of other nations was not the result of Jewish acceptance of the Torah; rather, the fact that the Jewish people accepted the Torah was itself the result of their unique nature.[4]

For those who shared this view, the problem of conversion to Judaism posed a serious dilemma. The tradition had been firmly established in talmudic times that a non-Jew could enter the Jewish fold through circumcision (for a male), ritual immersion, and the acceptance of the commandments of the Torah. At the same time, the view was generally held that the Jewish people was unique, separate, and innately different from all other peoples. It was difficult to reconcile these contradictory beliefs. The rabbis of the Talmud sought to explain away the contradiction by declaring that the convert was to be regarded as a child that had been newly born, and as if his former life had never been (T.B. *Yebamot* 22a). The kabbalists evolved the theory that a new soul entered the convert when he embraced Judaism. However, they believed that it was not of the same excellence as the souls of those born as Jews (Zohar, *Beshallah* 168a).[5]

It is evident from all of the foregoing that there persisted, throughout the centuries of the Dispersion, a great ambivalence toward converts and the desirability of admitting them to the fold. This ambivalence derived from a built-in tension which Judaism has manifested from the very earliest times. Is Judaism a universal religion or is it particularistic? Is the Jewish community a closed society or an open society? Are the Jewish people exclusivist and restrictive or are they open and hospitable to outsiders?

There is only one possible answer to these questions. Judaism is both universalist and particularist; the Jewish community is both closed and open, exclusivist and inclusivist. There is a constant tension between these polarities. There were periods in Jewish history when the universalist pull predominated, such as the Alexandrian era; there were times when the Jews retreated into extreme particularism, as in the seventeenth and eighteenth centuries in Eastern Europe. Judaism was most creative when it succeeded in maintaining an equilibrium between the two polarities, thereby escaping the dangers of both extremes. The prophetic period was such a time in our history; so were certain periods in the Greco-Roman era. Both Babylonian and Spanish Jewry enjoyed a golden era of Jewish creativity in which they lived harmoniously in two cultures and succeeded in enriching both of them.

In the pre-Holocaust period, American Judaism was beginning to emerge from its love affair with American culture and its dedication to universalism and world brotherhood into a self-conscious, creative force in American society. It was discovering the balance between the extremes of universalism and particularism. Its greatest teachers and leaders represented a harmonious blend of the two cultures. However, the shattering experience of the Holocaust tipped the balance, so that there has been, in many circles, a sharp swing to exaggerated ethnicity and extreme particularism. There is a heightened sense of Jewish uniqueness and separateness and a deepened feeling of alienation from the general society. There is a growing distaste for outsiders who seek to enter Judaism, and a dark suspicion of the motives of those who have been accepted. Though the rate of intermarriage is increasing, something that is inevitable in American society, the Jewish community has not been able or willing to develop a strategy for transforming this situation into an opportunity for bringing the intermarried families into the Jewish community.

The American Jewish community faces many threats to its continued survival. None, however, is more serious than its reluctance to open its doors and to admit those who are eager to enter "under the wings of the Shechina." We who declare ourselves modernists reject the view that there is a Jewish mystique, a special essence or a superior soul that belongs to the Jew. We believe, rather, that Judaism, the religion of this particular people, because of its unusual history and experience, has developed a way of life and a system of moral values which can bring spiritual fulfillment to all who adhere to it and practice it. It is open to all who seek it in truth and sincerity. As born Jews, we may guard our spiritual treasures very carefully, but the doors are not locked to those who would enter. We may impose some strict requirements for admission, but those who qualify should be joyously welcomed.

Many of us favor the proposition that we are a people with a mission, but not a missionizing people. In this respect, we follow the broad intent of the tradition, which teaches that we gladly accept sincere converts but we do not go out to proselytize. George Foot Moore expressed this thought as follows:

The belief in the future universality of the true religion [Judaism], the coming of an age when "the Lord shall be king over all the earth" . . .

led to efforts to convert the Gentiles to the worship of the one true God
. . . and made Judaism the first great missionary religion of the Mediterranean world. . . . the phrase must, however, be understood with a
difference. The Jews did not send out missionaries . . . to proselyte among
the heathen. They were themselves settled by thousands in all the great
centres and in innumerable smaller cities. . . . Their religious influences
was exerted chiefly through the synagogues . . . which were open to all
whom interest or curiosity drew to their services.[6]

We are properly concerned about the forces in our society which draw
Jews away from their heritage. Intermarriage, which is a fact of American
Jewish life that will be with us for the foreseeable future, may be destructive of Jewish identity and continuity, but it need not be. There is a
constructive way of dealing with the problem. Through the combined
efforts of the organized Jewish community, a climate of receptivity must
be created in all our institutions, and especially in the synagogue, to make
the intermarried families want to live as Jewish families. A Jew, male
or female, who marries outside the faith, has, by that fact, brought a
non-Jew into the Jewish family network. When that non-Jew is rejected
and the children of such a marriage are spurned, the Jewish community
has been robbed of a potential member. Threatened as we are by the
infertility rate of Jews and by many assimilatory forces, we cannot afford
such losses. In numbers alone, we need to keep the intermarried Jews
within our fold. Many of them will be persuaded, of their own accord,
to become converts to Judaism, and thereby enrich Jewish life with their
fresh loyalties and commitments.

In his monumental work *Judaism as a Civilization,* Professor Mordecai
M. Kaplan pointed out that so long as Judaism is a vigorous civilization,
it need not be fearful of intermarriage.

The power and vitality of a civilization are put to the test whenever the
members of different civilizations come into contact with each other.
When that contact results in intermarriage, the more vigorous civilization
is the one to whom the children will belong. . . . Judaism must be able
to imbue the Jewish partner to a mixed marriage with the willingness to
maintain a Jewish home. . . . Judaism should meet all situations that
might lead to mixed marriages not fearfully or grudgingly, but in the
spirit of encountering an expected development. . . . By accepting a
policy which does not decry marriages of Jews with gentiles, provided
the homes they establish are Jewish and the children are given a Jewish
upbringing, the charge of exclusivism and tribalism falls to the ground.

With such an attitude, there would no longer be any occasion for pointing to the racial pride of the Jews.[7]

In another age and in another place, a great Hebrew prophet gave expression to Judaism's vision and hope for Israel among the nations of the world:

> The strangers who join themselves to the Lord,
> To minister to Him, to love the name of the Lord, and be His servants,
> Everyone who keeps the Sabbath and does not profane it, and holds fast My covenant,
> Them I will bring to My holy mountain,
> And make them joyful in My house of prayer;
> Their burnt offerings and sacrifices
> Will be accepted on my altar;
> For My house shall be a house of prayer for all peoples.
> (Isa. 56:6–7)

NOTES

1. Yehezkel Kaufmann, *Golah V'Nekhar*, pp. 226 ff., and *Ha-Emunah Ha-Yisraelit*, vol. 4–5, pp. 702–6.
2. See Jacob Katz, *From Exclusiveness to Tolerance*, pp. 146–47.
3. See J. Guttmann, *Philosophies of Judaism*, pp. 126–27.
4. Katz, *From Exclusiveness to Tolerance*, p. 140.
5. Ibid., pp. 146–47.
6. George Foot Moore, *Judaism*, 1:323–24.
7. Mordecai M. Kaplan, *Judaism as a Civilization*, pp. 418–19.

THE WRITINGS OF IRA EISENSTEIN

By

RICHARD LIBOWITZ

Some may dismiss it as a truism, but the declaration that we are often the poorest judges of ourselves is nonetheless an accurate statement. Ira Eisenstein confesses to publishing a great deal of material, but explains it away with a "some of us seem to have ink for blood," while questioning whether any of his writing has lasting value. Because of this self-doubt, he never bothered to maintain a record of his soon burgeoning bibliography, a list which was begun in 1928 and today numbers hundreds of items, including books, essays, reviews, cantatas, speeches, editorials, contributions to symposia, etc.

The actual number of published writings is unknown; no attempt has been made to discern the authorship of the unsigned editorials which have appeared in the *Reconstructionist*. Although many of these statements were authored by Eisenstein, they were intended to reflect the consensus of the Editorial Board and have been so considered. With that one exception, the following chronology represents most—if not all—of Dr. Eisenstein's publications.

In perusing the titles, one is struck by the frequent use of *questions:* as an author, Ira Eisenstein raises questions before seeking answers. Those queries have touched upon the most pressing issues of the day; but for nearly half a century, the focus has always returned to the problems of the quality of Jewish existence. Thus, a voice was raised in 1928: "Judaism still contains the roots of a greater ethical culture. Judaism can realize not only the individual ethical personality; Jewish civilization can create the ethical state" (*SAJ Review,* 12/28/28, p. 15). The voice remained the same in 1949: "It seems to me that the question is not: to be or not to be? The question is: what kind and quality of Judaism shall there be?" (*Chalutz*, Summer 1949, p. 8). Another quarter-century passed, but the problem was still being confronted: "If Jews really wish to preserve the Jewish people they must take cognizance of the facts of contemporary life, and one of those facts is the fact of pluralism" (*Philadelphia Jewish Exponent*, May 24, 1974, p. 1). As Ira Eisenstein continues to work and write, the list continues to grow and the call resounds.

1928

"Unorthodox Fundamentalism." Review of *Judaism and the Modern Mind*, by Maurice H. Farbridge. *SAJ Review*, 7:26 (3/9/28), pp. 11–16.

"Life and the Synagogue." *SAJ Review*, 7:35 (5/11/28), pp. 15–23.

"Reformism and Christianity." *SAJ Review*, 8:6 (10/19/28), pp. 4–9.

"The Shock Troops of Orthodoxy." Review of *The Jewish Library, First Series*, edited by Rabbi Leo Jung. *SAJ Review*, 8:13 (12/7/28), pp. 17–20.

"Reform's 'Reversion'." Review of *The Democratic Impulse in Jewish History*, by Abba Hillel Silver. *SAJ Review*, 8:14 (12/14/28), pp. 19–20.

"Ethical Culture Sees It Through." Review of *Aspects of Ethical Religion*, edited by Horace J. Bridges. *SAJ Review*, 8:16 (12/28/28), pp. 13–15.

1929

"Wanted: New Motives." Review of *Motives of Men*, by George A. Coe. *SAJ Review*, 8:18 (1/11/29), p. 16.

"The Life of a Prophet." Review of *The Life of Moses*, by Edmond Fleg. *SAJ Review*, 8:20 (1/25/29), pp. 17–18.

"Some Latter-Day Saints." Review of *Leaders of Hassidism*, by S. A. Horodezky. *SAJ Review*, 8:21 (2/1/29), pp. 15–16.

"Unimpressive Aspects." Review of *Aspects of Judaism*, by Salis Daiches. *SAJ Review*, 8:22 (2/8/29), pp. 15–16.

"A Majority of Optimists." Review of *Whither Mankind*, edited by Charles A. Beard. *SAJ Review*, 8:24 (2/22/29), pp. 20–22.

"What Hath God Wrought?" Review of *CCAR Yearbook*, vol. 38. *SAJ Review*, 8:26 (3/8/29), pp. 19–20.

"The Gossamer of Civilization." Review of *Civilization*, by Clive Bell. *SAJ Review*, 8:27 (3/15/29), pp. 18–19.

"Unblushing Intuition." Review of *The Chosen People*, by Jerome and Jean Tharaud. *SAJ Review*, 8:29 (3/29/29), pp. 22–23.

"Reveries Over Things Past." Review of *Worlds That Passed*, by A. S. Sachs. *SAJ Review*, 8:30 (4/5/29), pp. 22–23.

"For Smart Children." Review of *The Burning Bush,* by Joseph Gaer (children's stories). *SAJ Review,* 8:31 (4/12/29), pp. 23–24.

"Living History." Review of *In the Days of the Second Temple,* by Jacob Golub (textbook). *SAJ Review,* 8:34 (5/3/29), pp. 19–20.

1933

"The Present Dilemma." *Opinion,* 3:8 (June 1933), pp. 8–9.

"Must Such Things Be?" Review of *Testament of Youth,* by Vera Brittain. *Opinion,* 4:2 (December 1933), pp. 30–31.

1935

Review of *A Common Faith,* by John Dewey. *Reconstructionist,* 1:2 (1/25/35), pp. 15–16.

Review of *Judaism,* by Morris Lichtenstein, *Reconstructionist,* 1:4 (2/22/35), pp. 15–16.

Review of *Jews in Palestine,* by A. Revusky. *Reconstructionist,* 1:6 (3/22/35), pp. 15–16.

"Should Jews Be Socialists?" *Reconstructionist,* 1:9 (5/3/35), pp. 8–14.

"The Place of Palestine in Jewish Life." *Reconstructionist,* 1:13 (11/1/35), pp. 6–11.

1936

Creative Judaism, New York: Behrman's Jewish Book House, 1936.

"Mr. Lewisohn's Misdirected Zeal." Review of *Rebirth,* by Ludwig Lewisohn. *Reconstructionist,* 1:20 (2/7/36), pp. 14–16.

"Jewish Narrative Literature." Review of *The Jewish Caravan,* edited by Leo W. Schwarz. *Reconstructionist,* 2:1 (2/21/36), pp. 15–16.

"Zionism and the Communists." *Reconstructionist,* 2:10 (6/26/36), pp. 7–13.

Review of *The Attitude of the Jewish Student in the Colleges and Universities Towards His Religion,* by Marvin Nathan. *Jewish Quarterly Review,* 27:2 (October 1936), pp. 189–90.

Review of *Religion and Its Social Setting,* by Abraham Cronbach. *Jewish Quarterly Review,* 27:2 (October 1936), pp. 190–91.

1937

"Dr. Kaplan Sails for Palestine." Editorial, signed by Editorial Board, including Ira Eisenstein. *Reconstructionist,* 3:10 (6/25/37), pp. 3–5.

"What Is the Jewish Problem?" *Reconstructionist,* 3:11 (10/8/37), pp. 8–14.

1938

What We Mean By Religion. New York: Behrman's Jewish Book House, 1938.

"Art and Jewish Life." *Reconstructionist,* 3:20 (2/11/38), pp. 6–9.

"A Note on Lag B'Omer." *Reconstructionist,* 4:7 (5/20/38), pp. 12–14.

"The Progress of Reconstructionism." *Reconstructionist,* 4:14 (11/18/38), pp. 13–16. (address originally given at Reconstructionist Summer Institute, Sept. 5, 1938)

"How the Other Third Lives." Review of *Land Without Moses,* by Charles C. Munz. *Reconstructionist,* 4:16 (12/16/38), pp. 15–16.

1939

"Toward a Sustaining Faith." *Reconstructionist,* 5:4 (4/7/39), pp. 5–9.

Review of *Prayers and Readings, Selected and Arranged,* by Solomon Goldman. *Jewish Education,* 11:2 (September 1939), pp. 143–44.

"The Significance of Jewish Survival." *Reconstructionist,* 5:13 (10/27/39), pp. 9–10.

"Henry George." *Proceedings of the Rabbinical Assembly,* vol. 6 (1939), pp. 86–93. (from a symposium, "Judaism and Contemporary Social Problems," delivered at 39th Annual Convention, 1939)

1940

"Shall We Have A Moratorium on Ideology?" *Reconstructionist,* 6:4 (3/29/40), pp. 12–15. (response to "A Moratorium on Ideology," by Jacob Agus, *Reconstructionist,* 6:3, 3/15/40, pp. 6–11)

"Preaching Modern Religion." *Proceedings of the Rabbinical Assembly,* vol. 7 (1940), pp. 143–49. (from a symposium, "The Rabbi and His Congregation," delivered at 40th Annual Convention)

1941

The Jordan: A New Frontier of Democracy (pamphlet). New York: Zionist Organization of America, ca. 1941.

The Ethics of Tolerance Applied to Religious Groups in America. New York: King's Crown Press, 1941. (Ph.D. thesis, Columbia University, 1941)

"Equity in Inter-Faith Relations." *Reconstructionist,* 7:12 (10/17/41), pp. 6–12. (from the recently published *Ethics of Tolerance*)

1942

The New Haggadah, edited by Mordecai M. Kaplan, Ira Eisenstein, and Eugene Kohn. New York: Behrman House. 1942.

"What Is Torah?" A cantata by Ira and Judith K. Eisenstein. New York: Jewish Reconstructionist Foundation, 1942.

"Judaism in America: 5. Reconstructionism." *Universal Jewish Encyclopedia,* vol. 6, pp. 245–46.

"Mordecai Menahem Kaplan." *Universal Jewish Encyclopedia,* vol. 6, p. 311.

"Oneg Shabbat." *Universal Jewish Encyclopedia,* vol. 8, p. 300.

"Society for the Advancement of Judaism." *Universal Jewish Encyclopedia,* vol. 9, p. 586.

Review of Publications of the National Academy for Adult Jewish Studies. *Jewish Education,* 13:3 (January 1942), p. 204.

"A Man of Integrity." A praise of Mordecai Kaplan, at age 60, signed by the Editorial Board, including Ira Eisenstein. *Reconstructionist,* 8:8 (5/29/42), pp. 3–4.

"Father of Jewish Reconstructionism." Written for syndication by the Independent Jewish Press Service, June 5, 1942.

"Reconstructionism and Zionism." *Reconstructionist,* 8:17 (12/25/42), pp. 7–9, 23–24. (later included in a Reconstructionist pamphlet, *Zionism)*

1943

Palestine in the Life of the Jew. New York: National Academy for Adult Jewish Studies, 1943.

Review of five books: *Introduction to Judaism,* by Beryl Cohon; *Folk and Faith,* by E. E. and Rabbi L. J. Levinger; *The Story of Jewish Holidays and Customs,* by Dorothy F. Zeligs; *Leading a Jewish Life in the Modern World,* by Rabbi S. M. Markowitz; *A Treasure Hunt in Judaism,* by Rabbi Harold P. Smith. *Jewish Education,* 15:1 (September 1943), pp. 45–47.

"The Centrality of the Synagogue." *Reconstructionist,* 9:13 (10/29/43), pp. 9–16. (originally delivered before the Joint Session of the Rabbinical Assembly and the Central Conference of American Rabbis)

"The Absolute and the Relative in Religion." *Reconstructionist,* 9:15 (11/26/43), pp. 23–24.

"A Note on 'Authority in Jewish Life.'" *Reconstructionist,* 9:20 (2/4/44), pp. 17–19. (response and comments on "Authority in Jewish Life," by Jacob Agus, *Reconstructionist,* 9:20 (2/4/44), pp. 9–17.

"The War's Brutality and Our Moral Sensitivity." *Reconstructionist,* 10:6 (4/28/44), pp. 15–17.

Letter. *Hebrew Union College Monthly,* 31:5 (June 1944), p. 12. (comments and contradictions of statements made by Sidney Morganbesser in March 1944 symposium "Reconstructionism After Ten Years")

"Introduction to 'Sabbath Services for the Modern Synagogue.' " *Reconstructionist,* 10:11 (10/6/44), pp. 9–15. (a reprint of the Introduction written by the Editorial Committee, including Ira Eisenstein)

"The Miracle of the Yiddish Theatre." Review of the play *Miracle of the Warsaw Ghetto. Reconstructionist,* 10:15 (12/1/44), pp. 19–20.

"The Centrality of the Synagogue." *Proceedings of the Rabbinical Assembly,* vol. 8 (1944), pp. 225–37. (delivered at 43rd Annual Convention [1943], in Joint Session with Central Conference of American Rabbis)

1945

Sabbath Prayer Book, edited by Mordecai M. Kaplan and Eugene Kohn, assisted by Ira Eisenstein and Milton Steinberg. New York: Jewish Reconstructionist Foundation, 1945.

"Excommunication Versus Freedom of Worship." In *A Challenge to Freedom of Worship,* (New York: Jewish Reconstructionist Foundation, 1945.) (a response to the herem pronounced upon Mordecai M. Kaplan).

"Our Bialik." A cantata by Ira and Judith K. Eisenstein. New York: Jewish Reconstructionist Foundation, 1945.

Reviews of *My Country,* by Russell W. Davenport, and *The Hitleriad,* by A. M. Klein. *Reconstructionist,* 10:18 (1/12/45), pp. 16–18.

"Reconstructionism: 10 Years Old." *National Jewish Monthly,* 59:6 (February 1945), pp. 180–181).

"Toward a Religion of Democracy in America." *Reconstructionist,* 11:1 (2/23/45), pp. 55–61.

Review of *Sabbath: The Day of Delight,* by Abraham E. Millgram. *Jewish Social Studies,* 7:2 (April 1945), pp. 173–74.

"Roosevelt's Ethical Will." *Reconstructionist,* 11:6 (5/11/45), pp. 10–12. (a tribute to FDR)

"Inter-Faith Relations and How to Improve Them." *Reconstructionist,* 11:12 (11/2/45), pp. 8–13.

"The Khalutz in America." *Jewish Frontier,* 12:12 (December 1945), pp. 22–24.

1946

Response to letter by Rabbi Louis Feinberg, in reference to article in *Reconstructionist* 11:12 (11/2/45), *Reconstructionist,* 11:17 (1/11/46), p. 23.

"Is Messianism Common Ground for a Jewish-Christian Coalition?" Review of *One Destiny*, by Sholem Asch. *Reconstructionist*, 12:5 (4/19/46), pp. 26–27.

"An Attempt to Define Conservative Judaism." Review of *Conservative Judaism*, by Robert Gordis. *Reconstructionist*, 12:8 (5/31/46), pp. 28–31.

Review of *Psychology of Religion*, by Paul E. Johnson. *Jewish Education*, 17:3 (June 1946), pp. 53–54.

"A Dog in Galut." *Jewish Frontier* 13:8 (August 1946), pp. 13–14.

"The British Are Not Nazis—A Reply to Mr. Duker." *Reconstructionist*, 12:14 (11/15/46), pp. 13–15. (response to article in *Reconstructionist*, 12:13 [11/1/46]. by A. G. Duker)

Review of *The Great Prisoners*, edited by Isidore Abramowitz. *Reconstructionist*, 12:15 (11/29/46), pp. 21–22.

"The Rabbi and the Jewish Community." *Proceedings of the Rabbinical Assembly*, vol. 10 (1946), pp. 108–11. (from a symposium, "The Rabbi as Communal Leader," delivered at 46th Annual Convention [1946])

1947

"Seven Golden Buttons." A cantata by Ira and Judith K. Eisenstein. New York: Jewish Reconstructionist Foundation, 1947.

Review of *The Arts and Religion*, edited by Albert E. Baily. *Jewish Education*, 18:3 (Summer 1947), p. 59.

"Psalm IX: A Song of Victory in the Third Year." *Reconstructionist*. 13:11 (10/3/47), pp. 18–20. (modern expansion of the psalm)

1948

High Holiday Prayer Book. Vol. 1, *Prayers for Rosh Hashanah;* Vol. 2, *Prayers for Yom Kippur*. Edited by Mordecai M. Kaplan, Eugene Kohn, and Ira Eisenstein.. New York: Jewish Reconstructionist Foundation, 1948.

"Keneset Yisrael." *Reconstructionist*, 14:4 (4/2/48), pp. 9–12.

" 'Dual Loyalty'—A New Approach." *Reconstructionist*, 14:12 (10/15/48), pp. 10–14.

"Towards a Philosophy of Conservative Judaism." *Proceedings of the Rabbinical Assembly*, vol. 12 (1948), pp. 110–11. (delivered at 48th Annual Convention [1948])

1949

"Jewish Life in the Diaspora." *Chalutz*, 42 (Summer 1949), pp. 5–8. (from "The Future of American Jewry—A Symposium")

"How Jews Can Contribute to American Democracy." *Reconstructionist*,

15:17 (12/30/49), pp. 10–16. (based on an address to the 1949 Convention of the Rabbinical Assembly)

"The New Diaspora and American Democracy." *Proceedings of the Rabbinical Assembly,* vol. 13 (1949), pp. 258–91. (paper and responses, delivered at 49th Annual Convention [1949])

1950

"A Message from Afikim, Israel." *Reconstructionist,* 16:1 (2/24/50), pp. 8–9. (editorial)

"Celebration in Afikim." *Reconstructionist,* 16:2 (3/10/50), pp. 17–19.

"The Sad News Reaches Jerusalem." *Reconstructionist,* 16:4 (4/7/50), pp. 13–15. (on the death of Milton Steinberg)

"Democracy Moves Forward in Israel." *Reconstructionist,* 16:7 (5/19/50), pp. 16–21.

"A New Approach to the Problem of Halutziut." *Hadassah Newsletter,* 31:2 (October 1950).

"Whose Freedom and Whose Responsibility?" *Reconstructionist,* 16:12 (10/20/50), pp. 22–24.

"Cultural Democracy." *Israel Life and Letters,* 6:5 (November 1950), pp. 2, 18.

"What Concerts Do to Israelis." *Reconstructionist,* 16:15 (12/1/50), pp. 14–16.

"Milton Steinberg." *Proceedings of the Rabbinical Assembly,* vol. 14 (1950), pp. 325–27. (a eulogy delivered at the 50th Annual Convention [1950])

1951

"Americans in Israel." *Reconstructionist,* 16:19 (1/26/51), pp. 9–14.

Review of *Jews in Transition,* by Albert I. Gordon. *Reconstructionist,* 17:2 (3/9/51), pp. 24–25.

Review of *The Jews of Charleston,* by Charles Reznikoff and Uriah Z. Engelman. *Reconstructionist,* 17:2 (3/9/51), pp. 25–26.

Letter Response: signed by Ira Eisenstein for the majority of the editors, to Rabbis Roland B. Gittelsohn and Sidney Jacobs re: an editorial (*Reconstructionist,* 2/9/51) urging admission of Spain into the United Nations. *Reconstructionist,* 17:2 (3/9/51), pp. 30–31.

"Some Israeli Haggadot." *Reconstructionist,* 17:5 (4/20/51), pp. 18–20.

"Mordecai M. Kaplan and the Zionist Movement." *New Palestine Magazine Section,* May 1951, pp. 2–3.

"Israel Zangwill." *Reconstructionist,* 17:8 (6/1/51), pp. 17–21. (written for Jewish Book Council, to appear in *Jewish Book Annual,* vol. 10, 5712, on 25th yahrzeit of Zangwill)

Untitled Paper. *Jewish Education,* 22:3 (Summer 1951), pp. 64–66. (excerpt of paper read at First National Conference on Jewish Education, January 13–15, 1951)

Review of *What the Jews Believe*, by Philip S. Bernstein. *Hadassah Newsletter*, July–August 1951, pp. 8, 11.

Review of *Man Is Not Alone*, by Abraham Joshua Heschel. *Hadassah Newsletter*, July–August 1951, p. 8.

"Religion." *Reconstructionist*, 17:13 (11/2/51), pp. 25–27. (a report on current goings-on)

"Religion." *Reconstructionist*, 17:16 (12/14/51), pp. 27–29. (a report on current goings-on)

Letter Response. *Reconstructionist*, 17:17 (12/28/51), p. 32. (response to letter from Shad Polier, regarding item in 17:16 review)

"Reform and Conservative Judaism." *CCAR Yearbook*, vol. 61 (1951), pp. 293–301. (presented at 62nd Annual Convention)

1952

Mordecai M. Kaplan: An Evaluation. Edited by Ira Eisenstein and Eugene Kohn, New York: Jewish Reconstructionist Foundation, 1952.

"Mordecai M. Kaplan and His Teachers." In *Mordecai M. Kaplan: An Evaluation*, pp. 15–25.

"The Unity of the Jewish People Throughout the World." *Proceedings of the Rabbinical Assembly*, vol. 16 (1952), pp. 119–23. (joint paper presented for the Committee on Jewish Unity in America and delivered at 52nd Annual Convention)

"Reborn." A cantata by Ira and Judith K. Eisenstein. New York: Jewish Reconstructionist Foundation, 1952.

Review of *The Sabbath: Its Meaning for Modern Man*, by Abraham Joshua Heschel. *Reconstructionist*, 18:1 (2/22/52), pp. 23–24.

"Religion." *Reconstructionist*, 18:4 (4/7/52), pp. 24–25. (a report on current goings-on)

"Primary Functions of the Jewish Community." *Jewish Social Service Quarterly*, 29:1 (September 1952), pp. 10–11. (summary of paper presented at the National Conference of Jewish Communal Service, Chicago, Ill., June 1, 1952)

"The Great American Experiment." *Reconstructionist*, 18:13 (10/31/52), pp. 7–13.

"Religion." *Reconstructionist*, 18:14 (11/14/52), pp. 26–28. (a report on current goings-on)

1953

Creative Judaism. Rev. ed. New York: Jewish Reconstructionist Foundation, 1953.

Review of *Milk and Honey* (Israel Explored), by George Mikes. *Jewish Social Studies*, 15:1 (January 1953), pp. 72–73.

"Sex Equality in the Synagogue." *Reconstructionist*. 19:2 (3/6/53), pp. 18–20.

Review of *Israel's Fate and Faith,* by Abraham M. Hershman. *Jewish Social Studies,* 15:3–4 (July–October 1953), pp. 318–19.

"Patterns of Living of the Jewish People on the American Scene." *Jewish Social Service Quarterly,* 30:1 (September 1953), pp. 91–99. (presented at the National Conference of Jewish Communal Service, Atlantic City, N.J., May 24, 1953)

"The Cantor in Modern Judaism." *Reconstructionist,* 19:13 (11/6/53), pp. 18–20.

Letter Response. *Reconstructionist,* 19:15 (12/4/53), pp. 31–32. (response to letter from W. Belkin Ginsburg, in reference to article on the cantorate, 11/6/53)

"President's Message." *Proceedings of the Rabbinical Assembly,* vol. 17 (1953), pp. 139–50. (delivered at 53rd Annual Convention [1953])

1954

"Thy Children Shall Return." A cantata by Ira and Judith K. Eisenstein. New York: Reconstructionist Press, 1954.

Review of *The Inner Eye,* by Hayim Greenberg. *Reconstructionist,* 20:3 (3/26/54), pp. 28–30.

"Moses—Creator of a Freedom-Loving People." *Hadassah Newsletter,* April 1954, pp. 3, 14.

"Jewish 'Center' in place of Kibbutz Galuyot." *Jewish Newsletter,* 10:13 (6/21/54), p. 3.

"President's Message." *Proceedings of the Rabbinical Assembly,* vol. 18 (1954), pp. 147–57. (delivered at 54th Annual Convention [1954])

1955

"New Directions in Jewish Education." *Reconstructionist,* 21:1 (2/18/55), pp. 50–54.

"My Philosophy of Judaism." *Reconstructionist,* 21:5 (4/15/55), pp. 8–12. (address delivered at Anshe Emet Synagogue, Chicago, Ill., December 3, 1954)

"A Community Council for Chicago." *Reconstructionist,* 21:8 (5/26/55), pp. 6–9.

Review of *Man's Quest for God,* by Abraham Joshua Heschel. *Reconstructionist,* 21:17 (12/30/55), pp. 24–26.

1956

Judaism Under Freedom. New York: Reconstructionist Press, 1956.

"From Over-Organized Chaos to Jewish Community." Major address, delivered at 18th Annual Meeting of the Jewish Community Council of Greater Washington, on January 29, 1956, pp. 13–18.

Review of *Essays in the Public Philosophy,* by Walter Lippmann. *Reconstructionist,* 22:3 (3/23/56), pp. 28–30.

Contributed to "An Analysis of Jacob Agus's *Guideposts in Modern Judaism.*" *Conservative Judaism,* 10:3 (Spring 1956), pp. 5–9.

1957

Editorials: "The Covenant Idea and Its Implementation"; "Revival of Reconstructionism in Chicago"; "Storm Over *Martin Luther.*" *Reconstructionist,* 22:19 (1/25/57), pp. 3–6. (signed editorials)

Review of *A Guide for Reform Jews,* by Frederic A. Doppel and David Polish. *Reconstructionist,* 23:6 (5/3/57), pp. 28–29.

"What's Wrong With 'Good Will' Movements?" *Jewish Digest,* 2:10 (July 1957), pp. 27–32. (extracted from *Judaism Under Freedom*)

1958

What We Mean By Religion. Revised and enlarged. New York: Reconstructionist Press, 1958.

Festival Prayer Book. Prepared by Mordecai M. Kaplan, Jack J. Cohen, Ludwig Nadelmann, Eugene Kohn, Ira Eisenstein, et al. New York: Jewish Reconstructionist Foundation, 1958.

What Is A Jew? Judaism Pamphlet Series. B'nai B'rith Youth Organization, 1958, pp. 1–23.

"Recent Books About American Judaism." Brief reviews of: *The Jews,* by M. Sklare; *Jewish Life in America,* by T. Friedman and R. Gordis; *American Jewry,* by E. Kohn; *American Judaism,* by N. Glazer; *Generation of Decision,* by S. Liptzin. *Jewish Heritage,* 1:3 (Fall 1958), pp. 45–47.

Review of *The American Jew: A Zionist Analysis,* by Ben Halpern. *Jewish Social Studies,* 20:4 (October 1958), pp. 247–48.

"The Need for Legislation in Jewish Law." In *Tradition and Change,* edited by Mordecai Waxman. New York: Burning Bush Press, 1958, pp. 447–454.

1959

"And Now The Editor." *Reconstructionist,* 25:11–25:17 (1/2/59–12/25/59). (a summary feature of each issue)

"Why I Am a Labor Zionist." *Jewish Frontier* 26:7 (August 1959), p. 21.
"The Great Debate Rages On: 'Who Is A Jew?' A Reply to Mr. Ben-
Gurion's Question." *Jewish Digest*, 5:1 (October 1959), pp. 42–44.
Review of *The Zionist Idea*, edited by Arthur Hertzberg. *Reconstructionist*,
25:16 (12/11/59), pp. 24–25.
"Some Beliefs of Reconstructionism." *Jewish Heritage*, 2:3 (Winter 1959–
60), pp. 43–48. (section II of article "Philosophy of Reconstructionism,"
selections from writings of Mordecai Kaplan, selected by Ira Eisenstein)
Whither?, by Mordecai Zeev Feierberg. Translated from the Hebrew by Ira
Eisenstein. New York: Abelard-Schuman, 1959.

1960

"And Now The Editor." *Reconstructionist*, 25:18–26:17 (1/8/60–12/30/
60.). (a summary feature of each issue)
Letter Response, to Rabbi Elmer Berger. *Reconstructionist*, 25:18 (1/8/60),
pp. 27–28.
"The Issues We Faced." *Reconstructionist*, 26:1 (2/19/60), pp. 7–11. (a
review of the contents of the initial volume of *Reconstructionist*)
Letter. *CCAR Journal*, 8:3 (October 1960), pp. 62–63.
"Milton Steinberg's Mind and Heart." Review of *Anatomy of Faith*, edited
by Arthur A. Cohen. *Reconstructionist*, 26:12 (10/21/60), pp. 23–30.

1961

"God, Israel and Torah." *Jewish Education*, 31:2 (Winter 1961), pp. 16–17.
(comment on "The Tangibles of Jewish Education," by Simon Greenberg, in that volume)
"And Now The Editor." *Reconstructionist*, 26:19–27:17 (1/13/61–
12/29/61). (a summary feature of each issue)
"Fraternal Delegates at the Congress." *Reconstructionist*, 26:19 (1/27/61),
pp. 6–7. (comments on the 25th World Zionist Congress; originally published in the *Jerusalem Post*, 1/4/61)
"Book Reviews in Brief." *Reconstructionist*, 27:7 (5/19/61), pp. 31–32.
(brief reviews of: *The Szolds of Lombard Street*, by A. L. Levin; *This Is
a Man*, by Primo Levi; *Old-New Land*, by Herzl, with notes by L. Levin-
son; *The Midstream Reader*, edited by Shlomo Katz; *Nachum Sokolow,
Servant of His People*, by S. Kling; *The Diary of David S. Kogan*, edited
by Meyer Levin and Dr. J. Nedava; *The Jews of Ancient Rome*, by H.
J. Leon; *The Psalms: Translation and Commentary*, by Rabbi S. R.
Hirsch; *How the Hebrew Language Grew*, by E. Horowitz)
"What Is Zionism?" *Reconstructionist*, 27:8 (6/2/61), pp. 5–9.
"Brief Reviews." *Reconstructionist*, 27:8 (6/2/61), pp. 28–29. (brief re-

views of: *My Faith and People,* by Theodore N. Lewis; *Living With Your Teen-Ager; A Guide for Jewish Parents,* by Simon Glustrom; *A Jewish Child Is Born,* by Nathan Gottlieb; *Zionism Under Soviet Rule,* by Guido G. Goldmann)

"Goals for American Jewry in 5722: A Collective Rosh Hashanah Wish." *Jewish Digest* 6:12 (September 1961), p. 3. (a collection of thoughts from many Jewish leaders, including Ira Eisenstein)

"An Imaginative Proposal to American Jewry." *Jewish Digest,* 7:1 (October 1961), pp. 1–4. הדאר, "קפלן בגבורות" מ. מרדכי vol. 21 (2 Kislev 5722 [Nov. 10, 1961]), pp. 21–22.

"In Passing." *Reconstructionist,* 27:12 (10/20/61), pp. 28–31. (comments on the concept of religious civilization)

"In Passing." *Reconstructionist,* 27:13 (11/3/61), pp. 29–30. (comments on havurot and the curse of Bigness)

"In Passing." *Reconstructionist,* 27:14 (11/17/61), pp. 30–31. (comments on what is required to draw reader responses to articles and editorials)

"In Passing." *Reconstructionist,* 27:15 (12/1/61), pp. 29–30. (comments on the havurah)

"In Passing." *Reconstructionist,* 27:17 (12/29/61), pp. 31–32. (comments on the havurah as more than a study group)

The Sabbath. New York: Reconstructionist Press, 1961. (a pamphlet)

1962

"And Now The Editor." *Reconstructionist,* 27:18–28:17 (1/11/62–12/28/62). (a summary feature of each issue)

"In Passing." *Reconstructionist,* 27:19 (1/26/62), pp. 28–29. (comments on a new definition of "peoplehood" included in the *Webster's Dictionary*)

"In Passing." *Reconstructionist,* 27:20 (2/9/62), pp. 24–25. (the 40th anniversary of the SAJ and its relationship with the Reconstructionist movement)

"In Passing." *Reconstructionist,* 28:1 (2/23/62), pp. 30–31. (comments on the 50th anniversary of Hadassah)

"The Attainable Goals." *Congress bi-Weekly* (Supplement), April 2, 1962, pp. 10–14. (from "Realistic Goals for Jewish Survival"; presentations made at the Fourth Conference on Jewish Values, February 22, 1962, at Stephen Wise Congress House in New York)

"In Passing." *Reconstructionist,* 28:13 (11/2/62), pp. 30–31. (critique of 1962 *American Jewish Year Book* article on Mordecai Kaplan)

"What Can a Modern Jew Believe?" *Reconstructionist,* 28:14 (11/16/62), pp. 6–11. (originally a broadcast on WRVR-FM [New York], Nov. 8, 1962)

"The Affirmation of Life and Its Possibilities." *Sermon Series* 1962–63, no. 4, December 9, 1962. Unitarian Church of Germantown (Pa.), pp. 1–4.
"The Story of a Search." Review of *Parallel Quest,* by Irma Lindheim. *Reconstructionist,* 28:16 (12/14/62), pp. 29–30.

1963

"Mordecai M. Kaplan." In *Great Jewish Thinkers of the Twentieth Century,* edited by Simon Noveck, pp. 253–79. (B'nai B'rith Great Books Series, Volume III) Clinton, Mass.: Colonial Press, 1963.
"And Now The Editor." *Reconstructionist,* 28:18–29:17 (1/11/63–12/27/63). (a summary feature of each issue)
"In Passing." *Reconstructionist,* 29:3 (3/22/63), pp. 29–30. (memories of Hayim Greenberg, on his 10th yahrzeit)
"A Community School for Teenagers." *Jewish Education,* 33:3 (Spring 1963), pp. 144–49.
Review of *In the Thicket,* by Solomon Simon. *Jewish Publication Society of America News Release,* July 19, 1963. (also appeared in *Chicago Sentinel,* 9/5/63, p. 13)
"Reconstructionism and Jewish Education" (part one). *Reconstructionist,* 29:12 (10/18/63), pp. 17–22. (drafted by Ira Eisenstein and revised by the Federation of Reconstructionist Congregations and Fellowships, at Annual Conference, May 2–5, 1963)
"Reconstructionism and Jewish Education" (part two). *Reconstructionist,* 29:13 (11/1/63), pp. 16–21.
"Intermarriage: A Growing Problem." Review of *Intermarriage and Jewish Life,* edited by Werner J. Cahnman. *Reconstructionist,* 29:13 (11/1/63), pp. 26–28.
"Jews Must Will the Future." *Jewish Heritage,* vol. 6, no. 3 (Winter 1963–64), pp. 50–52.
"The Reconstructionist Movement." In *Meet the American Jew,* compiled and edited by Belden Menkus, 1963.

1964

Intermarriage. Jewish Tract Series. National Academy for Adult Jewish Studies of the United Synagogue of America, 1964, pp. 3–23.
"And Now The Editor." *Reconstructionist,* 29:18–30:17 (1/10/64–12/25/64). (a summary feature of each issue)
Letter. *Jewish Spectator,* 29:3 (March 1964), p. 29. (comments on Rabbi Marc Samuels' article "Reconstructionism Reconsidered," in Feb. 1964 issue)
"More Questions Jews Ask." *Reconstructionist,* 30:2 (3/6/64), pp. 30–31.

"More Questions Jews Ask." *Reconstructionist,* 30:4 (4/3/64), p. 31.
"What Our Readers Think." *Reconstructionist,* 30:6 (5/1/64), pp. 31–32.
(responses to a readers' poll)
"What Our Readers Think." *Reconstructionist,* 30:7 (5/15/64), pp. 31–32.
(further responses to the poll)
"Poll Report III." *Reconstructionist,* 30:8 (5/29/64), p. 32.
"What The Shabbat Meant to Our Ancestors." *Jewish Digest,* 9:12 (September 1964), pp. 53–56. (condensed from the pamphlet *The Sabbath*)

1965

"And Now The Editor." *Reconstructionist,* 30:18–31:17 (1/8/65–12/24/65). (a summary feature of each issue)
"Almost a Reconstructionist." Review of *A Time for Christian Candor,* by James A. Pike. *Reconstructionist,* 31:1 (2/19/65), pp. 27–28.
"Modecai Zeev Feierberg: Forgotten Genius." *Jewish Heritage,* 7:4 (Spring 1965), pp. 59–63. (selected material, with an introduction by Ira Eisenstein)
"Interview With Professor Salo W. Baron." *Reconstructionist,* 31:9 (6/11/65), pp. 12–21.
"The Quest for Jewish Values—Part II: Questions for Thinking Jews." *Jewish Heritage,* 8:1 (Summer 1965), pp. 28–43. (a symposium, including Jacob Agus, Eugene B. Borowitz, Ira Eisenstein, B. Z. Goldberg, Robert Gordis, Steven S. Schwarzschild, C. Bezalel Sherman, and Judah Stampfer)
"Marvin Lowenthal: The Spirit of *Menorah.*" *Reconstructionist,* 31:13 (10/29/65), pp. 17–24. (an interview about the *Menorah Journal*)
"Reconstructionist Viewpoint—The Torah." *Reconstructionist,* 31:13 (10/29/65), p. 32. (reprinted from *Judaism Under Freedom,* p. 38)
"Intermarriage: For Jewish Parents." News Service of Commission on Synagogue Relations of the Federation of Jewish Philanthropies of New York. 1965.

1966

Varieties of Jewish Belief, edited by Ira Eisenstein. New York: Reconstructionist Press, 1966.
"And Now The Editor." *Reconstructionist,* 31:18–32:16 (1/7/66–12/23/66). (a summary feature of each issue)
"Alexander M. Dushkin at Seventy-Five." *Reconstructionist,* 31:18 (1/7/66), pp. 15–23.
"What to Do If Your Child Decides to Marry a Non-Jew." *Jewish Digest,*

11:6 (March 1966), pp. 73–76. (condensed from "Intermarriage: For Jewish Parents")

"Reconstructionist Viewpoint—Missionizing." *Reconstructionist*, 32:2 (3/4/66), p. 32. (from *Judaism Under Freedom*, pp. 239–40)

"Solomon Grayzel at Seventy: An Interview." *Reconstructionist*, 32:6 (4/29/66), pp. 16–25.

Response to Letter from Rabbi Jack Schechter. *Reconstructionist*, 32:10 (6/24/66), pp. 32–33.

"The State of Jewish Belief." *Commentary*, 42:2 (August 1966), pp. 85–86. (a symposium, later published in book form)

"Judaism and the 'Death of God.'" *Reconstructionist*, 32:11 (10/14/66), pp. 9–14. (expanded book review of *Radical Theology and the Death of God*, by William Hamilton and Thomas J. J. Altizer, to be included in forthcoming volume, edited by Richard L. Rubenstein)

"The Editorial Board Interviews Rabbi Kaplan." *Reconstructionist*, 32:11 (10/14/66), pp. 15–22.

"Reconstructionist Viewpoint—The Jewish Child." *Reconstructionist*, 32:11 (10/14/66), p. 28. (reprinted from "The Jewish Family Today")

"Reconstructionist Viewpoint." *Reconstructionist*, 32:12 (10/28/66), p. 30. (on Jewish laity's role in Jewish law: from "The Need for Legislation in Jewish Law," cited in *Tradition and Change*, edited by M. Waxman)

"Hazards to Dialogue." *Reconstructionist*, 32:16 (12/23/66), pp. 23–26. (review of *A Jew in Christian America*, by Arthur Gilbert)

Response to letter from Gershon Winer. *Reconstructionist*, 32:16 (12/23/66), pp. 27–28. (on autopsies in Israel)

1967

"And Now The Editor." *Reconstructionist*, 32:17–33:17 (1/6/67–12/29/67). (a summary feature of each issue)

Review of *Storm the Gates of Jericho*, by Abraham L. Feinberg. *Reconstructionist*, 32:17 (1/6/67), pp. 30–31.

"In Interview with Louis Kraft." *Reconstructionist*, 32:18 (1/20/67), pp. 10–21.

"Jewish Youth Wants to Know." *Reconstructionist*, 33:1 (3/3/67), p. 30. (explanation of Kaplan's concept of God)

"Jewish Youth Wants to Know." *Reconstructionist*, 33:2 (3/17/67), p. 30. (explanation of the concept of Jewish peoplehood in America)

"Jewish Youth Wants to Know." *Reconstructionist*, 33:4 (4/14/67), p. 32. (explanation of religion and philosophy)

"Jewish Youth Wants to Know." *Reconstructionist*, 33:5 (4/28/67), pp. 30–31. (the rationale for separate Jewish institutions)

"Reconstructionist Viewpoint—Pharaoh: The Arch-Tyrant." *Reconstructionist,* 33:5 (4/28/67), p. 31. (from *The New Haggadah,* pp. 50–51)
"An Interview With Yudel Mark." *Reconstructionist,* 33:10 (7/7/67), pp. 7–13.
"Whither Reconstructionism?" *Reconstructionist,* 33:11 (10/6/67), pp. 25–29. (on the possibility of creating a new training school for rabbis)

1968

"And Now The Editor." *Reconstructionist,* 33:18–34:6, 34:8–34:16 (1/12/68–5/3/68, 5/31/68–12/20/68). (a summary feature of each issue; on West Coast and unable to edit 34:7, 5/17/68)
Response to letter from Graenum Berger. *Reconstructionist,* 34:5 (4/19/68), p. 31.
Review of *Selected Essays of Ahad Ha'am,* edited by J. H. Neumann. *Reconstructionist,* 34:6 (5/3/68), p. 30.
"The Reconstructionist Rabbinical College Is Dedicated." *Reconstructionist,* 34:13 (11/8/68), pp. 28–31. (remarks from the opening, October 13, 1968)
"Jewish Youth and the Sexual Revolution." *Dimensions in American Judaism,* vol. 3, no. 2 (Winter 1968–69), p. 17. (from a symposium).

1969

Preface to Reconstructionism. New York: Reconstructionist Press, 1969. (a chapter in *Great Jewish Thinkers of the Twentieth Century,* edited by Simon Noveck)
"And Now The Editor." *Reconstructionist,* 34:17–35:13 (1/3/69–12/12/69). (a summary feature of each issue)
"Heroic Humanist." *Women's American ORT Reporter* 19:3 (January/February 1969), p. 5. (review of *Leo Baeck: Teacher of Teresienstadt,* by Albert H. Friedlander)
Letter. *Jewish Spectator,* 34:2 (February 1969), pp. 26–27. (included in "Open Forum" section)
"Mordecai M. Kaplan." *Jewish Heritage,* 11:3 (Spring 1969), p. 27. (reprint of praise, on Mordecai Kaplan's 80th birthday, 1961)
"Our Creative Colleagues." *Reconstructionist,* 35:5 (5/23/69), pp. 7–12. (reviews of: *God of Daniel S.,* by Alan W. Miller; *The Religious Imagination,* by Richard L. Rubenstein; *The Vatican Council and the Jews,* by Arthur Gilbert)
"The Future of Rabbinic Training in America." *Judaism,* 18:4 (Fall 1969), pp. 401–42. (a symposium)

The Condition of Jewish Belief: A symposium compiled by the editors of *Commentary Magazine.* New York: Macmillan Co., 1969, pp. 45–51. (reprinted from *Commentary,* 42:2, August 1966)

1970

"Jewish Law and the Ways of Judaism in Our Time." In *Contemporary Experience: Essays on Jewish Thought and Life,* edited by Alfred Jospe. (Schocken Books for B'nai B'rith Hillel Foundation, New York, 1970)

"And Now The Editor." *Reconstructionist,* 35:14–36:13 (1/2/70–12/25/70). (a summary feature of each issue)

"Dialogue on the Rabbinical College: With a Response." *Reconstructionist,* 36:3 (3/27/70), pp. 26–29.

"Dialogue With Dr. Horace M. Kallen." *Reconstructionist,* 36:5 (5/8/70), pp. 14–23. (on his retirement from active work at the New School for Social Research)

"Questions Jewish Youth Ask." *Reconstructionist,* 36:10 (10/23/70), p. 29. (on the Jews as a people)

"An Open Letter to Our Readers." *Reconstructionist,* 36:13 (12/25/70), pp. 3–6. (a call for financial aid for the Reconstructionist Rabbinical College)

1971

"And Now The Editor." *Reconstructionist,* 36:14–37:9 (1/15/71–12/17/71). (a summary feature of each issue)

"A Critique of a Critique: Comments on the Year Book Article" (part one). *Reconstructionist,* 36:14 (1/15/71), pp. 7–13. (review of Charles S. Liebman's article: "Reconstructionism in American Jewish Life," *AJYB,* 1971)

"Reconstructionist News." *Reconstructionist,* 36:14 (1/15/71), p. 30.

"Critique of a Critique—2." *Reconstructionist,* 37:1 (3/5/71), pp. 17–21.

"Critique of a Critique—3." *Reconstructionist,* 37:3 (5/7/71), pp. 17–21.

Response to letter from 11 RRC students, denouncing an editorial (*Reconstructionist* 37:1–3/5/71)—opposed to Jewish radicals. *Reconstructionist,* 37:3 (5/7/71), p. 35.

‫תגובה על המסה והמחקר של ישעהו (צ׳ארלס) ליבמן". תפוצות ישראל,‬ vol. 9 no. 3 (May–June 1971), pp. 65–78. (response to Charles Liebman *AJYB* article on Reconstructionism)

Review of *The Shaping of Jewish History,* by Ellis Rivkin. *Saturday Review,* October 23, 1971, pp. 86, 102.

"Reconstructionism and Zionism." *Encyclopedia of Zionism and Israel,* vol. 2, p. 937.

1972

"And Now The Editor." *Reconstructionist*, 37:10–38:9 (1/21/72–December 1972). (a summary feature of each issue)

"Paul and Psychoanalysis." Review of *My Brother Paul*, by Richard L. Rubenstein. *Reconstructionist*, 38:5 (6/30/72), pp. 30–31.

1973

"And Now The Editor." *Reconstructionist*, 38:10–39:9 (January-December 1973). (a summary feature of each issue)

"Werner Cahnman at Seventy." *Reconstructionist*, 39:5 (June 1973), pp. 24–33.

Review of *The Tenth Generation*, by George E. Mendenhall. *Review of Books and Religion*, July–August 1973, p. 4.

Review of *In The Beginning Love*, by Mark Van Doren and Maurice Samuel, edited by Edith Samuel. *Reform Judaism*, 2:2 (October 1973), p. 4.

1974

"And Now The Editor." *Reconstructionist*, 39:10–40:9 (January–December 1974). (summary feature of each issue)

"The Modern Appeal of Magic." *Friday Forum* (supplement to *Philadelphia Jewish Exponent*), no. 22, March 22, 1974, pp. 1, 8.

"Jewish Pluralism in Israel?" *Friday Forum* (supplement to *Philadelphia Jewish Exponent*), no. 24, May 24, 1974, pp. 1, 4, 8. (a symposium)

Review of *The Good Society: Jewish Ethics in Action*, edited by Norman Lamm. *Philadelphia Jewish Exponent*, September 6, 1974, p. 30.

"A Rabbi's Spiritual Odyssey." Review of *Power Struggle*, by Richard L. Rubenstein. *Reconstructionist*, 40:7 (October 1974), pp. 34–35.

"Jewish Law and Theology in Tension." Review of *Law and Theology in Judaism*, by David Novak. *Review of Books and Religion*, 4:2 (mid-October 1974), pp. 1, 16.

1975

"And Now The Editor." *Reconstructionist*, 40:10–41:9 (January–December 1975). (a summary feature of each issue)

"From School of Thought to Movement." *Reconstructionist*, 41:1 (February 1975), pp. 3–5.

"An Original Love Story." Review of *Golgotha*, by Chayym Zeldis. *Reconstructionist*, 41:2 (March 1975), pp. 28–29.

"A Meaningful Credo." Review of *Why Judaism?—A Search for Meaning in Jewish Identity,* by Henry Cohen. *The Reconstructionist,* 41:2 (March 1975), pp. 29–30.

"The Source of Our Hope." *Reconstructionist,* 41:6 (September 1975), pp. 7–10. (address at Third Graduation Exercises, Reconstructionist Rabbinical College, May 18, 1975)

1976

"And Now The Editor." *Reconstructionist,* 41:10–42:5 (January–June 1976). (a summary feature of each issue)

"Christians and the Holocaust." Review of *The Crucifixion of the Jews,* by Franklin H. Littell. *Reconstructionist,* 41:10 (January 1976), pp. 22–23.

Undated

What Can a Modern Jew Believe? New York: Reconstructionist Press. (a pamphlet, reprinting material from *Reconstructionist,* 28:14–11/16/62)

"The Havurah in Action." In *'The Havurah Idea,'* by Jacob Neusner and Ira Eisenstein, pp. 10–14. (New York: Reconstructionist Press, a pamphlet)

"Jewish Cultural Values." Publication of the Jewish Center Lecture Bureau of the National Jewish Welfare Board. pp. 4–5.

The Reconstructionist Movement. New York: Jewish Reconstructionist Foundation. (a pamphlet, reprinted from *Meet the American Jew,* edited by Belden Menkus, 1963.)

The Jewish Family Today. New York: Jewish Reconstructionist Foundation. (a pamphlet, based upon four lectures delivered to the Women's Organization, *JRF,* 1965–66)

ALPHABETICAL LIST OF CONTRIBUTORS

BEN-HORIN, Meir: Vice President for Academic Affairs and Professor of Modern Jewish Thought and Education, The Horace M. Kallen Center for Jewish Studies of Herzliah-Jewish Teachers Seminary, New York; former Professor of Education, The Dropsie University; author of *Max Nordau, Philosopher of Human Solidarity* (1956) and *Common Faith: Uncommon People—Essays in Reconstructionist Judaism* (1970); an editor of *Jewish Social Studies* since 1957.

BERNSTEIN, Philip: Executive Vice President, Council of Jewish Federations and Welfare Funds; Past President, National Conference of Jewish Communal Service.

BRAUNER, Ronald A.: Director of the Rabbinic Civilization Program, Reconstructionist Rabbinical College; Assistant Professor of Bible and History, Gratz College; Book Editor of *Reconstructionist* magazine and author of numerous studies in Semitic philology and Bible.

CAHN, Judah: Faculty, Springfield College and New School for Social Research; Rabbi, Metropolitan Synagogue, New York; President, New York Board of Rabbis.

CAHN, Steven M.: Professor of Philosophy and Chairman of the Department, University of Vermont; author of *Fate, Logic and Time* (1967), *A New Introduction to Philosophy* (1971) and *The Eclipse of Excellence: A Critique of American Higher Education* (1973).

CAINE, Ivan W.: Director of the Biblical Civilization Program, Reconstructionist Rabbinical College; author of reviews and articles, including "Numbers, Book of" in *Encyclopaedia Judaica* (1972); Ph.D. dissertation, *The Redaction of Numbers,* in progress.

COHEN, Kenneth, S.: Assistant Rabbi and Educational Director, Congregation Beth Shalom, Wilmington, Del.; Rabbi, Reconstructionist Rabbinical College (1975); Ph.D. candidate, Department of Religion, Temple University.

EISENSTEIN, Judith Kaplan: Faculty, Hebrew Union College-Jewish Institute of Religion; author of numerous cantatas (in collaboration with Ira Eisenstein), musical studies and *A Heritage of Music: The Music of the Jewish People* (1974).

FEINER, Harriet A.: Professor of Social Work, Wurzweiler School of Social Work, Yeshiva University; formerly a social caseworker in a Jewish family agency and a child guidance clinic.

GERBER, Jane S.: Assistant Professor of History, Herbert H. Lehman College, CUNY; Book Review Editor, *Jewish Social Studies;* author of articles on Jews under Islam.

GOLDIN, Judah: Professor of Postbiblical Hebrew Literature, University of Pennsylvania; author of *The Song at the Sea* (1971); editor of *The Jewish Expression* (1976).

GOTTSCHALK, Alfred: President, Hebrew Union College-Jewish Institute of Religion; Vice President, World Union for Progressive Judaism; author of *Your Future as a Rabbi* (1967), translator of N. Glueck's *Hesed in the Bible* (1967) and author of numerous studies on Ahad Ha-Am.

JANOWSKY, Oscar I.: Emeritus Professor of History, C.C.N.Y., C.U.N.Y.; Jacob Ziskind Visiting Professor, Brandeis University, 1966-67; author of *The Jews and Minority Rights* (1933), *Nationalities and National Minorities* (1945) and *The JWB Survey* (1948); editor of *The American Jew* (1965).

KAPLAN, Mordecai M.: Founder of the Society for the Advancement of Judaism, *Reconstructionist* magazine, the Jewish Reconstructionist Foundation; author of many studies of varied aspects of Jewish Civilization including *Judaism as a Civilization* (1934), *Ha-Emunah ve-ha-Musar* (1954), *Questions Jews Ask* (1956), *Judaism Without Supernaturalism* (1958) and *The Religion of Ethical Nationhood* (1970).

KESSNER, Carole: Assistant Professor of English, S.U.N.Y. at Stony Brook; author of articles in *The Milton Encyclopedia, Milton Studies, Milton Quarterly;* compiler of *An Annotated Bibliography for the Study of the Jewish Immigrant Novel in the U.S. Between 1865 and 1920, Bulletin of the New York Public Library* (Summer, 1977).

LACHS, Samuel Tobias: Associate Professor of History of Religion, Bryn Mawr College, Adjunct Associate Professor of Rabbinics, Gratz College; co-editor, *Gratz College Annual of Jewish Studies;* author of many studies on early Rabbinic literature and the Semitic background to the New Testament.

LIBOWITZ, Richard L.: Rabbi, Bet Am Shalom Synagogue, White Plains, New York; Rabbi, Reconstructionist Rabbinical College (1976); doctoral candidate, Department of Religion, Temple University.

LITTELL, Franklin H.: Professor of Religion, and Chairman of the Department, Temple University; President, Christians Concerned for Israel; author of *The Crucifixion of the Jews* (1975).

MILLER, Alan W.: Rabbi of the Society for the Advancement of Judaism, New York; Visiting Associate Professor, New School of Liberal Arts, Brooklyn College; author of *God of Daniel S.: In Search of the American Jew* (1969).

MORRIS, Henry D.: Assistant Professor, Department of Philosophy and Religion, Colgate University; Counselor to Colgate Jewish Community; Rabbi, Reconstructionist Rabbinical College (1975).

POPPEL, Stephen M.: Assistant Professor of History, Bryn Mawr College; Adjunct Lecturer in Modern Jewish Civilization, Reconstructionist Rabbinical College; author of *Zionism in Germany, 1897-1933: The Shaping of a Jewish Identity* (1976).

ROUTTENBERG, Max J.: Rabbi Emeritus, Temple B'nai Sholom, Rockville Centre, New York; editor, *The Eternal Light*, NBC-TV; Visiting Professor of Homiletics, Jewish Theological Seminary.

ZUCKERMAN, Arthur J.: Director of the Medieval Civilization Program, Reconstructionist Rabbinical College; author of *A Jewish Princedom in Feudal France, 768-900* (1972) and "Unpublished Materials on . . . Early Fifteenth Century Jewry" in *S.W. Baron Jubilee Volume* (1975).